The End of Modernism

UNC | COLLEGE OF ARTS AND SCIENCES
Germanic and Slavic Languages and Literatures

From 1949 to 2004, UNC Press and the UNC Department of Germanic & Slavic Languages and Literatures published the UNC Studies in the Germanic Languages and Literatures series. Monographs, anthologies, and critical editions in the series covered an array of topics including medieval and modern literature, theater, linguistics, philology, onomastics, and the history of ideas. Through the generous support of the National Endowment for the Humanities and the Andrew W. Mellon Foundation, books in the series have been reissued in new paperback and open access digital editions. For a complete list of books visit www.uncpress.org.

The End of Modernism
Elias Canetti's *Auto-da-Fé*

WILLIAM COLLINS DONAHUE

UNC Studies in the Germanic Languages and Literatures
Number 124

Copyright © 2001

This work is licensed under a Creative Commons CC BY-NC-ND license. To view a copy of the license, visit http://creativecommons.org/licenses.

Suggested citation: Donahue, William Collins. *The End of Modernism: Elias Canetti's Auto-da-Fé*. Chapel Hill: University of North Carolina Press, 2001. DOI: https://doi.org/10.5149/9780807875223_Donahue

Library of Congress Cataloging-in-Publication Data

Names: Donahue, William Collins.
Title: The end of Modernism : Elias Canetti's Auto-da-fé / by William Collins Donahue.
Other titles: University of North Carolina studies in the Germanic languages and literatures ; no. 124.
Description: Chapel Hill : University of North Carolina Press, [2001] Series: University of North Carolina studies in the Germanic languages and literatures | Includes bibliographical references and index.
Identifiers: LCCN 2001035150 | ISBN 978-1-4696-5742-4 (pbk: alk. paper) | ISBN 978-1-4696-5743-1 (ebook)
Subjects: Canetti, Elias, 1905- Blendung.
Classifications: LCC PT2605.A58 Z656 2001 | DDC 833/.912 — dc21

For my parents,
Dorothy and John Donahue

"Noch spür' ich ihren Atem auf den Wangen."

CONTENTS

Preface *xi*
Acknowledgments *xv*
Foreword to the 2020 edition *xix*
Introduction: Modernism in a Different Key *1*
1. The Novel(s) in the Novel:
   Modernism as Parody of Popular Realism *18*
2. "The truth is you're a woman. You live for sensations.":
   Misogyny as Cultural Critique *43*
3. Self-Indulgent Philosophies of the Weimar Period:
   The Use and Abuse of Neoempiricism and Neo-Kantianism *76*
4. The Hunchback of "Heaven":
   Anti-Semitism and the Failure of Humanism *106*
5. "An Impudent Choir of Croaking Frogs":
   Freud and the Freudians as the Novel's Secret Sharers *137*
6. Neither Adorno nor Lukács:
   Canetti's Analytic Modernism *174*
   Notes *207*
   Bibliography *257*
   Index *271*

ILLUSTRATIONS

1. Title page from a turn-of-the-century edition of Willibald Alexis's *Die Hosen des Herrn von Bredow* 23
2. Jewish men publicly ogle an "Aryan" beauty (from Kurt Plischke, *Der Jude als Rassenschänder*) 51
3. "The Martyr Abroad": visual background to Fischerle's escapist fantasy of American success (anti-Semitic cartoon from *Brennessel*) 52
4. "Der kleine Cohn" — The malformed shirker as Fischerle's cultural prototype (World War I–era postcard) 116
5. The stinking Jew: cultural reiterations of the "Fischerle type" (anti-Semitic caricature by Josef Plank) 121
6. "This total nose" (caricature from the anti-Semitic *Kikeriki*) 122
7. An anti-Semitic children's book, *Trau keinem Fuchs*, teaches lessons on "Jewish" and "Aryan" physiognomy 123
8. Blond Germanic Siegfried approaches the dwarf Alberich (from Fritz Lang's 1924 *Siegfried*) 126
9. "Jewish Metamorphosis" (a caricature of Jewish assimilation as essentially superficial) 132

PREFACE

Canetti's novel never fails to elicit rather strong opinions. Recently in the *New Yorker*, David Denby declared it "a long, provocatively odd, and emotionally demanding novel."[1] Remarkable amidst the variety of these distinctly unambivalent reactions is the fact that readers have tended to see *Auto-da-Fé* as a compellingly contemporary work, and in one notable case, even pronounced it a "postwar novel."[2] This is an understandable error. Canetti did not really gain wide recognition until the early 1960s, when his quixotic anthropological study *Crowds and Power* first appeared. Implicitly addressing the Cold War stalemate, and hailed as "above ideology," this much-discussed book was bound to encourage readers to associate Canetti in the first instance with the burning issues of that bipolar world, rather than with prewar modernist fiction. Yet placing Canetti the novelist alongside the likes of such unmistakably postwar writers as Grass, Böll, and Christa Wolf was probably more than an oversight. Those who read and reviewed the novel at this time, including those who certainly knew of its Weimar-era origins (such as Hans Magnus Enzensberger), were in fact quite prepared to view it as a work chiefly about contemporary society. It may be that "social relevance" was already becoming a dominant criterion of literary achievement, even before the student movement established it more firmly. And it may also be that some critics simply mistook the date of republication—it was reissued in the wake of *Crowds and Power* in order, in part, to capitalize on that book's success—for the original date. Whatever the case, nobody seemed to miss the modernist context of the early 1930s, when Canetti actually wrote what would be his only published novel.

There is more to this, of course, than merely a testimony to the novel's ageless appeal, though this would have pleased Canetti immensely since he aspired to nothing more than to be a writer who transcended his own times. This episode reflects an important fact about *Auto-da-Fé*: readers, even literary critics, are curiously disinclined to associate Canetti's novel with the classics of literary modernism. For this, as I endeavor to demonstrate, there is very good reason. Though surely part of the same anti-realist tradition that embraces Joyce, Musil, and Rilke, Canetti is indeed strikingly different. The novel's wicked humor, its analytic posture, and above all its concern for the diminishing public sphere set it far apart from what we would come to know as "aesthetic," or "high modernism."

In a graduate seminar on modernism, I recall asking about those estranged and world-weary aesthetes, the typical protagonists of high modernism: How did they navigate their *social* lives? My question, which arose out of my reading of *Auto-da-Fé* (a novel, incidentally, that was not on the course syllabus), was met with polite disinterest. As I began to work my way into the secondary literature, it occurred to me that critics often only complicated the matter by attempting to apply a high modernist template that just does not fit *Auto-da-Fé*. And, when the novel failed to measure up, they credited themselves with having discovered an "error" in its conception. Fortunately, just around the time of these musings, a paradigm shift occurred—in the case of German literature, one that is associated chiefly with Peter Bürger, Russell Berman, and Andreas Huyssen—that enabled me to approach the novel with an eye to its rich social and cultural context. This approach has proven most fruitful above all in taking the novel on its own terms, opening up a vista on a whole array of topics that up to now have only been addressed, if at all, in piecemeal fashion.

While this more capacious view of modernism structures the bulk of this study, allowing me to tap into Canetti's unwavering interest in social arrangements, it occurred to me that adhering to the traditional construction of literary modernism may, in its own way, prove just as instructive. What first helped me see the distinctive features of *Auto-da-Fé*, after all, was the marked *contrast* with aesthetic modernism. Thus in the final chapter of this study, I turn back the clock and place Canetti's novel in the context of high modernism. This exercise throws the novel into contrastive relief, revealing more clearly than otherwise possible all the narrative features that comprise what I have dubbed Canetti's trademark "analytic modernism."

Readers familiar with Canetti's engaging autobiography, the evocative North African travel memoir, or his far-flung anthropological study are typically struck by the breadth of the author's interests, the variety of his experience, and the quality of his erudition. These same expectations are fully met in *Auto-da-Fé*, yet up to this point there was no book available to guide the reader through the rich and complex contexts and intertexts that make reading this challenging novel such a rewarding experience. Despite some valuable monographs on particular aspects of the novel, as well as quite general surveys of Canetti's entire oeuvre, we have lacked a substantial study of the full range of topics broached by the novel: the Freud satire, the "cultural" case for misogyny, the virulent racial anti-Semitism in its relationship to a failed humanism, and a cluster of philosophical and pseudophilosophical movements of the interwar period.

Though Canetti's novel belonged to world literature long before it was reclaimed by German readers in the early 1960s, scholarship has tended to favor the German readership. I will attempt to serve two masters: both the generalist who knows the novel as *Auto-da-Fé* in the ordinarily quite excellent Wedgwood translation, as well as the more specialized Germanist, who will want to examine the original text in the context of my analysis. In order to accomplish both tasks I have arrived at the following solution: I have translated all quotations (or used available standard editions) from the secondary literature, including Freud, Adorno, and Lukács. For the novel itself, which is the principal object of my study, I have provided both the English (which in not a few cases represents my revision of Wedgwood) *and* Canetti's German original. While this may seem pedantic and cumbersome, it will, I think, prove worthwhile. For when it comes to humor and nuance, of which Canetti is an acknowledged master, even a talented translation can usually only capture one of an array of semantic options available in the original. Most of my alternate renderings appear, perhaps unsurprisingly, within the discussions of misogyny and anti-Semitism, topics which were not aired so openly in Wedgwood's day. Taken together, there now appears to be enough evidence that this "personally supervised" translation, while still of enormous value, cannot in fact have been line-edited by Canetti himself.

My interest in making this study of *Auto-da-Fé* available also to the nonspecialist and students of comparative literature has much to do with Canetti himself. Roger Kimball captures perfectly the intrinsic dual thrust of this enterprise when he describes Canetti's works as "scrupulously avant-garde yet 'large' enough in their ambition to command mainstream critical attention."[3] One of the things that makes Canetti so continually attractive is that he represents an ideal to which so many of us still, if only covertly, aspire— namely, that of the nonspecialist polymath. There may be no more memorable a skewering of academic overspecialization and pomposity in all of world literature than that which we find in *Auto-da-Fé*. Yet this is clearly not to be read as an anti-intellectual stance. On the contrary, Canetti steadfastly maintained that it is possible to be a serious intellectual generalist without necessarily devolving into a dilettante. The effort, at least, is necessary, Canetti felt, lest in our drive to master detail we lose sight of the larger social good. And those who are preoccupied with their own narrow specialty become vulnerable, as the novel unforgettably suggests, to the power grabs of the less scrupulous. Though *Auto-da-Fé* mercilessly critiques acquisitive bourgeois notions of German "cultivation" (Bildung), Canetti himself redeems—and refashions—the concept in his own literary-intellectual career. It is my hope, therefore, to enrich the reading experience of the more general reader, even as I engage my colleagues in fairly specific debates about the novel's complex relationship to the interwar period of Austrian and German culture, traditional literary modernism, and Canetti's own considerable body of social thought.

ACKNOWLEDGMENTS

I have profited immensely from all those who read the manuscript, or parts thereof, at various stages along the way. My sincere thanks to Russell Berman, Richard Brinkman, Dorrit Cohn, Alfred Doppler, Eric Downing, Sander L. Gilman, Gerhard von Graevinitz, Steven Grossman, Karl S. Guthke, Walter Haug, Noah Isenberg, Richard S. Levy, Sylvia Schmitz-Burgard, Walter H. Sokel, and Harry Zohn. I wish to thank in particular Stephen Dowden and Maria Tatar, who read the manuscript in the final phase on its way to becoming a book. If my argument has since become any sharper, it is due to their attentive criticism and generous commentary.

I completed the revisions on this book while a fellow at the Erasmus Institute (University of Notre Dame), and wish to record here a note of sincere gratitude to that institution—and to its directors, James C. Turner and Robert E. Sullivan—for a generous year of research, writing, and stimulating interdisciplinary discussion. I am indebted also to the UNC Press series editor, Dr. Jonathan Hess, and to editorial assistant Elizabeth Davis, both for expert editorial guidance and patient fielding of many anxious queries.

The Koret Foundation (San Francisco), the Littauer Foundation (New York), and the Rutgers Research Council (New Brunswick) made generous contributions to support the publication of this book, and I am grateful to each. Chapter 2 first appeared in a slightly different form in the *Deutsche Vierteljahrsschrift für Literatur und Geistesgeschichte,* December 1997.

Most important of all, I wish to thank my family—Marie, Molly, and Olivia—for their love, support, and patience throughout this project.

THE END OF MODERNISM

Foreword to the 2020 edition

Is it fair to ask, almost twenty years after its initial publication, whether this book is rightly titled "the end of modernism"? Is it too grandiose to claim that Elias Canetti's monumental interwar novel, *Die Blendung* (or *Auto-da-Fé*, as it would become known in the English speaking world), in any sense marked the *end* of modernism? The answer—a scholarly "yes and no"—sheds light both on Canetti as aesthetic innovator and social thinker and upon subsequent developments in literary and culture studies.

Auto-da-Fé is still rightly seen as a rejection of central tenets of what we once called aesthetic or high modernism. Arguably more than any of his literary peers, Canetti insists on the sheer durability and obstinance of our physical and social environments. This is not because he was invested in maintaining the status quo or in using literature to endorse traditionalist politics. Far from it. Canetti strongly opposed the Austro-fascism of interwar Austria, which he experienced firsthand as a young man, and he praised Karl Kraus's heroism in publicly denouncing the Viennese police commissioner's use of deadly force against unarmed civilian protesters at the famous 1927 demonstration in front of the Palace of Justice. And he would, of course, go on to pen an extended indictment against power itself, *Masse und Macht* (Crowds and Power)—his life's work—and the most far-reaching cultural investigation of power prior to Foucault.

No, the remarkable solidity of the social sphere the reader experiences in *Auto-da-Fé* is more of a warning, possibly even a threat. Diagnosing social arrangements as constructed—a typical move in literary and cultural studies during the reign of critique as the master interpretive paradigm—was often accompanied by an earnest optimism for social renewal. The unstated corollary to this finding went something like this: anything that is revealed to be *constructed* could be readily deconstructed or even reconstructed. Canetti—as if anticipating the critical debates of subsequent decades—answers with a cautious "not so fast." Like Brecht, he was not particularly sanguine about social progress emerging merely from the awareness of social constructedness. He had witnessed the persistence of Habsburg traditionalism long after the actual demise of the empire; the continuation of anti-Semitism after Jews had fulfilled all the requirements of assimilation, including in some cases baptism; and the perseverance of authoritarianism (not to mention the rise of fascism) during the putative democracy of the Austrian First Republic. There was plenty that he would have liked to see disappear, yet he was aware, perhaps particularly as a Jew, that wishing away the unwanted state of affairs was not only insufficient but also deeply problematic. A shrewd observer of entrenched power, he knew that social change was not a decisionist affair, and his modernist novel satirizes those who think it is.

The act of erasing intersubjective reality in *Auto-da-Fé* is therefore not high modernism's welcome release from the shackles of history and society, nor is it primarily the artist's soaring act of aesthetic reinvention. It is, more routinely, an ominous error: Peter Kien deploys scholarship (he is the world's foremost sinologist, or so we are led to believe) to enclose himself in a tomb of knowledge. In one of the most famous passages of the novel—a devastatingly humorous parody of academia still topical today—Professor Kien "explains" how ignorance of the world is not only justified but indeed required by the rigors of academic specialization. Therese, the misogynistically drawn housekeeper, pursues a husband and fortune through flagrant acts of what we might call selective seeing, or the culpable overwriting of major elements of the Viennese public sphere, as readers are meant to notice. And Fischerle, the poor little hunchbacked Jew, concocts a fantasy of becoming a debonair, rich American, a dream of assimilation meant to transport him out of the criminal underworld he has been confined to all his life. But he is only rendered sufficiently "un-Jewish" in a violent attack that ends his life.

In other words, *Auto-da-Fé* does not despair of the social world's reality or doubt its ontological status to the extent that many postwar scholars thought modernism should. The failure to fulfill this modernist criterion of epistemological uncertainty, it was argued (though sometimes only implicitly), rendered the respective work less sophisticated, less epistemologically radical, and moved it—ominously—in the direction of realism, with all of its allegedly unreflected assumptions about the real. Canetti's major contribution was to show—from within the movement itself—that dangers lay in the other direction as well. Although he could not have anticipated the critical discourse that would define and valorize modernism decades after writing his novel, *Auto-da-Fé* serves as an uncanny anticipation of, and response to, these very debates.

He was of course aware that his novel is dark (or "*duster*," as he would later refer to it in his correspondence)—difficult, and not easily consumable. He would often warn those who came to him by way of other more accessible writings (such as the autobiography) that the novel, with its extremist figures and challenging narrative technique (featuring serial interior monologue that frequently obfuscates the identity of the respective controlling consciousness), is simply not for everyone. It was not a book destined to become a bestseller, nor did it. He was also keenly aware of his place within literary modernism. James Joyce (whose grave at the Fluntern Cemetery in Zurich adjoins his own) was, Canetti observed, much more given to linguistic experimentation. In contrast, Canetti speaks of a need to respect the power and givenness of language; it proves sturdy enough, at any rate, to sponsor his own modernist satire in *Auto-da-Fé*. But this is by no means an unqualified endorsement. His profound skepticism focuses, rather, upon the *use* of language, particularly as an instrument of power and domination. The author of the modernist drama *Hochzeit* (in which intradiegetic confusion reigns supreme) was not naive about the propensity of language to fail. But neither was he absolutist about language's *inevitable* failure. This would cause disciples of Derrida, and other poststructural theorists responsible for the canonical view of literary modernism at the time this study was first published, to wonder if Canetti really belonged to the club after all. Unwilling to segregate language as a thing unto itself, Canetti always treated it holistically, which is to say in the context of its speakers, auditors, and readers. It is no coincidence, then, that he renders readers of *Auto-da-Fé* complicit in his language games by compelling them to decode the often malicious voices lurking within ostensibly third-person narration.

If it can be said that *Auto da Fé* identifies and opposes certain antisocial elements within the high modernist paradigm (and performs similarly diagnostic work for a literary-theoretical paradigm that valorized radical epistemological skepticism over other kinds of literary knowing), it is of course not true that the novel ended modernism per se. How could it have? Modernism mutated on its own, to be sure, but critics are to blame as well. Like doctors who have overprescribed antibiotics, they have, in overextending the term reduced its conceptual efficacy. How can one today explain to students, or to colleagues outside of the field, what the word should mean under these conditions of almost limitless elasticity? It is a terminological embarrassment that I tried to cope with by creating sub-genres (such as, in the case of *Auto-da-Fé*, analytic modernism). But I'm afraid that has not caught on—at least not yet.

In the introduction to this book, I lean heavily on David Hollinger's classic approach to the phenomenon. But I'm afraid that even his capacious dichotomy between the scientific, empirical knower and the aspirational, sometimes fantastic artificer no longer quite captures all that scholars now seek to place within this overburdened rubric. Still, given the apparent cache of the term, and the felt need to apply it to works of high innovation and achievement, there may be some wisdom in the pragmatic solution, proposed by David Harvey (in *The Conditions of Postmodernity*), to view modernism and postmodernism together as one large (and heterogeneous) aesthetic response to modernity.

Canetti of course is no innocent of the predicament in which we find ourselves. Rather than having ended the movement (which was of course never really his intention), he managed to expand it, ingeniously using modernist tools to dissect modernism. He forced open the gates of the genre, introducing a kind of hybrid satire that depends upon language to communicate reliably even while the novel radically questions language's communicative propensities. In *Auto-da-Fé*, it is after all one and the same narrative—a discourse that is repeatedly hijacked, sometimes covertly, by the novel's sundry figures—that gives us both a real world denied or misrecognized by its characters *and* a world of illusion and fantasy. In combining the knower and the artificer functions within a single work, Canetti prepared us for a richer, more complex understanding of modernism. Not one that need spin out of control indiscriminately, losing all definitional contours, but rather one that accommodates both dependable judgment about intersubjective reality and highly perspectivized, subjective flights of fancy. In light of the contemporary assault on truth, and what James Kloppenberg has aptly called the pervasive culture of irony, Canetti's is perhaps a particularly timely vision.

I dedicate this second edition of *The End of Modernism* to Alfred and Waltraut Doppler, who first introduced me to Canetti on a hike in the Green Mountains of Vermont when I was a student at Middlebury College. Their love of literature continues to sustain me.

William Collins Donahue
July 2020

Nobody can write as wickedly as you.
(So bös wie Sie kann niemand schreiben.)
—Friedl Benedikt to Elias Canetti

Introduction
Modernism in a Different Key

Auto-da-Fé is a brutal book.
— Roger Kimball[1]

After reading *Auto-da-Fé* Hermann Broch asked Canetti: "What are you trying to say?" Before the visibly stunned Canetti could reply, Broch continued, somewhat apologetically: "If you knew that, you wouldn't have written the novel. That was a bad question."[2] Yet it is the question that has occupied readers ever since the novel was first published in 1935. To lay out my own answer, I have had to write this book; yet it can be stated simply: *Auto-da-Fé* is profoundly concerned with the diminution of the social world. The "blinding" of the novel's original German title, *Die Blendung*, refers in the first place to the blocking out of social reality that manifests itself personally, but is in each case emblematic of a larger cultural practice. The novel evokes and hilariously debunks a whole series of cultural strategies that "address" social crises largely by, as the Germans say, "thinking them away" (*wegdenken*). These evasions take various forms, ranging from a child's magical thinking ("if I don't see you, you're not there") to the more subtle variety Canetti affiliates with escapist literature, popular philosophy, and, not least of all, Sigmund Freud. It was Canetti's deepest ambition to become the kind of author whose work, which, though perhaps not fully appreciated in its own day, would one day find lasting recognition. This aspiration may well be met in *Auto-da-Fé*. For though it should in the first instance be seen as responding to particular cultural crises of the Weimar era, as I will show at some length in this study, it would be difficult to name one object of the novel's parody that is not in some manner with us still.

What makes reading Canetti an exciting adventure is the fact that the perspectives he develops are never derivative and rarely expected, which perhaps accounts for some of the curious interpretations I will address below. Misogyny and racial anti-Semitism come under fire, therefore, not for the obvious reason that such practices are unjust. In fact, Canetti even exploits these topics for humor—a fact that may explain why so many readers admit only privately to laughing out loud while reading this novel. What proves to be so laughable (though not "funny" in the sense of trivial entertainment) is the intricate way in which misogyny is shown to be implicated in the much-heralded "crisis of subjectivity." Well before it was fashionable to do so, *Auto-da-Fé* portrays this classic event in high modernism—otherwise known as the "fragmented subject"—as a suspiciously gendered affair that is not merely a personal, but a decidedly widespread *cultural* malaise. Likewise anti-Semitism: it does not require great hermeneutic skill to decipher Fischerle (a major figure in Book 2 of the novel) as an icon of perverse anti-Semitic stereotyping. Yet Canetti complicates this issue by relating the fate of this hunchbacked Jewish pimp to the larger failure of humanism, indeed of the entire enlightenment project of "culture" as it was resuscitated in a particular way during the Weimar period.

At stake is not merely the efficacy of such peculiarly German enterprises as *Bildung* and *Kultur;* there are, of course, more specific targets. While the brothers Kien exhibit behavior that is perhaps most uncomfortably familiar to academics of our own day, they happen to represent specific aspects of two notable Weimar-era philosophical schools, neoempiricism and neo-Kantianism. Peter Kien (referred to henceforth simply as "Kien") is the most obvious culprit because he makes no secret of his cultural elitism. In his famous *Über die ästhetische Erziehung des Menschen in einer Reihe von Briefen* (Aesthetic Letters, 1795), perhaps the quintessential German document of idealist aesthetics, Friedrich Schiller had espoused a model of culture that would harmonize the requirements of the autonomous Kantian subject with the demands of the sensual and contingent social world. Though Kien claims to be an ardent partisan of this lofty cultural heritage, his professed love of Kant turns out to be little more than a specious justification for retreat and isolation from a dauntingly modern world. Though the "ivory tower" syndrome is indeed a perennial, if not universal, phenomenon, we will see that Kien's "idealism" takes on a specifically Weimar form. As a noted philologist—indeed, the world's most famous such specimen—he invokes precisely that discipline that was to play such a crucial role in Werner Jäger's interwar cultural renewal program known as the "Third Humanism." Needless to say, Kien's practice of scholarship gives us little hope of cultural rejuvenation from this quarter. Brother Georg is surely the more insidious of intellectual frauds, not in the least because he appears to be the sanest and most attractive of characters. He avidly seeks to portray himself as politically engaged by promoting his "innovative" psychological methods as subversively anti-bourgeois. But no less than his elder brother, Georg wraps himself in contemporary philosophical garb only to escape the very social world he claims to advocate. With these two highly educated brothers, Canetti reminds us how seductive fashionable modes of thought can be, and how easily they can be employed to mask hidden (as well as not so well concealed) agendas.

All of these constructions of culture are hilariously doomed: the pulp fiction that fosters nostalgic retreat into a national history that never quite was (an issue Canetti ingeniously intercuts by alluding to the then-bestselling novelist Willibald Alexis), no less than the veneration of an imperial "Vienna" that has been reduced to a spectral and insubstantial presence. In fact, the only truly durable municipal edifice in the whole novel turns out to be the "Theresianum," a building designed to evoke the economic dislocations and cultural contradictions of the interwar years like no other Viennese landmark possibly could. *Auto-da-Fé* leaves little doubt about what does not work. Neither turning back the clock (as Kien and company would have it) nor mindlessly chasing after the latest intellectual fad (as Georg does) will suffice as a foundation for the cultural renaissance the novel suggests we need so urgently.

Whence cometh our salvation? Once again, it is to Hermann Broch that we turn for common sense. He observed, quite correctly I think, that the novel ends in total destruction, harsh and merciless. Broch's penchant for answering his own questions is in evidence in the following query. Referring to the novel's rather bleak conclusion, he asks Canetti: "Do you *want* this collapse? It is evident that you desire precisely the opposite. You would gladly do your part to indicate a way out. But you don't show us any."[3] The novel does not in fact contain the answer to the question of culture and society it so complexly and relentlessly raises. Yet this point has eluded many critics, particularly in the last thirty-five years. And for this Canetti himself must take some of the responsibility. For that which has created so much confusion is of course the author's second major work, *Crowds and Power* (1960). Ever since the publication of this quirky and voluminous anthropological study, the novel has tended to be either rigorously segregated from it or relegated to a secondary, illustrative status. The former approach has been advocated by formalists such as David Darby, Robert Elbaz, and Leah Hadomi; but however much we stand to gain (and we undoubtedly gain the most from Darby), this perspective tends to neglect the novel's chief concern.

There has of course been no dearth of critics who read *Auto-da-Fé* in light of *Crowds and Power*. But while the social dimension is thereby rescued, another distortion inevitably arises: the novel is consigned to the unlikely role of anticipating the later social scientific theory. Critics of this school routinely cite the novel to illustrate a point made more discursively in *Crowds and Power;* and that point is often (and rather predictably) that Georg, or at least his protean conception of crowds, bespeaks Canetti's own ideas on the primal nature of social groupings—one of the foundational ideas of *Crowds and Power*. But rarely do these critics pause to notice that this is an essentially circular endeavor that accomplishes little except, perhaps, to attribute what I judge to be an unlikely degree of uniformity to Canetti's thought. Despite the fact that Georg's credibility has more and more come under fire in the last twenty years, this fundamental hermeneutic strategy has proved astonishingly tenacious. Gerald Stieg exemplifies this approach most recently in suggesting that the novel be read as a kind of encoded "fable" for the fundamental ideas of *Crowds and Power*.

My own approach is quite different. I believe we can have it both ways, without splitting the difference. We can read *Auto-da-Fé* as the German modernist novel with an inherently "social" agenda without reducing it to the status of prooftext in the service of *Crowds and Power*. For one, Canetti certainly did not know in 1930–31 what he would learn over the next thirty years. To assume he did is, I think, the proposition requiring the greater leap of faith. One could also point to the autobiography (still the most popular of all the author's works, by the way) to support this view, though I am conscious that this interpretive maneuver can easily function like the citation of scripture. Even as I write this line, I can imagine Canetti aficionados ready to pounce with passages from the autobiography where we read that the author's interest in crowds dates to the same period in which the novel was written; or eager to cite chapter and verse from the same work where we learn that the 1927 riot and subsequent massacre at the Viennese Palace of Justice were seminal historical events that inform both of these works. This much may well be true; I see no reason, at any rate, to doubt Canetti's word on this. But what he is claiming, it should be noted, is not that *Crowds and Power* provides the "theoretical key" to *Auto-da-Fé* (as Hans Magnus Enzensberger claimed in his *Der Spiegel* review of 1963), but rather that these two works are inhabited by a common spirit of inquiry. This, at any rate, is the formulation that best captures their actual relationship.

Since I am bucking a tradition that has dominated Canetti scholarship,[4] it seems worthwhile, even in this introduction, to say a few more words about my conception of this relationship. Grasping the novel's true relationship to *Crowds and Power* is in fact prerequisite to comprehending *Auto-da-Fé* in its own right and on its own terms. Without wishing to affiliate myself all too closely with the pompous philologist Kien (who, let us recall, proposes in all seriousness to write an authoritative and irrevocable exegesis of the New Testament), I do hope with this book to lay to rest the single issue that has most bedeviled Canetti scholarship. *Auto-da-Fé* no more anticipates *Crowds and Power* than it does the Nazi period (another recurrent claim in the literature). Rather, it comprises a complex critique of obsolete, ineffectual, and even reactionary ways of fending off modernity; it exposes a whole series of cultural practices as essentially subjectivist, escapist, and therefore fundamentally antisocial; and it provides a stark perspective on modern culture that unsparingly discloses all those things that mitigate against a tenable renewal of culture. But *Auto-da-Fé* does not yet provide the answer it seeks. Martin Jay has repeatedly adduced Adorno's residual Judaism as a significant factor in the development of his famous negative dialectic. The biblical injunction against divine images may have played some crucial role, Jay suggests, in Adorno's adamant refusal to provide positive, affirmative precepts.[5] A similar case could be made for Canetti, at least up to the point when he develops his notion of "*Verwandlung.*" For, like Adorno, he was an atheist Jew who remained stubbornly interested in Judaism (and fascinated by religion in general) throughout his life. But whether it was this factor alone, the dictates and limitations of the fictional literary form, or the fact that he simply did not yet know where his investigations would take him (or, more likely, some dynamic combination thereof), of one thing we can be sure: *Auto-da-Fé* negates bogus notions of public culture without offering anything to replace what Broch termed this "total destruction."

Enter *Crowds and Power*. Though the present study remains primarily concerned with *Auto-da-Fé*, I argue, particularly in the final two chapters, that the more accurate relationship between these two "life's works" is dialogic: the novel poses the great question, to which the anthropological study wagers a tentative, but passionately argued, answer. In short, *Crowds and Power* replaces the normative model of German *Kultur*, so richly pilloried in the novel, with an anthropological concept of culture. Such a move would of course have appalled idealist cultural conservatives like Kien, who viewed this approach (which was already widely discussed in the Weimar period) as dangerously relativistic, or worse, mindlessly historicist. After all, they reasoned, what do the primitive cultures have to say to that flower of European civilization, German *Kultur*? How could they serve as a font of cultural renewal? After the Second World War and the Holocaust, Canetti would face less difficulty in making his case. In opposition to that heretofore most influential thinker on crowds, Sigmund Freud, Canetti develops essentially two ideas that serve as bookends to *Crowds and Power*: the primary quality of social groupings (not, as Freud would have it, a secondary phenomenon essentially at odds with individual happiness); and a major revision of the Oedipus complex that Canetti calls "*Verwandlung*" (transformation). Both of these are fairly detailed concepts worthy of their own discussion, which I undertake below. But the point for now would be to note that the novel has already paved the way precisely for these conceptual innovations. In the penultimate chapter, I seek to show how Freud (and popularized Freudianism) was already an important intertext for the novel. Canetti's unremitting caricature of Freudian notions, which unsurprisingly centers on the novel's psychiatrist Georg, raises topics undeniably similar to those we will encounter in the later Canetti, namely issues of social organization and individual transformative potential, but in a strikingly different manner. As it turns out, Georg is the promoter of notions that are not only debunked in the novel, but also specifically superseded in the later anthropological work.

Though I work hard to overcome the fuzzy anachronistic thinking that reads the latter work into the former, neither do I wish to suggest that the works are radically different. The most obvious connection between the two is Canetti's enduring interest in power as an intersubjective, social practice, as well as his acute concern for an imperiled social world. It is this pronounced social orientation that marks *Auto-da-Fé* as distinctive, indeed as an *endpoint*, in the German modernist tradition. It should be stressed that this is not merely a chronological matter of *Auto-da-Fé* appearing at the end of the great novelistic output of German modernism (roughly 1910–30), though this fact cannot be entirely ignored since it provided Canetti the temporal vantage point to look back on, and react to, earlier developments in the German novel. Neither can we doubt that the young Canetti was anything but acutely aware of such matters. Knowing full well where to turn in these matters, Canetti sent off the novel in manuscript form to Thomas Mann. (Mann returned the bulky, unsolicited package without even having broken the seal, though once *Auto-da-Fé* appeared in print, he praised it profusely.)

One can undoubtedly give a political reading to Rilke's *Die Aufzeichnungen des Malte Laurids Brigge* (Notebooks of Malte Laurids Brigge, 1910), and it is certainly true that a menacing Berlin plays a crucial role in Döblin's *Berlin Alexanderplatz* (1929), but it is in *Auto-da-Fé* that we first encounter a fundamental challenge to that time-honored fixture of aesthetic modernism, the fragmented subject, who often takes the form of a sympathetically drawn, oversensitive aesthete misfit—one thinks, for example, of Rilke's Malte, Musil's Törleß (*Die Verwirrungen des Zöglings Törleß*, 1906), or even of Broch's own Pasenow (*Pasenow, oder Die Romantik 1888*, 1930). In the last chapter I argue that the novel's defiance of what would become the regnant paradigm of postwar modernism, most particularly in its rigorous examination of the social dimensions of fragmented subjectivity, explains in part why it was later marginalized by academic critics. Yet before this model of high modernism installed itself as normative under the aegis above all of Adorno, critics had no difficulty in recognizing *Auto-da-Fé* as self-evidently modernist. Indeed, it was one of the canards of the early criticism to affiliate Canetti's experimental novel with that touchstone of modernism, Joyce's *Ulysses*. And this is a connection later journalist critics would continue to make down to our own day.[6] Yet because it treats that sacred cow of aesthetic modernism with critical reserve, scholarly critics would withhold their imprimatur.

The second way in which *Auto-da-Fé* rings in an end to the high modernist tradition is via its deployment of a narrative structure that elicits and enables *analysis*. The presence of an "epistemologically strong" narrative, which I explicate also in the final chapter, would necessarily seem alien to those raised on a diet of canonical aesthetic modernism. Yet this need not signify a reactionary or regressive move, as some critics imply, especially if one considers that the novel does not simply mock one perspective (Kien's) in order to install another (Georg's). The critique is leveled evenhandedly across the board, as I show at some length throughout this study. It is a harsh and probing series of negations, not a "know it all" novel that contains its own standard of good behavior—not, in other words, a case of fictional "*Besserwisserei*." The novel's notable analytic propensity is an essential characteristic that can, however, all too easily obscure the simultaneous self-critique of reason enacted within the text. Indeed, if we are left with any single impression, it is that epistemological hubris, both the reader's and the characters', will inevitably be punished.

Nevertheless, we should not shy away from the fact that *Auto-da-Fé* represents a rupture in literary modernism, confronting the aesthetic (or "high") canon with what I have dubbed a variant strain of "analytic modernism." To find a suitable analogy—that is, a self-critical aesthetic program imbued with a modicum of analytic confidence that is focused intensely on the social world—one would have to step outside the genre to include Brechtian drama (and dramatic theory). But within the field of German prose modernism, Canetti's *Auto-da-Fé* stands in this regard conspicuously alone. Which evokes a second and important level of continuity in Canetti's oeuvre: both the early novelistic critique and the later anthropological rehabilitation of "culture" depend upon a fundamental allegiance to the enlightenment values of inquiry. Canetti's description of *Crowds and Power* in the 1965 interview with Adorno (which I discuss below) epitomizes this position perfectly: his project, he maintains, represents an "open system"—but a system nonetheless. The evils of Nazism and the Holocaust and the threat of Cold War nuclear annihilation—the real motivating forces behind *Crowds and Power,* by the way—demand a comprehensive revision of traditionalist European culture as well as a deep humility in the face of other, non-European "primitive" cultures. Hackneyed idealist notions of high culture, which imagine the German classics as an unproblematic wellspring of normative social values—a concept, by the way, very similar to that proffered in William Bennett's bestselling *Book of Virtues*—will simply no longer do. This dynamic combination of qualities we encounter in the novel—iconoclastic cultural critique conjoined with a commitment to analytic discourse—is in fact characteristic of the entire oeuvre. Canetti was to remain a skeptical rationalist throughout his life. Like Brecht's stance toward Stalin's Soviet Union—"Critical, but *for* it"[7]—Canetti affirmed rational critique as flawed but necessary. With this in mind, we can understand why those literary-critical paradigms predicated upon radical epistemological skepticism (I am thinking above all of deconstructionism) are *eo ipso* bound to miss (or dismiss) Canetti's distinctive contribution.

Did the young Canetti intend to put an end to aesthetic modernism? Clearly, he made no secret either of his own rather immodest artistic ambition to "make it new" (as Ezra Pound urged his generation), or of his disdain for commercially successful contemporary writers like Stefan Zweig, Franz Werfel, and Carl Zuckmayer. Yet it would be mistaken, I think, to confine our discussion strictly to literature, or to think of these innovations in primarily literary-aesthetic terms. Canetti critiques the sympathetic view of the fragmented modernist subject and structures his novel analytically for fundamentally *political* reasons. As an assimilated Sephardic Jew, born to a Ladino-speaking family in the small town of Rustschuk on the outskirts of the Austro-Hungarian empire, Canetti understood well that in reinventing one's self a whole lot more may be at stake than an aesthete's interior life. Canetti, I am suggesting, was biographically predisposed to understand the modernist decentered self as a potential problem, not something to be celebrated uncritically. Accordingly, *Auto-da-Fé* sounds a warning: If a self is reduced to a mere "bundle of sensations" (as Ernst Mach famously argued), then might it not become vulnerable to another's self-aggrandizement? If the perceiving subject becomes paramount, might that not render the rest of us more or less mutable objects of another's perception and power? Maybe these "fragmented subjects" were supposed to erode at precisely the same rate, giving no one an advantage over another; but *Auto-da-Fé* suggests that exactly this is *not* the case.

The significance of Jewish identity is of course not merely a matter of biographical speculation, but central to the novel. The self that Siegfried Fischerle desperately wants to shed is, not coincidentally, a stereotypically "Jewish" one. The fact that he cannot reinvent himself while the highly cultured Georg can enact any number of metamorphoses amounts to a grave indictment of a cultural program that only claimed to be universally accessible. As a politically astute Jew whose own assimilation to German culture was about to be revoked — *Auto-da-Fé* was published the same year the Nuremberg Laws were issued — Canetti was very much aware both of the politics of fragmented subjectivity and of the dangers of irrationalism.

To describe Canetti as essentially "political" requires an immediate caveat, for his was an intellectual's concern rather than an activist's engagement. This aspect of Canetti can best be gleaned (as can numerous others) from the author's encomiastic portrait of Dr. Isaiah Sonne (known perhaps to some readers under the pseudonym Abraham ben Yitzchak) which he draws in *The Play of the Eyes*: "Sonne had given up his worldly activities ... But he *remained* in the world, cleaved to its every appearance in his thoughts.

He let his hands rest, yet he did not turn his back on the world; even in the measured justice of his speech one could sense a passion for this world."[8] Clearly this is the way Canetti would have us think of him: intellectually removed, yet passionately committed. While he clearly hoped to intervene in actual sociocultural debates by means of his writing, one senses in Canetti a concomitant belief in the essential moral goodness of intellectual energy expended on behalf of the world.

Auto-da-Fé partakes of the moral seriousness that characterizes all of Canetti's work, yet it does not lack for rich comedy. In fact, Canetti evinces a great sense of humor about *Auto-da-Fé* as well as himself in one episode from *The Play of the Eyes,* where he describes how the novel ultimately came to be published. He had experienced not a little difficulty in finding a publisher, in great part, no doubt, due to the Nazi proscription of "degenerate" art (*entartete Kunst*), which by 1933 eliminated all the German publishers. But part of the problem surely also had to do with the fact that the novel makes substantial demands upon its readers. Finally, a wealthy newspaper publisher, a certain Jean Hoepffner of Strasbourg, stepped forward with an offer to put up the necessary subvention. Hoepffner's rationale for backing the book has nothing to do with the high-minded arguments I have been explicating thus far. Quite the opposite: he thinks the novel will enhance the status quo by making readers grateful that they do not actually inhabit a world quite so bleak as that of *Auto-da-Fé.* After hearing Canetti's résumé of the novel, Hoepffner responds: "I will never read that. But such a book should be available. That would have a good effect. Those who read it would awake as if from a nightmare and be grateful that reality is other than this dream."[9] Canetti goes on to explain that since Hoepffner was repulsed by the very description, and could not really support the novel for its actual content, "he [Hoepffner] thought up a pedagogical intention for the existence of the novel: that of deterrence."[10] In recounting this episode, Canetti betrays not only a rare self-deprecating sense of humor, but indicates also the Achilles heel of all political literature, namely reception. Even the most committed piece of prose could be disarmed by a mind-set like Hoepffner's and coopted as socially affirmative art. Here Canetti admits that his own aspirations for the novel, which he hoped would provoke rather than pacify his readers, are clearly beyond the novelist's control.

More important, perhaps, than Canetti's sense of humor *about* the novel is the novel's own humor, an aspect of the novel that was trumpeted by the early critics, particularly in the English press. If later German critics tended to pass over this salient aspect of *Auto-da-Fé,* the British reviewer Walter Allen did not hesitate to brand it "ferociously funny" and its author "a great comic writer."[11] It seems likely that the novel's noted humor was at loggerheads with the dominant existentialist readings of high modernism, an issue we will revisit in the final chapter of this study. Rudolf Hartung, for example, was apparently unable both to lament the novel's depiction of "the irreversible loneliness of the individual in an atomized world" *and* see the humor.[12] But Allen—along with many other readers—did. His judgment of the novel as "a truly savage comedy"[13] at once points up what is unique about Canetti's brand of modernism, and suggests a literary heritage à la Heinrich Heine and Friedrich Nietzsche, or, as Gerald Stieg has suggested for the Austrian context, à la Raimund, Nestroy, and Karl Kraus.[14] Reading the novel as a "great work of satire," as Allen does,[15] will require that we call into question certain epistemological assumptions about literary modernism.

By the time Herbert Reichner published *Auto-da-Fé* in 1935, at the prodding, apparently, of Stefan Zweig, the ideological climate had already become hostile to an experimental novel. The *Anschluß* of 1938 ensured that the novel's designation as "degenerate" extended to Austria as well. After the war, the Verlag Willi Weismann brought it out again, but this small publishing house suffered a great loss during the currency reform and soon went bankrupt, leaving stacks of unsold stock in Weismann's basement.[16] By the late forties Canetti's novel enjoyed a "wide press response in a broad spectrum of newspapers and periodicals" in England,[17] thanks to the Wedgwood translation, which Canetti supervised, and even garnered the coveted *Prix International* for the best foreign novel in France. But in the German-speaking countries it remained virtually unknown until its 1963 reappearance, now in the Hanser Verlag.

Reading the novel after the Second World War prompted interpretations both ahistorical and pseudohistorical. Reviewing the novel in 1947, Philip Toynbee counsels us, in a tone a preacher might take to urge his congregation to apply a scriptural passage to their lives, to accept the depiction of Peter Kien as an image of our darker selves. Canetti uses madness, Toynbee admonishes, "to isolate and intensify the obsessive elements in all of us. Hypocrite reader, he is forever insisting, this is *you;* yes, this disgusting, insane creature who makes you draw up your skirts, is you yourself."[18] In exhorting us to look into the distorting mirror of the literary grotesque,

Toynbee has fastened upon one of the novel's most memorable subjects, the academic parody, the meaning and humor of which can be grasped without making any special demands on the reader. The resilience of this take on the novel can be seen in the remarks of Germany's leading journalist-literary critic. Speaking in 1985 about Canetti's "Hauptwerk" (main work), Marcel Reich-Ranicki summed up the novel in the following manner: "It is a grand design concerning the tragedy of the intellectual in our century, a parable of the highest ambition."[19] Such a reading still has a good deal of appeal, even if we do not particularly wish to see ourselves in the image of the eccentric protagonist. The leftist social critic and poet Hans Magnus Enzensberger contributed to this universalizing, moralizing mode of criticism. But, as might be expected, Enzensberger switches our attention from the personal to the social: The novel's depiction of insanity has, as Enzensberger claimed in a *Der Spiegel* review of 1963, "everyman's face, and the battles, which are fought out in the slums and tenements, throw off giant historical shadows. Canetti shows the ubiquity of paranoid structures."[20]

Side by side with the universalizing gestures of Toynbee and Enzensberger appears what I would call the pseudohistorical approach, taken by those critics who see in the novel a prophecy of Nazism. Usually this takes the form of viewing the final scene of the novel in which Kien enacts his self-immolation as a foreshadowing of the Nazi book burning of May 10, 1933.[21] While it is surely tenable to maintain that Canetti, who visited Berlin twice in the years just before he wrote the novel, represents some protofascistic tendencies, such as the intellectual's inability—or refusal—to recognize the brute and murderous force of a Benedikt Pfaff, any more direct an analogy simply overreaches. We would do well in this regard to heed Canetti's own words. In one of the rare passages in the autobiography where we encounter fairly specific references to political events, Canetti observes: "At the end of January Hitler came to power. From this moment on everything that followed this event seemed uncanny and foreboding. Everything affected me personally . . . [but] nothing had been foreseen. Explanations and speculation, even the boldest of prophesies, appeared like mere straw when measured against reality. What happened was in every detail unexpected and new."[22] The interpretive strategy that views the novel as harbinger of Nazism fails therefore to persuade not only because it asks us to see Canetti as a fortune-teller (an assumption his autobiography clearly does not bear out), but also because it promotes the view of Kien as sympathetic victim. But the destruction of Kien's world is not so much lamented as celebrated in *Auto-da-Fé*. The burning of Vienna's "greatest private library" does represent a cultural disaster of the highest order—and one keenly felt by Canetti himself—but nevertheless one of a wholly different order than that instigated by the Nazis. In short, this pseudohistorical view of the novel as prophecy of Nazism is one of those hermeneutic shortcuts that does justice neither to history nor to the novel.

The End of Modernism: Elias Canetti's Auto-da-Fé comes at a time when neoconservative critic Harriet Murphy would have us believe that Canetti actually advocates the ivory tower intellectual.[23] Perhaps such confusion arises, as I have intimated above, because Canetti espoused a more genteel conception of intellectual engagement with the world than that which today enjoys wide currency. He certainly represents a standard of erudition that would be hard to maintain in the face of day-to-day political activism. It should also be stated that his noted critique of power may actually have prevented him from entering the rough and tumble of political agitation—may, in other words, have proved somewhat self-defeating. While this observation opens the door to a more critical perspective on Canetti, one we very much need, by the way, this should not be mistaken as Canetti's sponsorship of insular aestheticism. This book will, I hope, serve as a helpful corrective to those revisionist scholars who, in my judgment, seek to remake the author into one of his quite questionable characters.

Auto-da-Fé is a difficult and complex book in part because Canetti places demands upon the reader commensurate with those he laid upon himself. My own book seeks to place the reader in a position to grasp the multilayered parody of this ambitious work. Above all, this has meant explicating aspects of interwar European culture that may not be evident to contemporary readers, and then interpreting the novel against this backdrop. I have selected six fields of inquiry (each of which corresponds to a respective chapter) as most beneficial in this regard: (1) popular literature as an implicit contrast to the novel's own project; (2) misogyny and gender concepts, particularly as they intersect with the contemporary "crisis of subjectivity"; (3) Weimar-era philosophical schools and fads as "dignified" intellectual refuge from social concerns; (4) racial anti-Semitism as the barometer of humanist culture; and (5) Freud, as well as popularized Freudianism, as the novel's great negative influence. The sixth and final chapter fulfills two functions: it places Canetti's novel in the context of traditional literary modernism and permits me the opportunity to reprise the fundamental arguments of this study. As such, it serves in lieu of a more formal conclusion.

The title *The End of Modernism* risks conjuring the perhaps vintage Canettian attitude of grandiosity. (As Susan Sontag rightly reminds us, it was Canetti's unabashed aspiration to know everything, and *Crowds and Power* does indeed appear to harbor a "summa anthropologica" kind of ambition.) But this portion of the title will certainly mislead if taken to mean that *Auto-da-Fé* somehow receives and completes or transmutes all the various literary tributaries that lead into the muddy waters of what would become known as "modernism." Such would be an impossible claim in any event, since, as I discuss below, the term "modernism" would remain in considerable flux for decades after the novel's completion. The "end" to which I lay claim on Canetti's behalf is considerably less comprehensive, but can only be stated clearly once we extract ourselves from the conceptual morass that has developed around the term "modernism." *Auto-da-Fé* is an end; but to what precisely?

Fortunately, the intellectual historian David Hollinger has intervened to restore some conceptual order, arguing that alongside the perhaps better known literary figure of the "Artificer"—he takes Joyce's Stephen Dedalus as his prime example—was always the more analytically inclined figure of the "Knower." Modernism always harbored dual desires, Hollinger explains, both to create new meaning, in the smithy of one's soul, if need be, and to know a more or less objective order—or at least one that can be affirmed intersubjectively. These two pursuits were not, in the first third of the twentieth century, incompatible, and perhaps only now seem so, Hollinger shows, in the wake of postmodernist caricature. Hollinger's dichotomy is illuminating in general and provides in particular a rather useful way of viewing Canetti's distinctive achievement. More than any of the other great German prose modernists, Canetti sought to interrogate the assumptions of the artificer from the perspective of the knower—without, let it be noted, collapsing either position entirely. While others may implicitly suggest the need for the knower's perspective—one thinks of Musil, Broch, and Thomas Mann, all of whom offer powerful analyses of contemporaneous culture—none structures this into the very narrative to the degree of *Auto-da-Fé*. Canetti's novel distinctively ends the sole claim of the artificer—or of those artificer-smitten critics—to represent literary modernism.

My focus on fragmented subjectivity (as the target of Canetti's critique) and on the strong epistemic narrative structure (as the shibboleth of Canetti's "analytic prose") is meant therefore to highlight the ways in which *Auto-da-Fé* occupies a unique border position — an endpoint, surely, though not to a merely linear progression — and thus a fruitful perspective from which to view larger developments in literature and the arts. Though hardly capricious, my emphasis is necessarily selective and thus cannot do justice to all that modernism has come to connote.[24] By situating Canetti within a wide swath of Weimar-era modernist discourse (in the first five chapters) and into a discussion of certain salient aspects of postwar literary modernism (in the final chapter), I have, I hope, laid the groundwork for a clearer grasp of the place of *Auto-da-Fé* in twentieth-century German letters. But this is by no means the final word. And, while attempting to clarify Canetti's distinctiveness, I do not wish in the process to have propagated errors in the opposite direction. Though Broch and Kafka (for example) set themselves off from Canetti in ways I describe at some length below, we would be foolish to overlook their enduring similarities — that which, after all, argues for the comparison in the first place. Kafka's flat characters — despite their curious utility in Adorno's conception of modernism — remain in fact structurally similar to Canetti's. And Broch's noted lament about "partial value systems" — the critique of modernity that suffuses all three volumes of *Die Schlafwandler* (The Sleepwalkers, 1930–32) — certainly finds its counterpart in Canetti's aversion to the sometimes irritatingly unforgettable "private belief worlds" that characterize his novel. Pursuing these relationships in the present study, however, presents a temptation I have had to resist; the scope of my project has permitted only occasional asides and aperçus on authors to whom one could justifiably dedicate whole chapters. Alas, this is a task I must leave to others, or for another day. I hope with this book to have provided an analysis rich enough to provoke — and perhaps even to position — such further investigations.

I have drawn on Canetti's autobiography extensively in the preparation of this book, and thus it may be worth reflecting, at least briefly, on some methodological considerations. There is nothing of which Canetti scholarship is in greater need than a truly critical biography — not a mere restatement of the autobiography. When the estate papers are made accessible, presumably in 2004 (according to newspaper accounts as well as the Hanser publishing house), surely some of the widely accepted truisms about the

Canetti oeuvre—including those that appear in the present study—will need to be revised. To some extent, this is simply inevitable. But even now, it is clear that a great deal of scholarship—and not only that which draws directly on the autobiography—consists merely in classifying Canetti's fiction with Canetti's own theories of language and society. While some of this is manifestly erroneous, as I argue below, the greater danger may be that it is simply isolationist. Following the author's own least helpful example—Canetti famously fails to properly contextualize his social theory, or even fully acknowledge his intellectual predecessors—this kind of scholarship maintains a wall around the oeuvre. Ironically, this is a strategy that is diametrically opposed to Canetti's more laudable and often pathbreaking interdisciplinary interests.

I consider Canetti a privileged and inherently interesting, but not normative, interpreter of his own work, and wish therefore to take account of his views whenever this seems relevant to my argument. In no case, however, have I based an argument exclusively, or even primarily, on such material. I also deem it necessary to acknowledge here what most scholars know: Canetti was very interested in shaping critical responses to his work, though perhaps no more so than many other authors. One should therefore take the author's assertions of influence and the like—perhaps especially when they fit a critic's argument all too well—with a grain or two of salt.

My own interpretative approach derives furthermore from what I judge to be the quality and purpose of the novel's array of intertexts. In order to sketch in essential aspects of interwar culture I have not reinvented the wheel, but drawn liberally on the intellectual histories of Judith Ryan and Susan Marchand, the classic history of philosophy by Frederick Copleston, as well as specialist studies by Peter Gay (on Freud), and others too. I have endeavored, in other words, to bring the existing work of numerous scholars of various fields into conversation with the novel, and meet the reader at the level most commensurate with the intentions of *Auto-da-Fé*. What this means, as I explain below in my discussion of philosophy, is that the novel engages the educated reader and observer of wider cultural trends, but does not seek to intervene in scholarly philosophical debates per se. Such an approach is frankly discouraged by the mode of the allusion to interwar trends and figures: typically parodistic, this referential practice is simply not amenable to what one might consider an "objective" or dispassionate scholarly discussion. By drawing upon an array of authorities, I hope furthermore to evade the charge of capriciousness that has, not without reason, been leveled against cultural studies.[25] While I am keenly interested to note how *Auto-da-Fé* engages the wider culture, and seek to permit the novel the freedom to direct my attention, I turn to those more expert than I in the areas I have identified above to demonstrate that the respective phenomenon under discussion is indeed a salient and significant cultural feature of the interwar period independent of the novel.

Finally, a note of caution. *Auto-da-Fé* has been correctly characterized as harboring a kind of "relentless analysis" ("*bohrende Analyse*").[26] In attempting to follow Canetti, I have probably made myself guilty of the same crime. Again and again, the novel returns to its obsession with those questionable, even reactionary, cultural practices that contribute to the dissolution of the public sphere. *Auto-da-Fé* takes sometimes unexpected turns, engages in controversial and perhaps even objectionable argument, but always returns to this "social" agenda. I have undertaken to document and analyze each such turn. While individual chapters treat roughly discrete topics, there is inevitably some overlap. I have not, for example, been able to treat the topic of misogyny without raising issues that are more properly the province of subsequent chapters. Likewise, it has been necessary to treat the anti-Semitism of Willibald Alexis's text well before the major discussion of this topic in chapter 4. Nevertheless, the argument is on the whole structured so that readers can come and go as they wish; each chapter stands more or less independently, with numerous signposts to other chapters, which can be followed or ignored at the reader's leisure.

1   The Novel(s) in the Novel
Modernism as Parody of Popular Realism

A Different Kind of Novel

In 1930 an ambitious young author set out to write a different kind of book: a novel that would stand out against "the then regnant Viennese literature."[1] That twenty-five-year-old firebrand had, as the seventy-year-old Canetti recounts it, high aspirations, for this was to be "an austere book," "merciless," and, above all, a considerable cut above everything "that could be read as pleasant or pleasing."[2] With a healthy sense indeed of his literary importance, Canetti sought to distance his own work from the popular fiction of the day: "That which was accorded the highest praise was of operatic sentimentality, and among these were the most pitiful journalists and dilettantes. I cannot say that any one of these meant a thing to me; their prose filled me with disgust."[3]

His repulsion notwithstanding, Canetti seems to have been preoccupied with the popular realist and neoromantic literature of his day well before 1975, when he first published the essay in which these remarks appear. For he cites and thematizes popular novels throughout *Auto-da-Fé*, the novel that was to rise far above this humble fare. What is more — and infinitely more complex — he constructed his novel in a way that in some ways mimics the very realist narration he deplores. The point of these strategies is to repel what Canetti felt was the tendency of fiction to become an end in itself, and thus an obstruction to social awareness. Far from a cynical acquiescence in the unreadability of the modern world, *Auto-da-Fé* was to be a more truthful — or, at least, a less dishonest — vehicle for representing the menacing complexity of modernity.

When critics got around to analyzing the narrative structure of his novel, they discovered what Canetti already knew, namely that as experimental as *Auto-da-Fé* clearly is, it simultaneously evinces a traditional form. This led Dieter Liewerscheidt to complain of "A Contradiction in the Narrative Conception of Elias Canetti's Novel *Auto-da-Fé*."[4] More recently, David Darby divines a "rigidity of the narrative structure" lurking beneath the superficial chaos of the characters' rival belief worlds; and while the novel may seem innovative to untrained eyes, yet "this exclusive rigidity suggests an essentially traditional element in the narrative conception of the narrative structure of *Auto-da-Fé*."[5] Both critics have correctly noted the novel's affiliation with the traditional, or what Lennard Davis in *Resisting Novels* calls the "classic novel." What they miss, however, is the point that the relationship of *Auto-da-Fé* to popular realism is not accidental or insidiously atavistic, but quite conscious and parodistic.

Certainly none of this would have come as a surprise to Canetti himself, who repeatedly mentioned that his own novel was conceived as parodic imitation of Balzac: he did not plan simply to rewrite the French master's "human comedy," but to devise a "mad" new version — a "Comédie Humaine an Irren."[6] Indeed, in the same breath that he makes his bold claim for breaking new ground ("One day the thought occurred to me that the world could no longer be represented as in earlier novels"), Canetti divulges his predilection for firm narrative structure, perhaps thereby delineating his own work from Rilke's *Malte,* or, perhaps, from Döblin's already successful *Berlin Alexanderplatz* (1929), which had appeared just as Canetti was making notes for his own novel: "But that did not mean that one should create a chaotic book, in which nothing was to be understood any longer; on the contrary, one had to invent with the utmost discipline extreme individuals."[7] Precisely because Canetti's own "austere book" imitates the very literature it parodies, it will not suffice to describe his novel as merely latter-day, and perhaps even inadvertently, realist. If *Auto-da-Fé* is somehow "essentially traditional," it is so only in the sense that parody must, of necessity, incorporate that which it exposes to critique.

Willibald Alexis's *Die Hosen des Herrn von Bredow*

The novel as literary genre first becomes an issue in *Auto-da-Fé* when Kien meets Therese and decides she might just be educable: "Was it too late, he thought, how old can she be? It is never too late to learn. But she would have to begin with simple novels."[8] He selects a grease-stained copy of Willibald Alexis's *Die Hosen des Herrn von Bredow* (The Trousers of Mr. Bredow, 1848), a dog-eared volume that shows the wear and tear of having been passed around by numerous boyhood friends. A bundle of contradictions, Kien abhors the selfsame book he has never been able to discard. Though he first offers Therese the novel because he suspects that "she longs for culture,"[9] he loses no time in placing novels beyond the pale of true German "Geist":

> A novel was the only thing worth considering for her. But no mind ever grew fat on a diet of novels. The pleasure which they occasionally offer is far too heavily paid for: they undermine the finest characters. They teach us to think ourselves into other men's places. Thus we acquire a taste for change. The personality becomes dissolved in pleasing figments of imagination. The reader learns to understand every point of view. Willingly he yields himself to the pursuit of other people's goals and loses sight of his own. Novels are so many wedges which the novelist, an actor with his pen, inserts into the closed personality of the reader. The better he calculates the size of the wedge and the strength of the resistance, so much the more completely does he crack open the personality of his victim. Novels should be prohibited by the State.[10]

Kien's diatribe calls to mind serious questions about the status and value of novels (echoing a contemporaneous debate on the cultural role of vernacular national literatures at universities),[11] but this humorously paranoid tirade—especially as it culminates in a Platonic demand for state censorship of art—obviously cannot be taken as the novel's final word on the issue. Yet improbable as it may seen, Kien's warped fear of popular novels actually expresses the two points that will structure our own discussion of Alexis. In viewing novels as a kind of sexual seduction that leaves us dispersed and spent, a notion we will encounter again with Kien's brother Georg, the fearful professor correctly affiliates this kind of literature with escapism and passivity. More specifically, Kien's fear of sacrificing his own agency, even disintegrating his very self, by immersing himself in multiple pleasurable acts of readerly identification provides an important point of contrast, albeit comically exaggerated, against which *Auto-da-Fé* defines itself. Yet at this point, we must still greet these themes—Kien's fear of being bodily penetrated by novels, his horror at permitting the disintegration of his carefully cultivated *Charakter* by means of sympathetic overidentification with fictional characters, and his concomitant assumption that novels are just the right fare for women—with the deep suspicion they so richly deserve.

We encounter this same "sexual" orientation toward novels once again in Therese's reaction to Kien's gift. Misled by what she takes to be a suggestive title, "The Trousers of Mr. Bredow," she takes the book for a pornographic potboiler: "She opened the book and read aloud, '*The Trousers*' — she interrupted herself but did not blush. Her face bedewed with a light sweat."[12] Here Canetti slyly alludes to a very similar reception of this same novel in what is perhaps the most beloved instance of German realism, Theodor Fontane's *Effi Briest* (1895). Fontane's Roswitha, a simple domestic not unlike Therese, has been asked to borrow a whole list of books from the local library in order to carry Effi through her feigned illness designed to lengthen her stay in Berlin. But Roswitha balks at the last item on the list, which is of course Alexis's *Die Hosen des Herrn von Bredow*. "Roswitha read to the bottom of the list," the narrator informs us, "and in the next room cut off the last line; she was ashamed — both for herself and for her mistress — to hand over the list in its original form."[13] Like Therese, the semiliterate servant Roswitha assumes the novel is lascivious in nature and therefore disreputable. But unlike Roswitha, Therese eagerly lunges for the book; she does *not* blush, Canetti's narrator pointedly says, but only works up a little anticipatory sweat. With this one allusion, Canetti pithily indicates the problematic appeal of Alexis and his ilk. As Effi's request to Roswitha indicates, Alexis is sought out as a means to kill time, as a pleasant distraction from current problems; indeed Effi implores Roswitha to select "really old books," confusing perhaps the sixteenth-century setting of *Hosen* with its mid-nineteenth-century date of conception and publication.[14] And, as we have seen in both Roswitha and Therese, Alexis arouses a kind of misplaced sexual appeal, which we will explore further below.

While it is true that the core of Canetti's Alexis reception is already adumbrated in these first, brief reactions of Kien and Therese, these passages serve only to foreshadow an intertextual reference of tremendous significance throughout the novel. The Alexis intertext — which is cited no less than eight times[15] — clearly presents an illustration of the kind of novel *Auto-da-Fé* was meant to overcome: an example of culturally affirmative historical realism that offers solace to readers rather than a challenge to engage with contemporary cultural debates. The second — and related — point of contrast will be the narrative superciliousness of *Die Hosen*, a conceit that conceals, rather than problematizes, the use of invidious stereotypes. This "authoritative" endorsement of Germanic cultural unity proved highly seductive,

Canetti suggests, to an identity-deprived Weimar readership.[16] But we are far ahead of our story.

It may well be that for the post–World War II generation of readers neither the name Wilhelm Häring (1798–1871) nor his better known pseudonym Willibald Alexis rings a bell. Indeed by 1950 the Alexis scholar L. H. C. Thomas proclaimed that the bulk of the author's work, including his most popular novel *Die Hosen des Herrn von Bredow,* had "passed into oblivion."[17] Alexis, who began his literary career in 1822 with a translation of Sir Walter Scott and later wrote a series of eight historical "patriotic novels" (*vaterländische Romane*), never escaped the latter's shadow; indeed he had become widely celebrated as "the German Walter Scott."[18] After Fontane and Freytag, whose envy of Alexis's continuing popularity may have had something to do with the latter's eclipse, Alexis was the most popular realist author of the nineteenth century. Although his work was not always enthusiastically received by nineteenth-century critics, his "masterpiece" novel (Thomas) achieved instant and sustained success: "According to book lists, no fewer than sixty editions and reprints of *Die Hosen des Herrn von Bredow* have appeared since the date of first publication."[19]

When Canetti sat down to write *Auto-da-Fé* he could count on the fact that *Die Hosen* was still widely known.[20] The novel was published and reprinted throughout the twenties, reaching a high point in 1924 and 1925 with five separate editions appearing each year.[21] These editions seem to have targeted youthful and patriotic readers, for their publishers bore names such as the *Deutsche Jugendklub-Bücherei* (German Youth Club Library) and the *Deutsche Dichter-Gedächtnis-Stiftung* (German Poets Memorial Foundation; Dresden, 1927) and they were included in series such as *Lebensbücher der Jugend* (Lifebooks of the Young; Westermann, 1923–25), *Bücher der Deutschen* (Books of the Germans; Stiepel, 1922) and *Die bunten Romane der Weltliteratur* (Colorful Novels of World Literature; Verlag der Schillerbuchhandlung, 1925). In the previous decade the novel had been annotated for use in history courses and was joined in 1921 by another school edition from the presses of Velhagen and Klasing. In 1928 *Die Hosen* joined the ranks of *Reclams Universal-Bibliothek,* a well-known and respected series of inexpensive paperbacks designed to bring culture to the masses.[22] Though Fontane may ultimately have been correct when he prophesied in 1873 that Alexis would only be remembered by local fan clubs ("die kleinen W. Alexisgemeinden"), he completely missed the mark when it came to the enormous

Figure 1. Title page from a turn-of-the-century edition of Willibald Alexis's Die Hosen des Herrn von Bredow. *Harvard University Libraries.*

popularity of *Die Hosen* in the first half of this century.[23] What did those contemporaries of the twenty-five-year-old Canetti know, that we, in all likelihood, no longer do?

The story, which was once as familiar to Germans as Mark Twain's *Tom Sawyer* still is to Americans, is quickly told. While Götz von Bredow, a frontier nobleman of the early sixteenth century, is sleeping off a drinking bout held in celebration of the conclusion of a provincial diet (Landtag), his wife Brigitte sneaks off his famous trousers to give them a long overdue washing. Her moral dilemma, which she earnestly discusses with the *Dechant* (a clergyman), arises from the conflict between her duty as *Hausfrau* to uphold an exemplary standard of cleanliness and her obligation as *Frau* not to deceive her husband, who could never bear to be parted from his lucky trousers. Thus, contrary to the prurient expectations aroused in both Roswitha and Therese, this woman's interest in removing her husband's pants is totally lacking in erotic motivation; it is, rather, purely a "German" dilemma between two kinds of duty. Brigitte errs on the side of cleanliness and submits her husband's legendary elk skin pants (*Elenshosen*) to the annual outdoor fall laundry. A wandering peddler, or *Krämer*, arrives on the scene and arouses the attention of the laundry detail, which is starved for news and held in awe by his magnificent wares.

Some of the *Krämer*'s goods turn out to be fraudulent, a plot segment that exhibits a longstanding anti-Semitic trope about the deceitful Jew, as we will have further occasion to notice below. The ensuing displeasure sets the plot, at long last, in motion. Late that night in the Bredow castle *Hohenziaß* an unexpected guest arrives: it is Lindenberg, trusted advisor to the Elector Joachim I in Berlin, and a distant relation of the Bredows. Having lost in a crap game all the money entrusted to him by the prince for distribution to the poor, Lindenberg begins to cast about for ways to replenish his purse and avoid humiliation at court.

He mounts a diatribe—beginning with the young Elector and culminating with that upstart "bourgeois rabble" (*Bürgerpack*)—against all the social and political forces that threaten the traditional privileges of the landed aristocracy. This drunken harangue is clearly prompted by Lindenberg's gambling losses and is suspiciously framed by mention of the rich peddler Klaus Hedderich, who, it is said, could well afford to relieve the nobleman of his financial embarrassment. Lindenberg hatches a plan to initiate the adopted noble sons Hans-Jochem and Hans-Jürgen into the ancient—and now forbidden—*Faustrecht* of the aristocracy. Though Lindenberg claims that the reassertion of this now obsolete aristocratic practice of appropriating property at will is meant to redress the contemporary bourgeois affront to the *Junker* nobility, he will conveniently line his own pockets while taking this "principled" stand. That night they set out to ambush the peddler Hedderich, ostensibly to teach him a lesson for selling false wares, but actually to relieve him of his considerable wealth.

The brothers Hans (Hans-Jochem and Hans-Jürgen) are figures borrowed from the folk tale. All too predictably, one is good looking, well liked, and destined for knighthood and the world, whereas the other is distinctly plain, painfully shy, and marked for the monastery. Equally foreseeable is the eventual reversal: the handsome Hans-Jochem is crippled in the raid on Hedderich and is carted off to the cloister. Hans-Jürgen rises to the occasion, recovers von Bredow's pants (which the peddler had stolen), and becomes, by virtue of his unflinching honesty, the trustworthy advisor to the Elector, replacing the treacherous Lindenberg. Eva, once the object of Hans-Jochem's vain desire, becomes his brother's bride. With this marriage, Hans-Jürgen's ascent from neglected, orphaned son to privileged royal advisor is complete. It is a typical rags-to-riches fairy tale.

The story moves within carefully plotted moral coordinates: Hans-Jochem, the narrator instructs us, was given to "vanity and pride";[24] and the favored treatment he received from his adoptive family had suspiciously to do with a certain "substantial inheritance,"[25] which his brother lacked. His maiming injury was, therefore, foreordained by a narrative logic that punishes evil and rewards good. The treasonous Lindenberg pays for his disloyalty with his life, and even the ultimately good Elector-prince must pay for his youthful naiveté and gullibility. Though every figure must at some point withstand the scrutiny of the moralizing narrator, none acquits herself quite so well as the good wife Brigitte. After the know-it-all narrator, she is the moral standard bearer of the novel: A woman who knows her place, she can switch effortlessly from the role of "absolute ruler" ("unumschränkte Herrin") in household matters to the most subservient of women vis-à-vis men.[26] Indicating their essential consonance, the narrator says of Brigitte: "The housewife considered all manner of hard work a celebration, and we think so too."[27] It comes as no surprise, then, that Brigitte is the real hero of the novel: due to her ingenuity (and the practice she gained during the recent autumnal outdoor laundry), she is again able to deprive her husband of his heirloom pants, and thereby ensure his failure to take part in the rebellion against the Elector. Hans-Jürgen can decisively prove von Bredow's innocence because, thanks to Brigitte, he is able show that throughout the insurrection he had been in possession of "Die Hosen des Herrn von Bredow."

Those early readers of *Auto-da-Fé* who were still familiar with Alexis's novel, perhaps from their childhood reading, perhaps even from their school curriculum, would probably first have been struck by the humorous incongruity. Beyond the fact that Therese is virtually illiterate, it is clear that Kien, who read and reread *Die Hosen* as a child, mistakenly thinks of Therese as a harmless Brigitte figure. Like his cultural cousin Professor Rath (or, as his unappreciative students called him, Professor Unrath), Kien conceives of women in a painfully naïve manner that is thoroughly informed by the idealizing literature of a bygone era.[28] This comes as no surprise, for, as we shall see, Kien's conceptions of the material, sensual world—of which women are simply the chief exponents—are predetermined by the "higher" truths of books. Kien no more comprehends Therese as an erotic partner than Emanuel Rath does Lola-Lola's manifest sexuality (sleeping with Lola-Lola meant just that: sleeping). On the contrary, Kien anticipates in the first instance a model housekeeper, or *Wirtschafterin* (an expectation Therese initially fulfills in her solicitous treatment of *Die Hosen*), and a Brigitte-like woman, who knows her place. As we shall see in the following chapter, Therese grotesquely clashes with the gender expectations of both Kien and contemporaneous culture.[29]

The key aspect of *Die Hosen*, however, and one that would have been remembered long after plot twists and turns were forgotten, is that it is a historical novel at a double remove from the post–World War I period in which Canetti parodically cites it. Though it may seem hard to believe in the wake of the debate on history and fiction initiated by Hayden White, historical fiction was (and perhaps still is in some quarters) taken very seriously *as history*.[30] For Adolf von Grolmann, for example, Alexis's historical fiction represents an "internal contradiction" that nevertheless demands adulation when it is carried off well.[31] Despite the inevitable pitfalls endemic to the mix of history and fiction, *Die Hosen*, of all Alexis's "*vaterländische Romane*" (the subtitle of a whole series of his books) receives the highest marks for its faithfulness to history. Thomas even goes so far as to credit Alexis as a forerunner of the eminent positivist historian Leopold von Ranke.[32] Whatever we might today make of this novel's relationship to the early sixteenth century, the fact remains that German pedagogues and publishers of the Weimar period deemed it appropriate for the classroom.

This association of Alexis with the grand tradition of Rankian positivism may, however, distract from the more questionable ends to which such literature was routinely put, namely, as culturally affirmative purveyor of national(ist) tradition. Lynne Tatlock suggests that Alexis's historical novels were always simultaneously a means of coping with contemporaneous reality: it is a mistake, she says, "to see the historical novel and the novel of contemporary life as two distinct genres."[33] At the turn of the century, Thomas suggests, Alexis's "works may have been officially encouraged for political reasons. In the years following the unification of Germany an effort was made to build up a German tradition, something which older nations had created for themselves through the centuries. The importance of Prussia, now the center of the new state, required emphasis, and Alexis's novels were based on what little historical tradition Prussia had to offer."[34] The ideological value of the *vaterländische Romane* in shoring up the Prussian state seems clear enough; patriotism was at any rate the Alexian attribute emphasized both by Freytag and Fontane. The appeal of *Die Hosen* and similar historical fiction during the Weimar period cannot have been very different. At a time when national identity and political traditions were either lacking or hotly contested, novels in the mode of Alexis, which celebrate German historical traditions that perhaps never were, must have provided an anchor in an ideological maelstrom. In this regard, we would do well to recall that "the modernist and new objectivist aesthetics that emerged in Germany in the 1920s" were by no means typical of the time. In fact, as Wolfgang Natter points out in his study *Literature at War, 1914-1940*, traditionalist, patriotic, and nationalist literature was deeply entrenched and, indeed, promoted by virtually all the German cultural institutions in any way connected with literature.[35] For Canetti, at any rate, the recourse to historical fiction as an ameliorative for the identity crises of the interwar period represented one of those reactionary responses to modernity the greater novel parodies.

Canetti captures this flight into history above all by means of his protagonist, whose own practice of reading the world replicates that of the classic Alexian historical novel. Before Therese becomes his chief nemesis, Kien's confrontation with brutal reality takes the form of his relationship to Benedikt Pfaff, the retired police officer turned doorman. Though Kien would like to think of the monthly payments to this ogre as a generous gratuity, they amount in fact to the kind of bribe mafia toughs extort in return for "protection." Kien's method of coping with this menacing brute is to historicize him in a manner that both alludes to and reiterates the historical appeal of Alexis's novel. The period to which Kien assigns Pfaff, the early sixteenth century, underscores the connection to *Die Hosen des Herrn von Bredow*. Rumaging through a pile of books, Kien alights upon an academic strategy that will disarm this menacing beast:

> In the catalogue of the fallen books, there figured as No. 39 a stout antique volume on *Arms and Tactics of the Landsknechts*. Scarcely had it curvetted off the ladder, with fearful crash, than the trumpeting caretakers were transformed into landsknechts. A vast inspiration surged up in Kien. The caretaker was a landsknecht, what else? The fist had no more terrors for him. Before him sat a familiar historical figure. He knew what it would do and what it would not do ... Unhappy, late-born creature, who had come into the world a landsknecht in the twentieth century ... shut out from the epoch for which it had been created, stranded in another to which it would always remain a stranger! *In the innocuous remoteness of the sixteenth century the caretaker dwindled to nothing, let him brag as he would! To master a fellow-creature, it suffices to find his place in history.*[36]

It is of course not the sixteenth century per se that elicits such a sense of calm in the professor, but its safe remove from the rough and tumble of the interwar present. Recall that this was a time, as Thomas Mann records in his diaries, when military issue machine guns from the First World War fell into the hands of rival cliques, creating havoc in the once serene streets of Munich. Kien maintains this historicizing illusion about Pfaff throughout the bulk of the novel until his true brutality is no longer avoidable. When the brutish *Hausbesorger* apprehends Kien at the Theresianum (the state-run auction house cum pawn shop), Kien begrudgingly admits, in a pun that is characteristic of the novel's wit, "*Die Vergangenheit ist vorbei*"[37] (The past is over) — meaning that the ruse of employing history as prophylactic against a disconcerting present had now decisively failed. With Kien's enthusiasm for the "harmless distance" of the past, Canetti puts his finger both on a contemporary trend of the interwar period and on a bankrupt strategy of historical realism that is best summed up as escapism.[38] Kien develops this talent into a virtual cult of the past — at the expense, of course, of any engagement with his own contemporary polity.³⁹ Ironically, Kien, who set himself so far above Alexis's historical fiction, lives by the very same escapist principles.

Kien's brother Georg presents a strikingly similar view of belletristic novels: for him they represent an insular phase to be overcome, something he believes he has left behind in order to turn to the world of the mentally ill. Georg, too, associates novels with sex and women. But whereas Peter dreads novels as "wedges" (*Keile*) that would penetrate and dissolve the armor of his panzerlike *Charakter,* leaving him spent and distracted, Georg fondly remembers them as pleasurable occasions of sexuality: "Reading was fondling, was another form of love, was for ladies and ladies' doctors, to whose profession a delicate understanding of *lecture intime* properly belonged."⁴⁰

Such pleasures are, of course, private; in fact, Georg relates the joys of *"schöngeistige Lektüre"* (polite, usually belletristic literature) directly to its ability to smooth over the social divisions of the real world by reiterating empty but elegantly formulated sentences about "intimacy."⁴¹ In the following passage, we observe how Georg explicitly links novelistic escapism to mindless sex. Moreover, it appears that French novels served for him as a kind of instructional manual for seducing the clients of his gynecological practice, while providing the simultaneous pleasure of distracting him from the tragic and disruptive events of his own society:

> The best novels were those in which the people spoke in the most cultured way ... The task of such a writer was to reduce the angular, painful, biting multifariousness of life as it was all around one, to the smooth surface of a sheet of paper, on which it could pleasantly and swiftly be read off ... The more often was the same track traversed, the subtler was the pleasure derived from the journey ... Georges Kien had started as a gynaecologist. His youth and good looks brought patients in crowds. At that period, which did not last long, he gave himself up to French novels; they played a considerable part in assuring his success ... Surrounded and spoilt by innumerable women, all ready to serve him, he lived like Prince Gautama before he became Buddha. No anxious father and prince had cut him off from the miseries of the world, but he saw old age, death and beggars in such an abundance that he no longer noticed them. Yet he was indeed cut off, by the books he read, the sentences he spoke, the women who were ranged round him in a greedy close-built wall.⁴²

"Sealed off" (*abgeschlossen*), protected by an "unbroken wall" (*geschlossene Mauer*): There is probably no clearer expression of literature's problematic potential—here linked explicitly to male heterosexual gratification—to become an insular form of escapism. Georg's conception of novel reading as a sort of eroticized anaesthesia certainly takes the critique of Alexis's comforting historicism a step further. Yet, given the fact that Georg himself turns out to be a thoroughly questionable character, can we confidently say that this is the overall position of *Auto-da-Fé*?

Given the demonstrable social concerns of Canetti's novel, which are detailed further in subsequent chapters of this study, as well as the consistently skeptical attitude toward insular behavior we encounter in the novel, we can assume that Georg's rejection of belletristic novels as pleasurable diversions falls in line—though perhaps not quite in the way he intended—with the novel's larger position. But the question about Georg's reliability is nevertheless well placed, because it will lead us to a more precise distinction. The simple *pleasure* derived from identifying with a beautiful and trustworthy character, which is a standard feature of popular prose, becomes more complicated in *Auto-da-Fé*. It is not that Canetti sets out to deprive us of these gratifications utterly; rather he shows, above all in Georg, that identification is both a necessary and highly problematic process. The question of Georg's credibility regarding his views on novels, then, is itself part of a larger narrative strategy that is designed to entice the reader to identify with him. We are intended, in other words, to approve of Georg, at least provisionally; and thus it comes as little surprise that he here seems so right about novels. Ultimately, the point is neither to establish the brothers Kien as trustworthy nor as reliably and consistently untrustworthy; like all modernists, Canetti foregrounds the reader's role in making and revising such judgments. But he does so in ways that have not yet been fully appreciated. To elucidate this point will require us, temporarily at least, to leave our *Trousers* behind—but not without a promise to return.

Ascriptive Narration

Georg's musings on novel reading as an essentially antisocial mode of autoerotic gratification comes very close to the view proffered by the critic Lennard J. Davis, who, in *Resisting Novels* warns against novelistic seductions. He reminds us that "novels are not life . . . and [that] their function is to help humans adapt to the fragmentation and isolation of the modern world."[43] For Davis, as for Canetti, this function is highly suspect, because social fragmentation is typically overcome in novel reading not through engagement, but by means of pure avoidance. Thus the classic novel—the realist novel of the nineteenth century, which is the focus of Davis's study—offers a number of dubious defenses against modernity which, in turn, merit our vigilant supervision.

Central among these defenses is the process of identification.[44] Davis's remarks on this mechanism will help us understand what Canetti is up to with the asymmetrical figure of Georg:

> Now the issue of physical beauty becomes more understandable. Since the physical beauty of most protagonists is not accidental but taken as a functioning requirement of the classic novel, I would suggest its function is that it encourages the element of desire to enter the reading process. In making a character attractive, the author can draw the reader towards that set of signs much as advertisers can draw consumers toward a product by associating it with a physically attractive model. In effect, it is not so much that we identify with a character, but that we desire that character in some nonspecific but erotic way. In this sense, part of novel reading is the process of falling in love with characters or making friends with signs.[45]

With this in mind, the structural spoof on realist identification that attends the introduction of Georg Kien comes more clearly into view. Georg is not only the most likable character in a novel peopled with despicable and disgusting louts, he is also the most differentiated of the otherwise flat characters. Dagmar Barnouw observes correctly that "he is the most ambivalent, the most psychologically realistic figure of the novel."[46] Yet, above all, he is—or appears at first blush—"beautiful and kind."[47] "He was tall, strong, fiery and sure of himself; in his features there was something of that gentleness which women need before they can feel at home with a man. Those who saw him compared him to Michelangelo's Adam."[48] Only later will it occur to the reader that this glowing description, not unlike those laudatory program notes about actors and singers, has been authored by none other than the honoree himself.

Canetti's point in introducing the good, and good-looking, doctor four-fifths through *Auto-da-Fé,* is central to the novel's project of reflecting on—and distancing itself from—popular contemporary realism. Up until this point in the novel, Canetti has deprived us of any identification possibilities by serving up misers, cheats, and self-deluded megalomaniacs. With Georg we get for the first time someone like us, which is to say someone like our idealized selves, a person we can trust. More than that, as Davis would remind us, we receive with Georg the ideological comfort that comes from the belief in unitary characters, and from the conviction that individuals can effect social change—recall that Georg is a world-renowned psychiatrist, whose revolutionary methods of treatment are the envy of the profession and the promise of the future.[49]

Early critics of the novel took the bait, as I believe first time readers still do: Ernst Waldinger's review of 1936 asserts, for example, that Georg "symbolically represents—as we can easily guess—the writer himself with his interpretations and solutions."[50] Similarly, Walter Allen, in a review of 1947, writes of Georg as "the one sane character in the book . . . an eminent psychiatrist . . . who alone is aware of objective reality."[51] The novel does not ultimately support such an identification, as Barnouw has quite persuasively shown, but it does tease us. After all, as we shall see in the following chapter, Georg, who considers himself such a distinguished "connoisseur of men" (*Menschenkenner*), completely bungles his brother's cure.[52]

Why the tease? What Canetti has enacted at the structural level by having us lunge toward Georg to satisfy our craving for identification is a replay of an epistemological object lesson—this time between reader and text—that has already been played out a number of times at the level of story and that is part and parcel of realist fiction like *Die Hosen.* The pitfall, as we see again and again, is that identification, as a process for determining what is true, real, and valuable is an extremely problematic process. Whereas Alexis—as we shall soon see—proffers identification in a naive and unreflective manner, Canetti makes it the object of merciless parody.

In the following scene, Fischerle, the hunchback dwarf Kien meets when he is evicted from his library-apartment, attempts to ingratiate himself by showing exaggerated concern for the professor's unwieldy "mental library" (*Kopfbibliothek*). Before permitting this little man (*Männchen*) to take on this awesome responsibility, Kien inquires, as a standard precaution, whether this incorrigible thief has ever stolen. Kien receives the assurance he needs when he discovers that he and Fischerle share a lack of athletic prowess—that is, just at that moment when he establishes an identificatory bond:

> "You are no doubt a fast runner?" Fischerle saw through the trap and answered: "What would be the point of lying? When you take a step, I take half a one. At school I was always the worst runner." He thought up the name of a school lest Kien should ask him: in fact he had never been to one. But Kien was wrestling with weightier problems [namely the memory of his own physical shortcomings]. He was about to make the greatest gesture of trust of his entire life. "I believe you!" he said simply. Fischerle was jubilant.[53]

Later, in the course of Fischerle's scheme devised to fleece him, Kien chooses to believe a far-fetched tale concocted by the *Fischerin* (Fischerle's would-be lover) simply "because her indignation pleased him."[54] The novel is full of such scenes in which a misplaced identification of one figure with another results in hilarious misconstructions. Critics miss the point, therefore, when they stress exclusively the reader's epistemological superiority over the fictional world of *Auto-da-Fé*, forgetting that we, too, fall for Georg in a manner that has been rehearsed at the figural level throughout the novel.

Moreover, there is a certain warmth to this inclusive gesture that critics often overlook. While I stress the fact that Canetti subjects his readers to the very identification trap in which he enmeshes his repellent figures, there is perhaps a positive side to this technique: our condescension toward the novel's figures is pierced by the realization that we, too, are implicated in the very same hermeneutic process. As if to make the point that we are all subject to the Janus-faced potential endemic to identification, which holds out both the prospect of insight as well as the danger of vain distortion, Canetti comments in his autobiography on a rumor, passed along by an otherwise thoroughly untrustworthy gossip ("*Schwätzer*"), about his dear friend Dr. Sonne. "I accepted [the hearsay] without further investigation," he confides, "it simply pleased me so much, that I granted it credulity."[55] Of course, this rumor (which, incidentally, claimed that Sonne was a great philanthropist who attempted to keep his generosity anonymous) could prove false; Canetti is obviously no less vulnerable to error than anyone else. Considering the issue of identification from this retrospective view, the novel's position comes more clearly into view. The perceptual error Canetti seems so concerned with in the novel is perhaps not the essential epistemological dilemma, the "*erkenntnistheoretische*" problem attending any such act of judgment, but the fact that the typical case of figural identification implies a *willful* reduction of the other to the very limited parameters of the projecting self. Canetti's own identification with Sonne fails to arouse our condemnation not because it is any less fraught with possible error, but because this process directs Canetti outward and positively, far beyond his own abilities and interests. It is frankly true that the matter of identification is treated in *Auto-da-Fé* in primarily negative terms: here it is principally a danger that the novel will not let us forget. But this proves to be a central concept in Canetti's thinking that evolved significantly throughout this life. *Auto-da-Fé* frames the question, but it is not the last word on the hermeneutics of identification. Here as elsewhere, we are undoubtedly richer for considering the full scope of Canetti's thought; but it would be mistaken to assert crass equations. In opposition to Freud, as I endeavor to show in the penultimate chapter of this study, Canetti later developed a positive concept of transformative identification that he would famously dub "*Verwandlung*"—literally, "metamorphosis." As in other key areas, the novel's insistent negations would lead ultimately to more positive, though still cautious, affirmations. But once again, we are far ahead of our story.

When Davis writes of "novelistic identification," he is explicitly expanding the term to include both character *and* narrator, for the latter is also a source of seduction as well as an object of identification.[56] Indeed, Davis goes so far as to collapse the two when, for example, he maintains that "the character with whom readers most seek to connect is the narrator."[57] If we turn our attention now to that portion of *Die Hosen* which, we are told, Therese so meticulously reads and rereads, we are immediately confronted with an instructive contrast. Davis's observations on classic narration prepare us perfectly for the Alexian narrator: "The presence of the narrator is comforting and mature, and authorizes the restoration of order, community and communication by his or her very presence. This authority is made even more dramatic in the nineteenth century by the fiction that almost all narrators are male."[58] True to form, Alexis's patriarchal narrator opens with an expansive aerial shot of Brigitte's *Herbstwäsche* (autumn laundry), asks himself rhetorically what those specks of white could be, suggests a whole series of incorrect answers as he slowly moves us closer to the scene, and finally brings the great laundry enterprise into sharp focus. The narrator's mastery of space repeats itself when he momentarily occupies the perspective of the man in the moon.⁵⁹ When Brigitte later ventures out onto the roof, but is too preoccupied with her husband's pants to take in the breathtaking scenery, the narrator steps in to tell us what she *doesn't* see.⁶⁰

His magisterial spatial purview is matched by his temporal perspective: conscious of the intervening centuries, and constantly mediating between the past and the present, the narrator introduces a long descriptive passage with these words: "At that time the region was completely different than it is today."⁶¹ Most importantly, the narrator provides the moral fulcrum, stepping back occasionally even from his beloved Brigitte to remind us: "But the best woman remains a woman," ⁶² suggesting that even someone as sensible and practical as Brigitte cannot be assumed to transcend the inherent weaknesses of her gender.

Alexis's narrator, in other words, perfectly demonstrates Davis's soothing male authority figure, who provides seemingly reliable ethical and epistemological orientation to the reader. For Davis, this aspect of epistemological authority is the sine qua non of the classic narrator and explains our most fundamental attraction to this voice in the text: "As characters, then, narrators may not have physical beauty, but they are required to 'know the world.' The central myth here, as with the myth of beauty, is that if one is able to write a novel—to manipulate words into things—then one must be able to understand things and thoughts better than most other people." ⁶³ All of which only serves to magnify the contrast between the narrator of *Auto-da-Fé* and the narrator of *Die Hosen*. For though Canetti's narrator takes on the appearance of seductive omniscience, we soon come to see that he is driven and riven by incompatible figural interests.

The earliest and most apparent illustration of this can be seen in a key scene near the beginning of Book 1 of *Auto-da-Fé*. This situation, paradigmatic for the novel's narrative strategy—and therefore a point of reference later in this study—amply demonstrates the initial collusion of the narrator with the protagonist Peter Kien. For all we know, the professor is an innocent bystander witnessing the following exchange on a Viennese street: "Suddenly he heard someone shouting loudly at someone else: 'Can you tell me where Mut Street is?' There was no reply. Kien was surprised: *so there were other silent people besides himself to be found in the busy streets.* Without looking up he listened for more. How would the questioner behave in the face of this silence? . . . Still he said nothing. Kien applauded him . . . *Still the second man said nothing . . .* The incident was taking place on his right hand. The first man was yelling: 'You've no manners!' The second man was still silent. Then Kien felt a nasty jolt. The other man, the silent one, the man with character, who controlled his tongue even in anger, was Kien himself."[64]

This passage provides an early lesson on how to read the novel. Here (as elsewhere) the reader is duped, albeit temporarily, by a narrator who is repeatedly commandeered by his characters. Though we ultimately learn of the identity of Kien and "the second man," we will never again be able to read so trustingly. Like all beginner's lessons, this one is fairly elementary; later on we will not be told so directly that the narrator has conspired with— or been inhabited by—one of the characters. In fact, we are as readers encouraged to adopt the very cynical attitude that pervades the story itself. Far from the cosmic vantage point offered by the Alexian narrator, Canetti's narrator fails in his essential task "to know the world," a point I will return to in chapter 3. Rather than lulled into epistemic security, we are in fact called upon continually to engage in an active and not always very satisfying hermeneutic revisionism.

Having carefully sifted the claims and counterclaims of various critics regarding the narrative status of diverse passages of the novel, David Darby observes: "The conclusion one reaches from conducting such a survey of opinions regarding the extent of the different types of focalization is that the limits are extremely difficult to define... The effect of this almost ubiquitous ambiguity, along with the tendency of the narrator to slip between focalizers, undermines the authenticity of the information discoursed throughout the novel."[65] For Darby, the novel's crucial conflict is essentially internecine, namely that between the characters and the narrator. Following Dolezel's narratological lead, Darby postulates a battle between the characters, each intent upon installing his or her own private "figural belief world" as normative reality, and the narrator, who ultimately possesses the "authentication authority" of the greater novel. He declares the narrator the victor in this struggle, and thus solves what for him is the novel's great riddle—namely how relative clarity proceeds from such ambiguity.

Darby's close reading enriches our understanding of the dynamic nature of narration that characterizes *Auto-da-Fé*, but it does not solve the riddle entirely. For the intelligibility of these "inauthentic" rival belief worlds rests ultimately on their exclusion of any wider (and therefore more complex) vision of social reality. It is fundamentally the highly reductive and grotesquely stylized character of these mutually exclusive worlds that makes them in the end detectable and amenable to debunking. The panoptic view we gain on the characters' doomed solipsistic escapades proceeds less from a particularly knowledgeable or authoritative narrator, than from the characters' own highly problematic retreat from the intersubjective, social realm.

Narration in *Auto-da-Fé*, far from offering comforting structure, sets in motion a process of interrogation and ascription. When confronted with one of those moments of indeterminacy, the reader is put in the uncomfortable position of actively employing a set of conveniently discrete stereotypes—convenient, that is, from the point of view of the hermeneutic task. Crassly put, once inducted to the hermeneutics of suspicion and confronted with the set of stereotyped characters at our disposal, we must continually ask ourselves questions like these: Does this unit of narration sound like the lecherous *Wirtschafterin*? Is this scrap of speech attributable to the moneygrubbing Jew, the pompous professor, or the bestial *Hausbesorger*? Though we may in some cases decode the ostensibly third person narration differently (i.e., attribute it to another figural voice), we all draw on the stereotypes introduced by the novel to make sense of the voices which variously inhabit the narrator. The novel's success at combining pervasive narrative ambiguity with plot-level clarity, is therefore ultimately to be found not in narratological models, but in the culture which purveys the reductive and pernicious clichés on which Canetti so richly draws in the first place.

Auto-da-Fé provides its own antimodel in the form of the book given to Therese, which sets in motion the disastrous marriage, and thus the entire plot. Canetti's parody of narrative "Blendung" should therefore be understood against the blindness of the allegedly omniscient Alexian narrator, the most glaring example of which is his obliviousness to, which really amounts to his endorsement of, anti-Semitism. Despite his impressive geographic and temporal command, this narrator, who is otherwise full of truisms, judgments, and platitudes, fails to open his mouth on this (quite literally) central issue in the novel.

Book 1 of *Die Hosen* sets up a symbolic chain of signifiers, which employs the cliché of the deceitful Jew: the narrator explicitly associates the peddler with the devil and depicts him as conspicuously moneygrubbing.[66] Later, when Lindenberg inquires about the availability of a Jew to solve his financial worries, his hosts immediately suggest the hawker Hedderich.[67] In the meantime, the clergyman and Peter Melchior (of the Bredow clan) have a conversation that recapitulates the moral about the Jewish monger: the *Dechant* insists that it is acceptable to cheat the devil (read: the Jewish peddler), because he cheats us. Melchior concedes the latter statement, but insists that "One shouldn't even cheat the devil"[68] — thereby upholding the analogy between Jew and devil even while making a moral point. In each of these cases, it should be noted, the novel's morality extends only to the injustice of revenge; the cliché itself, the "guilty Jew," is never questioned. Lindenberg later tells a parallel story about the tailor Wiedeband; but, for obvious reasons, Lindenberg — who is about to attack Hedderich — fully endorses the execution of this deceitful and prideful tailor.[69]

Now all of this may seem overly subtle for a popular novel; and indeed it would be, were it not for the overt pronouncements made at the opening of Book 2. Speaking of von Bredow's arrest for having ambushed Hedderich, the Elector's bodyguard and the courtier Otterstädt exchange the following words: "Old man Krippenreiter has had such misfortune that he's ambushing a Jew who is travelling with his wares to Berlin." "A Jew." "Or something like that."[70] The confusion (or better, equation) of the deceitful, venal peddler with "the Jew" continues as the matter is discussed, and is picked up by Lindenberg as an obvious identification when he responds to the Elector's query: "Your Highness is referring to yesterday's attack on the Jew, about which I've heard."[71]

Up to this point one might still entertain the possibility that the politically progressive Alexis, who was loosely associated with the *Junges Deutschland* (Young Germany) group, may be thematizing rather than underwriting anti-Semitism.[72] Yet this assumption is misplaced: as Hal Draper has documented, many, indeed a majority, of Germany's liberals of this era were open anti-Semites.[73] The possibility of a critical perspective on anti-Semitism is definitively foreclosed when the idealistic young Elector (whose right-hand man the novel's young hero becomes) announces: "I hate the Jews, Lindenberg, and plan to tighten the reign on these unbelieving usurers, when their time comes. For they are and remain betrayers of the blood of our Lord and Savior. Yet, even if it were Simon the thief or Judas Iscariot, who took the thirty silver pieces, no one would have the right, and no one should even dare, to lay a hand upon him where I have reserved jurisdiction to myself."[74] The Elector would like to come across as noble: despite his pronounced religious anti-Semitism (which was widely held to be a defensible position up to, and in some cases even after, the Holocaust),[75] he energetically insists on banning rogue anti-Semitic vigilantes. But as his first sentence reveals, his hatred toward Jews is as much economic as religious, and he is really only reserving the right of such violent punishment to himself. Like Brigitte, whose only objection to beating that "knave of a peddler"[76] is that it will result in driving up the price of the goods of those peddlers who survive, the Elector's pronouncement has nothing to do with what he deems to be the essentially guilty and duplicitous Jew. Although Alexis does afford Joachim some depth by depicting weaknesses as well as strengths, the Elector remains an essentially positive figure.[77] His naivete regarding the Junkers' insurrection and his draconian punishment of Lindenberg—not, at any rate, his blatant anti-Semitism—constitute the sins for which he pays with loneliness.[78]

Conversely, neither does the eventual rehabilitation of Lindenberg affect the bigoted representation of the Jew.[79] That the novel's two great adversaries can so readily agree on this single issue, does, however, undercut any lingering supposition that Alexis's portrayal of anti-Semitism may somehow yet be critical. The clinching argument for *Die Hosen* is the narrator's complicity. Again in Book 2 he engages in diabolical description of the peddler, encouraging the semiotic link, already common at the time, connecting peddler, devil, tailor, and Jew.[80] Even more damning for this otherwise loquacious narrator is his sudden silence on blatant anti-Semitism. Recall that this is the same narrator, who, on other occasions, has not hesitated to supply us with such pearls of wisdom as: "The mind of man is changeable," to spell out the already evident cautionary tale inherent in Hans-Jochem's vanity, to jest about von Bredow's modest mental ability, or to preach his gospel of simple living.[81] Ironically, Hedderich's actual religious status remains in doubt to the end. Yet, given the ideological cast of the novel, the message is clearly not the relatively enlightened view that Christians, too, can be as rapacious as any others, but rather that one can justifiably be mistaken for a Jew if one behaves like the venal and dishonest Hedderich.

Of course Canetti, too, incorporates anti-Semitism in his novel, as we shall observe in some detail in chapter 4. But whereas Alexis goes to great lengths to naturalize bigotry, the racial and gender stereotypes of *Auto-da-Fé* virtually jump off the page. The reader of *Die Hosen,* as we have seen, is meant to identify with the racist narrator; the reader of *Auto-da-Fé* is painfully confronted with grotesque caricatures that cry out to be understood against the culture that fostered and propagated them. The Alexian text, I am arguing, serves up bigotry (and other comforting truisms) in the comfort of a hermetically packaged historical narrative that served in the interwar period to insulate readers from a disconcerting political and social reality. In contrast, Canetti's is virtually a know-nothing narrator, more placeholder than identifiable persona. Though there exists an undeniable narrative voice—as when Fischerle's murder and Kien's suicide are recounted—it is simply not the voice of pacifying authority. And if the narrator ultimately wins that "narrative battle" against the novel's characters, it is a Pyrrhic victory in which he remains their sometime hostage.

Perhaps the best evidence that narration in *Auto-da-Fé* is more a vexing question than a quenching font of epistemological authority comes from reception data. To use Davis's term, one can confidently state that this is not a novel that needs resisting—it seems to have provoked that response all on its own. Far from Georg's conception of reading as mindless sex, readers of *Auto-da-Fé* have often enough reported their *dis*pleasure: one thinks immediately of Hans Magnus Enzensberger's famous description of the novel as "a literary monster" (*ein literarisches Monstrum*), or of Marcel Reich-Ranicki's peremptory pronouncement that it is "ungenießbar"—unpalatable, not merely unenjoyable.

A good deal of this difficulty can be traced to the narrative strategy that fails to provide a ready-made perspective from which to view the insidious stereotypes that inhabit the novel. Reading, and rereading, is so annoying because just when we hope to pin some execrable assertion on the narrator, we discover that hiding in an apparently objective narrative voice is a focalized mind set after all—or at least the distinct possibility of one. What frustrates the reader is not the process of ascription itself—the attribution of some apparently gnomic statement to a particular figure—but the fact that it forces us, at least provisionally, to adopt as a necessary hermeneutic device the very stereotypes we would otherwise eschew. We must continually rehearse and deploy anti-Jewish, misogynistic, and other clichéd and base conceptions just to read the novel. Perhaps in so doing, we are unpleasantly reminded of the fact that, as Sander Gilman argues, we routinely employ such stereotypes in our everyday thinking.[82]

The novel is rife with pertinent examples.[83] But since a close reading of a more than five-hundred-page novel on this question is neither possible nor desirable (and because further illustrations will be given in subsequent chapters), one example, from a passage already quoted, will serve to demonstrate this phenomenon. In the discussion of Georg, above, we read what appears to be an obvious bit of narrator-based description: "In his features there was something of that gentleness which women need before they can feel at home with a man."[84] Once we discover Georg's incredible ego, his benevolent-sounding but unmistakable misogyny, and the ability he shares with his fellow characters to infiltrate the narrative voice, we will want to ascribe this portion of the description (and perhaps even more) to the self-aggrandizing consciousness of Georg himself. In this way, we are constantly challenged to ascribe what first appears to be authorial narration to one of the fictional characters who essentially has taken on the mantle of narrator. This ceaseless dynamic between the initial impression of "zero focalization" and the eventual determination of "internal focalization" comprises not merely a formal refinement regarding the representation of consciousness in literature,[85] but an important social admonition: Those authorities, like the Alexian narrator, who lay claim to magisterial cultural perspectives need to be examined critically for the special and partial interests that may be lurking beneath their "omniscience." There will inevitably be some disagreement in this mammoth text about precisely who is speaking where. What we are no longer permitted to do, however, is to ascribe unproblematically such foundational utterances to a trustworthy, neutral, and stable narrative voice. Adducing the narrator as the basis for a definitive interpretation of *Auto-da-Fé*—still a fairly common occurrence in the secondary literature—is therefore something readers should greet with suspicion. For in *Auto-da-Fé* we know only who these characters claim to be—not who they essentially are.

As a translator of three Upton Sinclair novels for the leftist Malik Verlag, a task he later described as a mere sustenance job ("eine Brotarbeit"), Canetti became an expert on popular, socially engaged realism in the interwar period. In citing and parodying the beloved Alexis in *Auto-da-Fé*, Canetti offers not a broadside on literary realism per se—for he continued to revere Balzac and Zola as exemplary practitioners of the genre[86]—but a much more specific critique of historicizing escapist tendencies and seductive narrative structures that conspire to make literature the very anesthetizing, insular activity Georg held it to be.

If truth be told, Canetti was not particularly interested in literary classifications, even if he was acutely aware of literary and cultural developments in general. Like his modernist contemporaries, he was interested in representing the modern world, the "new reality" (*neue Wirklichkeit*) of the post-

World War I era, which he felt demanded new modes of expression. In reflecting on the genesis of his novel, Canetti writes: "I told myself that I would build spotlights with which I could illuminate the world from outside."[87] This remains a valuable way of viewing *Auto-da-Fé*—as outside our everyday world, yet designed to illuminate it. Considering the various novels cited in *Auto-da-Fé* yields productive insights that clarify Canetti's own project. Yet this discussion also poses the danger of skewing the novel. For if *Auto-da-Fé* were to be read merely as a participant in a literary debate, this would only serve to reinforce the very insular escapism the novel seeks to challenge and overcome.

2 "The truth is you're a woman. You live for sensations."
Misogyny as Cultural Critique

> When Canetti finds in Broch the necessary attributes of a great writer—he is original; he sums up his age; he opposes his age—he is delineating the standards to which he has pledged himself.
> —Susan Sontag[1]

> You're always polite, you woman, you're like Eve . . . Take a rest from all this femininity! Maybe you'll become human again.
> —Peter Kien to his brother Georg[2]

False Starts: Toward a New Critical Paradigm

Recently, critics have begun to worry about misogyny in *Auto-da-Fé*. Rather than view it as part of the overall parodic structure of the novel, however, they tend to submit their findings urgently, like investigative reporters who have just discovered corruption in city hall. Richard H. Lawson alerts us, for example, to "Canetti's considerable misogyny,"[3] and regrets that the novel contains "a series of misogynistic aphorisms that perhaps passed as amusing in the 1930s; for example: 'Women are illiterates, unendurable and stupid, a perpetual disturbance.'"[4] If Lawson seems willing to let us off with a general sort of warning, Jenna Ferrara is less forgiving. She indicts the narrator for "submerging" women's voices, and Canetti himself for encoding in this fiction his own deep-seated hatred of women.[5] Ultimately, she contends, the novel recommends Anna—the sexually abused daughter of the building superintendent—as an exemplum of female subservience. Most recently—and most spectacularly—Kristie Foell has suggested that "the unfortunate message" of at least one scene of the novel "is that women want to be raped and [that they] make accusations of rape out of a sense of sexual frustration. Therese's confused desires play into the myth that women deserve what they get, whether rape, poverty, or murder";[6] similar pronouncements can be found throughout her recent monograph. If such critics have espoused disputable claims, they nevertheless deserve a good deal of credit for drawing our attention to a crucial and thus far rather neglected aspect of the novel.[7]

When confronted with this kind of ideological criticism—a sort of headhunting expedition for pernicious stereotypes—one is necessarily reminded of Shoshana Felman's pathbreaking corrective to psychoanalytic criticism, in which she reminded fellow critics (who were then churning out fairly predictable Freudian interpretations) that sex is not the answer, but the ongoing question.[8] Perhaps the same should be said of ideological criticism at this juncture: locating insidious stereotyping is not itself the end of the pursuit. What is needed, rather, is careful analysis of the larger matrix of ideas and literary strategies within which these stereotypes appear. Only then could we ask whether (and how) the reader is encouraged to accept, reject, or question the prejudice in question.

Yet such attention to the larger constellation of literary strategies is precisely what one misses. Overlooking what is perhaps the hallmark of this modernist novel, the ironically porous narrator, these critics have instead posited the traditional narrator of literary realism in order to anchor their respective argument about the "novel's misogyny."[9] While Canetti's narrator employs the formal prerogatives of the traditional storyteller (third person, the tense of narration, gnomic utterances), the novel itself pulls the rug of reliability out from beneath him, discrediting his putative authority and independence. Throughout the novel the narrator embodies more the desire to speak universally, objectively, or in the voice of nineteenth-century *Wissenschaft* than any unquestioned ability to do so. Canetti's mercurial narrator is repeatedly infiltrated by the novel's cast of characters, and the reader quickly learns to suspect that the claims issued by the narrator typically emerge from quite vested interests. At best, the narrator of *Auto-da-Fé* is reliably unreliable, and thus a foundation incapable of supporting such weighty allegations of misogyny.[10]

It remains a riddle how a reader could be interpolated or sutured into (to borrow terms from structuralism) this allegedly nefarious text. The failure to demonstrate this proposition is crucial; for the broad experience of readers indicates a continual "falling out" of the story rather than the experience of being comfortably buckled in. While Reich-Ranicki's pronouncement of the novel as "indigestible" may ultimately seem unfair, he is certainly correct that the reader is in no way seduced into a state of unreflective stupor. In fact, the novel's remarkable humor depends to a great extent on the reader's epistemic sovereignty over the distorted and limited worlds each character takes to be utterly real, natural, and universally valid. Perhaps these latter-day muckrakers should give some credit to the novel itself, for it is a text that foregrounds and questions those misogynistic stereotypes, rather than one that insidiously deploys them as natural.

Before proceeding directly to this argument, however, let us briefly revisit the question: Why the hesitancy to grant this parodic possibility in the first place? Part of the accusatory posture taken by the critics mentioned above may be attributable to two additional and related—though up to this point inexplicit—factors of feminist criticism of the novel. First is the failure to deploy with historic specificity the term misogyny, despite the fact that the meaning of the word has evolved significantly from the beginning of the century to the present day. One need not assume, for example, that Canetti evolved into a model feminist as the term came to be defined from the 1970s onward, in order to grasp his critique of misogyny as it was pressed into service during the early decades of this century to solve the celebrated "crisis of the self." The second factor that may have inhibited critics from seeing the novel's misogyny as part and parcel of the text's overall parodic structure is the premise of the Anglo-American approach to feminist literary criticism, which characterizes all the aforesaid studies. Such critics are forever trying to redeem the novel's women, particularly Therese. With regard to *Auto-da-Fé* this is frankly a doomed enterprise. Any attempt to recover Therese's supposed interiority is bound to be stymied by the hard fact that none of the characters is psychologically realistic. Stressing the novel's overt artifice in this regard, Canetti once said to Hermann Broch: "These are *figures,* not real people."[11] Moreover, the novel cannot be made over to be fundamentally about women: in point of fact, it is a rich parody of men's (particularly Peter and Georg Kien's) distorted views of women and "the feminine," and thus can never satisfy critics searching for a story centered on—or offering equal time to—female subjects. That would simply be a different novel.

Three Obsolete Women

If misogyny in *Auto-da-Fé* is neither some distasteful by-product of an otherwise great novel, nor merely the pernicious ideological vestige of a chauvinist author, one needs to confront the question with a new paradigm. Rather than the purveyor of retrograde thinking, *Auto-da-Fé* is in fact remarkably progressive. Not only because the self-conscious and pervasive deployment of misogyny takes critical aim at the contemporaneous clichés of gender—notably, as Pöder has shown, by citing and inverting Otto Weininger's widely read *Geschlecht und Charakter* (Sex and Character, 1903)—but also in its encoding of what is generally taken to be a fairly recent refinement in thinking on gender: the distinction between the social construction of gender roles and the biologically given status of sex. This disjunction of sex and gender is broadly evident in Therese's insistence on her conjugal rights as well as her adamant refusal to accept Kien's attempt to restrict her role to that of mother-librarian. The gender/sex distinction is perhaps nowhere clearer than in Kien's absurd (yet telling) pronouncement that his brother Georg is, essentially, a woman.

This rupture, however much it may contribute to the dislodging of traditional gender strictures, should be seen primarily in light of the novel's staging of the epistemological dilemma implied in the peculiarly *male* crisis of the self. The misogyny worthy of investigation consists therefore not in the fairly obvious derision of female figures, but in the novel's gendered structuring of the epistemological exchange, in which "woman" or the "feminine" figures throughout as the thing to be known. For the philologist Peter Kien she is both the inscrutable text (waiting to be authoritatively decoded) and China; for the psychiatrist Georg she is the quintessence of insanity, passively and appreciatively awaiting his marvelous treatments. She is, respectively, mother and demimonde. But what she may never be, of course, is a cognitively coequal partner capable of her own crisis of subjectivity.

Looking at the novel's misogyny in this way helps us to see the representation of woman not only as a synchronic, generalized critique of woefully sexist images, but also as a quite time-specific product of the historically conditioned crisis of subjectivity. Well before Hermann Bahr pronounced the self unsalvageable ("Das unrettbare Ich," 1904), Austrian intellectuals had been debating the implications of what Judith Ryan has dubbed "The Vanishing Subject." It was precisely this specter of an attenuated "empirical" self, Steven Beller argues, that inspired Otto Weininger's infamous opus; and though the contemporary debate on the self was perhaps most explicitly conducted in academic circles, it also had unmistakable political ramifications in the form of collectivist and irrationalist movements of the early part of this century.[12] Yet the more precise impulse behind *Auto-da-Fé*, which was begun in 1930, was not so much this ongoing anxiety about the self, but those questionable attempts (above all Weininger's) proposed to *solve* that crisis. The late modernist novel *Auto-da-Fé* can therefore be viewed most productively as an epiphenomenon of modernity, or as a kind of modernism once removed. Canetti's specific contribution, as we shall see in greater detail below, is not only to draw our attention to the gendered status of the subject, but more specifically to indict the canonical high German (and European) construction of culture for enshrining misogyny as both normal and normative. The only characters given enough psychological depth to sustain any kind of crisis of identity are, of course, Georg and Kien. And both attempt to use "woman" to manage their difficulties: to shore up a dissolving self (as in the case of Kien), or to trade in an obsolete self (Georg). "Woman" in the novel, let us be clear about this from the beginning, is largely the projection of desperate men. That these brothers can conduct their exploits under the dignified cover of high culture, however, broadens the novel's critique considerably.

First, it may be helpful to follow out the line of questioning implicit in the "image of woman" approach to feminist inquiry in order fully to appreciate the novel's critique of misogyny as a crutch to male identity. Where do the perverse images of woman originate? Certainly Kien is a quite fertile source for this kind of invective: indeed he literally reconstructs Therese as whore, reasoning that he had not fully understood her "true" profession until he recognizes her again in the person of the "Pensionistin" (Fischerle's prostitute, whose dependable patron has earned her this title), for Kien "a second Therese."[13] Fischerle, Pfaff, and even the purportedly good brother Georg all contribute their own inventive brand of misogyny. Although a considerable quantity of woman hatred emanates from the male characters, it would be quite mistaken to overlook the fact that the novel's women are rather simplistic types well before the novel's men get their hands (or, in the case of Kien, their minds) on them. It is also true that the narrator is no affirmative action employer: Therese does not command nearly as many pages as Kien, nor is her verbal repertory any match for the master philologist. The same could be said for Anna, the Fischerin, and the other female figures. Like the men, the women are comic types; unlike the men they are distinctly more limited in every imaginable way. Having noted the dual source of the novel's images of woman does not, however, reinstate the charge of narratorial or authorial misogyny. Those female images, as yet unmarked by the efforts of male figures to appropriate and refunction them, represent the cultural clichés of the day: woman as mother, housekeeper, whore, damsel in distress (Anna), martyr (the Fischerin). All, ranging from the combative and self-assertive Therese to the self-abasing Fischerin, serve to fulfill male fantasies, male careers, and male pleasures.

Let us first cast a glance at the novel's auxiliary female figures, Anna and the Fischerin. Both are holdover types from nineteenth-century culture, easily recognizable from popular literature and opera of the period. Canetti's deployment of these figures proceeds in the spirit of "hyperbolic parody," a term developed by Elisabeth Bronfen to describe the strategy of, for example, Margaret Atwood.[14] This approach—particularly well exemplified by Canetti's novel—attempts to overcome stereotypes not by avoiding them, but by giving them free berth to self-destruct. Obviously this method, which Bronfen calls "complicity as critique,"[15] does not produce many good women in the sense of models for extraliterary women. Canetti's portrayal of the absurdity of the female type is an assault on the cultural institutions that continue to purvey gendered straitjackets in the form of outmoded, sentimental female figures. In the figures of the Fischerin and Anna in particular, Canetti draws out the appeal and defining characteristic of the female martyr/victim: her utter expendability for male purposes.

The Fischerin, by all accounts a minor figure, suggests a tragic modification of the Papagena figure from Mozart's *Die Zauberflöte* (The Magic Flute, 1791). In that famous opera, Papagena is the luscious prize for Papageno, the buffoon counterpart to the protagonist Tamino. While an acknowledged musical masterpiece, *Die Zauberflöte* as libretto operates on a comically simplistic gendered binary opposition between the evil—and ultimately vanquished—Queen of the Night and the patriarchal seat of all wisdom and light, Sarastro. Papageno proves himself worthy of his look-alike bride by enduring certain abstentions (albeit with considerable shortcomings) enforced by the sacred priesthood. Essential for the intertextual allusion, however, is the memorable and entertaining childishness of Papageno. Unlike his counterpart Tamino, Papageno never quite matures. His life proceeds in an idyllic forest, and his work is nothing but play: he catches beautiful birds for the queen-mother and receives in return his daily bread and wine. If it is "delicious" (*köstlich*), as it always is when he behaves, he is content. In the make-believe world of perpetual childhood, Papageno has but one wish: a bride just like himself. The comic and fecund pairing of Papageno with Papagena parallels the opera's more serious coupling of Tamino with Pamina. True to Northrup Frye's conception of comedy, the opera ends in a double marriage. This much at least Canetti could have expected of his readership. The citation of Papagena in the figure of the Fischerin is not hard to recognize: the female hunchbacked dwarf with a "Jewish" long nose is simultaneously an evocation of the Papagena disguised as hideous crone (i.e., before her metamorphosis into the bucolic blond beauty), and Fischerle's exact physical counterpart. The modification, however, is double: not only does Canetti's hag remain a hag, but more important there is the alteration implicit in Fischerle's antagonistic relationship to the Fischerin. In Mozart's opera, Papageno gets his girl for obeying, more or less, the advice of the old woman (and, by extension, the guidelines of the priestly sect). He was, in other words, rewarded for being a good boy. Canetti draws out this aspect by making Fischerle perhaps even more a child than Papageno. Fischerle has no use for his look-alike would-be lover for two reasons: First, and foremost, he is attached to the Pensionistin (the "Capitalist" in the Wedgwood translation) as a boy to a mother. "For she loved him," he claims (infiltrating the narrator's voice), "he was her child."[16] At the pivotal moment when Fischerle might conceivably launch his voyage to America he is compelled to return to say goodbye to "mother," to spend one more comforting hour in the cradle under her bed. "He'd have liked to creep under the bed once more in farewell; that was the cradle of his future career . . . he'd found in it a peace unknown in any café."[17] It is from this protected site that Fischerle habitually experiences the Freudian primal scene ("*Urszene*") between his maternal Pensionistin and one or another of her paying customers.

The Fischerin's rejection is foreordained by a second, related factor. Fischerle represents a very self-consciously drawn caricature of the self-hating Jew. As such, Fischerle cannot possibly accept his veritable mirror image as spouse or lover. (His actual mirror image, one may recall, is only good for producing eminent, but beatable and despicably "Jewish," chess opponents.) His fantasy woman, with the emphasis on fantasy, is a rich, tall, American blond whose chief drawing card is her ability to finance Fischerle's own assimilation and acceptance in gentile society. Fischerle's make-believe bride is thus an "Aryan" beauty into which this misshapen and all "too Jewish" looking crone cannot possibly metamorphose. No chance in this fantasy—which resonates, as we shall see below in chapter 4, with the rising tide of racial anti-Semitism—for the hunchbacked, filthy, Jewish newspaper peddler.

In playing on the Fischerin/Papagena connection, Canetti draws out the essential component of male projection in creating a female *counterpart*. The principle of complementarity that underlies binary gender classifications in Western thought (and explicitly evident in Weininger's categories) is here pilloried as a merely apparent complementarity that is essentially a one-sided projection. Canetti cites and inverts the tradition of the "match made in heaven"—they meet in the pub "The Stars of Heaven" (*Zum idealen Himmel*)—by drawing the Fischerin as the object of abusive rejection, rather than as the comic resolution of plot. The Fischerin emerges as an outmoded female *type* who no longer serves to resolve the dramatic conflict, and thus elicits the humor of incongruity for those familiar with her cultural precursor(s). This is just one of Canetti's many "ernste Scherze" (serious jokes) told over the heads of his own characters.

It is characteristic and telling that in order to elucidate the role of the Fischerin one must tell the story of Fischerle: that, in a nutshell, is the point. Canetti is drawing our attention to female figures who are little more (in the case of the Fischerin, *nothing* more) than the reflection of male characters, mere adjuncts to male development plots. The Fischerin is significant not only in what she invokes and fails to fulfill, but also in her additional role as martyr. For she stands by her man until death does them part, a sacrifice not remotely hinted at in the role of Papagena. This tragic turn results precisely from the identical outward appearance of Fischerle and the Fischerin. The event follows upon the encounter between Kien and the book-pawning team of Pfaff and Therese. Kien apprehends Therese, Pfaff restrains Kien, and the police are called in straight away. The crowd outside draws its own ever-changing conclusions, deciding ultimately that the dirty little man with the "Jew nose" (*Judennase*) is the guilty culprit deserving of vigilante-style justice. They proceed to beat him quite severely; he is saved only when the Fischerin shows up and is mistaken for Fischerle. She is murdered in his stead.

Critics accustomed to viewing the novel through the optics of *Crowds and Power* tend to see in this scene a criticism of crowd behavior, of the "Masse"

Figure 2. Fischerle's rejection of his look-alike Jewish paramour in favor of a tall, blue-eyed blond is echoed in the anti-Semitic caricature of the day, as in this circa-1935 cartoon from Kurt Plischke's Der Jude als Rassenschänder. *United States Holocaust Memorial Museum Photo Archives.*

whose thirst for excitement and revenge is blind. True enough. But the critique is more complex: the death of the Fischerin is the death of the type, a revelation of the essential nonliving status of woman as a male look-alike projection. In fashioning the Fischerin, Canetti seeks to retire an obsolete cultural representation of woman, as well as explore its motivations. Yet this understanding of the Fischerin as a female character type clearly does not exhaust her meaning in the novel. In fact, focusing exclusively on the topic of misogyny can easily distract from the concrete anti-Jewish fervor, which so clearly contributes to her murder. Moreover, Fischerle's rejection of this virtual mirror image because of her inescapably "Jewish" physical markers in favor of an imagined Aryan beauty suggests the pertinence of the Fischerin to our discussion of racial anti-Semitism below in chapter 4.

None of the novel's figures evokes empathetic identification, with the temporary exception of Georg, as we have noted. But if the Fischerin elicits any reaction from the reader, it is probably foremost the feeling that she is pathetic. This much at least she has in common with the figure of Anna, the unfortunate daughter of the brutal Hausbesorger Benedikt Pfaff. To under-

Figure 3. Fischerle's fantasy of American success includes a fancy chauffeured car, as in this 1935 cartoon, titled "The Martyr Abroad," from the magazine Brennessel. *These onlookers, however, are not the adoring crowds of Fischerle's vain imagination, but resentful observers who immediately identify the prosperous man as a Jew (as Fischerle suspected would happen even in America), and suggest (in the German caption) that Jews who emigrate with such wealth could not have faced much hardship in Germany in the first place. Bildarchiv Preußischer Kulturbesitz; photo courtesy United States Holocaust Memorial Museum Photo Archives.*

stand how in the figure of Anna Canetti is drawing on a mainstream of German literary tradition, it will be necessary first to review the folktale milieu that is clearly the inspiration for this daughter in distress. We turn, of course, to the Brothers Grimm, those intrepid folktale collectors and wordsmiths of the nineteenth century whose philological fervor was deeply rooted in the German nationalism of the day. As in the case of the Fischerin/Papagena, the citation is mixed but unmistakable.

Anna is a folktale figure who cannot become a fairy tale heroine: she is stuck in that realistic first part of the fairy tale marked by naturalistic exposition. In this case it is an account of brutal victimization at the hands of her own father. But her story fails to abide by that "fundamental law [of fairy tales] requiring the reversal of all conditions prevailing in its introductory paragraphs."[18] Anna does indeed dream of a rescuing hero in the form of the local grocery boy, but the fictional world of *Auto-da-Fé* simply fails to respond to her romantic desires and fantasies of revenge: the grocery clerk botches the burglary and fails to deliver Pfaff's head on a platter. The "fairy tale's movement from victimization to retaliation"[19] therefore takes place only in the imagination of the beaten and beleaguered daughter.

Instead of rescue she suffers numerous beatings, rape, and pregnancy. Finally she is left by her father to die. Anna is, in a sense, the modern incarnation of "Allerleirauh" (Thousandfurs), but without any of the supernatural assistance accorded that heroine. Again, the reference is all but subtle. In the Grimms' tale, "the father of young Thousandfurs (Allerleirauh) . . . promises his wife on her deathbed that he will remarry only if he finds a woman whose beauty equals that of his quickly fading spouse. When the king's envoys return from a worldwide search for a second wife to announce that they have failed in their mission, the king's eye lights on his daughter, and he is overcome by passion for her."[20] Benedikt Pfaff of *Auto-da-Fé* is not so scrupulous: "Soon after this change his wife died, of overstrain . . . On the day after the funeral his honeymoon began. More undisturbed than before, he treated his daughter as he pleased."[21]

In *The Hard Facts of the Grimms' Fairy Tales*, Maria Tatar explains the suppressed centrality of the incest theme in this genre: it is the obverse of the more frequently noted "jealous evil stepmother" motif. Since the relationship of the two tale types may not be widely understood, it is worth quoting her elucidation at length: "In tales depicting erotic persecution of a daughter by her father . . . mothers and stepdaughters tend to vanish from the central arena of action. Yet the father's desire for his daughter in the second tale type furnishes a powerful motive for a stepmother's jealous rages and unnatural deeds in the first tale type. The two plots thereby conveniently dovetail to produce an intrigue that corresponds almost perfectly to the Oedipal fantasies of female children. In this way fairy tales are able to stage the Oedipal drama even as they disguise it by eliminating one of its two essential components."[22] Whereas a tale such as "Allerleirauh" might permit us to speculate whether we are reading about a daughter's "fantasy of an amorous father" as opposed to an actual "father's perverse erotic attachment,"[23] Canetti's reinscription of this fairy tale figure allows no doubt as to the origin of the desire and violence. The benefits to the child, which, as Bruno Bettelheim famously expounded them, result from psychologically working through the oedipal drama, are of absolutely no value if the fantasies and desires are all the father's. Anna's drama is relegated to the feckless fantasy of a nonexistent male savior. Pfaff's is the real drama, and in this Anna has a mere supporting role.

As in the case of the Fischerin/Papagena, the cultural allusion becomes in the hands of Canetti a rather more complex alloy. If the male projection involved in the construction of the Fischerin was primarily visual, here it takes the form of a cruel verbal game. Anna must reinforce Pfaff's self-image as "the good father" (*der gute Vater*)—in a chapter of the same name which Canetti remembers having performed at frequent public readings—by completing his sentences. It is a debased version of that type of polite Viennese conversation espoused by Altenwyl (of Hofmannsthal's *Der Schwierige*), the purpose of which is "to provide your partner the key conversational prompt" (*dem andern das Stichwort [zu] bringen*):

"She gets her keep from . . ." ". . . her good father."
"Other men do not want . . ." ". . . to have her." . . .
"Now her father's going to . . ." ". . . arrest her."
"On father's knee sits . . ." ". . . his obedient daughter."
"Her father knows why he . . ." ". . . thrashes her."
"My daughter isn't ever . . ." ". . . hurt."
"She's got to learn what she . . ." ". . . owes to her father."[24]

This exercise is a form of verbal and semiotic extortion and serves to underscore Anna's enforced role as reflector or function (in the mathematical sense) of her father's ego. Like the fairy tales that harbor father-daughter incest in their subtext (or in alternate versions),[25] Anna herself is enlisted to cover over the father's violence and remake him in the image of "the kind father."

If Canetti's point with respect to the Fischerin is to desentimentalize forever the submissive, self-sacrificing representation of woman, with regard to Anna it is to demonstrate the absurdity of the notion that a woman's power and freedom is rooted primarily in imagination and fantasy. In both cases he draws our attention to clichéd cultural representations of women that served — until, perhaps, their refunctioning in *Auto-da-Fé* — to disguise their source in male interests. Yet here, too, Canetti's critique is multivalent. Anna belongs therefore not only to the discussion of female types and stereotypes, but also plays a central role in the novel's rejection of Freudian notions that interiorize real, intersubjective violence — as I argue below in greater detail in chapter 5.

As in the cases of the Fischerin and Anna, let us consider Therese first as she is "given" to us by the narrator, apart from the misogynistic aspersions generously heaped upon her by Kien and Pfaff. For she is a type before she enters the plot — indeed she remains virtually unchanged throughout. She is a lower class, fairly obese, and imposing woman, who has spent her entire career as a domestic servant. She is in addition a social climber for whom marriage is the means of entering the respectable middle class; and, of course, she is a woman with an unabashed and largely unsatiated sexual appetite. She is drawn, on the surface at least, as the diametrical opposite of Kien. In her materiality, fleshliness, greed, and thick affiliation with commerce and money she represents the antithesis to her husband's putative intellect, "*Geist*," and overall aloofness to things of this world. Not surprisingly, this opposition is advanced ironically, consisting largely of Kien's own manifest self-delusions.

Therese makes her debut as a fifty-six-year-old *Wirtschafterin*, a maid who cooks and cleans for the forty-year-old scholar. She makes her greatest impression, however, in providing fastidious care for Kien's books. It is this which earns her the short-lived epithet, "a sublime spirit" (*eine großartige Seele*).[26] Indeed, "her touching solicitude for *The Trousers of Herr von Bredow*"[27] moves Kien to propose marriage: "With some ceremony she selected a suitable piece of paper and wrapped it around the book like a shawl round a baby . . . He had underestimated her. She knew how to handle a book better than he did."[28] The comparison of book to baby is apt: for this is precisely the function Kien envisions for her—mother to his library. But if he marries to gain a maternal figure to nurture his charges, he is very quickly disabused of this notion. On his wedding night Kien finds to his dismay that lurking within the apparently loyal, motherly domestic is a "monstrous" sexual appetite. Up to this point Therese may be said to incorporate a good many contemporary cultural clichés regarding women as, for example, catalogued by Weininger. Yet to those familiar with the German literary canon, Therese evokes a more specific literary predecessor: she is the reincarnation and revision of Lene from Gerhart Hauptmann's widely read *Bahnwärter Thiel* (Stationmaster Thiel, 1888).[29]

Eric Downing has suggested that in reading the literature of the German nineteenth century we look to the female figures for the encapsulation of the respective aesthetic program.[30] With regard to Hauptmann, it is clear that Lene is advanced as the bearer of that "really real" realism, namely Naturalism. She provides a stark contrast not only to the ethereal first wife, Minna, but also to the more sensitive and spiritual Thiel himself. True, the stationmaster is no intellect; yet he is the village pedagogue and cultivates an inwardness totally alien to Lene. The dichotomy is therefore essentially the same as in *Auto-da-Fé*. Until the brutal final scenes of Hauptmann's novella, at which point Thiel is in any case coded as insane (and thus not his former self), Thiel represents the higher, spiritual values of the Romantic past, while his robust and corpulent wife stands for the brutal violence of modern life. It is surely no coincidence that Tobias's death is due as much to the negligence of Lene as to that harbinger of technical modernity, the locomotive.

It is of course also no coincidence that Thiel (like Kien) marries in order to get a good mother and receives something quite undesirable into the bargain: "Without realizing it, he had, however, accepted three things in his wife: a harsh, tyrannical temper, truculence, and a brutal temperament. After six months it was common knowledge who ruled the roost. One pitied the stationmaster."[31] The sympathies of the villagers for Thiel, as opposed to Lene, whom they brand a whore ("*das Mensch*") and an animal ("*So ein Tier*"), correspond to those of the implied reader. Thiel is the beloved companion of the village children, their informal teacher and friend, while Lene is the greedy wife who cannot sleep for her excitement about the potato patch to be planted on the railroad right of way. In contrast to Thiel's gentle instruction—given, not coincidentally, in a rich bucolic setting meant to contrast with the new industrial landscape—Lene's pedagogy consists of cruel corporeal punishment, the traces of which Thiel observes in the red markings on the face of his son Tobias. Lene, too, is the seat of sexuality, and as such she paralyzes poor Thiel. This sexual dependency seems to explain his visceral attachment to her even after he has witnessed her physical abuse of Tobias. All in all, one can safely argue that the novella advances Lene, the monstrous wife and representative of a "naturalistic" and brutal reality, quite without irony. But this only works as long as the other term in the gender binary — namely Thiel — is drawn with relative sympathy.

Canetti's citation of Lene in the figure of Therese draws out the phony premise in such gender dichotomies. By making Kien (and others) equally monstrous, he lays bare the absurdity of heaping the evils (or "realities") of the age at the feet of woman. Rereading Lene in light of Therese allows us to see how the former is set up to take the fall: like the Fischerin and Anna, Lene is doomed from the start. In her very construction — that is, as she enters the narrative — we find a crass distribution of character traits designed to put a female face on the stark realities of the day.

In *Auto-da-Fé* such a possibility is precluded from the start. Kien is no sympathetic or innocent figure, such as Thiel has often been construed to be. Therese's sexuality is even more pronounced than Lene's, but the simplistic model of sexual stimulus (= woman)/response (= man) is in *Auto-da-Fé* dramatically altered by an array of sexual proclivities and perversions: Pfaff's brutal incest, Kien's frigidity, Georg's flagrant seduction of his patients, and so on. The citation of Lene in the figure of Therese serves to recall and explode a simplistic gendered economy of vices and virtues, though it is surely also true that this rejection of the Thiel/Lene model arises from the larger cast of characters, which will be explored in greater detail below. It is notable that a number of critics have only realized half of the intertextual potential: Therese's entrance has sometimes unproblematically been hailed as the intrusion of the "world" into the realm of Kien's rarefied intellect.[32] Yet nothing could be more appalling to the arch anti-realist Canetti than the prospect of any one figure — male or female — representing adequately so much reality.

In arguing that Canetti is citing Hauptmann's Lene in the figure of Therese, I am suggesting a rather specific allusion. Can Therese, then, still be said to represent a type? In so far as Lene herself is drawn as a nonindividual type, the answer is an emphatic yes. It is not merely that Lene is given no psychological depth and considerably less attention than Thiel, which qualifies her for the status of the typical rather than the individual. It is also the narrator's use of the ancient arachnid trope to designate her femininity. In fact, one of the principal images which for the reader aligns the ominous train with the brutal wife is that of the ensnaring, predatory spider. Lene's pronounced physicality and sexuality spreads a "web of iron" over the trapped husband: "Her full, half-naked breasts heaved with excitement and threatened to burst her brassiere, and her gathered skirt made her broad hips appear even broader. This woman appeared to emanate a power—unconquerable, inescapable—to which Thiel felt unequal. Light as a fine spider's web and yet firm as a net of iron, it surrounded him, binding, overwhelming, debilitating."[33] The ensuing description of telegraph wires and poles as "the web of a gigantic spider"[34] that runs along the train tracks only underscores the text's juxtaposition of Lene and the train as ambivalent forces of modern life, both intimately involved in the demise of Tobias.

By partaking in the traditional allegorization of woman as spider (and the implied corollary of man as trapped victim in her web), the narrator of Hauptmann's novella places Lene in a venerated tradition of misogynistic representation in German literature. The most obvious predecessor in the German canon would of course be Gotthelf's *Die schwarze Spinne* (The Black Spider, 1842), a story Canetti read as a youth and recounts in some detail in his autobiography.[35] Though there are surely notable differences in the realizations of the arachnid trope—Hauptmann makes Lene more the Naturalists' stimulus of instinct than the Gotthelfian seducer to moral evil—all representations of this type suggest a crudely dichotomized distribution of character traits invariably unfavorable to the woman.[36]

Like Lene, Therese is constructed as an unlikely, obese femme fatale. Therese's physicality, for example her "gorgeous hips" (*prachtvolle Hüften*) noted by the furniture salesman Herr Grob, along with the voluminous blue skirt, receive repeated attention. Furthermore, her wedding night expectations, the relentless pursuit of Herr Grob, as well as her apparently willing acquiescence in Pfaff's advances, all attest to an unabashed sexual appetite. But the type stops here, at least as far as the narrator is concerned. Kien, as we have already seen, is in no way portrayed as the passive victim of the woman's web of intrigue. True, Therese is called a spider (as well as Medusa and a good many other things), but this is all Kien's doing: "In the spider, the most cruel and ugly of all creatures, I see an embodiment of woman. Her web shimmers in the sunlight, poisonous and blue."[37] Whether we look, then, at the specific gender economy of Hauptmann's novella or consider

Lene as a representative of a broader type, it seems rather clear that Canetti's interest in the allusion is to subvert the traditional binary gender classification. For whereas it was the omniscient narrator of Hauptmann's novella who advanced the arachnid link between Lene and the killer train, it is the very questionable Kien in *Auto-da-Fé* who pathetically employs his rhetorical skills to paint himself as the true victim of the "monstrous" housekeeper.

Therese distinguishes herself from the Fischerin and Anna in her ability to manipulate images and intervene on her own behalf. She rejects Kien's intended role for her as the eternal mother, she makes a pass at Herr Grob, and she meets her match in Pfaff. It is not that she is better or worse than her more simply drawn sister types, but that, beyond the already circumscribed role given at the level of narrator, she is able to contest further reductions in her role that are assigned (or denied) her at the level of character. This act of contestation (modest though it is, since it still operates well within the mother/whore dichotomy) introduces to the novel the more nuanced notion of gender as an imputed, but by no means natural role. Therese's achievement, if we can call it that, is to place the gender stereotype into question by reversing the expectations Kien harbored for her. Kien, too, seems to realize that "the feminine" need not refer to women per se. In a manner consonant with the parodistic cast of the novel as a whole, Kien untethers the concept of gender from its biological moorings. How else could he discover that his brother, deep down, is really a woman? The representation of the feminine — whether or not female figures are at issue — comprises an important strand of narrative in *Auto-da-Fé*.

Before turning to the novel's treatment of this more elusive topic, let us take stock of the ground covered so far. In the Fischerin we saw how the notion of woman as preordained prize or crown for the male protagonist's successful completion of a test of maturity (the Papagena function) is self-consciously inverted in Fischerle's rejection of his female counterpart precisely because she is made to appear as his unacceptably Jewish double. In the figure of Anna we witnessed the shortcomings of romanticized illusions and passive fantasies in the face of actual abuse: no prince comes to the rescue of this incestuous ruler's daughter. Finally, in Therese we are invited by allusion to the Lene-Thiel model to rethink the gendered binary distribution of vices, and to question the validity of explaining the brutal side of modernity as, essentially, female monstrosity. Which is another way of saying that Kien's diagnosis of his own sense of exile in the modern world—

a predicament faced by so many other intellectuals of the Weimar era — is frankly untenable. Canetti suggests that none of these outworn literary topoi is adequate to capture the complexity of post–World War I society.

The Brothers Kien Discover "the Feminine"

The male characters' own misogyny is detectable almost without analysis; the only hesitation one might provisionally have would be the attribution of any particular misogynistic observation to an unambiguous source, as we noted above in surveying the novel's peculiar narrative situation. This obvious form of misogynistic representation and behavior — be it Kien's "inspired" pseudophilosophical grounding of misogyny, Pfaff as incestuous father and wife-beater, Fischerle as pimp, or even Georg's more insidious abuses — need not detain us here. For, to borrow Justice Potter Stewart's dictum on pornography, we know it when we see it.[38] What is perhaps less clear is that notions of the feminine constructed and employed by each of these figures are by no means limited to biological women. Such representations range from China, to the novel's quixotic "gorilla man," indeed, as we have seen, to the male protagonist(s) themselves. To understand the function of the feminine on this level — and to appreciate Canetti's critical engagement with contemporaneous intellectual debates — it will be necessary to digress a bit and sketch in the "crisis of subjectivity" in fin-de-siècle Austria.

In "The New Psychologies," the first chapter of *The Vanishing Subject*, Judith Ryan outlines the major figures in the pre- and non-Freudian psychological movements of the late nineteenth and early twentieth centuries: Franz Brentano, Ernst Mach, William James.[39] The crisis of subjectivity that followed from the new "neoempiricist" views of the self — for example, from Mach's conception of the self as "a bundle of sensations" — proved disconcerting, to say the least. Ryan explains: "As empiricist thought began increasingly to filter into the consciousness of the educated public, panic began to spread. If there was no such thing as the self, the basis for decisions and actions seemed to have been removed. If there was no real distinction between subject and object, the familiar structures of language seemed to have been eroded. Many contemporaries felt virtually paralyzed, unable either to act or to speak."[40] Ryan's survey of psychologies covers the period from 1870 to 1930 (though for the literature under consideration she extends this period to 1940); thus Canetti clearly comes in at the tail end of this movement. In his *Vienna and the Jews, 1867–1938,* Steven Beller concurs in the urgency of this Weimar-era debate, pointing out that this question occupied leading Jewish intellectuals such as Freud, Schnitzler, Broch, and others, who addressed this disconcerting rift between the "empirical" (Machian) disunified self and the "ethical" self presupposed by liberal political culture in a variety of crucial ways.[41] Canetti's contribution to this debate is manifold, but first and foremost was his realization that the crisis was not of subjectivity per se, but of *male* subjectivity. *Auto-da-Fé,* I will argue, thematizes the suspect conjunction of rabid misogyny with attempts to shore up the dissolving self.[42] When one thinks of these two problems — the "vanishing self" along with misogyny — in the early twentieth century with special attention to the Austrian context, it becomes clear that Canetti was not, by far, the first to treat these two issues in tandem. His predecessor was of course the widely read Otto Weininger, whose immensely popular *Geschlecht und Character* was already beyond its thirtieth printing by the time Canetti sat down to write his novel.[43] Intellectually and culturally, this is undoubtedly the novel's great intertext, one with which Canetti and his friends were well acquainted. "What Weininger is essentially doing," Beller explains, "is using sexual types to describe psychological states, a procedure that was deeply embedded in Western culture . . . [and] part of a tradition that reached its apogee in Jungian psychology."[44] Weininger's legendary misogyny — "his obsessive identification of all that he fears with the feminine"[45] — is integral to his attempt to salvage the self (as the genius, value legislating "Man") and banish those traits associated with its dissolution to the category "Woman."[46] Whereas Weininger sought to salvage the "liberal" self — a self defined by reason and ethical thinking — by recourse to misogyny (as well, of course, as anti-Semitism), Canetti's project is to expose this putative solution as highly problematic.

Viewing the feminine in this larger sense helps us to see the male characters — especially Kien and Georg — as having more in common than has usually been seen. Kien has been treated as the ascetic academic, who stands in contrast to his lecherous and hedonistic brother, Georg. Certainly the novel itself invites such a polarization on one level: Kien is represented as the self hermetically (that is to say academically) sealed off from the threatening stimuli of the outside world. Georg, in contrast, is the winsome man of the world, who willingly engages, even incorporates, the most aberrant of human behavior in his work with the insane. This opposition, however, is undercut in a number of ways, but most obviously by the manner in which both make use of the feminine. Simply put: both brothers represent the self in crisis; only the method of self-rescue is superficially different. For Kien it is a radical elimination of the feminine, for Georg it is the radical incorporation of the very same—a strategy he thinks will work like a preventive inoculation against disease.

Kien's academic pursuits are not incidentally misogynistic, they are intrinsically so. Canetti's decision to make Kien a master philologist in the nineteenth century tradition frames the issue in terms of interpretation. Kien himself sees the matter of interpreting texts in a fairly simplistic, though no less self-contradictory, manner: all semiotic power emanates from the master interpreter who fixes for all time a heretofore incomplete or corrupt text. Let us not forget that this is the man who plans a final, and, needless to say, irrefutable, exegesis of the New Testament, in which he proposes to demonstrate that Jesus was at heart a bibliophile like Kien himself: "Since the philologist in him still lived, he decided to devote himself, when peaceful times should again bless the land, to a fundamentally new textual examination of the gospels . . . He felt himself equipped with enough knowledge to guide Christianity back to its true sources, and though he was not to be the first to pour the true words of the Savior out to humanity, . . . he might indeed hope, with sufficient inner conviction, that the interpretations he set down would be final."[47] Kien's interpretive audacity stands in stark inverse proportion to the credibility he arouses in the reader: because his claims to authority often refer to well known extrafictional texts (such as in this case the Bible) of which the reader has independent knowledge, Kien's pretension to definitive accuracy is immediately recognized as mere bombast. Yet as long as Kien's powers of interpretation are trained exclusively upon abstruse Oriental texts, and as long as no one can challenge his claim to the title of the "world's foremost sinologist," he meets with little opposition. Like the "Philosophie der Blindheit" (philosophy of blindness) he concocts when confronted with Therese's intransigent bedroom set, Kien's intellectual conceptions are eclectic, inconsistent, and fundamentally self-serving. Though Kien's relationships with mere mortals are at best secondary to his intellectual pursuits, he clearly tries to employ the same process in reading people: a unilateral, authoritarian projection of himself onto the other. Though small-minded projection is widespread in the novel, one can safely argue that for Kien woman is—or should be—the philologist's text par excellence. The equation in fact reads both ways: it is both a matter of the feminization of the text and a textualization of woman.

If Kien is on the one hand full of overweening confidence in his interpretive aptitude ("Whatever he sets his hand to succeeds, submits to his proofs"),[48] he is also plagued by lingering doubt. In fact, his overly confident assertions of demonstrable univocal textual meaning—as opposed to Saussurian multivalence—reveal an untenable epistemological desperation. Unconvincingly, but no less hilariously, Kien pronounces: "Knowledge has freed us from superstitions and beliefs. Knowledge makes use always of the same names, preferably Graeco-Latin, and indicates by these names actual things. Misunderstandings are impossible."[49] In addition to the humor this remark arouses amidst the plethora of patent misunderstandings, it bespeaks a pervasive epistemological anxiety.

Earlier yet Kien reveals a hairline crack in his self-image as master meaning-maker when, following the great dispute with Therese concerning the will, he finds himself stymied and capable only of incomprehensible drivel: "Time and again he had to force himself to reach for the Japanese manuscripts on his desk. When he got so far, he would touch them, and immediately, as if repelled, draw his hand back again. What is the meaning of them? . . . On the half-written sheet before him he had drawn, quite contrary to his habit, characters which had no meaning whatever."[50] It is of course no coincidence that woman—here in the figure of the novel's principal woman, Therese—represents the challenge to fixable, stable meaning, even while she represents the fantasy text that elicits the very prowess boasted by the philologist. Indeed these are two sides of the same coin. The exact same oppositional relationship—though here the tables are turned—is evident in the situation below where Kien is enjoying a temporary victory over Therese: "It was enough for him that she was silent. Poised between China and Japan, he paused to assure himself that this was the outcome of his clever diplomacy . . . In these days he was fertile in happy conjectures. An unspeakably corrupt text he had rehabilitated within three hours. The right characters simply streamed from his pen . . . Word by word, older litanies came back to him and he forgot hers."[51] Therese is "an affront to scholarship," therefore, not merely in the mundane sense of pestering the great scholar engaged in his lofty "mission of enlightenment" (*aufklärende Mission*)[52] with petty material requests, though this is the way Kien perceives it much of the time. In her nagging inscrutability, she represents, more importantly, the dark side of *Wissenschaft,* and as such she is a constant threat to Kien's very *raison d'être.*

Kien has been attempting, with ever dwindling success, to read Therese since the beginning of the novel. Just before proposing marriage, Kien, thinking he is about to marry a maternal librarian, reflects: "She is the heaven-sent instrument for preserving my library ... Had I constructed a human being according to my own designs, the result could not have been more apt for the purpose."[53] What he fails to see, however, is that he has all along been attempting to construct her according to his own design. Both the desire to render Therese a patently decipherable text *and* the inability to do so are evident in the scene where Kien lies in bed recovering from the sound beating Therese has just given him: "At that time she repeated herself over and over again; he learnt her words by heart and was thus, in the truest sense, her master ... but Therese suddenly began to talk again. What she said was incomprehensible, and therefore held despotic sway over him. It could not be learnt by heart, and who could guess what would come next?"[54]

None of this dissuades Kien from his effort to textualize Therese: in fact his efforts to write her off, or out of the scene, form the central event of the novel. In what is deservedly the most celebrated chapter of the novel, "Private Property" (*Privateigentum*), Kien mounts his lengthy "Defense of Learning," in which he hopes to prove "that Therese's death was *essential*" — "*daß Therese zugrunde gehen mußte.*"[55] His self-defense is selfless and noble, for his is really a "*Verteidigung für die Wissenschaft*" — that is, for science and truth against this female adversary. Therese, of course, is far from dead, and is all the while standing behind her would-be murderer. Although we will want, below, to consider precisely how and why scholarship itself demanded her death, what concerns us here is Kien's characteristic conception of Therese — for him, now, a mere mirage — as a corrupt text awaiting his interpretive genius. The equation of woman with text, and the view of both as eminently conquerable, is evident throughout Kien's thinking, but perhaps nowhere so obvious as in the following: "He would examine this mirage until he had convinced himself of what it really was. He had followed trails no less dangerous, imperfect texts, missing lines. He could not recall ever having failed. No problem he had undertaken had ever been left unsolved. Even this murder he must needs regard as a task accomplished. It took more than a hallucination to shatter Kien."[56]

Kien's failure to bring Therese under semiotic control is deeply implicated in his final suicide. Very near to his demise, Kien extols the virtues of books over people: "Books are dumb, they speak yet they are dumb, that is the wonder."[57] Therese proves less tractable than Oriental manuscripts: she talks back, thwarting the unilateral direction of meaning-making envisioned by Kien. The obstacle to the master-slave (philologist-text) model, which Therese poses in her unpredictable, incomprehensible, and therefore uncontrollable prattle is in fact very much like the rebellion of the books in the final conflagration scene. Those formerly docile, decodable ciphers mount a semiotic insurrection.

Here Kien's world turns upside down. The passive recipient of meaning, the text, takes on a life of its own, wreaking vengeance on the once tyrannical and now quite mad master reader: "A letter detaches itself from the first line and hits him a blow on the ear. Letters are lead. It hurts. Strike him! Strike him! Another. And another. A footnote kicks him. More and more. He totters. Lines and whole pages come clattering on to him. They shake and beat him, they worry him, they toss him about among themselves. Blood ... Help! Help! Georg!"[58] Kien is ultimately undermined by the feminine, beaten now not by Therese but by the binary rigidity of an epistemological system that seeks to sort out the knower and the known along predictable gender lines, a system that in the case of Peter Kien self-destructs. A great library burns and it is a grand farewell not to a collection of irreplaceably rare books, but to a system of thought pregnant with its own destruction.

Focusing on the person of Kien—who is intentionally drawn rather sparsely—can distract us from the novel's more profound critique of contemporary culture. In her most recent study, *Lustmord: Sexual Murder in Weimar Germany*, Maria Tatar remarks, "The profusion of images of Eve, Circe, Medusa, Judith, and Salome in art and literature around 1900 gives vivid testimony to an unprecedented dread of female sexuality and its homicidal power."[59] This concatenation brings to mind Kien's own subsequent dredging of the mythological, literary, and philosophical canon meant to make his final case against Woman.

Kien's great speech at the police station, the novel's most hilarious scene, is of course delivered for a crime he never committed, but ardently wishes he had: the murder of Therese. He clearly presents it as a murder; but is it in any sense *Lustmord*? There can be no doubt that the aggression between Therese and Kien dates from the unconsummated wedding night, when Kien, in response to his bride's sexual overtures, locks himself in the bathroom and sobs uncontrollably. Certainly Kien's physical trouncing at the hands of this "phallic mother" (as Foell dubs her) comes as a direct response to his failure to follow up on the sexual advances Therese perceived him to have initiated. If the sexual source of this murderous aggression is not yet sufficiently evident, Canetti provides a gloss in the form of the protagonist's flashback. Just as Kien's wedding night anxieties come to a head, our world famous sinologist recalls in vivid detail a childhood visit to the beach during which his curiosity about the soft, slimy inside of a mussel drives him to utter distraction. His frenzied destruction of the sea shell (*"die Muschel"*) — when he cannot properly pry it open, he simply smashes it to smithereens — is as much an act of *Lustmord* as Döblin's "Murder of a Buttercup" (*Die Ermordung einer Butterblume,* 1913) which Canetti may in fact have had in mind.[60] At any rate, the incident gains significance in the novel in so far as it is elevated to a chapter title in Book 1. Canetti is clearly capitalizing upon popularized Freudian ideas in this passage; but as we shall see below in chapter 6, this tongue-in-cheek borrowing does not imply an endorsement of Freud.

Kien's strikingly learned justification of this imagined murder provides an ironic case study of the phenomenon Tatar finds so striking in Weimar-era culture: not so much the historical cases of Lustmord themselves (numerous enough, to be sure), but the wider, post–World War I cultural tendency to reduce complex sociohistorical causality to archaic misogynistic myth. In *Auto-da-Fé* we catch Kien in the act: the rumors of Therese's death have been not only greatly exaggerated, but fabricated before our very eyes. Kien's feeble attempts to coopt victim status, simultaneously to suppress the female victim, and to obscure the fact of his own agency — all traits Tatar identifies as seminal aspects of the Lustmord phenomenon[61] — are the target of the novel's critical humor. Clearly we are not in danger of falling under the ideological sway of a man who claims, almost in the same breath, (1) to have murdered Therese in self-defense, (2) that Therese actually killed herself in a grotesque act of autocannibalism, and (3) that it was finally scholarship itself which required her death — all, of course, while Therese is physically pushing herself on her confessed murderer.

If Kien's frustrated Lustmord is rooted in a crisis of male subjectivity, which, according to Tatar, intensified dramatically in the post–World War I era,[62] he finds plenty of cultural fodder for his hatred in the books he reads and collects. In the end of his great defense, Kien credits his library with

Therese's murder. Similarly, Pfaff seeks to dismiss Kien's ranter by explaining to the detectives that "things like that are in books."[63] And both are, in a sense, quite right.

As if to bear out the veracity of Pfaff's claim, Kien mounts in the novel's penultimate chapter, not coincidentally entitled "Warywise Odysseus" (*Listenreicher Odysseus*), a veritable tour de force, ostensibly for the benefit of his brother Georg, proving the rich cultural pedigree of misogyny. Beginning with Confucius, Buddha, and Homer, Kien wends his way through the great books taking (and mistaking) misogyny wherever he can find it. At one point during this woman-hating harangue, the overconfident psychiatrist thinks he has found the key to Kien's disquisition: "Georg here saw himself as an important part of the mechanism which another person had set in motion for the maintenance of his threatened self-respect."[64] While Georg correctly perceives Kien's "threatened sense of self" as a key precondition for this cultured exhibition of misogyny, this is probably no longer the insight we need. What strikes the reader at this point is not Kien's quirky perversion of texts, but the large-scale cultural availability of misogynist narratives. Unlike modernist novels such as Döblin's *Berlin Alexanderplatz*, which employ misogynist myth to exculpate the *Lustmörder* (sexual murderers),[65] *Auto-da-Fé* foregrounds the cultural excess of such myth and showcases the protagonist's efforts at self-exoneration in the pathetic and desperate figure of Peter Kien, that impotent would-be Lustmörder. "What kind of man would not have murdered such a woman?" he asks, rhetorically.[66] As Kien brings his cultured tirade to a close, Georg observes correctly, in a statement that exceeds his own comprehension, that "the [cultural] material was more ample than his hatred."[67]

Madness, as Foucault has taught us, may be more a suspect catchall designation that expands and contracts to meet the interests of those in power than some eternal, objectively determined classification. Defining madness can be deployed polemically to marginalize those who would threaten the semiotic and social order. This is precisely the way in which the narrator casts Kien's diagnosis of Therese's madness: "He felt at his best when he could relegate her to the one category where there was room for everything which he was unable, for all his education and understanding, to explain. Of lunatics he had a crude and simple idea; he defined them as those who do the most contradictory things yet have the same word for all. According to this definition Therese was—in contradiction to himself—decidedly mad."[68] The conjunction of women and madness has, of course, its own well-worn tradition in European literature, as Gilbert and Gubar have long since shown.[69] This novel's specific feminization of mental illness is carefully laid out, particularly with regard to the gynecologist-psychiatrist Georg Kien. An important thread running throughout this narrativization of madness is the markedly "feminine" threat to stable semiotics, that is, the menace posed by "those who do the most contradictory things yet have the same word for all."

In his rigid insistence on "the accepted terminology" of "official psychiatry" and in his conviction that the insane are only good insofar as they can be used to corroborate the existing scientific system, Georg's predecessor at the Paris insane asylum comes very close to Kien himself: "He took it for his real work in life, to use the vast material at his disposal to support the accepted terminology . . . He clung to the infallibility of the system and hated doubters. Human beings, especially nerve cases and criminals, were nothing to him . . . They provided experiences which authorities could use to build up the science. He himself was an authority."[70] This egotistical director elaborates a definition of madness as ludicrous as Kien's philosophy of blindness. Like Kien's own rather suspect pseudophilosophy, the predecessor's psychiatric principles are unmistakably rooted in a conflict with "real" women: "Madness, he said with great emphasis, and looked at his wife with penetrating and accusing gaze (she blushed), madness is the disease which attacks those very people who think only of themselves. Mental disease is the punishment of egoism . . . He had nothing else to say to his wife. She was thirty years younger than he and cast a glow over the evening of his life. His first wife had run away before he could shut her up—as he had done with the second—in his own institute; she was an incurable egoist. His third, against whom he had nothing save his own jealousy, loved Georg Kien."[71] Just as the quack philologist locates the disruption of meaning in woman, so too this self-important psychiatrist finds madness to consist of excessive female egoism, for which his ex-wives provide the prime examples.

Although Georg would have us believe he is the great alternative to his predecessor's rigidity and arrogance, we come to understand (as we realize the extent to which Georg has commandeered the narrator's voice) how fundamentally similar they really are. Not unlike his predecessor (and not unlike his elder brother) Georg sees himself as a savior figure; that his methods differ is not really the point. He casts himself (by means of the infiltrated narrator's voice) first as an inverted Moses figure, then as Yahweh himself: "He did them [the insane] the service, and led them back into Egypt. The ways he had found to do so were no less wonderful than those of the Lord when he set free his people."[72] Reminiscent of Kien's cooptation of the narrator to express his worldwide eminence among sinologists and philologists is Georg's claim to his own fame, deceptively ensconced in authorial narration: "His colleagues admired and envied him . . . They hastened to break off little fragments of his fame, by proclaiming indebtedness to him and applying his methods to the most different cases. He was bound to get the Nobel Prize."[73]

Georg's immense ego and putative fame rest no less than his brother's on the exploitation of the feminine. But whereas Kien felt compelled to exclude it in order to protect the purity of his precepts and the integrity of his much vaunted *Charakter*, Georg's manipulation takes the form of radical cooptation. This was true from his earliest days as a gynecologist when he exploited his good looks to attract female patients. In his "own" words, he was "surrounded and spoilt by innumerable women, all ready to serve him; he lived like Prince Gautama before he became Buddha."[74] What shall concern us presently is precisely this conversion experience in which he apparently learns to forego the pleasures of real women, only to take on the mantle of malleable femininity.

Though he claims to have parted ways with women at age twenty-eight, we should not understand this as total abstention.[75] It is true, however, that Georg's infatuation with the so-called gorilla man (the insane brother of the rich banker) coincides precisely with his attempt to fend off voluptuous female sexuality in the person of the banker's wife. This erotically neglected spouse lures Georg to the upper chambers of her mansion in order to seduce him by means of a sexually suggestive painting, which, in deference to appearances, had been relegated to the gorilla man's garret quarters. But this strategy fails: the extensive overtures of "Madame"—the banker's wife— prove fruitless against the charm of the gorilla man: the man who has, in Georg's eyes, successfully appropriated the feminine while remaining male. For Georg it is love at first sight: "If only the gorilla would speak again! Before this single wish all his thoughts of time-wasting, duties, women, success had vanished, as if from the day of his birth he had only been seeking for that man, or that gorilla, who possessed his own language."[76]

In a study of quite different texts (namely, horror films), Carol Clover has shown that the typical story of male development, deeply entrenched in the Western tradition, is marked by an appropriation of culturally defined feminine traits.[77] Thus, whereas a woman exhibiting male attributes would more likely be seen as aberrant (and thus incite horror), it is entirely possible for a male hero—while retaining a fundamentally masculine identity—to exhibit development in his character by becoming somewhat feminized. The developmental arc of one male character (in *Auto-da-Fé:* Georg) can be made to look more reasonable, Clover demonstrates, by contrasting it with a more radically gender-mixed character (here, the gorilla man). In portraying Georg's great conversion, this pivotal growth experience made possible by the incorporation of the feminine, Canetti is lampooning this very tradition. But to understand this parody better, we must first ask what precisely this gorilla man represents.

Part of the humor, of course, is the apparent incongruity of images. We are invited to see this bestial man evincing a considerable sexual appetite (recall his ever-present "scantily dressed" Parisian "secretary" on call to tend to his every whim) as somehow essentially feminine. But in his primitiveness, animality, and predilection for hedonistic pleasures, he is a quite precise realization of Weininger's fears regarding the "surrender of the 'masculine' bastions of logic and ethics to the 'feminine' realm of feelings and sexual desire, which he saw occurring all around him in turn-of-the-century, 'modernist' Europe."[78] Indeed, one could not ask for a clearer illustration of a forfeiture of logic and intersubjective rationality than the gorilla man's solipsistic "system" of language.

Georg falls not for the sexualized, macho ape-man, but for his allegedly revolutionary and whimsical system of language, in which the signifiers no longer match up with the signifieds. In fact, the gorilla man's linguistic innovations, viewed in their entirety, can accurately be seen as a caricature of Saussurian insights on the relationship of *langue* to *parole.* Since the experience of the gorilla man is what causes Georg not only to reconsider his previous promiscuity, but also to privilege madness over sanity, it will be worth examining the gorilla man's enterprise in some detail. This is the linguistic marvel that so captivates Georg, not to mention many critics of the novel:

> Each syllable which he uttered corresponded to a special gesture. The words for objects seemed to change. He meant the picture a hundred

times and called it each time something different; the names seemed to depend on the gesture with which he demonstrated them ... Objects ... had no special names. They were called according to the mood in which they floated. Their faces altered for the gorilla, who lived a wild, tense, stormy life. His life communicated itself to them, they had an active part in it. He had peopled two rooms with a whole world. He created what he wanted, and after the six days of creation, on the seventh took up his abode therein. Instead of resting, he gave his creation speech.[79]

The free-floating signifiers notwithstanding, the gorilla man is essentially a Peter Kien in a monkey suit. The gorilla's language production, a grand spoof on the neoempiricist theories of the day (as we will see in greater detail below in chapter 3), has two essential qualities: (1) it is apparently capricious, fluid, and spontaneous, but (2) anchored in the consciousness of the (ever-changing) gorilla man himself. The gorilla's speech is indeed an act of free creation over which he himself exercises sole domain. The fluidity and lack of clear definition between self and other that characterizes this language is in fact a parodistic evocation of Weininger's infamous shibboleth of "*Weiblichkeit*," or femininity, namely the so-called "*Henide*."[80] It may be a tautology to unveil the gorilla man's language system as pure nonsense; yet insofar as Georg himself—who has been seen by a number of critics as the novel's only sane character, even as the voice of Canetti himself—makes so much of it, we, too, need to be very clear about it.

For Georg this is a crucial experience: he publishes a formal "thesis on the speech of this madman"[81] and alters the entire course of his life from this point on. Georg's enthusiasm for the gorilla man's language is fundamentally analogous to the peculiar brand of empathetic psychiatry he practices: he treats his patients by taking on their manias, by playing a role in their psychodrama, by becoming a pure function of their needs. He plays the Fischerin to their Fischerle, the Anna to their Pfaff, and, quite literally, the "Jeanne" to their Jean.[82] In short, in both the narrower and metaphorical senses, he plays the role of woman. Yet just as the gorilla's language capriciously shifts in meaning according to his mood or passion but never spins out of *his* control, so, too, is Georg covertly always in charge. He *plays*, but never really becomes, the "*Weib*" Peter accuses him of having become.[83] The malleable mask he dons merely serves to camouflage a rather unified, ego-dominated, "male" self.

His therapy amounts to playacting, as his elder brother repeatedly charges. "Kings he addressed reverently as Your Majesty . . . He became their sole confidant . . . He advised them . . . as though their wishes were his own, cautiously keeping their aims and their beliefs before his eyes . . . never authoritative in his dealings with men . . . Was he not after all their chief minister, their prophet or their apostle, occasionally even their chamberlain?"[84] Careful to appear submissive and humble to men, and to fulfill their delusional wishes, Georg clearly occupies a feminine role in the treatment of his patients. In one of the novel's most memorable images Georg envisions himself as "a walking wax tablet" (*eine spazierende Wachstafel*),[85] which expresses precisely his self-conception as passive receptacle rather than domineering determiner of meaning. On the surface this would indeed seem to be quite the opposite of his elder brother's self-image; indeed, it tellingly coincides with the philologist's conception of the ideal, masterable, text.

Georg's principal undoing in the reader's eyes is his bungling of the treatment of his own brother. Like the renowned philologist who fails accurately to read Therese, the famous psychiatrist unravels before our eyes as he makes one idiotic diagnosis after another. Despite (or perhaps because of) his vaunted ability to assume the manias of others, he cannot really see much beyond himself. When he arrives on the scene and hears Therese's tale about Kien having murdered a previous wife, he refers the crisis back to himself. In the blink of an eye, he shifts our focus from the ailing brother to the specter of a disgraced, internationally renowned therapist:

> Georg the brother of a sexual murderer [*eines Lustmörders*]. Headlines in all the papers . . . His retirement from the direction of the institute. Indiscretion. Divorce. His assistants to succeed him. The patients . . . They love him, they need him, he cannot leave them. Resignation is impossible. Peter's affairs must be seen to . . . *He* was all for Chinese characters, Georg for human beings. Peter must be put in a home . . . It is evident that he is not responsible for his actions. Under no circumstances will Georg retire from the direction of the institute.[86]

In passages such as these it becomes clear that Georg's careful learning of the language of the insane is not essentially different from Kien's motive in memorizing Therese's every utterance. The effect of emphasizing that "*He* was all for Chinese characters, Georg for human beings" simply encourages us in our reading of these two phenomena, Oriental texts and the insane, as parallel instances of the feminine, though of course Georg means to suggest the much greater importance of his endeavor. Yet it is clear enough that both brothers seek control and confirmation of their own preeminence and genius by exploiting the interpretive potential of their speciously feminized objects of inquiry. This essential identity of the two brothers is evident once more in Georg's "yearning for a place where he too was no less absolute master than his brother in the library."[87] To sustain this illusion of absolute sovereignty both employ the very clichéd, contemporary conceptions of the feminine that achieved such widespread notoriety during the interwar period. Peter Kien, in a vain effort to shore up an obsolete, positivistic epistemology, tries desperately to textualize his woman, to make her the unmistakable object in the subject-object binary, and thereby to assuage his own anxieties via "culture." When she fails to comply, when the threat of incomprehensibility persists, his system collapses and he goes mad. Georg attempts to coopt the feminine as a type of madness and malleability that claims to subvert an ossified, conservative political culture. His endeavor, no less than his brother's, is principally one of interpretation and meaning-making. But the subversive, countercultural, and antibourgeois stance that Georg's conversion experience initially seems to signify is ultimately exposed for its rootedness in a profound egocentrism. Like Kien's, Georg's use of the feminine proves to be a profoundly unsuccessful way of defining himself. In the end Kien immolates himself and Georg departs, ignorant of his own disgrace.

This analysis raises new questions about canonical readings of *Auto-da-Fé*. Until the seventies it was not uncommon to find Georg interpreted as the novel's only identification figure, even as the author's *raisonneur*, an idea Foell resurrects in her recent study of 1994. One of the principal reasons for siding with Georg is of course his relative congeniality toward the greedy, self-centered, and brutal cast of characters. More important to interpreters such as Walter H. Sokel, however, was the alleged correspondence between Georg's reflections on crowds and Canetti's own theory on this topic as elaborated at great length in *Crowds and Power*.[88] Though more recent evaluations of Georg have taken him down a peg, uncovering him for the charlatan he is,[89] none has penetrated to the principal point of identity between the brothers Kien: the exploitation of the feminine to resolve a male ego crisis.

The reading I have developed here might also dampen the kind of enthusiasm, which, for example, Russell Berman expresses in *The Rise of the*

Modern German Novel (1986), where he adduces *Auto-da-Fé* as an instance of "charismatic modernism."[90] This interpretation hinges on a rather sanguine reading of Georg, who is portrayed as the key exponent of the novel's "utopian character." Berman's perspective on Georg and the novel as a whole seems to be rooted in a strain of literary theory that sees—if only implicitly—a source of social liberation in both the linguistic theories of Ferdinand de Saussure and Freud as he was read in the late sixties, and beyond. The liberation of the signifier from the signified as well as a belief in the emancipatory potential of unrepressed libidinal energies have indeed served to inspire the literary theory of leftist critics as diverse as Foucault, Cixous, Barthes, and some members of the Frankfurt School. Saussurian linguistics, it would seem, has helped deconstruct the naturalness not only of language, but that of larger social and gender arrangements as well.

This linguistic/psychoanalytic infusion into criticism, notwithstanding the many lasting contributions it has made and continues to inspire, may be precisely what has blinded us for so many years to Canetti's parody in the figure of Georg. Neither Georg's enthusiasm for a language that is nothing more than a child's, nor his espousal of fighting insanity with insanity, can really be taken seriously today. His authoritarian occupation of "feminine" madness is hardly a harbinger of the new charismatic community—unless we really want to emulate the gorilla man's semiotic whimsy, to which, let us not forget, his sex-slave secretary must subordinate her every desire. Indeed, without the overwhelming context of emancipatory literary and cultural theory that values the marginal, oppositional forces thought to stand "outside the law" (and which Berman felt were present in Georg), it is quite difficult to imagine how one could have been so enthralled with Georg. Canetti's parody of Georg's appropriation of the feminine (first in the seduction of his gynecological patients, then in his adoption of the language of the insane) also gives us reason to reevaluate Georg's ruminations on the crowd. Sokel may be quite right to emphasize some thematic parallels with *Crowds and Power,* but with one important caveat: for the ethnologist/sociologist Canetti, "*die Masse*" (meaning "mass" or "crowd") is a fundamental category of social analysis applicable to all human beings. For Georg, it is clearly—and therefore speciously—feminized.[91] The best evidence of this may be Georg's conviction that his own course of self-feminization has inured him to the dangers of an unannounced eruption of the feminine: "Countless people go mad because the mass in them is particularly strongly developed and can get no satisfaction . . . Once he had lived for his private tastes, his ambition and women; now his one desire was perpetually to lose himself. In this activity he came nearer to the thoughts and wishes of the mass, than did those other isolated individuals around whom he lived."[92] Georg never gives up either his own rather firmly developed sense of individuation nor his lascivious appetites. His newfound love of the crowd is just another instance of erotically charged playacting. Below in chapter 5, within a discussion of the novel's response to the contemporary Freud mania, we will observe how Georg's muddled ideas about societal ontogeny form a pointed and humorous target of satire. More immediately, we will see how both Georg and Kien wrap themselves in the respectable garb of Weimar-era philosophy, a process that in the end only demeans the larger cultural project to which both pay such effusive lip service.

3 Self-Indulgent Philosophies of the Weimar Period
The Use and Abuse of Neoempiricism and Neo-Kantianism

> By the time he wrote *Auto-da-Fé,* Canetti had arrived at a devastating insight: not only is all speech self-serving but all listening is self-serving. We remake the world in our minds as a phantasmagoria of our desires.
> —David Denby[1]

With the noted exceptions of the revered Dr. Sonne and a few other elect, Canetti recalls the bulk of the Viennese intellectuals he encountered during the interwar period as problematically self-absorbed: "One has to imagine this city and this coffeehouse ethos, this flood of self-reference, self-assertion, confession and self-aggrandizing. Everyone spilled over with sympathy for himself and for his own significance. Everyone grumbled, everyone chimed in and trumpeted. Yet all remained huddled together in small groups, even publicly, because they needed and suffered each other for their [self-important] speeches."[2] Particularly this final sentence, which portrays these gatherings not as bearing intrinsic communal value, but useful instead only insofar as they prop up the solipsistic individual, resonates profoundly and hilariously in *Auto-da-Fé*. It is precisely this "selfishness" (*Eigenutz*), the polar opposite of everything Sonne (and, by extension, Canetti) stands for, that Canetti saw as the expression of a dangerous and widespread lack of concern for society. Canetti singles out Eastern philosophy—or, to be more precise, a particular mode of reception of Eastern thought—as the culprit for this asocial behavior on the part of so many intellectuals of this era. "Eastern wisdom," he contends, provided a popular and respectable way of abandoning social responsibility: "In renouncing sympathy for the world of one's immediate environs, one also surrendered responsibility for it."[3]

But in *Auto-da-Fé* it is not really Eastern philosophy—despite our protagonist's prominence as a world-renowned sinologist[4] — that serves as intellectual cover for a retreat from social concerns, but rather two specific philosophical movements that flourished in the interwar period: neoempiricism, which in the novel is associated principally with Georg; and a loosely practiced neoidealism, which of course centers on Kien himself. These two highly educated brothers both wrap themselves in popular (and popularized) philosophy in order to authorize their spurious withdrawal from an increasingly bewildering social reality. Contrary to what Lukács would later claim about modernism — that it abuses the dignity of philosophy to endorse its own subjectivist ideology — *Auto-da-Fé* pointedly questions the use of philosophy employed to legitimize the denigration of social awareness. Moreover, Kien and Georg represent two sides of the same philosophical coin. Both the radicalization of the Idealist subject (as caricatured in Kien) as well as the empiricist premise of inductive epistemology (as practiced by Georg) tend to grant priority to the thinking/percipient subject at the expense of those objects of thought and sensation. In the end, these "self-legislating" subjects greatly exceed Kant's prescription for autonomy; they proceed unhindered in their abusive and solipsistic behavior by virtually any kind of checks and balances and, worse yet, do so as adherents of high-minded philosophical schools.

Before pursuing this line of thought, a word on method. Previous critical discussion of philosophy in *Auto-da-Fé* has focused on classical empiricism, taking its cue from the protagonist himself, who, in a moment of philosophical confusion, quotes the famous eighteenth century British empiricist Bishop Berkeley.[5] While Darby's discussion of Kien's misappropriation of Berkeley remains instructive, it may also be misleading insofar as it takes the novel for an academic philosophical tractate. There are two problems with this assumption. First, Canetti repeatedly discounted this intention, protesting that he was not in the first place a philosopher. Though he exhibits an impressive but general familiarity with the Western philosophical tradition, one that could be assumed in an educated person of his day, he nevertheless yielded on particular points to the philosophically more expert Hermann Broch, who, according to Canetti, gave himself over to philosophy as willingly as others yielded to nocturnal pleasures.[6] One can furthermore deduce from Canetti's total oeuvre that Canetti was indeed well acquainted with those areas of philosophy that impinged upon the social concerns dearest to him, that is, issues related to crowds and power. Of course we should not now err in the opposite extreme by assuming that the numerous philosophical references in *Auto-da-Fé* are superfluous or mere background music, as they surely are, for example, in Isaac Bashevis Singer's novel *Shosha*. On the contrary, they continue to be quite meaningful, as we shall see below, though not as interventions in professional academic philosophy, but rather insofar as they illuminate the individual's relationship to society and culture as a whole. Second, the fact that neoempiricism and neo-Kantianism make their appearance by way of caricature suggests that we will be better served by seeking their meaning broadly, that is, in the manner in which they serve to characterize the respective figure, rather than as an independently valid assessment of the respective philosophical movement. Finally, in this regard we should note that Canetti simply did not know directly the work of Franz Brentano, a major figure in neoempiricism, at the time he wrote the novel.[7] The novel cannot therefore be read as an academic, source-based engagement with this—or, indeed, any particular—philosophical school. In elaborately reconstructing a philosophical system of, say, Bishop Berkeley in order to elucidate a quip that Kien tosses off opportunistically, one clearly risks hermeneutic overkill. Or worse, it can lead us away from the novel's principal concerns, and, however inadvertently, present a kind of evasion of the novel's central critique. Instead, I will proceed on the assumption that Canetti imbibed neoempiricism as something that was, as he himself puts it in a piece of correspondence, simply "in the air."[8]

Empiricism and Neoempiricism

Judith Ryan has shown that, with psychology just beginning to emerge from philosophy as a discipline in its own right, "empiricist psychology" was the great and as yet neglected impetus for modernist writers up to 1940.[9] Let us begin by asking how Canetti's novel of 1930–31 fits into this matrix of ideas.

Ryan sets out to distinguish between the "experimental psychologists" and the "empiricists" of the latter half of the nineteenth century.[10] The former, represented by Wilhelm Wundt, inquired into human sensation by means of experimentation and overlapped with the interests of physics; such inquiries "led to new investigations into the various forms of illusion perpetrated by the senses."[11] By contrast, the empiricists (and in particular Brentano) prized introspection over experimentation. It is this second group, "the philosopher-psychologists, the empiricists," that Ryan credits with "the greatest impact on writers and artists at the turn of the century."[12] Here is Ryan's précis of the ideas that were to prove so influential on modernist poets: "What did it mean to be an empiricist in the late nineteenth century? Primarily, it meant that the only admissible evidence for the existence of something was that of our senses; the only reality was that of our consciousness. The empiricists attacked metaphysics as postulating a reality 'behind' or 'beyond' that of the senses. Similarly, they rejected the dualism of subject and object. For them, there was no separate 'object-world': everything that was, subsisted in consciousness itself."[13]

The towering figures in this group were, as we have already noted, the Austrians Franz Brentano and Ernst Mach, as well as the American William James. Although there are important differences among these thinkers,[14] the denominator common to all is a diluted, less substantial self. Brentano championed a more systematized view of the poetic theory of correspondences, in which neither the subject nor the object exists absolutely and independently, but only in mutual interdependence. This relationship he called "intentional." Mach's famous definition of the percipient subject as a "mass of sensations, loosely bundled together" goes a good deal further in unraveling the traditional conception of the self. And though William James tempered the effect of such radical ideas by means of his philosophy of pragmatism, he nevertheless shared such fundamental concepts as the intentionality of perception. "His answer to those who saw empiricism as a life-inhibiting philosophy was to propose a strategy of accepting any notions that actually helped us in our practical lives, even though they might not accord with the more sophisticated philosophical views we also held."[15]

Ryan's most important contribution, for our purposes, concerns the pervasiveness of empiricist thinking. She shows, for example, how Brentano's teaching seeped into the Austrian *Gymnasien* (university preparatory schools) by way of his numerous students who later took teaching positions there. In general, it seems well established that empiricist thinkers such as Mach, Brentano, and James did indeed set the intellectual agenda on this issue at least through the early decades of the twentieth century—that is, if we are careful to include not only their disciples, but their opponents as well. While it is true that Canetti later claimed to have had only an "insufficient conception" of Brentano's "widespread influence" (*die Vielfalt seiner*

Austrahlung) on contemporary thinkers,[16] he acknowledges that the Viennese air was still thick with free-floating neoempiricist notions during the interwar period.

Though Ryan presents a quite differentiated spectrum of literary responses to the problem of "the vanishing subject" — some authors enact the trauma, others parody it, still others oppose it — her survey of contemporary philosophy and psychology pays scant attention to that prominent intellectual movement that effectively (though indirectly) opposed empiricist psychology, namely neo-Kantianism — a movement that is importantly relevant to *Auto-da-Fé*. Nowhere are these schools more clearly opposed than in their conception of subjectivity. While the neoempiricists trumpeted the erosion of the boundary between self and world, the neo-Kantians sought to reestablish the line of demarcation separating the *Verstandeswelt* (world of intellect) from the *Sinneswelt* (world of sensory experience), a division that was held to be prerequisite to the expression of Kantian autonomy of the individual. An additional amendment to Ryan's account seems in order when appraising the work of Canetti, namely a greater emphasis on the experimental psychologists within the neoempiricist movement as opposed to the introspective philosopher-psychologists. We ought to remember in this connection that Canetti spent five years studying chemistry and allied sciences just prior to writing *Auto-da-Fé*. Though he could not flee quickly enough from the laboratory, this experience appears to have left its imprint on the novel. Indeed we shall see below that a striking analogy exists between the approach taken by experimental psychologists such as Wilhelm Wundt and the form of the novel as designed by Dr. rer. nat. Elias Canetti.

The novel's attitude toward empiricist accounts of subjectivity is, as we shall see, richly parodic. Kien is at best a fair-weather empiricist, Georg a farcical caricature of the empirical self. Canetti's main concern is to show that the empiricist conception of the self may be fine for world-weary aesthetes and lonely lyric poets, but is overtaxed in confronting the demands of intersubjectivity, that is to say in imagining humans as essentially social beings. In drawing out the implications of empiricist thinking, often by means of merciless hyperbole, the novel suggests that this manner of thinking undermines the sociopolitical realm. In terms of individual psychology, moreover, it implies a kind of self-evisceration, even a *Selbstmord:* for only a self can get rid of a self.

Peter Kien is neither the isolated individual in the vertiginous metropolis fumbling to make sense of self and world (e.g., Rilke's Malte), nor the artist as a young man (Musil's Törleß), nor the hapless young hero forced to live out the clichés of a previous generation (Broch's Pasenow). Writing in the wake of rising social unrest—whose violence, as we have noted, Canetti witnessed personally—and in the wake of his own experience of the isolating nature of an overspecialized academia, Canetti is preoccupied with the dissolution not of the self per se, but of the connection between the individual and society. Or, to put it another way, he problematizes a conception of the self, which from the outset is unsuited to interpersonal and social engagement.[17] His response to the matrix of empiricist psychology is not, therefore, a sympathetic literary reenactment of the vanishing subject, but a critique of inauthentic strategies of self-assertion, a parody of illegitimate efforts to overcome the subject-object dichotomy and, ultimately, a rejection of empiricist psychology as solipsistic.

Empiricist as well as experimental psychology were, as we noted, very much concerned with the matter of perception. But whereas empiricists such as Brentano (much like his eighteenth-century empiricist predecessor Berkeley) stressed the interdependence of existence and perception, the experimental researchers such as Wundt emphasized the distinctions between the individual's perceptions and a scientifically observable reality. Both theories have a certain validity: the former stresses the symbiotic relationship, the constitutive power of perception (and thus the inextricability of reality and perception), while the latter stresses the distorting potential inherent in perception.

At first glance, Therese's creative reworking of the sign at the furniture shop seems to give us a scene from classical comedy, of which Gottsched himself—were it not for the farce—might heartily approve: "She came to a halt in front of his shop. The letters in the shop front came close to her eyes. First she read Gross & Mother, then Brute & Wife. She liked that. She even wasted some of her busy time just looking at it . . . The letters danced for joy, and when they had finished dancing she read suddenly, Gross & Wife. That didn't suit her at all."[18] The scene is a spoof on Brentano's "inner perception," which grants a reality to consciousness, whether or not the items of consciousness correspond to an external reality. Having just witnessed Therese's elaborate reverie of bedding the handsome "Mr. Brute" (Wedgwood's rendering of "Herr Grob"), one does not hesitate in convicting her of allowing her runaway fantasy to rewrite reality in a manner commensurate first with her own erotic desire and then with her greatest fear—namely that he is already married.

How is this different from Gottsched's dictum that in comedy the point is to mock ("*auslachen*") aberrant characters, that is, to laugh them back into a morally acceptable place? The question is pertinent in light of Canetti's use of comic types: Therese might, for example, be labeled according to her ruling passion(s): she is a lecherous version of the miser ("die Geizige"). But while this type of generic, moralizing reading of *Auto-da-Fé* is not invalid, neither should it eclipse Canetti's stinging, hilarious, and far more general critique of empiricist thinking. For it is not up to Therese alone to remedy this failing; the neoempiricist atmosphere lies heavy over the entire cast of characters. As a broader, cultural phenomenon, it is not amenable to individual remedy. Ultimately, this latter critique is of greater moral—rather than moralizing—import.

Though Brentano's theory was not in itself subjectivist, it had this effect nevertheless. Brentano, we recall, held that "we can consider the object precisely as *intended* and as *inexistent*, without raising questions about its extramental nature and status."[19] Brentano's avoidance of ontological questions and extramental reality gave priority, if only by default and eventual misapplication, to the subjective perceptions of individuals. What the neoempiricists of the late nineteenth and early twentieth century lacked, and what their eighteenth-century forebears (such as Berkeley) supplied, was a guarantee against such relativism. Berkeley anchored his system, as Darby amply documents, in God.[20] The neoempiricists, as Ryan points out, were pointedly antimetaphysical, and thus this option was lost to them. Yet, as Copleston observes, the reigning and still topical problem in Western philosophy is, as Kant well understood, the conformity between mental concepts and extramental objects.[21] The neoempiricist attempt to sidestep this puzzle in eliminating the subject-object dichotomy by granting reality only to consciousness is, as Canetti's novel wickedly illustrates, not without problems.

In what is perhaps the most memorable of Therese's misprisions, Canetti provides an ironic twist to Brentano's "intended" but "inexistent" objects. This occurs during Therese's visit to what we know as the Cathedral of St. Stephen; the scene marks an interlude in her dogged attempt to wrench a testament from Kien, who, in turn, believes she is referring to a great sum *she* stands to inherit independently. Just after learning of Kien's meager net worth, Therese takes her problem to prayer:

> She sought out the largest church in the town, the cathedral... There hung a picture of the Last Supper, painted in expensive oil colours... The money-bag looked as though you could touch it, thirty beautiful pieces of silver inside... Judas held it tight. He wouldn't let go, he was so greedy. He grudged every penny. Just like her old man... Her old man is thin, Judas is fat and has a red beard. In the middle of it all sits the superior young man. Such a beautiful face, all pale, and eyes just as they should be. He knows everything... Her husband's a dirty miser. To do such a thing for twenty schillings... She is the white dove. She is flying just above his head. She shines white, because of her innocence. The painter would have it that way... She is the white dove. Let Judas try any of his tricks. He won't catch hold of her. She will fly wherever she wants. She will fly to the superior young man, she knows what's beautiful. Judas can say what he likes. He can go and hang himself... The money belongs to her... Soon the soldiers will come... She will step forward and say: "This isn't our Lord. This is Mr. Brute, a simple salesman in the shop of *Gross and Mother*. You mustn't lay a finger on him. I'm his wife..." Judas can go and hang himself. She is the white dove.[22]

Therese's rewriting of this cardinal scene should not be read merely in a manner that would characterize *her:* as a virtual stock character, she is already quite amply developed. The satire aims instead at empiricism, for which every mental image is "actual," even if it is not otherwise "real." It is perhaps pedantic to spell out Therese's misreading. Yet we should be clear that it involves not merely an identification of her beloved Herr Grob with Jesus, but ultimately an utter substitution of the latter for the former.

Canetti specifically parodies the process of mental correction (the way the mind corrects for perceptual illusions was a central concern of the experimental psychologists) in having Therese first see Judas as the physical opposite of Kien (i.e., corpulent and red-bearded), and then somehow his very likeness. Notice also how she first savors the thirty shillings in the purse insofar as she envisions having the money herself. But once she projects Kien onto the Judas figure, who, as everyone knows, actually receives the moneybag, the sum suddenly drops to twenty. This is no accident, since immediately after naming this new, lower figure, Therese angrily recalls her obdurate allegation that Kien had attempted to cheat her out of her rightful inheritance by correcting the arithmetic in his bankbook—another sum that, she believes, sank before her "very eyes." Though she is compelled for other reasons to remake Kien into Judas, she is not about to grant him the full thirty shillings. The third instance of "mental correction" from the passage cited above has to do with Herr Grob: because he is at first the beautiful love object, Therese eagerly assigns him the role of Jesus. Shortly thereafter, however, under the pressure of the Passion narrative itself, she is constrained to distinguish her beloved Herr Grob from Jesus—who, of course, is about to be crucified—so that she can script a happy ending to her own erotic fantasy.

The point of such scenes is not, in the first place, to scold the two-dimensional figure back to moral perfection, but wittily to indicate what is lost in the empiricist conception of the self: namely a firm sense of the other, and of the larger social world. Though Canetti is certainly not concerned to restore Christianity as a dominant cultural narrative, he demonstrates by means of exaggeration the threat inherent in empiricist thinking: in this case, the loss of common cultural goods, of images that (for better and worse) can bind a community together. Writing at the end of a long period during which the subjective side of experience had, in the German canon at least, been highly valorized, Canetti raises in *Auto-da-Fé* an objection, not against that vaunted German *Innerlichkeit* (inwardness) and authentic subjective states per se, but against the implicit claim that nothing else matters quite so much. Therese's heretical, personalized version of the Last Supper is easily unmasked and corrected (now, by the reader) because she and the object of her devotion are extremely well-known quantities. She, a highly stylized type; the Last Supper, a tableau from the Christian masterplot. Only such extremes can produce a parody of empiricism that does not itself risk becoming a celebration of the empiricist self. Canetti's recourse to a relatively stable cultural signifier should not be seen as nostalgia for a type of literature (or worldview) where everything has its unquestioned, preordained place. Nor does it reflect an inherent preference for two-dimensional figures as opposed to full-blooded *Menschen*. Canetti's self-conscious use of these extremes is dictated rather by his task, which here is to illuminate the potential risk in uncritically embracing the faddish neoempiricism of the day. This critique of what we might call "mental privatization," which takes aim at the progressive erasure of the public domain as an independent ontological entity, is particularly evident in the novel's spectral and fleeting evocation of Vienna.[23]

Therese's burlesque reading of the Last Supper painting satirizes the empiricist effort to collapse the subject-object dichotomy. In contrast to Malte's celebrated, imaginary reconstitution of the semi-demolished house, a process we are meant to affirm, Therese's undeniably imaginative reading of the painting is rendered decisively inauthentic. Her visit to the cathedral suggests that the empiricist conflation of mental conception and extramental object, the reduction of reality to consciousness, is flawed because it overlooks the potential inequality of the two terms. Anticipating one of his own great themes in *Crowds and Power* (as well as the work of Foucault), Canetti points out that what one sees (as well as what one fails to see) is already enmeshed in power. Or, to put it otherwise: power—and therefore the abuse of power as well—begins at the point of (mis)perception.

Nowhere is this more obvious than in the case of Kien. We have seen already how Kien's empiricist pronouncements, in particular his epistemological skepticism expressed above all in the "esse percepi" outburst, are rooted in his skirmish with Therese. It is beside the point, however, whether, or to what extent, Kien is a *sincere* empiricist. More importantly, he—like Therese—is an occasion for playing out some of the more questionable implications of empiricist conceptions.

One cannot approach Kien without encountering the classic empiricist agenda. He is, as we observe throughout the novel, obsessively concerned with the strength of his eyes and with overcoming the subject-object bifurcation. Furthermore, he maintains a doggedly antimetaphysical stance and explicitly subordinates existence to consciousness. Yet though all the issues line up, Kien is nevertheless the novel's least likely empiricist. Deeply fearful of any except the most solitary experience, Kien cuts himself off from the empiricist font of meaning. His eyes actually reverse the order of Democritus's atomism: his optical apparatus seems to assign rather than receive the data of experience. And, though the empiricists included introspection (in addition to sense perception) as a source of meaning, this hardly makes Kien an exemplary empiricist. If we associate a diffuse ego with empiricism, a sense of self and other as embedded in an indivisible flux, then it becomes clear that Kien is at best a misfit, autocratic empiricist. When we read, for example, that "he reserved consciousness for real thoughts; they depend upon it; without consciousness, thoughts are unthinkable,"[24] it becomes clear that the empiricist program is lurking there, even if at times it appears more to threaten than to characterize the protagonist. Indeed, Kien could only represent an authentic empiricist by giving up the critique of empiricism which he embodies.

One could visit a multitude of scenes where perception is fundamentally at issue, as near the end of the novel where Kien declares the meal Therese serves him an illusion. Having the meal thrown at him does little to convince him of its material reality; neither does his act of self-mutilation (he cuts off a finger) prove persuasive. But all such scenes, and in particular this act of self-impairment, harken back to Kien's paradigmatic denial of Therese. Indeed, the act of digital self-dismemberment recalls Kien's act of self-blinding, and the attendant *"Philosophie der Blindheit"* discussed above. It echoes (and inverts) the famous mutilations of Abelard and Origen, who only escaped the snares of (female) material reality—and were thus free to continue their meditative lifestyle—by means of castration. And it accentuates the proximity of empiricism to escapism, a nexus we will notice in connection with Georg, below.

Kien's prototypical problem is his failure to apprehend figures who enjoy as much fictional reality as he does himself, and, more importantly, his attempt to employ the dignity of philosophy and scholarship to underwrite these failings. When Kien applies his philological prowess to obscure oriental texts, most of us can only guess at the distortion. But when he trains his powers on the *tabula rasa* for which he takes Therese, we catch him red-handed; for her fictional existence, no less than his own, has already been inscribed by the narrator and no effort of the world-renowned philologist can erase her with impunity. In other words—to reconnect briefly to an aforementioned debate—if there really is a struggle between Kien and the narrator for what Lubomir Dolezel calls the "authentication authority" in this narrative, its resolution must be sought not only in narratology, but also in the novel's broader critique of popularized neoempiricism.

Once again, the problem is not so much an individual moral failing as a shortcoming endemic to empiricism, which since its eighteenth-century incarnations has been notoriously ill equipped to affirm the existence of other coequal subjects. Though Berkeley never doubted what he referred to as the "spiritual" reality of percipient subjects, his difficulty of affirming fellow humans can, perhaps, be grasped from the provocative claim in the

Principles "that the existence of God is far more evidently perceived than the existence of men; because the effects of Nature are infinitely more numerous and considerable than those ascribed to human agents."[25] When the neoempiricists of the nineteenth century jettisoned theism and metaphysics, this prop to "finite spiritual substances," incredible even to some of Berkeley's contemporaries, was lost as well. Which may explain in part why Brentano, immediately after his neoempiricist phase, became a Catholic priest.

There is an additional, though closely related, intrinsic weakness to the basic conception of all varieties of empiricism, including the neoempiricist incarnation, which makes the apprehension of fellow individuals depend on an *a posteriori* assembly of sense data. To this way of thinking, fellow human beings are secondary phenomena, mere inductions from sensory experience. Copleston's critique of Berkeley on this fundamental point applies *mutatis mutandi* to the later forms as well:

> [Berkeley] does not tell us how we can be certain that the ideas which we take to be signs of the presence of finite spiritual substances [i.e., people] really are what we think they are. Perhaps, however, he would reply that ... from ideas or observable effects which are analogous to those which we are conscious of producing, *we infer the existence of other selves;* and this is sufficient evidence. But if anyone is dissatisfied with such an answer and wishes to know what justification there is, on Berkeley's premises, for making this inference, he will not receive much help from Berkeley's writings.[26]

The conception that other selves need to be built up from "effects which are analogous to those which we are conscious of producing" poses the danger of seeing others as mere projections, a notion that the novel extensively parodies. When the neoempiricists blurred the contours of the self, moreover, they concomitantly blurred the perceptibility of other selves as independent entities. While Mach's "idea of a fluid, unbounded self essentially composed of sense impressions, a self that was not distinct from its surroundings"[27] may in some sense be seen to overcome or master a painful dichotomy between subject and object—a kind of liberation, as it were—it simultaneously erodes the essential distinction between subject and subject. Shorn of its eighteenth-century metaphysical underpinnings, neoempiricism can ultimately only speak of the other as object of one's own consciousness, or, to use more contemporary terminology, as a mental construct, rather than co-equal subject. From the neoempiricist point of view, the *percipient* subject is structurally favored over the *perceived* subject.

And this is precisely the critique we see played out again and again in *Auto-da-Fé*. The combined evidence of all his senses fails to convince Kien of his wife's existence:

> He had seized Therese; not tentatively, but with all his strength he clutched at her skirt, he pushed her from him, he drew her to him, he enclosed her in his long, lean arms. She let him have his way . . . Before they are hanged, murderers are allowed one last meal . . . He turned her round once on her axis and forewent the embrace . . . He glared at her from an inch off. He stroked her dress with all ten fingers. He put out his tongue and snuffled with his nose. Tears came into his eyes with the effort. "I suffer from this hallucination!" he admitted, gasping.[28]

The overwhelming sensory data notwithstanding, Kien stands by his previous conclusion: "*I live for truth. I know this truth is a lie.*"[29] Canetti goes to great lengths to include all five senses here. Prior to the so-called experiment narrated above, Kien had already perceived a Therese-like voice: "At present she is silent, but earlier she had the voice of the murdered woman too."[30] In fact, it is this singularly disturbing voice that leads Kien to disprove her existence in the first place. His learned argument in favor of a spectral Therese ("*Schein-Therese*") therefore presents an embattled empiricist agenda; for the professor, as we shall see presently, is really intent upon asserting his own pseudo-Kantian autonomy and defeating the heteronomy implied in his sensory experience of Therese. Ironically, empiricism is here vindicated; Therese really does exist. Yet it has introduced and authorized a subjectivism that, the novel implies, can be turned against itself. Moreover, as we shall soon see in greater detail, it invites a neoidealist backlash, as already adumbrated in the passage cited above.

The misrecognition of Therese is paradigmatic of figural misapprehension throughout the novel. Kien misperceives Pfaff's essentially violent nature (at least until Kien becomes his prisoner) by historicizing him as a sixteenth-century "*Landsknecht*," as we noted above. Georg similarly misreads the brutish caretaker by aestheticizing him into a state of mythological impotence: "All the murders, all the anxieties, all the malevolence in the world had vanished: The caretaker pleased him. His head reminded him of the rising sun of early that morning. He was crude, but refreshing, an untamed, stout fellow such as one rarely sees now in the cities and homes of civilization. The stairs groaned. Instead of carrying it, this Atlas smote the wretched earth."[31] The construction of an acceptable caretaker proceeds along the same lines as Therese's reinscription of the Last Supper: bits and pieces of the original are incorporated into an image determined predominantly by the needs of the percipient subject, and therefore result in pure distortion. Georg's prettifying misprision of the caretaker in fact strays far more from the wife-beating, child-molesting brute we know than does Kien's putative hallucination, the *Schein-Therese*, from the real Therese.[32]

The inability to see people, or to see them for who they really are, repeats itself in virtually every figural constellation: Fischerle takes Kien for a Jew, and assumes that practically everyone else is the swindler he (that is, Fischerle) in fact is. The parody reaches its height in Fischerle's construction of a chess opponent who is literally his own mirror image. Pfaff renames his daughter "Poli," a shortened form for the *"Polizist"* (policeman) he once was, forcing her to wear his pants and play the role of the criminal he in fact is. When the daughter finally rebels, Pfaff denies her existence, claiming she is an impostor: "She was no daughter of his! . . . By mistake he referred once to a certain Polly. But his muscles made up for that mistake immediately. The name of the female he was disciplining was Anna. She claimed to be identical with a daughter of his. He did not believe her. Her hair came out in handfuls and when she defended herself two of her fingers got broken."[33] The "blinding" of the novel's title, then, can be read as an indictment of the empiricist blind spot for fellow human beings. Though Brentano stressed the unity of consciousness, and Mach envisioned a sort of sensory monism, the egalitarian, leveling tendency of this thinking does not account for the *de facto* experience of separate, antithetical agents. It may be fine to speak, as William James did, of a super-consciousness in which we all somehow participate; but such a heady view fails to accommodate the experience of clashing, rival subjects.

In peopling his novel with Hobbesian louts, Canetti is saying neither that the world is really so utterly brutish (as Peter Russell famously claimed),[34] nor that perceptual error is so rampant or so typically detectable. He is instead drawing attention to a widespread manner of thinking about the self and other that is essentially apolitical, perhaps even antipolitical. The empiricist failure to affirm the other a priori, as it were, paves the way toward a mental expansion of the self at the expense of the other. In the novel we see this in the mental cocoons, "the rival belief worlds," as Darby deftly dubs them, that each character weaves around him/herself—individual refuges in which fellow subjects are merely so much material to be affirmed, denied, or reworked according to the respective reigning monomania.

The result of such thinking, when taken to the extreme, is the eclipse of the social world. In a massive novel of roughly five hundred pages, set in a metropolis we might as well call Vienna, there is surprisingly little attention to community, city, commerce, and so on. The great contrast would of course be Döblin's *Berlin Alexanderplatz,* in which the capital city is itself a rival subject, as Marilyn Silbey Fries has argued. But *Auto-da-Fé* is a novel in which the narration is largely determined by the characters. The narrator moves the characters on and off stage, supplies the characters with enough rope to hang themselves in self-contradictory babble, and splices in a number of key cultural intertexts. But he does not provide a sustained, independent vista. The characters, unable to see each other, cannot begin to construct a social world. This accounts for the simple fact—to give just one example—that on Therese's way home from the furniture store the city suddenly fades to black, and we get none of the municipal ambiance that Fontane would surely have provided. Instead, we are restricted to Therese's consciousness, constrained to observe her as she reworks her humiliation into dubious acclaim. Retaining her inward focus, she expends every ounce of mental energy in an effort to place abusive mockery in a more favorable light, which becomes apparent to the reader when she stretches the auditory data beyond belief in concluding that the assembled customers "laughed at her out of respect" (*lachten vor Stolz*). Preoccupied with such "introspection," Therese perceives not a representative slice of city life and local color, but a highly selective assortment of scenes (such as her fascination with the marching band leader) which in the end serves primarily to reiterate her own venal proclivities and desire for erotic fulfillment.

This warrants bearing in mind in light of Canetti's repeated comment that his novel was inspired by Balzac's *Comédie humaine.* The first question one might raise, especially when one thinks of the best-known of that series, *Père Goriot* (1834), is, Where is Canetti's Paris? In Balzac's novels one encounters similar base passions, but one also experiences a vibrant metropolis and a palpable society, however much this society may be excoriated for its injustice, greed, and vain pursuits. The municipal and social lacunae in

Auto-da-Fé follow in good empiricist fashion from the consciousness of the subjects. As Kien put it, when he found it convenient to strike an empiricist pose: "*Esse percipi,* to be is to be perceived. What I do not perceive, does not exist."[35]

Though empiricism never claimed to supply an adequate political theory, any theory that seeks to define the subject must ultimately be held accountable for the implications of that theory on the polis. *Auto-da-Fé* spins out those consequences mercilessly. After all, a vanishing subject does not accord well with the notion of civic responsibility; a Machian dissolute self merely dissolves the question of ethics, both personal and social. If an empiricist sympathizer were to object, claiming that the author tramples upon the nuances of empiricism in straining the theory beyond the intent of its original philosopher advocates, one could only agree. *Auto-da-Fé* does indeed present a caricature of empiricism, with all the reductionism and distortion that term implies. Yet this observation only serves to clarify, rather than nullify, the novel's distinctive intervention. *Auto-da-Fé* is concerned with the questionable social uses of the neoempiricism that was bandied about Viennese salons and coffee houses during the interwar period, not with an esoteric professional debate among philosophers.

Canetti's creation of headstrong fictional figures should not be misunderstood as a nostalgia for an outmoded will-dominated psychology. His figural constellations do however bear a pertinent and still relevant warning: ego strength does not simply disappear in the face of empiricist notions of the self. Here we must take stock of the fact that empiricism never established itself as a widely accepted theory, to the extent, for example, of Darwin's theory of evolution. That the debate was widespread, I do not dispute. But what began as a theory of the self, rooted both in experimental psychology and philosophical reflection, quickly became something else in addition: something we might call a mood, a set of conceptions that one adopted. We need, in short, to account for empiricism's Janus face: it was both a scientific theory (i.e., something discovered) and a mood (i.e., something donned). It is necessary to grasp this dual aspect in order to appreciate Canetti's final critique contained in the figure of Georg.

If one has been up to this point hesitant to accept empiricism as a vital intertext to the novel, Georg should remove all doubt. Unlike the other figures, Georg is characterized specifically to allegorize (and caricature) the empiricist self. In explicit opposition to his well-armored brother, Georg is drawn as the great recipient of sensual reality. Both as gynecologist-womanizer and as psychiatrist, he is portrayed as essentially drawn to, if not dependent upon, the voluptuousness of material reality. Explicit references to empiricist concerns are replete. After studying the gorilla man, we learn that this man of science, who, by the way, metamorphoses from "Georges" in France into the Germanic "Georg" as he passes the border into Austria, "was learned enough to publish a thesis on the speech of this madman. A new light was thrown on the psychology of sounds,"[36] a publication that evokes a typical neoempiricist research project. More specifically, Georg's elaborate praise of the insane for firmly holding to the actuality of their hallucinations is a satirical reference to a subcategory of Brentano's celebrated theory of intentionality, namely "inner perception," a point we see reflected in the following lecture Georg delivers to his fawning assistants:

> "You see, gentlemen," he would say to them when they were alone together, "what miserable single-track creatures, what pitiful and inarticulate bourgeois we are, compared with the genius of this paranoiac. We possess, but he is possessed; we take our experiences at second hand, he makes his own. He moves in total solitude, like the earth itself, through his own space . . . He believes in the images his senses conjure up for him. We mistrust our own healthy senses . . . But look at him! He is Allah, prophet, and Moslem in one. Is a miracle any the less a miracle because we have labeled it *Paranoia chronica?* We sit on our thick headed sanity like a vulture on a pile of gold. Understanding, as we understand it, is misunderstanding. If there is a life purely of the mind, it is this madman who is leading it!"[37]

Georg's endorsement of such inner perception is at once a playful perversion and a critical citation of Brentano's ideas; for although Brentano acknowledged hallucination and idiosyncratic mental images, his theory of the "unity of consciousness" failed adequately to distinguish between delusion and reality. What strikes us immediately about this passage is that Georg diagnoses the empiricist self as essentially insane and for this very reason capable of offering a credible critique of bourgeois society. Georg, of course, thinks he is tendering a precious paradox to his worshipful listeners. But the novel suggests the contrary. Given the withering critique of neoempiricism we have already encountered, we are instead inclined to inquire into the sanity of attributing political subversiveness to an already weak, marginalized, and largely institutionalized group of people. Questions of power, particularly as they are secreted by erudite-sounding philosophy and psychology, are never far away in this novel.

We realize before long that Georg is in effect praising himself, or the self he had become since his conversion experience with the gorilla man. His entire method, such as it is, lies in the putative permeability of his consciousness, his ability to enter into — and take on — the selves of others. In this he is the very image of the Machian self, a self that merely serves as the locus for the constant reconfiguration of sense impressions: "When he was tired and wanted a rest from the high tension with which his distracted friends filled him, he would submerge himself in the soul of one of his assistants. Everything that Georg did, he did in the character of someone else."[38] Recall that Georg dates the shedding of his mundane, bourgeois self to that fateful meeting with the gorilla man, who is the great inspiration for his revolutionary psychological treatments. Yet, as we noted in some detail above in chapter 2, if the celebrated gorilla language represents a collapse of subject-object relations, if it suggests a much more elastic relationship between signifier and signified than Peter Kien could ever abide, it does so at the expense of everything and everybody but the author of this make-believe universe, the gorilla man himself. Canetti's criticism of empiricist thinking as embodied in Georg is, then, both old and new: he continues to raise questions about reality reduced to consciousness and he challenges the assumption that empiricism is innocent of power relations. New with Georg, however, is a critique of what we above called empiricism-as-mood. It is not Georg's disingenuous shedding of traditional subjectivity alone, or even primarily, which is at issue. Though it is true that the brothers Kien both suffer from savior complexes, and that only Peter is a self-acknowledged elitist, there is a deeper question at stake. The empiricist satire associated with Georg aims in the first place at the *possibility* of such a conversion to empiricism.

Once again, the issue antedates the empiricism of the late nineteenth and early twentieth centuries, but continues into our own day as well. The problem can be stated thus: the phenomenal treatment of the human being, which neoempiricism espoused, fails to account for the individual's experience of being separate from, and yet acting on, the world. Copleston explains how this dual aspect of experience, of being both separate from and part of the world, has structured much of the Western philosophical tradition. Since this point is foundational not only for the present argument, but also for our later discussion of modernism (chapter 6), it will be worth quoting here in full:

> Considered as spirit, as standing out from the world, he [i.e., the human being] is able, and indeed impelled, to raise metaphysical problems, to seek unity behind or underlying the subject-object situation. Considered as a being involved in the world, he is naturally inclined to regard these problems as empty and profitless. In the development of philosophical thought these divergent attitudes or tendencies recur, assuming different historical, and historically explicable, forms . . . Inasmuch as man can objectify himself and treat himself as an object of scientific investigation, he is inclined to regard talk about his standing out from the world or as having a spiritual aspect as so much nonsense. Yet the mere fact that it is he who objectifies himself shows, as Fichte well saw, that he cannot be completely objectified, and that a phenomenalistic reduction of the self is uncritical and naïve.[39]

This last sentence bears particular relevance for our understanding of Georg. The very conception of the empiricist (or here, phenomenalistic) self implies, as Copleston illustrates, the potential existence of the idealist self that would thereby be negated. In other words, this represents an aporia in the philosophical discussion of subjectivity in which each option implies the possibility of the other. Neither the spiritual nor the phenomenalistic view of the self can be adopted to the exclusion of the other without oversimplifying an issue that has perplexed the Western philosophical tradition down to our own day, and which, according to Foucault, constitutes the central conundrum of the modern episteme.[40] Neither will *Auto-da-Fé* let us rest easy in uncritically adopting what was then the intellectual fashion of the day and still circulates in various guises. Canetti suggests in the figure of Georg, without in any way proposing a simplistic return to idealist metaphysics, that it may take a self to lose a self.

Though Kien spouts key empiricist terms, and Therese exhibits — in an admittedly hyperbolic fashion — the perceptual concerns of empiricism, Georg is the only figure who self-consciously adopts an empiricist self. Ironically, he is impelled to such a makeover for the same reason his brother is moved to quote the famous *esse percipi*: troublesome women. His fascination with the gorilla man comes at a time when he professes to be bored with his career as gynecologist and with his licentious lifestyle, both of which tend for him to merge into a single undertaking. His fling with empiricism, then, is deeply imbricated with an attempted escapism. Yet, as we saw in the previous chapter, Georg's conversion is a case of "back to the future." As psychiatrist he is no less careerist, and to the extent he has sworn off women — and that is indeed debatable [41] — he has replaced that sensual gratification by continually slipping into the psyches of his maniacal patients.

When considering the target of Canetti's parody embodied in Georg, we would do well, finally, to recall the marriage of empiricist thinking to fin-de-siècle aestheticism, as Ryan has encouraged us to do. Georg's unique art of healing is derived from the nonreferential, nonutilitarian language of the gorilla man. This faux primitive man, though maintained by a rich and corrupt banker, is held up as the consummate critique of bourgeois venality, moral hypocrisy, and narrow-mindedness. His own free use of sounds with no regard to the mundane requirements of communication is opposed to a bourgeois commodification of language. Relegated to the attic because of his family's embarrassment, the so-called gorilla brother is a scathing parody of the garret artist ostensibly at odds with and misunderstood — yet all the while supported — by the middle-class world.

Georg carries his message forward, founding by means of his revolutionary psychiatric methods a select group in which membership implies neither collegiality nor equality, but depends on the good graces and condescension of its leader. Dedicated to a small cadre of those privileged with the gift of insanity, Georg takes it as his mission to preserve them from the degradations of the dull-minded bourgeoisie. Outside the confines of his asylum and in the real world — for example, at the abode of his beleaguered brother — Georg is utterly helpless. Given all these parallels between Georg and the most famous aesthete of the day, one is tempted to conclude that the Georg Canetti has in mind is perhaps Stefan George (1868–1933).

Georg certainly demonstrates that empiricism's vanishing subject is not exclusively a scientifically found object, and is by no means a neutral stance free of ideology. With Georg, Canetti raises once again the question of empiricism's collaboration in escapism, apoliticism, and in effete bourgeois protest, as well as the more fundamental question involved in the uncritical espousal of the phenomenal self. If the empiricist self is traditionally associated in high modernism with privileged states of consciousness (such as the quasi-mystical union of self and other), it can just as well, as we see in Georg, be affiliated with a kind of false consciousness. That "wax tablet" may not be so malleable and accommodating as one would like to think; in fact, it may have a mind of its own.

The novel's answer, therefore, to the question posed by William James in an essay of 1905—"Is Radical Empiricism Solipsistic?"—is an emphatic "yes." But we should be careful in stating this to emphasize the term "radical." For in raising communal, ethical, and political issues Canetti confronts the empiricist evanescent self with questions it is ill suited to answer. It would be premature, however, to conclude that with *Auto-da-Fé* Canetti rejects en masse the great modernist novels that either feature a lone, or virtually solitary, protagonist, or focus primarily on the rich consciousness of one figure among many others. We are concerned, rather, in *Auto-da-Fé* with a substantially different set of problems that nevertheless impinges on aesthetic modernism. One could perhaps more correctly say that *Auto-da-Fé* picks up where a novel like *Berlin Alexanderplatz* leaves off: Döblin portrays Franz Biberkopf brilliantly as passive player, as the capital city's truly hapless *spazierende Wachstafel*, if you will. But that novel provokes a critical clamor just at that point when we are asked to envision Franz as a credible political agent. This mystically reconstituted self is, apparently, to be redeemed in the politics of socialism, though some critics have wondered if the drums we hear at the end of the novel are calling Franz to dance to the step of a quite different—perhaps even fascist—drummer. How suited is this fragmented and buffeted protagonist—however reconstituted he may be—to the demands of politics and public culture? This question, as *Auto-da-Fé* makes clear, is very well placed.

Below we will explore how neo-Kantianism, which grew up side by side with (and in partial opposition to) neoempiricism, is present in the novel in a way that both underscores the critique elaborated above and suggests ways of rethinking some of the central problems associated with empiricism: namely, the isolation of the individual and the eclipse of the sociopolitical world.

Neoidealism

KIEN: THE MAN WHO WOULD BE KANT

In the essay "The First Book, *Auto-da-Fé*," Canetti recounts the curious fact that his protagonist once bore the name "Kant."[42] What is so astonishing in this account, in which Canetti conceals as much as he tells, is the fact that this appellation was no mere momentary fling. The novel was completed, circulated in typescript form, and read publicly on numerous occasions with the name Kant still in place. Even the novel's original title, foretelling the protagonist's doom, suggested the well-known forebear: *Kant fängt Feuer* (Kant Catches Fire). Since the author dropped this hint in 1975 there has been no lack of speculation on the protagonist's supposed affinities with his philosopher ancestor; nor has there been a paucity of inventive, if rather unconvincing, conjecture on the transformation of that name into "Kien."[43] In this regard, I would not overlook the obvious, even if mundane, convenience of replacing the original name with one of the exact same length in an already prepared typescript. Understanding the sense in which Kant remains integral to the novel will require a brief digression; but since Kien's nominal precursor has so often provided the occasion in the secondary literature for raising the novel's philosophical issues, it seems appropriate to discuss the question here.

Those critics who maintain that the similarity between Kien and Immanuel Kant is rather slight, limited to a few biographical details, are essentially right. But this determination does not in itself solve the problem. For what is the point of those parallels that do exist: the early-rising, prolific bachelor intellectual given to strict routine, the persnickety punctuality, the daily walk one could set one's watch by? Why did Canetti expunge merely the name, but not the substance of the comparison?

To assume both that there are indeed some residual similarities between the character Kien and the philosopher Kant and that it was a good idea for the author to change the name, apparently on Hermann Broch's insistence,[44] would suggest either that Canetti was a little lazy, perhaps less than thorough in making the correction, or that the characterization should be understood as a sort of capricious, postmodern citation that doesn't quite add up to anything. Yet if we distinguish between author and character, we may find a third, more compelling, solution, which requires us neither to impugn the author's craft nor suggest an anachronistic and rather far-fetched periodization.

Tellingly, the similarities that do obtain between Kien and Kant are of Kien's own making: just as he tosses off a Berkeleian quote when in need of a philosophical justification for the tactics he employs in his feud with Therese, so too does he elsewhere fancy himself as following in the footsteps of Germany's most celebrated intellectual. We have already seen that, although consistency and accuracy are not attributes of Kien, self-importance and philosophical opportunism certainly are. To see Kien as a self-styled Kant figure squares well with what we otherwise know about the protagonist. Indeed one could posit further similarities, which, we can assume, would only please the arrogant *Privatgelehrte* Kien. Kien's pride in the inscrutability of his work does indeed ring a certain intertextual bell: for, "as Hegel remarks, it is only when we come to Kant that we find philosophy becoming so technical and abstruse that it could no longer be considered to belong to the general education of a cultured man."[45] Furthermore, when Kant was forty years old—precisely the age of the protagonist—he refused several university posts that were offered to him, just as Kien *claims* to have done: "Whenever any chair of oriental philology fell vacant, it was offered first to him. Polite but contemptuously, he invariably declined."[46] Instead of taking positions incommensurate with his research interests, Kant worked both as a *Privatdozent* and as a librarian.[47]

If we consider each of these points of similarity, it becomes clear that Kien is only Kant in his uncorroborated but grandiose claims to academic status and in his inconsequential daily habits. To leave these similarities in place in the face of the obvious differences between the historical and fictional figures characterizes the protagonist's inflated self-image while simultaneously giving the reader some comic distance between the real Kien and the Kien who would be Kant.[48]

Of course characters do not name themselves; authors do. It is tempting to think that Canetti, who allows his figures to occupy the narrator to an extraordinary degree, simply allowed his protagonist, for a while, to inhabit his own consciousness. But to permit Kien to remain Kant would indeed have been a great mistake because it would validate the actual conflation of the protagonist with the great philosopher. Leaving Kien as Kant would, in other words, have suggested that the author shares in his character's delusions of grandeur. Such, apparently, was Broch's concern. He was extraordinarily irritated by the original title and name of the title figure, Canetti recalls, "as if I meant thereby to imply that the *philosopher* Kant was a cold, insensitive creature now condemned in this book to catch fire."[49] Canetti certainly meant for his protagonist to think of himself in such complimentary terms, but did not intend to endorse them. He grasped this distinction just in time.

KIEN AS A PARODY OF NEOIDEALISM

This point must be made delicately, because while *Auto-da-Fé* parodies certain reactionary implications of interwar neoidealism, it also shares some of the fundamental concerns of this movement's most distinguished philosophers, namely the neo-Kantians, who dominated philosophical and academic discussions of the day.[50] Like Canetti, the neo-Kantians (to the extent one can make any such generalization about this loosely knit group) were profoundly concerned about the atomization of culture, and earnestly sought to legitimate the humanities (*Geisteswissenschaften*) as an antidote to this process of cultural disintegration.[51]

As both a Ph.D. chemist appalled at the narrow-mindedness of scientific specialization and a creative author asking the big cultural questions, Canetti, too, was concerned to bridge the widening gap between the prestigious natural sciences (*Naturwissenschaften*) and the increasingly beleaguered humanities. If there is any one theme that unified the neo-Kantians, it was surely their effort to overcome both the crude materialism of the scientific positivists, while simultaneously opposing the metaphysical extravagances that had marked German idealist philosophy from Fichte to Hegel — all with a view to establishing a new cultural unity. It was the last grand attempt of Western philosophy to establish a unified Weltanschauung before the rise of radical pluralism, or what we now call the postmodern condition.

If Canetti and the neo-Kantians shared the same point of departure, however, they soon parted ways. In *Auto-da-Fé*, and particularly in Peter Kien, Canetti chose to parody not the neo-Kantians themselves, but certain reactionary tendencies for which neo-Kantianism provided a respectable, philosophical cover. Thus I do not contend that the novel targets the sophisticated (if problematic) systems of Cohen, Windelband, Cassirer et al., but the more simpleminded recipients (such as Kien) who saw in this movement an opportunity to retreat from the disconcerting materialism and political turmoil of Weimar-era culture into the rarefied realm of German idealism. Though Kien is enough of an intellectual opportunist to make occasional use of the surfeit of neoempiricist thinking that swirls about him, he is much more prevalently an ardent idealist, albeit according to his own lights. Though one could justifiably take issue with his use of idealist philosophy, this is the vocabulary with which he is most comfortable.

While he cloaks himself in idealist phrases, Kien employs these more as a shield against an unwanted reality than as a designation for something he seems to understand or value in its own right. For Kien the realm of true being is neither the Platonic form nor the inscrutable Kantian *Ding an sich*, but simply learned books. The printed word—not any Berkeleian "substrate"—represents the primary ground of reality; our sensory world is only secondarily real, a wan shadow thrown off from the realm of great books. A few examples of Kien's "idealism" are memorable for their humor. While taking an uncharacteristically relaxed walk one day, Kien hears the cooing of pigeons, whose real existence he can only recognize and confirm thanks to his special access to the printed word: "'Quite so!' he said softly, and nodded as he always did *when he found reality bearing out the printed original.*"[52] The birdsong is only true because the sensory data ratifies the prior and higher truth emanating from the printed page, which thus functions as a kind of Platonic form. In a similar fashion, Kien recognizes the roses presented to him by Fischerle only because he had first encountered them in that realm which is the source of all truth and reality, his library: "He took the roses from Fischerle's hand, remembered their sweet smell which he knew from Persian love poetry, and raised them to his eyes; it was true, they did smell. This soothed him completely."[53]

Clearly, for him the neoidealist sanctum sanctorum is the library itself. The flight from the anxieties of contemporary culture is abundantly evident in Kien's effusive enthusiasm for his well-fortified library:

> Through the lofty skylights poured illumination and inspiration . . . Through the glass above him he could see the condition of the heavens, more tranquil, more attenuated than the reality. A soft blue: the sun shines, but not on me. A grey no less soft: it will rain, but not on me. A gentle murmur announced the falling drops. He was aware of them at a distance, they did not touch him. He knew only: the sun shines, the clouds gather, the rain falls. It was as if he had barricaded himself against the world: against all material relations, against all terrestrial needs, had built himself an hermitage, a vast hermitage, so vast that it would hold those few things on this earth which are more than this earth itself, more than the dust to which our life at last returns.[54]

As numerous commentators have noted, Kien literally blocks out reality with books: save the skylight overhead, he has all the windows cemented up in order to make room for more bookshelves. Whenever he leaves the library-fortress, Kien takes a little protection with him: every morning before his signature walk (to bookstores, by the way) he carefully selects the right volumes, which he then carries as close to his body as possible, a kind of biblio-prophylaxis "against all material relations." Once Therese deprives him of access to his beloved books, Kien agilely develops the mobile "mental library" (*Kopfbibliothek*).

Though a caricature to be sure, Kien repeatedly identifies himself as an idealist. He is given, for example, to praising the timeless and durable nature of his own *Charakter*, which he opposes to a variety of protean beings such as actors, the masses, women, and so forth. Here is an early illustration: "Punctually at eight his work began, his service for truth . . . You draw closer to truth by shutting yourself off from mankind. Daily life was a superficial clatter of lies . . . Who among all these bad actors, who made up the mob, had a face to arrest his attention. They changed their faces with every moment; . . . *His* ambition was to persist stubbornly in the same manner of existence. Not for a mere month, not for a year, but for the whole of his life, he would be true to himself."[55] This elitist, self-congratulatory encomium culminates in a declaration of Schillerian idealism. Echoing the famous idealist motto "*Es ist der Geist, der sich den Körper baut*" (It is Spirit which builds itself a body), Kien affirms: "Character, if you had a character, determined your outward appearance" and then proceeds to describe himself as appropriately "narrow, stern and bony."[56]

Later in the novel Kien emerges as an explicit defender of German idealism. A poor student arrives at the *Theresianum* with the intention of pawning an eight-volume set of Schiller's works. Kien intercepts him with this question:

"What do you want?"
"I . . . er, I wanted the book section."
"I am the book section." . . .
"What do you intend to do upstairs?" asked Kien threateningly.
"Oh . . . er . . . only Schiller."[57]

Kien pays an excessive price for a worthless, used edition, which he then returns to the student with this admonition: "'Never repeat this action, my friend! Believe me, no man is worth as much as his books!' . . . 'Why Schiller? You should read the original. You should read *Immanuel Kant!*'"[58] Once again, we observe the confusion of the central term "value" (*Wert*), whose economic and normative-cultural meanings are continually at loggerheads.

Kant will surely return the besieged Kien to a more secure world of traditional values, but Kien thinks he can help bring this about only by paying ransom—he uses precisely these terms—to the very market forces that have undermined traditional culture.

Kien reveals a similar affinity for his erstwhile philosopher namesake when, at the apex of his misogynistic diatribe, he arrives at what for him is the root of the problem, the creation of woman. "It irritates him the more that he can only believe in the Categorical Imperative and not in God. Otherwise he could transfer the blame to Him."[59] Yet in each case where Kien evinces an idealist (or pseudoidealist) inclination, the deeper motive for his philosophical loyalties peeks through: fear of masses, modern society, and women—all of which for him are metonymically related. This suspect form of idealist enthusiasm—neoidealism as escapism—emerges clearly from what at first seems a paean to Enlightenment supranationalism:

> Every human being needs a home, not a home of the kind understood by crude jingoistic patriots, not a religion either, a mere insipid foretaste of a heavenly abode; no, a real home, in which ground, work, friends, recreation, and the spiritual realm of ideas [geistiger Fassungsraum] come together into an orderly whole, into—so to speak—a personal cosmos. The best definition of a home is a library. It is wisest to keep women out of the home. Should the decision however be made to take in a woman, it is essential to assimilate her first fully into the home, as he had done.[60]

Kien, who clearly focalizes this narrative segment, begins by celebrating that classic Enlightenment realm open to all men willing to shed their particularist national or religious affiliations. Without transition, however, this enlightenment reverie spills over into explicit misogyny. The "heteronomy" that for Kant meant the reception of laws from an external source (and which thus abrogates the idealist autonomous subject) becomes in Kien's eyes a prospect preeminently associated with women. As we saw in chapter 2, it is above all Therese who stands in for the dreaded "*Sinneswelt*" (the world of senses and materiality) that threatens to overpower Kien's "*Verstandeswelt*" (world of the intellect). Though employing quite assailable definitions of these concepts, Kien obdurately clings to the Kantian distinction between the intelligible world and the world of the senses as if to a lifeboat. It is in this sense that Kant represents a home, or "*Heimat*," to Kien. "*Zurück zu Kant*"

(Back to Kant) was the motto of the neo-Kantians of the interwar period; one can almost hear it here in Kien's philosophically inflected longing for a secure conceptual home. The abrupt transformation of this fantasized library, this *"geistiger Fassungsraum,"* from universal intellectual gathering place into a blatant refuge from modernity, a "personal cosmos," signifies the critique *Auto-da-Fé* offered to the wider cultural debate of the Weimar era. Kien's desperate expression of "Kantian" autonomy proves no less dangerous, it should be noted, than the empiricist pose struck by his brother. Before this inflated "idealist" self, the quotidian world threatens to dissolve just as assuredly as it does under Georg's neoempiricist dispensation.

While the novel's parody of neoidealism is practically insulated from the more serious work of the professional philosophers (by dint of Kien's sloppy and opportunistic thinking), it simultaneously targets an inherent weakness of the neo-Kantian program, namely its own insular proclivities. As much as it may have hoped to provide the epistemological basis for a new cultural consciousness, it remained ghettoized in university philosophy departments. On the other hand, to the extent that it held an appeal for a wider audience in the interwar period, it proved eminently cooptable by conservatives who wished to turn back the clock. If Kien can be seen as one of Fritz K. Ringer's "mandarin intellectuals," as I think he should be, then this problematic professor may represent one instance of that backward looking *Bildungsbürgertum,* which witnessed the eclipse of its own relevance and yearned for the return of the more secure days of yore.[61] To ears such as these, and according to Ringer they were many and influential in the interwar period, the entreaty to return to Kant provided a welcome rallying call that often had little to do with formal philosophy.

In this context it would be apt to underscore Kien's obsession with the past, a proclivity we have already had occasion to notice. Here, in his hymn to the past (*Vergangenheit*), the professor's problematic adherence to idealist philosophy comes into full view. Just before he is ousted from his beloved *Bibliothek,* we read:

> The present is alone responsible for all pain. He longed for the future, because then there would be more past in the world. The past is kind, it does no one any harm. For twenty years now he had moved in it freely, he was happy. Who is happy in the present? If we had no senses, then we might find the present endurable . . . He bowed before the supremacy of

the past... A time will come when men will beat their senses into recollections, and all time into the past. A time will come when a single past will embrace all men, when there will be nothing except the past, when everyone will have one faith—the past.[62]

The conjunction of love of the past (or what Ringer in his study calls "past mindedness") with a distinct predilection for neoidealist slogans (no matter how misunderstood) should give us some pause, for this had a real-world counterpart in contemporaneous academic circles in the wake of neo-Kantianism. Though Kien will presently profess supreme faith in the Kantian categorical imperative—to the exclusion of the biblical diety—he is at this point still willing to pay tribute to God as guarantor of the past: "God is the past. He *believes* in God."[63] This of course indicates where this pseudo-philosopher's real concerns lie, even as it points to another entrenched phenomenon in German culture, namely the infusion of post-Kantian idealism with a misplaced religious aura.[64]

Now historians of philosophy might well view Kien as a straw man, perhaps little more than a one-sided polemic, and they would be partly right. For Canetti has singled out only those two aspects of contemporary neoidealist thinking which he held to be most suspect: (1) the tendency toward self-insulation and historicizing retreat, which tempted less discriminating devotees to bracket out rather than embrace the modern world; and (2) the inherent propensity of all idealist philosophy to subordinate the "world" to abstract and potentially self-serving formulations. With Kien we are reminded that philosophy—even idealist philosophy—is never wholly above the world, and certainly never innocent of power.

Yet just as we noted above (in chapter 2) that Kien and Georg are ultimately not that dissimilar, so, too, would it now be mistaken to exaggerate the differences between neoempiricism and neo-Kantianism. Both represent latter-day forms of the great Copernican revolution in Western philosophy, which began to understand perception as constituent of reality, though obviously in quite different ways. Both are forms of philosophical modernism, and as such challenge simplistic notions of objective reality that were fueled by the dominant natural sciences of the mid-nineteenth and early twentieth centuries.[65] Both neoempiricism and neo-Kantianism, the latter more systematically to be sure, sought to combat what Ollig terms "the objectivism of popular materialist philosophy" of this period,[66] the same unproblematic assertion of objectivity, it should be noted, that is so much with us still today. Thus it should not be surprising at all that Kien, groping for a learned way to oppose the materialism of mass culture, should light upon a Berkelian quip, even though he otherwise clothes himself in idealist apparel. In fact, the incident that inspires Kien's philosophy of blindness, the incursion of Therese's furniture into his library, is accompanied by a lengthy reflection on the onerous "excess of sensory stimuli" (*Sinnesexzesse*) inflicted upon him by modern nuclear science. On top of everything else, he now is intruded upon by "fools who fiddle with electricity and complicated atoms," and has to worry about electrons racing around his formerly peaceful pages.[67] The coupling of unwanted furniture with the then-latest discoveries in physics under the rubric "sensory overload" is a reminder that Kien, transparent as his motives may ultimately be, cannot simply be dismissed. Like it or not, he is but an avatar of broader cultural phenomena, a fact nowhere more evident than in his flawed attempts to salve his discomfort in the modern world with the consolation of traditionalist philosophy. While these two specific philosophical schools have faded from the intellectual scene, the potential for abusing intellectual pursuits as flight from social responsibility is clearly very much with us still.

Kien's prescription of old-fashioned, philologically based *Bildung* to a modern world that seems to be spinning out of control in fact places him in a specific group of idealist respondents to the interwar crisis of culture. Though Kien would be appalled to be associated with a movement deeply concerned with the reformation of secondary school curricula, his strident espousal of philology as a cultural cure-all situates him precisely there. The identification of this group, once a preeminent cultural force headed by Werner Jäger, will be the initial task of the following chapter, which has as its larger concern the elucidation of the novel's representation of racial anti-Semitism.

4 The Hunchback of "Heaven"
Anti-Semitism and the Failure of Humanism

> It was of course the Prater, which gave rise as well to that monstrous figure Siegfried Fischerle from *Auto-da-Fé* . . . yes, that horribly doomed attempt at assimilation under extreme conditions.
> —Gerald Stieg[1]

Bildung, Assimilation, and the "Crisis of Values"

Canetti's Jewish figures are frankly hideous: filthy, rank, hunchbacked, underclass dwarfs intent upon cheating a blue blood gentile out of a family inheritance. *Auto-da-Fé*'s principal Jew is of course Siegfried Fischerle, the pimp from a lowbrow Viennese pub called The Stars of Heaven (*Zum idealen Himmel*), who strikes up a conversation with Peter Kien in the hope of drumming up business for his prostitute wife, *die Pensionistin*. Needless to say, Fischerle fails in his effort to entice Kien, who after all could not bring himself to sleep with Therese on their wedding night. In a manner perfected by Canetti (both in the novel and the contemporaneous drama *Hochzeit*), Kien and Fischerle converse at length without ever really understanding who the other is. Failing to grasp the true occupation of either Fischerle or his wife, Kien concludes that the persecuted little man desperately aspires to the attainment of that highest of German cultural goods, *Bildung,* only to be thwarted at every turn by his fleshly and greedy wife. In diagnosing Fischerle's ills as a lack of proper cultivation, Kien touches upon one of the most salient cultural debates of the interwar period. If Fischerle proves impervious to Kien's *Bildung*-remedy, it is because, as the very embodiment of virtually every contemporary anti-Semitic stereotype, he is by definition forbidden that universal avenue of human ascent held out by this Enlightenment ideal.

In no time at all, Fischerle metamorphoses in the mind of the protagonist into a junior Kien, and the Pensionistin into another Therese. This disfigured little man becomes the professor's protégé on terms that are thus by now quite familiar. Accordingly, as the suffering husband of this duo, Fischerle is assigned the role of the Faustian spirit hindered in his lofty pursuits by his venal and concupiscent "wife":

> He [Kien] knew nothing of the rituals of the place, but one thing he recognized clearly — this stainless spirit in a wretched body had struggled for twenty years to lift itself out of the mire of its surroundings . . . Therese [*die Pensionistin*], no less determined, dragged him for ever back into the slime . . . He has clutched at one tiny corner of the world of the spirit and clings to it like a drowning man. Chess is his library . . . Kien pictured to himself the battle this down-trodden man fought for his own flat. He takes a book home to read it secretly, she tears it in pieces and scatters it to the winds. She forces him to let her use his home for her unspeakable purposes. Possibly she pays a servant, a spy, to keep the house clear of books when she is out. Books are forbidden, her own way of life is permitted . . . She flings open the door and with her clumsy foot kicks over the chessboard. Mr. Fischerle weeps like a little child. He had just reached the most interesting part of his book. He picks up the letters scattered all over the floor and turns his face away so she shall not rejoice over his tears. He is a little hero. He has character.[2]

Kien's efforts at recreating Fischerle in his own self-image are transparent. As in the case of Therese — who reworks the mocking laughter of the furniture store employees into dubious praise — we are witness here to an imperfect projection still in process. Determined to see Fischerle as a pure spirit and seeker of truth (that is, as a neoplatonist academic like himself), Kien superimposes the image of a book on the chessboard so that when "Therese" brutishly overturns it, Fischerle scrambles to collect "scattered letters" (*die herumliegenden Buchstaben*) as he would so many chess pieces. It would be a great mistake to dismiss this passage as merely the distorting projection of one figure upon another, though of course this is once again the case. In misreading Fischerle as hungry for humanistic *Bildung,* Kien engages a specific controversy about humanism's prospects as a source for German normative values after the great defeat in World World I. Fischerle, as we shall see, incarnates the failure of this humanism to translate its values into social policy.

As background to this calamity, I will paint in a few broad strokes a complex story that has been told much more extensively elsewhere.³ Though the German "crisis of values"—the deep sense of cultural anxiety occasioned by the rift between the natural and social sciences on the one hand and the humanities ("*Humanenwissenschaften*") on the other—dates back to the last decades of the nineteenth century, it occupied the post–World War I imagination with particular intensity.⁴ Following Winckelmann in the Enlightenment, German intellectuals had widely turned to Greece as the font of normative cultural values. To what extent could this Schillerian model of aesthetic education continue to function as a cultural stabilizer in postwar Germany? Was it possible to turn to classical philology for the cultural moorings that were so necessary in these turbulent times? Commenting on the situation in post-1918 Germany, intellectual historian Suzanne Marchand observes:

> Never before had the gap between scholarly research and the cultivation of the individual seemed so wide; never before had the Humboldtian aim of reconciling the interests of both within the German system of higher education seemed so implausible . . . During and particularly after the war, this critique of scholarship for its own sake found a large and increasingly diverse circle of advocates . . . Critics charged the scholarly community of the 1920s with abdicating its role in establishing social values and building character. The scapegoating of "specialists" for the "soullessness" of modern German culture went hand in hand with the conviction that "pure intellectualism" would destroy social unity—as well as the integrity of the human character.⁵

During the interwar period, there were a number of attempts to address this crisis, ranging from the amorphous vitalist movement advocating "*Lebensphilosophie*" (life philosophy) to the more sophisticated efforts of philosophers aimed at reinstating Kantian philosophy as an anchor for cultural cohesion and meaning.

Alluding to Goethe's *Faust*, and no doubt wishing to see himself as a Faustian spirit striving for truth amid Weimar decadence, Kien dubs Fischerle his "Famulus."⁶ In order to grasp the meaning of this would-be spiritual ("*geistig*") apprenticeship, we must first understand more clearly what Kien, as a self-styled idealist academic in the throes of the interwar crisis of values, stands for. As we noted in the previous chapter, brother Georg is the novel's preeminent carrier of neoempiricist sentiments, Kien his idealist counterpart. But just as we differentiated above between actual empiricist philosophers and psychologists (such as William James and Franz Brentano) and their more questionable epigones, so, too, ought we to differentiate here. Kien's appropriation of idealist notions is, as we have noted above, a desperate attempt to hold on to something solid at a time of monumental social, political, and intellectual upheaval.

The academic group with which Kien might more precisely be identified, however, is suggested by his specialty as master philologist. For it was classical philology, according to Marchand, that came under fire in the interwar period for what reformers decried as its elitism and irrelevance to the modern world. Marchand observes:

> "Philology" had become a metaphor for the numbing drudgery, authoritarian discipline, pedantic obscurantism, while classical language training remained, for the bulk of the professoriate, the sine qua non of both *Bildung* and humanistic *Wissenschaft*. This combination of declining social status and the increasing sense that the *Gymnasium* alone held back a culture-destroying flood of superficiality, decadence, and utilitarianism prepared the backdrop for a kind of classicist morality play, in which philologists were sacrificed on the altar of modern materialism.[7]

It is easy to imagine Kien in this latter role of sacrificial lamb, particularly since he so willingly portrays himself and his scholarship as valiantly and inveterately opposed to mass commercial society. This is, after all, how he ends up standing guard before the Theresianum in an attempt to intercept anyone attempting to pawn books. Before one too precipitously exempts Kien from this context because of his primary interest in sinology, it should be noted that Kien is also a classical and biblical philologist, as his grandiose plan to write the final exegesis of the New Testament illustrates. Indeed Kien's specialty as an Orientalist may above all signify the very "pedantic obscurantism" Marchand notes above.

Today it may seem curious indeed to suggest that one would turn to the humanities for a consensus on cultural and social values. We are in our own time — and perhaps particularly in France and the United States — more accustomed to viewing these disciplines as a theater of contention rather than a wellspring of cohesive and binding norms. Yet in what is perhaps the last great attempt at a German cultural synthesis, the so-called "Third Humanism" of the interwar period, Werner Jäger attempted precisely this: to anchor postwar politics (broadly conceived) in what he held to be the secure foundations of classical philology. The goal, as Marchand explains, was to "rejoin *Wissenschaft* to *Bildung,* historical research to the generation of values, and modern 'rootless' Germans to the serene and morally superior Greeks; a new German Golden Age, a Third Humanism, might commence in the shadow of military defeat and political chaos."[8] While Kien's practice of desiccating scholarship represents exactly that which Jäger wanted to overcome, Kien also registers those very scientific challenges with which Jäger's ambitious program was ill equipped to contend. Kien's consciousness of the "millions of atoms" racing around in what in the good old days appeared to be a quite stable piece of text signifies, as we noted above, a scientific modernity of which the protagonist is only dimly aware. Pausing long enough only to express his anxieties, the old-fashioned philologist reminds the reader how utterly incongruous modern science had become for the traditional scholar. Refracted through Kien's partial understanding and palpable trepidation are some of the most revolutionary breakthroughs of the early twentieth century science: the theory of relativity, quantum mechanics, and the Heisenberg uncertainty principle. In this context, Kien's embrace of a pseudo neo-Kantianism — to the extent even that he mimics the daily habits of Immanuel Kant — and his unconvincing espousal of neoidealist principles clearly signifies a questionable retreat, rather than a new cultural synthesis. Ultimately, Jäger's vaunted Third Humanism, which set out to salvage Kien's discipline and place it at the center of the new German republic as the "provider of cultural norms," foundered on its inability to contest vulgar, exclusionary definitions of Germanness;[9] failed, in other words, in roughly the same way Kien would.

It is against this background that Kien's offer to elevate the handicapped Jew via high culture needs to be seen. If Fischerle's wife transmogrifies in Kien's jaundiced eyes into "a second Therese," it is nevertheless true that Fischerle himself becomes for the reader a kind of second Therese insofar as he is destined to fulfill the role Kien had once assigned to his bride: junior librarian. For Therese, too, Kien had once held out the hope that, illiterate as she was, the sheer proximity to such a magnificent library and, of course, to himself, might raise her to a higher level of humanity. Yet because she is a woman, Kien is never so sanguine about Therese's prospects for *Bildung* as he is about Fischerle's.

From the very beginning, Kien worries about his ability to keep up his end of the *Bildung*-bargain: "He feared coming into collision with the little fellow's thirst for education. He might reproach him, with apparent justification, for letting his books lie fallow. How was he to defend himself?"[10] Shortly thereafter, the narrator—infiltrated again by Kien—worries that "through daily contact with so vast a quantity of learning the little man's hunger for it would grow greater and greater; suddenly he would be caught secreting a book and trying to read it . . . He would have to be prepared for it orally."[11] These practical matters of proper pedagogy notwithstanding, Kien never doubts the equation of *Bildung* with humanity: "If it were possible to infuse these [like-minded creatures] with a little education, a little humanity, this would certainly be an achievement."[12] Of course this bias cuts both ways: those with little or no learning (such as Therese) are by the same standard judged to be subhuman.

When Fischerle feigns deep concern for his employer's *Kopfbibliothek*— the phantom counterpart to the library Kien was forced by Therese to vacate—the self-styled "Privatgelehrter" (a term meaning "private intellectual" without an official academic post, but ironically emblematic of the protagonist's noted asocial "inwardness") can only assume that the dwarf's education is proceeding just as he had expected. In fact, he seems to acquire cultivation virtually by osmosis: "Under the pressure of the books, which he did not even read, the dwarf was changing before his very eyes. Kien's old theory was receiving notable confirmation."[13] Of course, nothing could be further from the truth. The entire novel is structured by the comic principle of incongruity, and this is no exception: Fischerle is merely playing along with Kien in order more systematically to rob him of the balance of his inheritance. Yet the fact that Fischerle fails to take seriously his own *Bildung* does not at all detract from the fact that Kien's repeated and lofty claims regarding the transformatory power of learning—hypocritical though they may well be—define the sociocultural agenda for the reader. Though he lacks the self-awareness and sophistication of Schnitzler's *Professor Bernhardi* (1912), Fischerle nevertheless serves to draw our attention to the conflict between the rising tide of racist nationalism on the one hand, and the cosmopolitan core of Kantian humanism that was being revived in various hues in order to shore up German identity after the First World

War, on the other. Comically unaware of this larger cultural nexus, Fischerle nevertheless poses the serious question about Jewish assimilation by means of German *Kultur.*

In the interwar period Jewish assimilation as well as the increasing opposition to it were burning issues. In 1922 Karl Kraus reissued his 1913 essay "*Er ist doch e Jud,*" in which the master satirist reiterated his faith in assimilation through *Bildung.* "He tried to deal with the claim that he was Jewish," writes Steven Beller in *Vienna and the Jews, 1867–1938,* "by demonstrating that he possessed none of the supposedly Jewish qualities. The world of *Geist* in which he lived, he continued, had no room for race or racial characteristics. He did not even know what Jewish characteristics were. Nevertheless, he demonstrated to his own satisfaction that he had none ... In other words Kraus was saying that the Jews who lived in the world of *Geist* could avoid the problem of 'jüdische Eigenschaften' ... by not having any, for they were irrelevant in that world." [14] But Kraus's claim, especially by 1922, was more a desperate argument for the way he wished things were than a reflection of contemporaneous reality. Kraus's "continuation and radicalization of the Enlightenment ideal of pure humanity," [15] no less than Kien's own phony espousal of these ideals, point to a liberal tradition already long under siege by, for example, the open anti-Semitism of the Austrian Christian Socialists led by the notoriously anti-Semitic mayor of Vienna, Karl Lueger.

What people like Kraus, Theodor Gomperz, and Hermann Cohen (the latter in his role as one of the founders of the neo-Kantian school) were hoping to articulate in the post–World War I era was thus not merely a *general* response to the larger crisis of values, but, more particularly, a response to the challenge to their identity as German Jews.[16] Their tenacious loyalty to the German philosophical tradition since Kant can in large part be explained, Beller argues, "because the tenets of German idealism contained the one vital prerequisite to assimilationist theory, the autonomy of the will." [17] Indeed, for humanists of the *Aufklärung,* Jews offered a test case of the efficacy of *Bildung:* "The sheer radical nature of the transformation needed to create a human being from an oriental such as the Jew would be proof of education's power in creating a purer human, the 'new types of humanity' which would form the rational society of the future." [18]

Fischerle as Mascot for Racial Anti-Semitism

This "society of the future," however, bore little resemblance either to the Weimar Republic or the First Austrian Republic. Indeed the rise of racial anti-Semitism, which had its roots in the later nineteenth century but achieved particular virulence in the post–World War I period, contested precisely that "one vital prerequisite to assimilationist theory, the autonomous will" of each human being. In *Auto-da-Fé* the diminished opportunity for assimilation is represented less in the plot—it is certainly not a matter of a Jew's thwarted attempt to join German culture—but in the very characterization of the novel's principal Jew, Siegfried Fischerle. Without a doubt Fischerle worries about being recognized and treated as a Jew, and he is in fact snubbed by a waiter in The Stars of Heaven because of his Jewishness. Yet, as in the case of Therese, it is vital to note that Fischerle enters the narration—that is, even before he becomes the object of prejudice and abuse at the level of plot—as a veritable stockpile of contemporaneous anti-Semitic stereotypes. Chief among these, as we shall see, are the physical attributes that mark him as a Jew. This is how we first encounter him:

> Suddenly a vast hump appeared close to him and asked, could he sit there? Kien looked down fixedly. Where was the mouth out of which speech had issued? And already the owner of the hump, a dwarf, hopped up on to a chair . . . The tip of his strongly hooked nose lay in the depth of his chin. His mouth was as small as himself—only it wasn't to be found. No forehead, no ears, no neck, no buttocks—the man consisted of a hump, an immense nose and two black, calm, sad eyes . . . Suddenly [Kien] heard a hoarse voice underneath the table: "How's business?"[19]

Needless to say, this description comprises a veritable catalogue of contemporary anti-Jewish clichés, the best known being the large-nosed Jew, which is reiterated tirelessly throughout Book 2 of the novel. This coarse and strident use of stereotypical characteristics seems to have cowed some critics, who appear more disposed to view Fischerle as just one more in a series of self-absorbed characters unable to communicate meaningfully with his fellow human beings. Yet it would be a mistake to muffle the novel's critique by generalizing Fischerle in this manner.

In her 1991 study *Die Figurenkonstellation in Elias Canettis Auto-da-Fé*, Jutta Paal has suggested that Fischerle's Jewish identity need not detain us at all: "Except for the 'consumptive waiter' no one at the Stars of Heaven is bothered by his heritage. Therefore it would be mistaken to attribute too much meaning to the religious persuasion of this figure."[20] Yet the manner in which Paal refers to Fischerle's Jewishness is flawed from the very outset. For the kind of racial anti-Semitism this figure is made to represent has little to do with the euphemizing term "heritage" (*Herkunft*) and nothing to do with religion. Ironically, if Paal really means "religious confession" (*Religionszugehörigkeit*), her assertion would be correct; for Fischerle has no connection whatsoever to Judaism as religious faith. Instead, this phrase — and similar ones appear elsewhere in the criticism — functions merely as an evasive surrogate for the very Jewish identity that has become so problematic. Indeed, this eagerness to dismiss the issue overlooks Kien's own initial aversion to Fischerle's Jewishness. Shortly after the introductory passage on Fischerle, we read that Kien "considered the all-pervading nose of the manikin, it inspired him with mistrust."[21] A little later Fischerle intentionally drops the word "Jewish" while attempting to defraud Kien of some funds: "Fischerle made a minute pause in order to observe the effect of the word 'Jewish' on his companion. You never can tell. The world is crawling with anti-semites. A Jew always has to be on guard against deadly enemies. Hump-backed dwarfs and others, who have nevertheless managed to rise to the rank of pimp, cannot be too careful. The swallowing did not escape him. He interpreted it as embarrassment, and from that moment decided that Kien must be a Jew, which he certainly was not."[22] Here Fischerle registers a street-smart awareness of pervasive anti-Semitism, even if this "sharp observer" (*scharfer Beobachter*) completely misconstrues Kien's body language at the same time. As we already know, Kien is able to put aside the repugnance he feels in the company of Fischerle and see his own "pure spirit" reflected — albeit somewhat more dimly — in the disfigured dwarf. But if Paal is right in that the central figures do not themselves actively cast anti-Semitic aspersions upon Fischerle, this apparently does little to allay the Jew's own acute awareness of widespread anti-Semitism. It occurs to him, for example, that it would be particularly inadvisable to draw attention to himself in a church: "He forgot he was in church. He was usually respectful and cautious in churches, for by his nose he was very obviously marked."[23] A little later Fischerle whisks Kien off a busy Viennese street into a church, and a similar fear recurs: "Fischerle was caught off his guard; in a church he felt uncertain of himself. He almost pushed Kien out again into the square . . . Let the church collapse, he was not going to run into the arms of the police! Fischerle knew terrible stories of Jews buried in the wreckage of falling churches because they had no business to be there. His wife the Capitalist had told them to him because she was devout and wanted to convert him to her faith."[24] Yet it is not only this type of superstitious anti-Semitism registered by Fischerle himself, but also the patronizing philosemitism of the proprietress of "The Baboon" (*Zum Pavian*), which keeps our focus on the character's "Jewishness" throughout.

The question that has been assiduously swept under the rug in the discussion of *Auto-da-Fé* is, Whose anti-Semitism is it? Just as we were required to confront the misogyny evident in the narrative construction of Therese, so, too, must we ask about the anti-Semitism inherent in Fischerle's very characterization. Recall that his very first words are "How's business?" (*Wie gehn die Geschäfte?*). Though he is far from singular in his avarice, he is the preeminent entrepreneur in the novel, and, of course, a swindler par excellence, not to mention a systematic exploiter of the gentile workers in the "Firma S. Fischer." It seems only natural to him to refer to investment funds as "Jewish capital" (*das jüdische Kapital*), which he does repeatedly.[25] Furthermore, though no one character is particularly attractive in this novel, Fischerle alone (with the necessary exception of his look-alike accomplice, *die Fischerin*) is consistently described as an animal, outfitted with simian arms ("*lang wie die eines Gibbon*") and a croaking voice ("*er krächzte*"), who sniffs out ("*wittert*") both money and danger and, like some trained circus animal, even gathers up cash with his tongue.[26]

The matter is perhaps complicated by the fact that the novel's greatest anti-Semite is Fischerle himself. He sees Jews as essentially criminal, and when Kien tries to fire him, he retorts: "Grateful, aren't you! You Jewish swine! . . . You can't expect better from a Jew swine!"[27] Still under the impression that Kien is himself a Jew, Fischerle reiterates the epithets he has presumably heard in abundance directed at himself. Above all, Fischerle is forever dressing down imaginary chess opponents who are none other than projections of his own "Jewish" self. After one such match — Fischerle is literally addressing his mirror image — he dispatches his opponent with these words: "At home in Europe we call this galloping chess! Go begging with that nose!"[28]

Are we entitled to dismiss all this by claiming, however incredibly, that Canetti was oblivious to contemporary anti-Semitism?[29] An alternate,

Figure 4. "Der kleine Cohn" (Little Cohn): Fischerle's cultural prototype in a World War I–era postcard.

though equally insufficient, way of accounting for this discourse is to suggest that it is merely an expression of Canetti's own Jewish self-loathing.[30] These opposing explanations share a common strategy of subsuming the anti-Semitic discourse under debatable questions of biography, and thus distract us from Fischerle's iconic role as the grotesque amalgam of almost every contemporaneous anti-Semitic stereotype.[31] Looking back to the first half of the century, it is not hard at all to find anti-Jewish caricatures strikingly similar to Fischerle himself. Figure 4, for example, gives us "*Der kleine Cohn*" (Little Cohn), a Jewish dwarf whose physical deformity disqualifies him from military service. Sander Gilman observes that the "ill-formed 'little Mr. Kohn' [was] the eponymous Jew in German caricatures of the period," a kind of anti-Semitic mascot of Wilhelmine culture.[32]

The alleged Jewish physique exhibited in Little Mr. Cohn/Fischerle is not at all new in the long history of anti-Semitism; but racial—or better, corporeal—anti-Semitism was on the rise in the early part of the twentieth century and gains infamous prominence in Germany and Austria during the interwar period,[33] a development clearly in evidence in the famous caricatures of the period. Though not every Jew is necessarily represented as quite so small as *Der kleine Cohn*, most are indeed stunted, bowed over, and egregiously malformed.[34] Furthermore, a preponderance of contemporary anti-Semitic caricature shows Jews to have notoriously bad posture, a trait that in Fischerle receives its hyperbolic expression in the form of the great hunchback.[35] Using the language of philology, which as we noted was at this time charged in a particular way with propagating the very Enlightenment values that should have liberated Fischerle from his entrapment in anti-Semitic stereotypes, Kien rationalizes Fischerle's imprisonment in a cursed genealogy. Referring here to the Capitalist's persecution of poor Fischerle, Kien notes that "her destructive activity . . . was directed at the man opposite, whom nature by means of a dismal etymology had, at any rate already made a cripple."[36] Just prior to this episode, Kien tellingly remarks, in response to Fischerle's curious explication of the term "Stipendium" as "Jewish capital":[37] "By their etymology shall ye know them."[38] It is worth noting that Kien has in fact reversed the enlightenment formula for assimilation: whereas once particularity was to be absorbed in universal human potential, here the philologist employs the tools of his trade to explain away the Jew's physical abnormality. He speaks like a Jew, Kien reasons, so it makes sense that he looks like the quintessential Jew; nature, sanctified by the nomenclature of high cultural *Bildung*, has made him thus. Clearly, the suggestion that etymology, that central trope of philology, could be used to rationalize and naturalize Fischerle's fate as a Jewish cripple is deeply ironic in light of the central cultural mission attributed to philology during the Weimar era.

Hunched over, often bow-legged, frequently short, and almost universally supplied with a grotesque, oversize nose—these characteristics correspond to a tee with those assigned to Fischerle, and largely make up the physical charm he holds for the madam of The Baboon, the whorehouse cum cafe where Fischerle procures his bogus passport: "The landlady embraced Fischerle's hump. She overwhelmed him with words of affection; she'd been longing to see him, longing for his queer little nose, his crooked little legs, she'd longed for his darling, darling chessboard."[39]

Neither the visual nor the narrative clichés are by any means coincidental; on the contrary, they reflect the specific doctrines of an increasingly widespread racial anti-Semitism. Gilman reports that physical degeneration was a scientifically accepted fact of Jewish life at this time; the only debated question was whether such deformity was attributable to genetics or to a baneful environment, such as the Jewish ghetto.[40] Within the fictional world of *Auto-da-Fé* it is therefore not surprising that the brawny Benedikt Pfaff rhetorically suggests that he is "becoming a Jew" just as he begins to fear that he is being perceived as a physical weakling.[41] For, as Gilman notes, German medical handbooks from the first half of this century are rife with assertions about the innate feebleness of the Jewish body.[42]

Siegfried

Canetti's critique in *Auto-da-Fé* of corporeal anti-Semitism takes what is at this point in this study a familiar form: hyperbole. As in the case of traditional misogynistic stereotypes, Canetti records putatively Jewish physical attributes and explodes them by means of grotesque exaggeration: the poor posture becomes an outrageously prominent hunchback, the large nose becomes "this total nose" (*diese ausschließliche Nase*). But that is not all. Built into Fischerle's characterization is another aspect of contemporaneous Jewish life, a trace of assimilationist striving of which Fischerle himself is hardly conscious: his name.

Before proceeding it may be helpful to recall that in *Auto-da-Fé* the characters do not develop in any Aristotelian sense: their possibilities—like those of musical instruments—are pregiven, and the plot is therefore a mere playing out of predictable (and often quite meager) potentialities.[43] This is worth keeping in mind when reflecting on the significance of Fischerle's first name: Siegfried. For this is not to be seen as revelatory of Fischerle's inner striving—Canetti's figures do not at any rate have any discernible inner life[44]—but as a signifier of a social and cultural event that stands in parodic contrast to the actual career of Fischerle: namely, successful Jewish assimilation to German culture.

If Canetti meant merely to repeat the negative stereotypes, he might have given Fischerle one of the more common epithets from the abundant stock of anti-Semitic nomenclature: Israel, Jacob, or Itzig.[45] But instead he chose "Siegfried," the quintessentially Germanic name from that quintessentially Germanic epic, *Das Nibelungenlied*. What today may seem a quaint subtlety (or, indeed, a mere detail) was in fact a matter of no small import at the beginning of the century.[46] During the Wilhelmine period, Ruth Gay reports, "Siegfried became one of the most popular names among Jewish boys," a fact she explains as a direct expression of Jewish veneration of German culture: "To the German Jews *Bildung* represented a new kind of intellectual and emotional home after the physical confines of the ghetto and the closed scholarly world of Jewish learning."[47] Which illuminates, perhaps, why the infamous protagonist of Oskar Panizza's *Operated Jew* (1893), Itzig Faitel Stern, crowns his grotesque series of efforts to remake himself into an "Aryan" look-alike with the new name "Siegfried Freudenstern."[48] Both as a magnet for virtually every anti-Semitic stereotype and in his determination to recreate himself physically, this Itzig/Siegfried is richly reminiscent of Canetti's later Fischerle—a connection encouraged insofar as Panizza was championed in the Weimar period by both Kurt Tucholsky and Walter Benjamin.[49]

Yet if the Jewish predilection for the Germanic name Siegfried once signified a confidence in German culture as a home for Jews—an assertion Panizza puts in question already at the turn of the century—this clearly no longer applies to Fischerle, who can envision a future for himself only by means of escape, not assimilation. Though he does not aspire to authentic *Bildung*, Fischerle's name (as well, of course, as his association with Kien) invites us to remember a not-too-distant time when allegiance to German culture provided an entré, a venue for shedding the particularist garb of Judaism. In a masterful stroke of naming, Canetti has captured the contradictions of post–World War I German culture: "Siegfried," the signifier of successful assimilation, coupled with "Fischerle," a designation of indelible ethnicity that simply could not be escaped.[50]

If Jews at this time were increasingly defined in terms of genetic and physical features, so, too, were Germans. The slouching, limping figure of "Israel" was, in the popular imagination, contrasted with the idealized "German" body of Siegfried. "Blond Siegfried types," for example, became the physical—if secret—ideal of the Jewish foreign minister Walther Rathenau, even while he accepted "many features of the anti-Semites' caricature of the Jew."[51] Indeed, in the Wilhelmine and Weimar periods there would have been an inescapable association with Richard Wagner's immensely popular *Siegfried*, whose title figure did much to propagate the image of the nordic man as the quintessential German.[52]

Ernst Hanisch, who has investigated "The Political Influence and Appropriation of Wagner," points out that during the First World War "*Siegfried* came to be identified with the essence of Germanness, the world war was seen as the *Götterdämmerung* of the West."[53] Hanisch goes on to explain that during the First World War, "inevitably, the famous sentence from Wagner's *German Art and German Politics* is invoked, to the effect that to be German means to do something for its own sake, a sentiment that had acquired an almost sacrosanct status in nationalist circles. Siegfried, symbol of victory (*Sieg*) and peace (*Fried*), appears as the poetic exemplification of this thought, whereas Mime, the symbol of all that is un-German, of the enemy powers, is motivated only by considerations of egoistic utility and self interest."[54] Shortly after the outbreak of the First World War, Wagner's son-in-law Houston Stewart Chamberlain identified Wilhelm II as the age's new Siegfried, authorized to uproot all that is "un-German" and lead the battle against "the corroding poison of Judaism." "Opposed to this diabolical race" Chamberlain wrote to the Kaiser, "stands Germany as divine champion: Siegfried versus the worm."[55] Given the widespread cultural resonances of Wagner's opera in this period, it may be instructive to view the novel in this light.[56]

Fischerle's physical description in itself suggests the connection, for while he may be named for the handsome and powerful hero (of both the Germanic saga and the Wagner operas), he is clearly drawn more to the specifi-

Figure 5. This rough draft for an anti-Semitic cartoon by Josef Plank counterposes a judge from Kien's social class with a stooped-over, malodorous Jew who could have been drawn from the pages of Auto-da-Fé. Similarly repulsed by Fischerle's filth and deformity, Kien nevertheless senses in this misshapen dwarf the hunger for transformative Kultur. Library of Congress; photo courtesy United States Holocaust Memorial Museum Photo Archives.

Figure 6. "*Diese ausschließliche Nase*" (This total nose). Two of Fischerle's cardinal attributes are reflected in this cartoon from the anti-Semitic Viennese magazine Kikeriki. These "Jewish" drones are marked most obviously by a grotesquely oversized nose, but are characterized no less by their parasitic practice (as the German caption instructs) of exploiting the worker bees—echoing Fischerle's abuse of his gentile employees in the "Firma S. Fischer." United States Holocaust Memorial Museum Photo Archives.

Figure 7. This page from the 1936 anti-Semitic children's book Trau keinem Fuchs auf grüner Heid, und keinem Jud bei seinem Eid *provides a stark visual contrast between idealized "Aryan" masculinity and the putatively physically degenerate Jew. The accompanying poems teach schoolchildren the following lessons: "The German is a proud man, who can work and fight. Because he is so handsome and full of courage, the Jew bears him an ancient grudge. This is the Jew, one sees that immediately—the biggest scoundrel in all the land. He thinks he is the handsomest of all, and all the while is so ugly." United States Holocaust Memorial Museum Photo Archives.*

cations of the hideous dwarf Mime. Early on, the young Wagnerian Siegfried informs his surrogate father that he finds him physically repulsive:

> I am repelled
> by the sight of you;
> I see that you're evil
> in all that you do.

> I watch you stand,
> shuffle and nod,
> shrinking and slinking,
> with your eyelids blinking—
> by your nodding neck
> I'd like to catch you,
> and end your shrinking,
> and stop your blinking!
> So deeply, Mime, I loathe you...
> Everything to me
> is dearer than you: birds in the branches
> and fish in the brook—
> all are dearer to me,
> far more than you.[57]

Physical polarity, expressed in terms of "racial" physical attributes that contemporaneously defined Germans and Jews, is the crux of Siegfried's break with Mime. The telltale signs are familiar to us from Canetti's description of Fischerle: an awkward, almost animal gait combined with a grasping, probing visage. When the young hero recognizes the incongruity of his own "Aryan" beauty with the unpleasant appearance of his putative father, he begins to question his true parentage. He learns the truth while gazing at his own splendidly Germanic image reflected in the waters of a pond:

> And there in the stream
> I saw my face—
> it wasn't like yours,
> not in the least,
> no more than a toad
> resembles a fish.
> No fish had a toad for a father![58]

Mime, clearly the toad (*Kröte*) in this dichotomy, is forced to admit that he is no blood relation: "You're no kin to me."[59] Under great duress, he vouchsafes the story of his charge's naming, suggesting a nominalist causality (or proleptic etymology) that issues forth in physical beauty:

> The wish of your mother—
> that's what she told me:

as 'Siegfried' you would grow
strong and fair.⁶⁰

Moreover, Mime's reputation — particularly in Wagnerian circles — as essentially greedy, materialistic, treacherous, and therefore "un-German" only strengthens the connection between him and Fischerle. Like Mime, Fischerle attempts to deceive and rob his master while he sleeps, but unlike his Wagnerian double, Fischerle contemplates murder only to dismiss it as an impossibility for a Jew. Marc Weiner goes further to argue that Wagner differentiates Siegfried from Mime — both tenors — by assigning them distinctive voices that connote, respectively, a healthy, manly Germanness and a degraded, effeminate Jewishness: "[Mime's] elevated tessitura, contrasted with the lower vocal writing for Siegfried, gives him away to Wagner's contemporary audience schooled in a culture that understood the Jewish voice to be high, nasal, and different."⁶¹ Perhaps Mime (or, for that matter, Alberich) is not essentially an anti-Semitic figure in the sense that later audiences in different cultural settings would easily recognize. Yet, given the broader semiotic economy of the Weimar period, he is eminently amenable to this interpretation, and in fact functions in this manner as an intertext to *Auto-da-Fé*.⁶² The decisive factor in establishing this intertextual relationship may be the fate Mime and Fischerle share: both die by the sword because of their irrepressible venality: "If I fail to kill you," Mime asks Siegfried, "how can I be sure of my treasure?"⁶³ But Siegfried, of course, prevails. "Taste then my sword, / repulsive babbler!" he cries and afterwards "grabs Mime's corpse, drags it to the knoll at the entrance to the cave, and throws it down inside."⁶⁴ Underscoring the higher principle at stake in this execution, Siegfried apostrophizes the now deceased Mime:

In the cavern there,
lie with the hoard!
You schemed so long
and strove for gold;
so now take your joy in that treasure!⁶⁵

Fischerle meets his end somewhat less operatically: he is dismembered with a bread knife and then shoved under a bed. Yet the justification for murdering the disfigured dwarf is essentially the same: as retaliation for betraying his former employee for lucre. And, like Siegfried, this executioner turns (or

Figure 8. Fritz Lang's 1924 Siegfried *powerfully reiterates the "Aryan" ideal of Germanic masculinity as unattainable by hideous misshapen dwarfs like Fischerle—despite the assimilationist aspirations ironically encoded in his first name, Siegfried. The film's intertitle reads: "He is wondrous fair," a commentary that hardly seems necessary in light of the stark visual contrasts in this scene. Museum of Modern Art/Film Stills Archive.*

returns) to amorous pursuits, once this venal little antagonist is thus dispatched.

Wagner was still a favorite in the interwar period, particularly of Viennese Jews. Further, Fritz Lang's Weimar-era filming of the Nibelung saga can only have circulated the story to even wider audiences. Lang's 1924 *Siegfried* in fact underscores powerfully the iconic physical polarities described above. There is therefore little doubt that *Siegfried* would have echoed meaningfully within the fictional chambers of *Auto-da-Fé*. But in considering the specific meaning of this intertext, we should not forget that the novel's irony—and, thus, the critical vantage point—resides in the fact that Fischerle is neither Mime nor Siegfried, but both. Or, better, he is a *Mime who would be Siegfried,* a Jew who would like to be freed of his physical markers, but, within the strictures of corporeal racism, can only dream of such freedom. Bearing the name Siegfried thus incarnates one of the novel's bitter ironies that reverberates with wider cultural significance.

All of this may elucidate the dilemma present in the very exposition of one *Siegfried Fischerle,* an ostensibly simple character in whom a complex unit of Weimar-era culture is encoded. If, on the one hand, Fischerle reflects the truth of what Peter Gay calls the greatly imperiled prospects for Jewish assimilation after the First World War, this dwarf also suggests by his very being that the intra-Jewish debates of the era were tragically quite moot. While no novel—let alone a modernist novel—can ever quantify the social and cultural issues it may engage, we are nevertheless left to wonder about the significance of those controversies between the assimilated Western Jews and the Orthodox Jews of the East, or the debates between the Zionists and the acculturated Austro-German Jews in the face of implacable racial anti-Semitism.[66] For such anti-Semites, after all, a Jew was a Jew was a Jew. The cultural loyalties, political aspirations, or religious beliefs of the individual Jew mattered not at all.[67]

Inescapably "Jewish"

Despite Canetti's noted aversion to concepts of dramatic development, *Auto-da-Fé* does contain some narrative progression. In fact, of all the parallel plots that comprise the novel, Fischerle's is perhaps the most traditionally linear. In addition to the constraints of his unavoidably "Jewish body," Fischerle apparently also lacks the intelligence to qualify for Kien's spurious *Bildung* program (he mistakes Plato, for example, for a wealthy mogul),[68] and is therefore prevented on this count as well from aspiring to traditional assimilation. Instead, Fischerle fosters a fantasy of escape to America, which he plans to finance by methodically robbing Kien.

Because he has internalized the malicious physiognomic premises of the corporeal anti-Semites, Fischerle believes that freedom means freedom from his "Jewish" body. His self-hatred takes darkly comical turns, as when he beats himself for stealing Kien's wallet, and expresses itself in a disarmingly straightforward manner: "He had no articles of faith, or only one — that 'Jew' is a genus of criminal which carries its punishment with it."[69] Canetti offers up this bitter satire at a time when, by all accounts, real-world Jewish self-hatred had never before been so virulent.[70] Certainly the phenomenon was of great enough significance to warrant a controversial study by Theodor Lessing, whose 1930 title *Der jüdische Selbsthaß* (Jewish Self-Hatred) actually coined the term.[71]

Characteristically, Canetti takes a complex social phenomenon and reduces it to its core absurdity. For Fischerle this means the pursuit of two somewhat inconsistent, though oddly compatible, goals: removing the physical markers of Jewishness from his body, and fleeing to a country where his Jewishness will not count so much against him. America is the place where Fischerle sets his fantasy about striking it rich both by winning big at chess and by marrying a blond heiress, a sort of Horatio Alger myth minus the work ethic. But Fischerle worries, in one of the earlier installments of this reiterated fantasy, about being treated as an outsider even in this land of outsiders. In imagining his own American success story, he finds it necessary to confront anti-Jewish stereotypes: "Let them say Jews are cowards. The reporters ask him who he is. Not a soul knows him. He doesn't look like an American. There are Jews everywhere. But where does this Jew come from, who's rolled in triumph over Capablanca?"[72] America nevertheless holds out the offer of better times; it is a place, Fischerle imagines, where hotels offer clean sheets even to Jews, and where a big, beautiful, blue-eyed Mae West–type blond can fall for a little guy with an extraordinarily long nose: "'Darling!' said the millionairess and pinched it, she loved long noses, she couldn't stand short ones."[73] This dream bride seems in fact to be an idealized version of the philosemitic proprietress of the pub The Baboon, who expresses a similar weakness for Fischerle's "special" nose.[74]

These fantasies aside, Fischerle is greatly concerned that his body will give him away. Early on he considers surgery to repair his back, but has no way to finance it. Georg actually first enters the narrative in this connection: Fischerle determines that Kien's brother will certainly be able to perform this long-awaited operation and thereby alleviate him of his Jewish appearance. He knows for certain that the removal of his hunchback, either by surgical or sartorial means, will require more money than he has, and therefore ardently pursues his scheme to bilk Kien of his remaining net worth. This plot segment offers Canetti the opportunity to heap every remaining anti-

Jewish stereotype on the already hunched back of this little man. Fischerle becomes the exploitative businessman who makes a huge profit while his gentile employees remain impoverished. It can be no coincidence that just as Fischerle announces the formation of the "Firma Siegfried Fischer," explicit references to the First World War and its aftermath begin to appear in the novel: the "blind" beggar, we learn, spent three long years at the front, and, as a result, cannot bear the stench of carbon to this day; Fischerle maintains that Kien went mad in the war and still retains an army-issue revolver; and the same employee who will later murder Fischerle turns out to have a war injury that curiously affects his memory.[75]

Sandwiched between two books that play primarily within interior space, Book 2 alone provides a more sustained opening to the social setting. It may therefore be advisable to pay some attention to the social environment metonymically signified by these references. First of all, the war and its aftermath saw a marked increase in anti-Semitism, as Jonny Moser explains: "With the agitation against the Jewish war refugees commenced the renewed attack on the entire community of Austrian Jews . . . The Jews were represented as racketeers, black marketers, war profiteers and shirkers."[76] As the Jewish entrepreneur, Fischerle incorporates each of these charges in some way. His physical disfigurement obviously disqualifies him from military service and thus has garnered him the status of shirker during the Great War even before the action of the novel commences. As an exploiter of handicapped war veterans and a dealer in fraudulent goods (recall that he sells the same packet of cheap paperbacks to Kien over and over, representing them in each case as something quite different), he incarnates the cliché of the dishonest Jewish businessman. Of course the postwar era brought with it a plethora of more general social ills and anxieties, many of which can be observed in the scene where the great crowd gathers outside the Theresianum just after Kien catches Pfaff and Therese in the act of pawning his great private library.

Some readers have no doubt assumed that Fischerle's concern for his appearance may have nothing more to it than this: as a known thief, he fears being recognized by the police on account of his trademark hunchback. But the novel belies this innocent assumption. There is a distinct danger, it appears, in looking "too Jewish," especially when a Viennese crowd, roiled by rumors of a great crime, and already suffering the shortages of a lagging, inflation-ridden postwar economy, is looking for a scapegoat. When Fischerle first sees the crowd he is emboldened by the prospects for pickpocketing, thus confirming his own image of Jews as essentially criminal: "Among such a mass of people a mass of money might be made."[77] Yet in very short order he becomes the object himself of this agitated crowd's ire: "Fischerle heard the reproaches heaped upon him . . . A dwarf would get twenty years. Capital punishment ought to be re-introduced. Cripples ought to be exterminated. All criminals are cripples. No, all cripples are criminals . . . Why can't he earn an honest penny. Taking bread out of people's mouths. What's he want with pearls, a cripple like him, and that Jew nose ought to be cut off."[78] In unmistakable terms, the invective of what has become a wrathful lynch mob culminates in corporeal anti-Semitism. The indirect speech of the German gives perhaps a better impression of the way the novel hosts what is at first a richly confused polyphony of voices and gradually galvanizes them into a homogenous anti-Semitic choir—giving rise, ultimately, to the antithesis of Bakhtin's progressive notion of *heteroglossia*.[79] Fischerle escapes their rage, when, just in the nick of time, *die Fischerin* (the Fishwife in the Wedgwood translation)—Fischerle's female double—appears elsewhere in the crowd. Owing to their uncanny physical resemblance, the Fishwife takes the blows intended for the other little Jew: "The crowd falls upon her . . . The Fishwife falls to the ground. She lies on her belly and keeps quite still. They mess her up terribly . . . No doubt about the genuineness of the hump. The crowd breaks over it . . . Then she loses consciousness."[80]

Reflecting on "the role which the Jews play in the cultural world of Christianity as the ultimate object of projection," Sander Gilman remarks: "The Jew, caught up in such a system of representation, has but little choice: his essence, which incorporates the horrors projected on to him and which is embodied (quite literally [sic]) in his physical being, must try, on one level or another, to become invisible."[81] This is precisely what Fischerle attempts to do. In what amounts to a caricature of the old formula for assimilation, "wealth and cultivation" (*Besitz und Bildung*), Fischerle seeks a doctoral title to accompany his newly acquired wealth, in the conviction that this will gain him, if not invisibility, then at least some respect in the eyes of the police. In the following we notice how Fischerle clings to the illusion that culture— here metonymically represented by the revered German *Doktorwürde*—can mitigate his physical "Jewishness": "All the same, he was afraid. He couldn't help his shape. Now if only he were called Dr. Fischer instead of plain Fischer the police would respect him at once."[82] Although the men of the underworld pub try to convince Fischerle that such a *Doktortitel* would do little good for someone so misshapen as he, Fischerle vehemently disagrees, and launches into a drunken, ludicrous tale about a tiny doctor even more disfigured than he. Fischerle prevails on this point, procures the passport, and proceeds to the tailor, where he orders a suit that will render his hunchback invisible. "His new suit fitted him like the most splendid of combinations. Whatever trace was left of his hump disappeared under the coat."[83] Fischerle's efforts to eradicate his Jewishness by sartorial subterfuge reverberate in the anti-Semitic caricature of the day, placing him squarely within the tradition of the ridiculed Jewish parvenu.[84]

While waiting for his wonder suit — a kind of "Tarnkappe" for his deformed torso — to be properly fitted, Fischerle attempts to learn the language of his future home, "Amerikanisch." Practicing loudly in the park, Fischerle arouses the attention of a number of passersby. Because he believes already to have dispensed with the hunchback — "his hump was on its last legs"[85] — Fischerle hopes, but cannot really convince himself, that the attention he receives is just innocent curiosity. These self-taught language lessons are intended to put the final touch on a physical transformation of which he does not himself seem fully confident. Still, his hope is to jettison his all-too-revealing Jewish-Viennese dialect by acquiring English. When evening comes, a group of menacing youths approaches Fischerle, and he immediately assumes the worst:[86] "A few boys herded themselves together and waited until the last grown-up had gone. Suddenly they surrounded Fischerle's bench and burst into an English chorus. They yelled 'Yes' but they meant 'Jew' [the German — Ja/Jude — is alliterative and makes the aural confusion more plausible]. *Before* he decided on his journey, Fischerle had feared boys like the plague . . . [but now] he was neither a Jew nor a cripple, he was a fine fellow and knew all about wigwams."[87] Fischerle survives the harassment, and returns to pick up his new set of clothes. Fully decked out in a garish outfit — a black and white checked suit, bright blue coat, and canary yellow shoes — he becomes a walking parody of the Jewish parvenu. The tailor gazes proudly down upon his own sartorial miracle, the very "image of a well-bred dwarf,"[88] but attributes this transformation, ultimately, not to his craft, but to humanist culture. It is the tailor, oddly enough, who reminds us one last time of the emancipatory promises of German culture. In good idealist fashion (and with an irony meant only for the reader), he sonorously opines that it is not the body, in the final analysis, that has the last word: "the education of the heart is all."[89]

Figure 9. Jewish "Metamorphosis." Though Fischerle believes that his ingenious tailor has removed all vestiges of his Jewishness, he of course remains physically marked — just like the figure in the cartoon above — as a Jew.

Affecting a German accented with American intonation, Fischerle manages to convince a train ticket salesman that he is indeed an American businessman. Appearing, he hopes, as "a smartly dressed person, rejuvenated and well born,"[90] Fischerle delights in his great "success" in deceiving the train official into believing that he is a highly desirable foreigner, rather than one of the great unwashed, that mass of Galician Jews that flooded the Austrian capital during and after the First World War: "From this Fischerle assumed rightly and with pride that he was no longer recognizable."[91]

All of which does him precious little good, however. For when he returns home to recover an address book in which he will carefully inscribe his new title and place of residence ("Doktor Fischer, New York"), Fischerle's new set of clothes and newly acquired English fail to conceal his identity from a vengeful former employee. His longstanding desire to have his hunchback removed is finally granted, but certainly not in the manner he had hoped. Fischerle becomes the "Operated Jew" of the late Weimar period, whose doomed assimilationist efforts cannot even get him over the border: "A fist shatters his skull. — The blind man hurled him to the ground and fetched from the table in the corner of the little room a bread knife. With this he slit his coat and suit to shreds and cut off Fischerle's hump. He panted over the laborious work, the knife was too blunt for him and he wouldn't strike a light . . . He wrapped the hump in the strips of the coat, spat on it once or twice and left the parcel where it was. The corpse he shoved under the bed."[92] He is thus murdered as unceremoniously and as brutally as was the Fischerin — the only figures explicitly slain within the action of the novel, and both Jews.

Long after Fischerle makes his bloody exit from the novel, his voice reemerges, if only momentarily, by way of a telegram he had earlier sent to Georg. Fischerle settles upon this plan because he thinks Georg might be able to surgically remove his hunchback, and is therefore keen on luring him under false pretenses to Vienna. He composes a succinct cable in Kien's name, indicating that he urgently requires the professional assistance of his younger brother. The words Fischerle carefully selects betray the very Jewishness he so assiduously shuns.[93] When Georg rips open the telegram and reads aloud the words, "Bin total meschugge. Dein Bruder" ("Am completely crackers. Your brother"),[94] the Yiddish word "meschugge" strikes him — correctly, as it happens — as totally uncharacteristic of his learned philologist brother. But for us it serves as one last reminder that Fischerle, despite his recently acquired *Bildung,* language lessons, and new set of clothes, remains tragically and inescapably Jewish in an environment increasingly hostile to Jews.

It is true that Canetti felt some discomfort about Fischerle in the wake of the Holocaust. Might he have contributed to the very anti-Semitism he sought to document? Could the novel's depiction of Fischerle as a repugnant, self-hating Jew have played into the hands of those who implemented or sought to justify the mass killings of Jews? Or might this book have simply entertained and titillated anti-Semites? That Nazi officials chose to ban the novel rather than exploit it for propaganda purposes would suggest that it did not lend itself very easily to such a use. But Canetti was of course aware of the wide range of responses evoked by art, particularly modernist art, and knew that his readers might draw conclusions from the novel that differed markedly from his own intentions. He later wrote that he dreaded running into people who had just read *Auto-da-Fé,* because they inevitably tended to locate the wretchedness of the novel in the author himself. Not coincidentally, I believe, Canetti puts his defense of Fischerle into the mouth of the revered Hebraist Isaiah Sonne, who justifies this potentially offensive characterization in this way: "People will bristle at Fischerle because he is a Jew, and will reproach the author with the charge that this figure can be misread as if in support of the odious sentiments of the times. Yet this figure is true, as true as the narrow-minded, rustic housekeeper [Therese] or the abusive building superintendent [Pfaff]. When the catastrophe is over, all charges of this kind will fall away from the figures and they will stand revealed as that which led to the catastrophe." This is the important passage that precedes Canetti's more frequently cited line regarding his regret about Fischerle: "I mention only this one detail because later, with the progress of events, I often felt discomfort regarding Fischerle; and then I always sought refuge in this early justification."[95]

This defense is interesting not because it comes from Sonne—that we may never be able to corroborate—but because it contains an awareness on the part of Canetti of the essential instability of parody. If Canetti really did suffer pangs of conscience, however, I suspect that it was due not only to the potential misunderstandings that his book might inspire, but because he really does target Jews, at least in part, as complicit by way of Jewish self-hatred. Complicit, however, in the rising tide of racial anti-Semitism of the early 1930s—not in the organized destruction of European Jews that commenced in the early 1940s. This distinction might well be lost in the post-Holocaust era and thus give rise to the author's quite understandable "uneasiness" (*Unbehagen*).

Yet we should not permit this to obscure the novel's broader frame of reference. Kien's betrayal of Fischerle, which he grounds in philological humanism, commences almost from the moment they meet. It is then that we witness Kien distorting the idealist Schillerian sentiment, "It is the spirit which builds itself a body," into a justification for Fischerle's deformed "Jewish" body rather than employing it as a motto of liberation from such irrational prejudice. In other words, Sonne's contention, that Fischerle, along with this gallery of despicable figures, indicts not the author but the times from which he drew them, does in the end ring true. Specifically, his insightful formulation concerning these characters as "that which led to the catastrophe" seems apropos of Fischerle. Canetti may still be right to worry that even serious humor about grotesque attempts at assimilation will be rejected by some readers as simply in poor taste. Yet the larger perspective, which demands that we see Fischerle not only as an icon of racial anti-Semitism, but more specifically as a product of a bankrupt, socially irrelevant humanism, raises this handicapped Jew to a tragic sign of the times.

While Fischerle is, I think, best understood in terms of this larger problematic, he remains a locus of multivalent tension. When Nicola Riedner, one of the few critics intimately familiar with the novel's anti-Semitic discourse, argues that we should view Fischerle as punished for an overweening assimilation drive, she founders on numerous counts, not the least of which is her curious imposition of a rational choice model to the virtual exclusion of the very complex matrix of social and political forces she herself has documented. Yet her argument powerfully communicates the distinctly distasteful degree of excess in this figure. Though our post-Holocaust vantage point has much to do with it—one cannot simply bracket out the historical fact that Eastern European Jews were murdered at much higher rates than German Jews—Canetti's practice of grotesque caricature perhaps exceeds his own narrative intentions. In discussing the novel's attitude toward misogyny (chapter 2), we noted Canetti's use of hyperbolic parody, a technique that risks a measure of complicity as critique. The same holds true here. It would, however, be an unfortunate mistake to permit this observation to obscure the fact that in the end it is indeed Fischerle, and not the voluble and self-pitying Kien, as some early critics would have it, who becomes the novel's real victim of modernity's crisis of values. Yet it would be equally mistaken to overlook the way in which Siegfried Fischerle outstrips his didactic function and continues to haunt the novel long after he is murdered.

Up to this point in this study we have seen how Canetti has left a trail — perhaps something more like an elaborate web of trails — linking this novel to broader social and intellectual concerns. The next chapter will be concerned less with positive traces of intertextuality than with a palpable but curiously obscured presence, namely that of Sigmund Freud. For readers of the 1930s, Freud hardly needed to be evoked. Among later critics who fell under the author's own anti-Freudian spell, Freud seems unaccountably absent. In either case, the novel's relationship to Freud and popularized Freudianism cries out for elucidation.

5 "An Impudent Choir of Croaking Frogs"
Freud and the Freudians as the Novel's Secret Sharers

> Freud, however, was not concerned with politics, not even sexual politics.
> —Peter Gay[1]

An Anxiety of Influence?

Canetti's hostility toward psychoanalysis is legendary, yet it is a fact usually mentioned in the context of his much later *Crowds and Power* (1960), and seldom in connection with the novel of 1931. Though commentators on the novel could scarcely have missed Canetti's disdain for Freud, they seem on the whole to have assumed that the novel dismisses rather than confronts Freud; few, at any rate, have paid any kind of sustained attention to the novel's thick web of Freudian allusions. Though Gerald Stieg proposes that both *Auto-da-Fé* and *Civilization and Its Discontents* (1930) be seen as quite specific and contrastive responses to the 1927 riot/massacre that followed the burning of the Viennese Palace of Justice, he is unable, in the end, to show how the novel really "answers" Freud.[2] Yet Freud is already present in *Auto-da-Fé*, and it will be the task of this chapter to show how powerful even—or especially—a negative influence can be. How, indeed, could a novelist as intellectually ambitious as Canetti ignore one of the most influential thinkers of his own time?

What complicates our inquiry, however—and this may explain the hesitance of critics to take this path—is the fact that Canetti never set out to refute Freud directly, for that might on the one hand imply an acquiescence in the Freudian agenda, and on the other would be inappropriate to a *literary* engagement. A more direct confrontation would indeed have to wait thirty years for *Crowds and Power*. Furthermore, Canetti's impatience with Freudian grand theories is, at this time, inextricably bound up with his critique of Freud's disciples, whom he held to be overzealous, to say the least. His targets in the novel, therefore, will never be pure instances of unadulterated Freudian dogma. Instead the novel's evocations of Freud will always include an element of popularization, deviation and misprision. While this ensures that the novel resonates more richly with the widespread cultural reception of Freud, it will no doubt irritate Freud purists—to the extent that such a group is to be found among Canetti aficionados in the first place.

Surprisingly, there are a few instances in which Canetti acknowledged an intellectual debt to Freud. The most memorable of these is in a 1962 radio interview with Theodor W. Adorno, who was keen to rectify what he perceived to be a glaring lacuna in the recently published *Crowds and Power*. Canetti completed this lengthy anthropological study without once mentioning Freud by name, who, after all, had written the most influential essay to date on the topic of crowd formation and social psychology, namely his *Group Psychology and the Analysis of the Ego* (1921). In response to Adorno's persistent query—he returns to Freud throughout the interview—Canetti musters a few gracious words for the founder of psychoanalysis: "As you speak of Freud—I am the first to admit that the innovative way in which Freud approached things, without allowing himself to be distracted or frightened, made a deep impression on me in my formative period. It is certainly the case that I am now no longer convinced of some of his results and must oppose some of his special theories. But for the way he tackled things, I still have the deepest respect."[3]

This diplomatically worded homage—intended, I would wager, to placate those critics who read Canetti's omission as an arrogant dismissal of a worthy predecessor—may ultimately only confuse the matter. For it suggests that Canetti's opposition to Freud is both of recent vintage (e.g., "I am *no longer* convinced") and partial ("*some* of his results . . . [and] *some* of his special theories").[4] In fact, neither claim is true. For the earliest of Canetti's writings, *Auto-da-Fé*, already reveals a pattern not of positive influence, but of thoroughgoing dissent. Twenty odd years after the interview with Adorno, an elderly Canetti—the esteemed Nobel laureate approaching his eightieth birthday—seems to have been at greater ease in reflecting on the place of Freud in his life. The final volume of his autobiography, *Das Augenspiel: Lebensgeschichte 1931–1937* (The Play of the Eyes), is strewn with observations that leave no doubt that the young author of *Auto-da-Fé* was already determined to do battle with Freud.

The Dispute with Broch

The context for such reflections is frequently a reminiscence about the author Hermann Broch, whom Canetti loved and admired despite his devotion to Freud: "He had really fallen for Freud, in a religious manner I would say; I don't mean to say that he had become a zealot, like so many others whom I knew at the time. Rather, he was permeated by Freud, as by a mystical teaching."[5] In speaking with Broch, Canetti sounds central objections that will reverberate throughout his work. Again and again he maintains, though not always as civilly as in this friendly debate, essentially two points: (1) Freud is too readily cited and believed, when in reality the phenomena he attempts to explain remain complex and puzzling; and (2) Freud's theories tend to interiorize and personalize *social* reality. The following passage, taken from an exchange between Canetti and Broch, is meant to rebuff the latter's claim that a modernist novel should incorporate Freudian insights by presenting psychologically realistic characters, something Canetti in *Auto-da-Fé* obviously chose not to do. To Broch he counters:

> You gladly appeal to modern psychology. It seems to me that you are proud of it because it arose, so to speak, out of your own intimate milieu, from this special area of the Viennese world. This psychology has for you the familiar feel of home [*Heimatgefühl*] . . . Whatever it declares, you find on the spot in yourself. You don't even need to go in search for it. Precisely this psychology strikes me as completely inadequate. It concerns itself with the individual, and in this it has accomplished something; what it cannot comprehend is the crowd [*Masse*], and that is the most important entity, about which we need to learn. For all new power that arises *today* draws its sustenance from the crowd. In practice, everybody who is after power knows how to manipulate the crowd.[6]

The one concession Canetti makes here to individual psychology may be nothing more than a polite way of differing with a respected friend; on the other hand we should be careful not to exaggerate the dispute. As we shall see below, Canetti will *use* Freud to critique Freud and what he perceived to be the broader Freud mania. Apart from this double-edged tribute, however, we notice the classic laments. The first, that Freud's theories are all too easily confirmed, indeed, that they are assumed to be correct from the outset, should be judged as much a critique of Freud as of his uncritical followers. The significance of the second point for the novel, which at this time is still lying around in typescript form, could be easily overlooked because Canetti is so clearly using the language we associate with his later work on *Crowds and Power*.[7] Yet we should not overlook the fact that Canetti pointedly places these remarks in the context of a discussion of modernist novels. Broch has just read *Auto-da-Fé* and criticizes Canetti for failing to avail himself of the latest discoveries in psychology. Canetti responds that Broch's brand of psychological realism leads not to critical distance, but serves instead as a kind of anodyne. In a carefully worded passage, Canetti suggests that Broch's psychological realism brings insight, but also soothes ("*beruhigt*") readers in a manner that he finds problematic.

This exchange, however much it may have been stylized or perhaps even invented in hindsight, is crucial in understanding Canetti's relationship to Freudian psychology, at least as he saw it. Broch is not an easy opponent, and presses his point: "There is a modern psychology and it says things about people that we simply cannot ignore. Literature must be on the intellectual level of its day. If it falls behind, it becomes a kind of kitsch."[8] Canetti persists in advocating his use of schematic figures over Broch's psychologically realistic people ("*Menschen*"), a point we have touched upon already in chapter 1. What is essential to underscore at this juncture is the fact that Canetti predicates the entire design of his novel upon a considered rejection of Freudian psychology: "I, too, believe that the novel of today must be *different*, but not because we live in the era of Freud and Joyce. The *substance* of the times is different, and can only be represented by way of new figures."[9]

Let us return to that second objection with the assurance that it has an important place in the discussion of the novel: this is Canetti's assessment of psychoanalysis as essentially an individual, personal affair ("*befaßt sich mit dem einzelnen*"), which is therefore constitutionally incapable of addressing the social and political, particularly when it comes to the exercise of power. For these are precisely the themes which had already found expression in *Auto-da-Fé*, as we have had occasion to see thus far in this study. Revealing an intimate familiarity with Freud's *Group Psychology and the Analysis of the Ego*—the earliest sustained and perhaps the most important effort on

Freud's part to come to terms with the social—Canetti once tried to convince Broch of the error of his, and more importantly Freud's, ways. Otherwise tolerant and patient with his interlocutor, Broch drew the line when it came to assailing Freud; indeed "he seemed angry when I criticized Freudian conceptions."[10] For our discussion of the novel, it is significant to note that Canetti's critique here—he argues that crowds are ontologically different and not sufficiently explained by individual psychology—articulates once again his basic objection that Freud overextends the personal. Even as sympathetic a biographer as Peter Gay, himself a fairly orthodox though not uncritical Freudian, comes to a similar conclusion regarding the *Group Psychology* essay when, in offering this précis, he remarks: "The crowd, as crowd, invents nothing; it only liberates, distorts, exaggerates, the individual members' traits . . . In short, crowd psychology, and with it all social psychology, is parasitic on individual psychology; that is Freud's point of departure, to which he persistently held."[11] For Gay, this is a fairly neutral observation; but for Canetti, this was war.

It is not surprising that the antagonist Freud was on his mind when Canetti sought out his beloved Dr. Sonne as a sounding board for some of his evolving ideas on social phenomena, a project Canetti had already come to see as his "life's task" (*Lebensaufgabe*).[12] Canetti succeeds, however, only in eliciting guidance on what—or whom—to avoid. Wondering what it must have been like for Sonne, the known Freud opponent, to suffer Broch's enthusiasm for psychoanalysis, Canetti muses: "He was friends with Broch, whom he respected and perhaps even loved. Whenever he spoke with him, the conversation will certainly have turned to Freud, to whom Broch was addicted [*dem Broch verfallen war*]. I would have loved to learn how Sonne withstood that without interjecting a wounding protest."[13] Canetti did not need to imagine such scenarios, however, for he knew from personal experience that Sonne had no truck with Freud: "That he had crucial disagreements with Freud, I experienced once when I vehemently attacked the 'death drive' in his presence,"[14] a concept, we might note in passing, which though tentatively introduced already in *Beyond the Pleasure Principle* (1920), became a cornerstone of the extremely popular *Civilization and Its Discontents* of 1930. Sonne, at any rate, steers his young protégé away from Freud: "He warned me of doctrines that are everywhere present but explain nothing. Better than any he understood how much they stand in the way of gaining insight into public matters."[15] All of these anecdotal remarks tell us, if nothing else, that Canetti saw himself and others as crucially engaged with Freudian thought at the time he wrote *Auto-da-Fé*.

As we have seen on numerous occasions in this study already, *Auto-da-Fé* is nothing if not centrally concerned to diagnose our blindness to "public things"—"*öffentliche Dinge*," as Canetti puts it. And thus it is not surprising that it is within this context that the novel's confrontation with Freud most clearly emerges. I have selected three episodes for analysis: the notorious chapter entitled "The Good Father" ("The Kind Father" in Wedgwood), as well as two less well known segments that have unjustly suffered neglect in the secondary literature: the incident involving the mad village blacksmith Jean Préval; and finally Georg's curious "Parable of the Termites." Each of these passages takes as its target a central Freudian tenet: the Oedipal complex; transference (and countertransference); and sublimation, respectively. Though the novel undoubtedly contests these notions, it would be erroneous to read *Auto-da-Fé* as an attempt to directly disprove Freud. This is an aim surely inconsistent with imaginative literature in general, and furthermore one that would make the author guilty of the very crime of which he accuses the Freudians: overreaching. In concluding with an analysis of Georg as a parodic vehicle for Freudian ideas and associations, the relationship of *Crowds and Power* to the novel—an affiliation which thus far has not redounded to the favor of *Auto-da-Fé*—will emerge in a clearer light. We will see that while both challenge fundamental Freudian notions, they do so in quite different ways.

Father Knows Best: Unseating the "Electra Complex"

"Sadism in the evening is refreshing and bracing!" Max Pulver's response, the first on record to what is perhaps the best-known chapter of *Auto-da-Fé*, "The Good Father," apparently broke the silence of an agitated and bemused salon audience, which had gathered in Zurich to hear the young author read from his yet unpublished work.[16] At a later reading of this same piece in Vienna, Canetti would be accused of "inhumanity" (*Unmenschlichkeit*); indeed, sometimes the most positive remark Canetti's auditors could muster was the assurance that the author would one day outgrow this kind of writing.[17] Well before feminist critics would draw our attention to the violence perpetrated upon women in this novel—sometimes in the process accusing the author himself of promoting the misogyny depicted here (see above, chapter 2)—Canetti had been subjected to "a real scolding" (*eine wahre Schelte*) by his contemporaries for this stark and unsparing portrayal of child and spousal abuse.[18]

"The Good Father" (*Der gute Vater*), an ironic reference, of course, to the very bad father Benedict Pfaff, contains only the most concentrated part of a story that in fact extends throughout the novel. It is in this chapter, however, that we are confronted with a critical mass of incriminating evidence against an abusive father who has been trying (and will continue to attempt) to suppress, distort, and trivialize the extent of his sexual violence. Contemporary readers may be tempted to attribute the attention accorded this chapter to the rise of critical paradigms informed by second-wave (i.e., post-1968) feminism, and to some extent this is perfectly true. Yet as we have seen, *Der gute Vater* already enjoyed an unmistakable prominence—and not only in the eyes of the author, as we shall see—even before the novel appeared in print. Canetti, at any rate, referred to this chapter as the "indispensable" part of the novel,[19] and later as an "obligatory" component of his performance repertoire.[20]

Our "good father" is of course Kien's Hausbesorger—a kind of doorman cum building superintendent—long known to us as an unambiguous woman-hater. When Kien first calls upon his services, well before the chapter in question opens, Benedikt Pfaff assumes his assignment is to beat Therese: "For years he had longed in vain for an opportunity to smash up a piece of woman's flesh."[21] Pfaff is quick to assure us that his motto, "Women ought to be beaten to death. The whole lot of them,"[22] is based on personal experience: "My old woman now, she was black and blue to the end of her days. My poor daughter, God rest her, I was that fond of her, there was a woman for you now, as the saying is, I started with her when she was that high."[23]

Pfaff's sexual abuse of his daughter takes on new dimensions starting on the day of his wife's funeral. Tellingly, Pfaff is reminded of the sexual relationship with his daughter just as he begins sleeping with Therese, a comparison that clearly does not favor the older woman: "If only she [Therese] were forty years younger. His daughter, God rest her, she had a heart of gold. She had to lie down beside him while he watched out for beggars. He used to pinch and look. Look and pinch. Those were the days! . . . Cry, she used to. Didn't do her no good. You can't do anything against a father. Ah, she was a love. All of a sudden she died . . . He simply couldn't do without her."[24] The

Hausbesorger's sporadic but insistently bad conscience slowly reveals a pattern of father-daughter assault and molestation. Prodded by the likelihood that the authorities will imminently appear at the Theresianum, where he and Therese are attempting to pawn Kien's library, Pfaff imagines himself punished not for dealing in stolen property, that is, for his current and evident infraction, but for sexually abusing and murdering his daughter years ago: "The caretaker stood stock still. He saw it: on every first of the month someone would come to take away his pension instead of paying it out to him. They'll lock him up as well ... Everything will come out and the plaintiffs will continue to violate his daughter posthumously. He isn't afraid ... He is retired on a pension. He isn't afraid. The doctor said himself, it's her lungs. Send her away! How would I do that, mister? He needs his pension just to eat ... Health insurance — the idea! Suddenly she'd return to him with a baby. In that tiny room. He isn't afraid!"[25]

With the phrase "and the plaintiffs *continue* to violate his daughter in the grave" (*und die Parteien schänden seine Tochter* noch *im Grab*), his fear that "everything will come out" (even while he repeatedly denies being afraid), not to mention his foreboding that Anna will return with a baby from a medical exam supposedly made necessary because of her lungs, Pfaff convicts himself in his own idiom. For this narrated monologue clearly belongs to his linguistic and mental repertory. When the police actually arrive, Pfaff immediately thinks, "My daughter!" and during the ensuing police inquiry he refers the murder that Kien insists having perpetrated upon Therese back to his own guilty conscience: "The Professor was talking about a wife, but he meant my daughter."[26] Kien is lying about a murder he never committed (though he fervently wishes he had); Pfaff dissimulates about a murder he actually committed but cannot fully suppress. All of this leads up to the episode in question.

"The Good Father" chapter gives a more complete picture of this unsavory incestuous abuse, but one that has rarely been fully acknowledged in the critical literature until recently, as Kristie Foell documents in *Blind Reflections*, her Canetti monograph of 1995. This may be due to the fact that Pfaff, whose denial of the crimes against his daughter is only occasionally and inadvertently punctured by feelings of guilt and concomitant moments of honesty, is largely in linguistic control of this chapter. This fact, combined with a hesitance on the part of critics — acting, perhaps, on the same feelings of disgust registered by Canetti's early auditors — to address such issues, may explain why Kien has so often been portrayed as the principal victim of Pfaff's aggression. At any rate, as the famous father-daughter dialogue referred to above in chapter 2 illustrates, Pfaff's power over his daughter is mediated by a kind of semiotic extortion. A central point for Canetti, here as in the contemporaneous play *Hochzeit* (The Wedding), is that language does not merely represent power relations, but actively structures them. While true, we should also acknowledge that language is simply an easier topic for critics to handle; the venerated "crisis of language" (*Sprachkrise*) whose pedigree reaches back at least as far as Hofmannsthal's *Lord Chandos Brief* (1902) provided a critical context for the discussion of "The Good Father" that often led away from the substance of this infamous exchange. One of the central points of that one-sided dialogue is after all the father's pointed prohibition of *other* romantic interests—there shall be no other suitors beside him—a point that is all too easily lost in more abstract discussions of referentiality and linguistics. The exchange commences with Pfaff talking to himself and does not essentially change, despite the coerced inclusion of Anna's voice:

> "A father has a right to . . ." ". . . the love of his child." Loud and toneless, as though she were at school, she completed his sentences. [. . .]
> "For getting married my daughter . . ."—he held out his arm—". . . has no time."
> "She gets her keep from . . ." ". . . her good father."
> "Other men do not want . . ." ". . . to have her."[27]

With regard to the implicit Freud debate, it is of obvious import that the exclusion of other erotic interests is an unambiguous function of the father's unseemly desire for the daughter, and not vice versa. The extent to which Anna is reduced to a function of her father's fantasy world is made abundantly evident by the fact that she is compelled not only to speak like her father, but to dress like him as well. Wearing his pants, doing his job, and ultimately bearing his name—he renames her "Poli" ("Polly" in Wedgwood) to remind him of the "Polizist" he once was—Anna's independent existence is effectively obliterated. And this, Pfaff opines, is the way to handle women after all: "Since he had nominated her Polly, he was proud of her. Women were good for something after all, men just have to understand how to make Pollys of them."[28] The "other" whom Anna impersonates is merely a figment of her father's narcissistic imagination, a sadomasochistic stimulant to his sexual fantasy. Having subjugated her in this manner, Pfaff was inclined to pleasure: "For hours he fondled her."[29]

Just as he has scripted his own wife's death,[30] Pfaff actively—but unsuccessfully—attempts to camouflage the incest as some kind of acceptable paternal solicitousness. Given this imbalance of narrative power, we must sometimes piece together the actual abuse from revelatory fragments scattered throughout the narrative. For example, in a passage clearly describing the father-daughter relationship *subsequent* to the mother's death, we encounter the astonishing phrase—clearly attributable to Anna's consciousness—"in the long years of *their marriage*" (*in den langen Jahren* ihrer Ehe).[31] "Marriage" is of course the most arresting term here, whereas the descriptive phrase "long years" indicates the daughter's subjective experience of time in this oppressive relationship. If this might quickly be passed over, then we need only turn to Pfaff's blunter formulations. For he uses within the space of three pages two separate terms for the illicit "honeymoon" (*Wonnemond* and *Honigmond*) he shamelessly conducts with his daughter since his wife's premature demise.[32]

Furthermore, when Anna engages in her doomed fantasy of redemption, she attends to a sartorial matter that might seem extraneous until we realize her need to appear to her would-be savior, the "black knight" Franz, as the virgin she no longer is: "She takes all the money with her, over her nightgown she slips on her own coat, the one she's never allowed to wear, not the old cast-off of her father's, thus she appears to be a virgin."[33] The significance of this apparent detail becomes clearer when we turn our attention to the culmination of Anna's fantasy: just as Franz declares his determination to marry her and her alone, Anna has him take approving notice of her "new coat."[34] Again, if Anna's subaltern language permits alternate and less repellent interpretive possibilities, her father's less subtle manner of speech proves stunningly less ambiguous. Inhabiting the narrator's voice, he relates: "While she beat the steak for his dinner, he could thump her to his heart's content. His eye did not know what his hand did."[35] Thus we can easily surmise the reason for her unmistakable fear of the marital bed, "the fear which this piece of furniture instilled into her."[36] In the end we learn that, after being beaten almost to death, "she lived for several more years as her father's servant and wife,"[37] at which point the term "Weib" (wife, woman) as designation for Anna should no longer surprise us—yet it does. We are left to wonder only if the guilt-ridden Pfaff, in an intertextual reference to Poe,[38] has walled up his daughter's corpse in the adjoining room. Certainly the evidence of his escalatingly guilty conscience, whose demands increasingly intrude upon his consciousness and culminate in his confession to Georg,[39] calls to mind the unforgettable "Tell-Tale Heart."[40]

But domestic violence was not Canetti's only—or, perhaps, even principal—point here, and the contrast with Kien, whom Pfaff threatens with a similar fate of domestic interment, clarifies the issue. Particular to Anna's story are two factors: the incest itself, and the concomitant, elaborate effort to reconstruct her as a mere supporting actor in Pfaff's psychodrama. These two elements propel the story into conflict with an influential cultural narrative already firmly entrenched at the time of the novel's writing and one that, if we can believe Adolf Grünbaum's pronouncement on "the present stunningly ubiquitous cultural influence of the Freudian corpus," is largely with us still.[41] In plotting this story, Canetti goes to some lengths to insure that this narrative both conjures and collides head on with Freud's account of fathers and daughters. In naming his fictional daughter after Freud's own daughter, Anna, Canetti may indeed have earned the compliment proffered by Friedl Benedikt: "Nobody can write as wickedly as you."[42]

It is this single father-daughter relationship, in fact, that can be said to have given birth to psychoanalysis, despite the fact that Freud would already in the Weimar period be accused of a myopic preoccupation with men— that is, with sons and mothers—and of having founded a "masculine psychology."[43] In the beginning, however, Freud derived much of his theory from the analysis of what was then known as female hysteria. Though Freud encountered case after case of incest and sexual assault by fathers and father figures, he interpreted these stories as defenses against a deeper truth: the daughters' unacknowledged sexual desire for their fathers. And in this way he was able to confirm that cornerstone of psychoanalysis, the Oedipus complex. Later, Freud would contend that any serious detractor would have to come to terms with this central tenet: "Every human newcomer has been set the task of mastering the Oedipus complex. Whoever cannot manage it falls prey to neurosis. The progress of psychoanalytic work has sketched the significance of the Oedipus complex ever more sharply; its recognition has become the shibboleth that separates the adherents of psychoanalysis from its opponents."[44] Thus Freud, who by now had placed the Oedipus complex squarely at the center of his controversial account of the rise of civilization (*Totem and Taboo*), drew a line in the sand. And Canetti, with his frequent public renditions of "The Good Father," meant to cross it.

Freud's account of the girl's passage through the Oedipus complex has of course proven notoriously controversial. Even in his own words, Freud seems to suggest that the girl does not so much pass through as remain mired in her erotic attachment to the father. True, she transfers her love from mother to father; but where does she go from here? Freud's own pronouncement does not offer much hope: "She slips — along the line of symbolic equation, one might say — from penis to a baby. Her Oedipus complex culminates in a desire, which is long retained, to receive a baby from her father as a gift — to bear him a child."[45] Indeed, as Judith Lewis Herman argues, Freud's model posits girls who are predisposed to father-daughter incest.[46] It is not difficult to see how this side of the Oedipus complex would prove useful to Freud in dispelling the claims of sexual trauma made by his female "hysterics": their stories only served to conceal their own illicit desire. Though it would be unfair to suggest that Freud actually sanctioned the sexual assault of daughters by fathers (and father figures, like uncles and older male friends of the family), or that he completely denied such abuse, his theory would serve powerfully to disguise such molestation as the fantasy of maladjusted women. In the *Introductory Lectures,* Freud recounts rather candidly why he was moved to recant his own seduction theory, an interpretation that accepted at face value the accounts of his female "hysterics," in favor of the allegedly deeper explanatory power of the Oedipus complex: "Almost all of my women patients told me that they had been seduced by their father. I was driven to recognize in the end that these reports were untrue and so came to understand that the hysterical symptoms are derived from phantasies and not from real occurrences . . . It was only later that I was able to recognize in this phantasy of being seduced by the father the expression of the typical Oedipus complex in women."[47] In a footnote appended to a subsequent edition of *Studies on Hysteria,* Freud did admit to falsifying a case study by suppressing the fact that a father was in fact the perpetrator of the molestation of his daughter.[48] But this was of little consequence in light of his continued trumpeting of the female Oedipal complex, which in effect suggests that if the daughter does not wholly imagine the abuse, then at least she can be thought to have elicited it on account of an unresolved erotic attachment to her father.

What Freud had driven inward, Canetti was determined to bring into the light of day. "The Good Father," with its blunt portrayal of Pfaff's abuse of Anna, challenges the Freudian internalization of this father-daughter conflict. Despite obvious thematic parallels that would at first invite a Freudian reading, Anna's predicament cannot possibly be grasped by means of the Freudian prefabricated postulate of daughterly desire. And, as if it were not already abundantly clear that Freud is the spectral antagonist in "The Good Father," the title itself seems designed to cement the allusion and clarify the target. For though it is the beleaguered daughter who is forced to bestow the epithet "the good father" on the villainous Pfaff, we come to see by means of the intertextual dynamic implicit in this chapter that it is none other than Freud who makes this appellation culturally available—and problematic.

In bequeathing this title to the patriarchal society of his day, Freud authorizes—however inadvertently—a kind of blindness to social reality, one of the principal varieties of "Blendung" arraigned in this novel. Viewing "The Good Father" as a counternarrative to what Jung later dubbed the "Electra Complex" expands our understanding of Canetti's critique of contemporary misogyny, explored above in chapter 2. In the case of Pfaff it is clearly not a matter of an individual's use of the feminine to shore up a dissolving self—he, like many lower-class personages of literary modernism, does not possess enough of a self to be taken seriously in this regard—but a larger cultural narrative that is here put on trial. From this perspective, the stability and affirmation the Viennese patriarchy derives from Freud's Oedipus complex—despite the surface clamor and claims of outrage—comes at the price of repressing a reprehensible social reality.[49]

Apropos of overreaching theory and in particular of his reception of Freud, Canetti once observed:

> Among the most uncanny phenomena of human intellectual history is the evasion of concrete experience [*das Ausweichen vor dem Konkreten*]. There exists a striking penchant to go after the most distant of things first and to overlook everything that one continually knocks up against in the immediate vicinity. The soaring arc of grand [interpretive] gestures—the adventure and audacity of expeditions into the unknown—masks the motivations for going there. Not infrequently, it is simply a matter of avoiding the most immediate reality because we are not equal to it.[50]

This "evasion of the concrete" is, I would suggest, the rubric that best captures Canetti's Freud critique, here and in subsequent passages considered in this chapter. Freud's promulgation of the Oedipus complex comes under fire in *Auto-da-Fé* not because it is inherently wrong as a model for individual psychology—that is simply not at issue here—but because it is overextended in a manner inconsistent with observable social facts. It is quite true that Canetti would later reject the Oedipus complex outright—replacing it in *Crowds and Power* with the more positive concept of "*Verwandlung*" (transformation)[51]—but the novel's disavowal of this central Freudian notion is already conspicuous.

Canetti is fully aware that *his* father-daughter narrative shifts the sympathy to the "tortured daughter" and toward the recognition of the intersubjective reality of power. As he approvingly remarks in noting the response to a public reading, "The auditors were moved by the 'Good Father,' there was the opportunity for sympathy with the tormented daughter."[52] Moreover, Canetti is fully convinced that his version of the story resonates with palpable Viennese reality: "The frightful 'Good Father' provoked horror; the Viennese were well aware of the power of their building superintendents [*Hausbesorger*] and I don't believe that anyone would have dared doubt the truth of this figure as long as everyone in the room was in his [Pfaff's] power."[53] Actual—not just fictionalized—child abuse was in any case a great sensation in fin-de-siècle Vienna, as Larry Wolff has documented. "The Viennese cases," Wolff observes, "provide us with an extraordinary picture of how child abuse was perceived and interpreted in an age that had not yet accepted the fundamental concept of child abuse."[54] Canetti's stark reinscription of this issue in the Pfaff-Anna conflict might therefore be seen not merely as a sobering evocation of this as yet unrecognized social pathology, but also as an inquiry into "why it had to be obliterated and forgotten."[55] The social resonance of Pfaff-like violence is further corroborated by the modernist sculptor Fritz Wortruba, who, remarking on the same reading of "The Good Father" Canetti refers to above, is said to have quipped "that nothing was *more* Vienna, the real Vienna, than that which [was] selected for this reading."[56] And later Dr. Sonne will testify to the irreducible truth of the Pfaff figure.[57] It can hardly be a coincidence that when Canetti later set down his own definition of "hysteria," he would eschew all references to intrapsychic disturbances, and view it instead as a woman's frequently unsuccessful attempt to escape male violence and domination.[58]

To appreciate Canetti's revision of the Freudian masterplot does not require that we fully endorse it. Faithful Freudians could easily exempt themselves from the novel's critique by crying foul. Though Anna is clearly disturbed and apparently delusional, she does not seem to exhibit classical symptoms of "hysteria." And is not Pfaff a kind of extreme, tailor-made exemplum? While Canetti never wavered in his insistence that "The Good Father," nourished by the "darkest aspects" of Viennese society,[59] exhibits a quantum of social truth, devout Freudians could claim that Canetti holds Freud to a standard that is simply incommensurate with the latter's own claims.[60] Whatever the case may be, it should be noted that Canetti sounds a critique here (and in the instances discussed below) that will echo throughout later Freud reception. Even—or especially—those who wish to redeem Freud for use in social theory will have occasion to address what is seen as psychoanalysis's inherent propensity to privatize what properly belongs to the social. In the end, of course, *Auto-da-Fé* is limited in its engagement to the tools of fiction: it can merely provoke, satirize, and suggest; clearly, it cannot disprove in a purely analytic sense.

If the assessment of the novel's Freud critique must to some extent remain in the eye of the beholder, there can be little doubt as to the narrative's almost heavy-handed allusion to Freud. Anna imaginatively refashions the sickly and slight grocery clerk into an avenging black knight, creating a fairy tale with a thick network of Freudian motifs that would seem to rival any of Bruno Bettelheim's examples from *Kinder brauchen Märchen* (published as *The Uses of Enchantment*). Franz gives Anna a treasured cigarette, which she caresses and nuzzles as if it were a baby, stowing it on her person in a place her father would never think to violate (just below her breasts); but of course he does. Franz, "the noble knight" (*der edle Ritter*), declines the opportunity to elope quietly, insisting instead on the honor of ceremoniously beheading the father, which in turn triggers an additional Oedipal desire. Suddenly Franz feels impelled to bring "the father's red head" to mother (albeit to Anna's mother): "'To mother,' he says, 'she should also have some happiness.'"[61] Upon winning his "virgin" bride in this manner, Franz comments in a way that seems to exceed his own understanding: "Today . . . I'll carry you off back home."[62] But just as Canetti explicitly invokes the fairy tale atmosphere only to parody it, so too does he evoke the language and imagery of psychoanalysis only to undermine it.[63] For in the chapter's parting gambit, it becomes clear that the expectations aroused by these Freudian allusions are not only unfulfilled, but reversed. Pfaff's naked aggression fully suffices to motivate the unmistakable masochism of Anna's richly imagined revenge fantasy; we have little need for Freudian notions that posit masochism in pubescent girls and women as a product of the female Oedipus complex.[64] Franz's utility to Anna lies not in his function as father replacement, or even as erotic love object, but purely in his role as potential patricide. When we read "She wants to get a husband in order to get away from home,"[65] we fully realize that Anna is not just any teenage girl anxious to make her way in the adult world. Quite in contrast to the powerful black knight of her fantasy, the real Franz turns out to be a common thief who is thrown in jail, whence he is unable to perform his rescue function. Because he is impotent to deliver her from paternal harm, Anna dismisses Franz as immaterial to her real concern.[66]

If "The Good Father" disputes the dominant Freudian narrative on fathers and daughters, it does so without the intent of creating sustained sympathy for Anna, or for similarly abused girls, as an end in itself. Though aware that his narrative revision cast the daughter in a relatively more compassionate light, Canetti's aesthetics demand here as elsewhere a cool, unsentimental consideration of the issues at stake. By abjuring the aesthetics of identification, that is, by eschewing a lachrymose portrayal of the brutalized daughter, Canetti prevents us from "dissolving ourselves"—to echo Kien's fears about popular novels—in empathy for an Anna, who of course to some extent remains a comic cipher. Instead (and, like Brecht, Canetti saw this as an either/or situation), the novel's strikingly dispassionate depiction of father-daughter violence invites a response whose energies would not be discharged within the story, but directed outward to the world the novel seeks to engage. To put it simply: Anna's stark unreality contrasts productively with the reality of the social problems to which she points. In confronting Freud's "Dora" with his own Anna, Canetti strikes a blow at the explanatory power of the Oedipus complex, the very centerpiece of Freud's whole theory. Pfaff's sexual violence is undeniably real and inescapably "out there": "To be sure he took his stepdaughter off the bed and beat her bloody."[67] No less than Georg's neoempiricism and Kien's elitist conception of scholarship and idealist culture, psychoanalysis makes its appearance in *Auto-da-Fé* as a popular but fatally flawed brand of blindness to a world that will not be ignored.

Georg and Countertransference: The Machiavellian Analyst

The figure of Georg, the gynecologist turned psychiatrist, might seem at first glance the most obvious place to begin an investigation of the novel's engagement with Freud. But are we justified now in viewing Georg as a kind of Freudian analyst, especially in light of our prior association of him with the explicitly non-Freudian psychological movement known as neoempiricism? Can we have it both ways? Canetti's undogmatically and capaciously drawn figure does indeed evince several key Freudian concepts and practices, as we will see below; but we must keep in mind that Georg both evokes and exceeds this role. He is not merely a cipher, as in a *roman à clef*, for the psychoanalyst; as we have seen, he is a crystallization site for a whole cluster of cultural movements, including neoempiricism, primitivist "life philosophy" (*Lebensphilosophie*), and, yes, Freudian analysis as well. Though Canetti goes to some lengths to satirize the psychoanalyst as unacknowledged power broker—reprising one of his favorite themes—the parody ultimately functions to discredit Georg as the oracle of crowd theory. In other words, in this case Canetti actually *employs* Freudian notions, though only provisionally, in order to undermine Georg's pseudosolution to the crisis of modern culture.

The chapter that introduces us to Georg, "A Mad House" (*Ein Irrenhaus*), is laced with Freudian references, as perhaps any sustained treatment of psychology by 1930 would inevitably be. Georg's jealous assistants, for example, link their director's unorthodox methods and unbridled ambition to a disturbed childhood and in particular to a fear of sexual impotence.[68] Earlier in the novel, too, we notice the broad influence of popularized Freudian ideas in the comic portrayal of the wedding night—a subject to which Georg himself will later turn in an effort to analyze his brother. After the wedding ceremony, Therese produces the key, which Kien cannot find despite desperate fumbling in his pant pockets. She proceeds to dominate sexually, albeit unsuccessfully, in a manner that has led one critic (Foell) to view her as a "phallic mother." Kien clearly recognizes that his chief nuptial task (*"seine Aufgabe"*) is now to initiate sexual intercourse, and attempts to build up his courage to do so.[69] Ultimately, he reaches the conclusion that sexual intercourse, presumably by means of the Freudian "principle of constancy," will bring him relief from the nightmares he attributes to his abstemious lifestyle: "The bad dreams of these last days were doubtless connected with the exaggerated austerity of his life. Everything would be different now."[70] Thus, sex is for Kien a necessary evil, a kind of pressure release valve that will allow him to carry on his service to culture more efficiently.

Evoking similar notions of popularized Freudianism, Georg, on his way to Munich to aid his beleaguered brother, wonders what could possibly be ailing his virtually sexless older brother. Revealing the Freudian conception that personality disorders are rooted in the psychic management of sexual instincts, Georg queries: "What could be oppressing him, an almost sexless creature?"[71] Peter's apparent sexlessness only momentarily stumps the stellar psychiatrist, who quickly modifies his diagnosis to madness brought on by exaggerated repression (rather than absence) of sexuality: "Peter belongs in a lock-up facility. He has lived chastely for too long."[72] These and numerous other episodes that evoke the general atmosphere of Freudian psychology are more than witty and wicked instances of the novel's comic background music. Indeed, they set the stage and direct our attention to the question of Georg's relationship to psychoanalysis.

On closer consideration, however, we discover there is much that sets Georg apart from Freud, at least on the surface. Most important is Georg's conviction that his whole approach to psychology is fundamentally antibourgeois, not to mention his deepest desire to leave the mentally ill, as far as possible, in their state of intense and "authentic" (if psychotic) delirium. While some critics may wish to view precisely these characteristics as inverted references, respectively, to Freud's own pronounced political conservatism and to psychoanalysis's reputation as an essentially "bourgeois discipline,"[73] it may be more correct to say that it is specifically Georg's misplaced belief in his own radicalism that constitutes the parody.[74] That is, just as Freud fancied himself a bourgeois critic in certain matters of sexuality, he actually served to undergird that class at a deeper level. This aside, there is a more obvious point of contact with Freud: Georg's lauded form of treatment consists exclusively of the "talking cure." Gerald Stieg, at any rate, does not hesitate to refer to this practice as "Georg's psychoanalytic therapy" and to the practitioner himself as a "psychoanalyst."[75]

An example of Georg's "Freudian" approach can be gleaned from his attempt to cure Kien by taking him back to the origins of his misogyny in order then to rid him of this disturbance:

Georg noticed very well every time Peter's voice went sharp. It was enough that his thoughts returned to the woman upstairs. He had not said a word about her, but already in his voice there betrayed itself a screeching, shrill, incurable hatred . . . He must be induced to give vent to as much of his hatred as possible. If only he would simply retrace the events as they had appeared to him from their origins onwards in a simple narrative! Georg knew well how to play the part of the eraser in such a retrospect, and to wipe from the sensitive plate of memory all its traces.[76]

Here we see Georg intent upon helping Kien manage his irrational hatred not with drugs or electroshock therapy or even by means of incarceration (despite an earlier temptation to do just that), but by listening to and interpreting the stories of his patient. The very image of Georg as eraser (*Radiergummi*) may already contain the novel's caricature of this practice, yet "erasure" is not all that far from the term Anna O. would famously give to the Freudian talking cure: "chimney sweeping."[77] This attempt to have Peter "talk away" his problems[78] raises the question of Georg's overall track record with patient treatment, his own claims to unqualified success notwithstanding.

The hallmark of Georg's spectacular new treatment consists not merely in talking (and then erasing), but in his active encouragement of that central event in psychoanalytic therapy known as "transference." Freud once described transference as the therapeutic revival of "a whole series of psychological experiences . . . not as belonging to the past, but as applying to the person of the physician at the present moment."[79] This process of inappropriate projection onto the essentially unknown person of the psychoanalyst provides crucial insights into the patient's personal history and is considered to be indispensable to the psychoanalytic cure. Psychologist and Freud expert Stephen Frosh explains that "transference has increasingly come to be seen as the central element in the psychoanalytic situation, encouraged by the passivity and 'blank screen' behaviour of the analyst."[80]

Georg considers himself, as we observed above, to be precisely such a neutral recipient of his patients' manias, his preferred self-appellation being *eine spazierende Wachstafel* that passively registers only his patients' needs: "Instead of working over things or responding to them, he received them mechanically."[81] Canetti could hardly have devised an image more likely to conjure Freud's own figure for the properly objective and distant analyst. "The physician," Freud writes, "should be opaque to the patient and, like a mirror, show nothing but what is shown to him."[82] Though Georg's claim to objectivity and neutrality is ultimately belied, as we saw above, by his own behavior, his effort to engage his patients' fantasies and desires does evoke (even if it simultaneously misconstrues) the Freudian "reliance of analysts on making an alliance with the patient's ego."[83]

Notice in the following passage, part of which we have already visited in another context, how the encouragement of the patient's fantasy projections is intimately linked to the therapist's exercise of power. Here Georg, clothing himself in the narrator's voice, is describing his most promising patients, whom he (like Freud) would treat in his own apartment:

> There he would easily win, if he did not enjoy it already, the confidence of those who, towards anyone else, would hide behind the screen of their insanity. Kings he addressed reverently as Your Majesty; with Gods he would fall on his knees and fold his hands. Thus even the most sublime eminences stooped to him and went into particulars. He became their sole confidant, whom, from the moment they had recognized him, they would keep informed of the changes in their own spheres and seek his advice. He advised them with crystal cleverness, as though their wishes were his own, cautiously keeping their arms and their beliefs before his eyes . . . Was he not after all their chief minister, their prophet or their apostle, occasionally even their chamberlain?[84]

It hardly needs to be said that Georg, his self-image notwithstanding, hardly fulfills the psychoanalytic contract: rather than assisting his patients to resolve their conflicts, he actively encourages their delusions by taking on and playing out their fantasies. Without a doubt, Georg's evocation of transference simultaneously contravenes the fundamental Freudian precept barring analysts from abandoning their neutrality: "On no account must the analyst live up to the transference," writes Frosh, paraphrasing Freud's own warnings of 1915 contained in a paper titled "Observations on Transference Love": "every departure from analytic distance and the pure pursuit of truth supports the patient's resistances and makes the analytic work more difficult."[85]

The caricatured nature of this allusion to Freudian analysis may be held by some to exonerate authentically practiced psychoanalysis. But the opposite may in fact be true: For the caricature only draws out the structural imbalance endemic to the patient-analyst relationship. Frosh elucidates this inherent potential for abuse, of which Georg makes rich use: "[Psychoanalysis] accentuates the power of the therapist to such a degree that it appears to validate authoritarianism . . . The real distress engendered in the patient by experiences which s/he has undergone are taken up into the person of the analyst so that all reality is lost and everything is understood in terms of the transference relationship—an astonishing piece of megalomania, if nothing worse."[86] Canetti satirizes this aspect of analytic hubris in Georg's purported ability to cure schizophrenia precisely by hosting, as it were, the patient's rival personalities in his own consciousness: "The scientific world argued vigorously over his treatment of schizophrenia of the most varied kinds. If a patient, for instance, imagined himself to be two people who had nothing in common or who were in conflict with each other, Georg Kien adopted a method which had at first seemed very dangerous even to him: he made friends with both parties . . . Then he would proceed to the cure. In his own consciousness he would gradually draw the separate halves of the patient—as he embodied them—closer to each other, and thus gradually would rejoin them."[87] It does not much matter that the bulk of Freud's patients were neurotics, not psychotics like Georg's clientele. Nor is it ultimately important that Freud specifically cast doubt on the effectiveness of analysis for psychotics. For this caricature is clearly not drawn out of a concern for scrupulous fairness to Freud, but to ridicule the tyranny of the analyst. Indeed, Freud's own dictatorial certainty that Dora's adamant denials of the master's diagnosis were actually covert affirmations of his insights may not have been far from Canetti's mind.[88] The last sentence of the passage quoted above indulges in comic hyperbole, to be sure, yet it also expresses Canetti's conviction that psychoanalysis, authorized in this instance by the privilege of the all-powerful analyst, is complicit in the reduction of social to mental phenomena. The patient, after all, no longer even exists for Georg, except as a function of the analyst's consciousness. As in the case of Pfaff's attempt to subordinate Anna's existence to his own, we are meant to recognize psychoanalysis as a dubious accomplice in this process. Despite considerable liberties, then, Georg's "quite controversial" treatment captures rather effectively the problematic role assigned to the Freudian therapist, namely to "take up into the person of the analyst" (Frosh) all the patient's fantasies and desires in order then to assist in the resolution of psychic disturbances. It should come as no surprise, then, to learn that Canetti would later describe the psychoanalyst's "blank screen" behavior as "cold" and "power-hungry" and the analysand, conversely, as "helpless" and "exposed."[89] From this perspective, Georg's celebrated method of mending a split ego serves as a kind of cautionary tale about the potential for ontological reductionism implicit in the therapeutic relationship.

But Georg is not merely a walking illustration of the imbalance of power intrinsic to the transference phenomenon. He crosses the line and commits the cardinal psychoanalytic sin of countertransference in allowing his own response to one of his favorite patients to influence the treatment outcome of that patient. Jean Préval is one of the doctor's model patients, and as such serves well in characterizing Georg. The assistants at the psychiatric institute marvel at and envy their leader's ability to treat this particularly intractable case. Georg's phenomenal success consists of nothing more than encouraging Jean's delusion that his absent wife is indeed present, when she has in fact disappeared long ago, having run off with a young officer. Georg's encouragement is clearly the key factor in the diurnal conjuring of an imaginary Jeanne: "'But Jean, she's in the net, don't you see her?'" the analyst would insist; and, lo: "He was always right. His friend opened his mouth and look, his wife was there."[90] Although the assistants try the very same trick ("*die Zauberformel*"), only the trusted Georg can fulfill this fantasy: "Every day he helped Jean produce her."[91]

While this may already constitute psychoanalytic malpractice, it is not yet countertransference. This first occurs at a point in the novel celebrated by other critics as Georg's eloquent disquisition on the futility of individuality and the inevitability of the crowd—a passage that, as we noted above, has consistently been seen as an expression of Canetti's own views on the crowd, and therefore has endowed Georg with an ill-deserved authority. Basking in his ability to mediate the multitudinous roles imagined for him by his psychotic patients, and despairing at his assistants' constitutional incapacity to do so, this preeminent psychiatrist is inspired to explain what distinguishes him from these mundane colleagues. Georg decries their overly restrictive, unidimensional psyches ("*ihre flachen Seelen*"). What these overly cultivated apprentices refuse to acknowledge, claims Georg, and here he is echoing the *Lebensphilosophie* that first converted him to psychiatry, is the primal drive toward the crowd: "Of that far deeper and most essential motive force of history, the desire of men to rise into a higher type of animal, into the mass, and to lose themselves in it so completely as to forget that *one* man ever existed, they [the assistants] had no idea. For they were educated, and education is in itself a *cordon sanitaire* for the individual against the mass in his own soul."[92] As we noted above when we first began to glimpse the fundamental similarity between Georg and Kien, Georg's espousal of the crowd is calculated initially to evoke readerly sympathy. Not only is the bearer of this message the novel's first — and only — really attractive character, but the message itself seems correctly to diagnose Kien's own abuse of high culture, namely as a "Festungsgürtel" (fortress belt) against a feared modernity envisioned by the elitist professor precisely as the province of the masses. Kien's fortress-like library, the walled-up windows of which are meant to keep the world at bay, is only the most obvious of symptoms and symbols in this regard. Add to this Canetti's later analysis of crowds — in pointed but unacknowledged opposition to Freud — as fundamentally positive human groupings fulfilling primal urges, and one can easily grasp the temptation of so much Canetti scholarship to view Georg as the mouthpiece of the author of *Crowds and Power*.

This view, actively encouraged by the novel on the one hand, is substantially qualified by the very context of these remarks, thus creating a stimulating narrative dynamic, a push and pull that makes us aware of our own readerly desire inherent in the hermeneutic process. Some critics, beginning with Barnouw, had early on begun to suspect that Georg is hardly the dispassionate voice of reason, as we have noted. Yet apart from what has been said about Georg's questionable practices and general unreliability elsewhere in the novel, no one has yet observed how the very passage that is supposed to elevate Georg's trustworthiness as bearer of crowd theory actually undermines his status considerably. For it is within the context of an egregious instance of countertransference onto his star patient Jean that Georg delivers this vaunted soliloquy on the crowd.

Madness, says Georg, is attributable to an untenable repression of the masses within. In what sounds like an instinctual theory à la Freud — substitute "libido" for "crowd" and it would be hard to tell the difference — our psychiatrist postulates the following: "Countless people go mad because the crowd in them is particularly strongly developed and can get no satisfaction. In no other way did he explain himself and his own activity. Once he had lived for his private tastes, his ambition and women; now his one desire was perpetually to lose himself. In this activity he came nearer to the thoughts and wishes of the crowd, than did those other individuals who surrounded him."[93] Whereas Georg had previously claimed to be interested also in historically real crowds—"*die Wirksamkeit der Masse in der Geschichte*"[94]—he ends up interiorizing this social phenomenon. Like his philologist brother, Georg's advocacy of grand explanatory theories turns out to serve his immediate (and, as we will presently see, changing) needs. Here Georg is claiming to have successfully circumvented the dangers of an erupting crowd by assimilating the porous, malleable self he so valued in the gorilla man; in other words, by his therapeutic practice of "perpetually losing himself." We might note in passing that this conception implies a humorous reversal in which patients serve as fodder for the analyst's own self-therapy—a preparatory step in the process of countertransference that will follow. But at this point, which represents the grand finale of Georg's oration about crowds, what is essential to notice is that the crowd has become an intrapsychic phenomenon. Precisely by playing out the many roles assigned him, above all by successfully mediating the presence of the spectral Jeanne that inaugurates this discourse on the crowd in the first place, Georg claims to have appeased his own "inner crowd." Like the psychotic patients he treats, Georg has become the crowd, and therefore need not fear its vengeance.

All such "philosophical" musings on crowd theory are of course bracketed by the story of the unfortunate village blacksmith turned mass murderer, Jean Préval, whom Georg approaches once again on evening rounds. But Georg's fortunes have suddenly turned: his assistants are no longer enamored or even jealous of their leader, and the once fawning patients have become indifferent: "A sad day, he said softly to himself . . . He always breathed in the stream of other people's feelings. Today he could feel nothing around him, only the heavy air."[95] In this depressive mood, Georg encounters Jean's relentless and now tiresome preoccupation with his long-since-departed wife. Reminded of his own flagging marriage—Georg will soon confess: "My wife bores me"[96]—he mounts the countertransference. Annoyed specifically by the connubial loyalty he observes in his patient, Georg takes his revenge on the imaginary wife Jeanne: "'Hit her over the head,' said Georg, he was sick and tired with this thirty-two years of faithfulness. Jean hit her hard and performed the screams of help for her."[97] Though Jean's behavior is initially no different today than on any other day, his request elicits not the blank screen analytic behavior even Georg sometimes musters, but functions instead to trigger a crisis in the analyst's own life. Georg's cherished self-image, the very therapeutic structure, let us recall, that permits him to host his inner crowd and cure his patients, is now endangered: "Besides, the wax tablet was melting."[98] Now not even indulging in a fantasy of his own future fame can cheer him up, for he must face the fact that such reveries only delay what he desperately wants to avoid entirely, namely going home to his wife: "Why don't I go home? Because my wife's there. She wants love . . . The wax tablet weighed heavy."[99]

This instance of imaginary wife-beating probably has very little to do with raising readers' consciousness about actual domestic violence, particularly since Jean himself supplies the screams for his imagined victim. Yet it represents an important point of convergence for the themes we have been thus far considering. The only Jeanne we know, and the one Jean batters, is after all largely the product of the omnipotent analyst. As such, she underscores her creator's depoliticizing tendency, already in evidence during the interpolated monologue on crowd theory. In deploying "Jeanne," Georg clearly employs his power to enforce the internalization of a problem enmeshed in the iconic events of economic modernity. Though trapped now in psychotic delusions, Jean Préval's woes originate of course in his economic displacement. As village blacksmith, he has been ruined by the arrival of automobiles. "His wife, after a few weeks of acute poverty, could no longer endure her life with him and ran off with a sergeant."[100] Though he claims to want to find the actual wife, Georg is constitutionally ill equipped to do so; as a psychologist he is disinclined to attend to the socioeconomic causes of his patient's symptoms.[101] Rather than persuade Jean to learn a new trade more promising in the late industrial period, Georg encourages him to see himself not as socially embedded, but as an eternal type, that is, as the wronged and vengeful husband from ancient mythology, Vulkan, who catches his wife in the act of infidelity. Alluding to Freud's own well-known love of ancient mythology, and his tendency to build psychoanalysis around archetypical situations prefigured in myth, Canetti endows Georg with a similar passion. This is why Georg, even when he speaks of Jeanne as a real-world woman, incites his star patient to imagine his regained wife as Venus, trapped in Vulkan's incriminating and punishing net.[102] Though a specific act of countertransference triggers the intertextual connection to Freud, what is principally on trial here is Georg's larger transference of a fundamentally social problem—one pointedly rooted in the industrial dislocations of the early part of this century—to the realm of fantasy and universal myth. At issue, by extension, is Georg's entire conversion to psychiatry. Recall that he then claimed to leave behind the debauchery of easy sex and anesthetizing French literature, a kind of *"schöngeistige Literatur"* he felt papered over the cracks of the real world, in order honestly to confront a more complex and diverse reality. In his treatment of Jean Préval we see that Georg's earlier commitment to multiplicity and difference is belied by his method of subsuming individual cases under prefabricated mythological constructs, a charge that precisely coincides with one of Canetti's central and repeated critiques of psychoanalysis as master narrative—"the aridity of a single theory that would apply to all human beings."[103] In the end, then, Georg's apparent abandonment of gynecology in favor of psychiatry proves to be a homecoming—itself a kind of humorous Freudian allusion. Yet as much as Canetti may wish to loosen the grip of Freud on the popular imagination, it is noteworthy that the novel also capitalizes on this widespread cultural narrative. For it is partly due to the unwitting help of an admittedly bowdlerized Freud that we come to see Georg's crowd theory as the opportunistic cant it essentially is.

In the Termite Colony

Alluding to the extremely popular *Civilization and Its Discontents,* Canetti has his fictional Freudian analyst concoct and apply his own, roughly parallel, account of the rise of society and culture. The context of Georg's tale of the termite colony, which is meant to coax Kien into revealing his own libidinal drives, is at least as important as the story itself. Rather than rendering Kien a cooperative patient, however, Georg's efforts only incite the learned scholar to ever greater heights of misogynist erudition. At the heart of this sibling rivalry, in which Kien ultimately gains the upper hand, are competing notions of culture. Kien's rebuttal of Georg's termite parable illustrates the shortcomings of the Freudian account: culture is not so much the achieved *product* of sublimation, we learn, but the *site and record* of ongoing conflict.

Though Freud had already rehearsed his fundamental ideas on societal ontogeny in *Totem and Taboo* (1912–13), these views received fresh articulation and widespread circulation in 1930, the year Canetti began work on the novel. "Freud could take comfort in his book's astonishing popularity," notes Gay; "within a year, its first edition of 12,000, exceptionally large for a work of Freud's, was sold out."[104] Georg's anthropomorphic tale, which envisions a society founded upon the renunciation of the sexual drive, could thus scarcely have failed to evoke Freud at this time. Reflecting his primitivist orientation and the influence of his guru (the gorilla man), Georg displaces his story onto the animal kingdom. The very choice of termites seems calculated, as Stieg has suggested, to evoke Freud; for at one point in *Civilization* Freud muses about termites as having achieved an ideal state of stable sublimation that forever eludes humans.[105] Though Freud distinguished human from termite society, he simultaneously presents it as an ideal of sorts and therefore comparable in some respects. Georg's humorous explosion of the Freudian metaphor affords us the critical perspective we have come to expect in Canetti. Above all, the use of termites permits Canetti the opportunity of targeting one of the weakest links in Freudian theory, namely a notoriously unspecific theory of drives.[106] Contrary to Stieg, who argues that Canetti's cultural critique actually rests upon the Freudian theory of psychic economy, we will see how the novel parodies this foundational conception of drives.[107]

But first let us have the tale—or at least the first half—in Georg's own words:

> Even some insects have it better than we do. One or a very few mothers bring into being the entire race. The rest remain underdeveloped. Is it possible to live at closer quarters than the termites do? What a terrifying accumulation of sexual stimuli such a stock would produce—if the creatures still possessed their sexuality! They do not possess it; and have the related instincts only in small quantities. Even what little they have, they fear. When they swarm, at which period thousands, nay millions, are destroyed apparently without reason, I see in this a release of the amassed sexuality of the stock. They sacrifice a part of their number, in order to preserve the rest from the aberrations of love. The whole stock would go aground on this question of love, were it once to be permitted.[108]

While broadly alluding to Freud, this is clearly a rather imperfect clone of that master narrative. Yet it is precisely in those ways in which Georg's tale alters its original that it becomes interesting as critique. Repression and sublimation are for Freud the *sine qua non* of human society, whereas the instincts of termites represent unalterable, genetically determined behavior patterns. A termite's sociability is as predetermined as a moth's attraction to light; there is never a question of their forgetting or remembering a sexuality sacrificed for the benefit of society. The pseudoscience again pokes through as we observe Georg's unabashed anthropomorphism: the termites, we are told, fear even the residual sexual instinct still in their possession.

Canetti's use of the termite parable could be dismissed as another instance of the novel's "hyperbolic parody," a perhaps gratuitous burlesque on contemporary ideas. But to do so would be to fail to grasp the way in which this perhaps illegitimate transposition nevertheless raises valid and fundamental questions about Freud's theory of drives. Freud of course observed a distinction between hardwired animal instincts (what Laplanche calls the "zoological" viewpoint) and those human drives (*Triebe*) deemed to be malleable and redirectable to other ends;[109] yet Freud himself remained unclear on this crucial point. In having Georg espouse the patently absurd view that termites can somehow manage their own instincts, Canetti raises a serious set of questions regarding the process in humans. What is the domain of the "Instinkt" and what that of the "Trieb"? Where does biological determinism leave off, and where (and how) can analysis intervene in the economy of drives? If the actual determinants of sublimation remain shrouded in uncertainty, then what can be said about the civilization to which these repressed drives have supposedly given rise? These are some unresolved and perhaps unresolvable aporias of psychoanalysis implied in Georg's blatantly incommensurate example.

The parody achieves sharper focus in the second half of the story, in which Georg's fixation on a potential termite bacchanalia reflects his own unabated prurient interests as much as it continues to assault the Freudian notion of drives. Tellingly, the hard-wired *Instinkt* we noted above metamorphoses into the *Trieb* just at the point when the termites begin to act like the humans Georg really has in mind. The following passage, which in the novel follows immediately upon the one quoted above, begins as pure speculation but modulates by way of the historical present verb tense into a very immediate scenario:

> I can imagine nothing more poignant than an orgy in a colony of termites. The creatures forget — a colossal recollection has seized hold of them — what they really are, the blind cells of a fanatic whole. Each will be himself, it begins with a hundred or a thousand of them, the madness spreads, *their* madness, a mass madness, the soldiers abandon the gates, the whole mound burns with unsatisfied love, they cannot find their partners, they

have no possibility of sex, the noise, the excitement far greater than anything usual, attracts a storm of ants; through the unguarded gates their deadly enemies press in, what soldier thinks of defending himself, they only want love; and the colony might have lived for all eternity—that eternity for which we all long—dies, dies of love, of that drive [*Trieb*] through which we, mankind, prolong our existence! A sudden reversal of the wisest into the most foolish.[110]

This "sudden reversal" dramatizes the conflict inherent in the Freudian explanation of culture: in so far as we are civilized at all, we are doomed to unhappiness. Georg's specter of the advance of the killer ants may distort the threat (since Freud did not envision the peril as coming from without), but it does so in a manner that draws our attention to the fundamental trade-off implicit in the Freudian model of repression. If the termites seek to fulfill their deep sexual urges, this leads inevitably to social disintegration and certain death. Frosh could be speaking about Georg's make-believe termites, but he is of course commenting on Freud's view of civilization when he observes: "Before society there is only the unremitting and potentially calamitous libertarianism of the instincts; as soon as these instincts become bridled, society is formed... The theory that society is ineluctably opposed to individuality is one of the most pessimistic strands of thought associated with the bourgeois era. For Freud, the passions of the individual were primordial and dangerous, the work of civilisation being to control them—a justifiable work in the interests of the perpetuation of human existence."[111]

It is not merely the termite story that mocks Freud's global explication of society and culture, it is Georg himself. He has positioned himself, as we recently saw, as the novel's bold proponent of the crowd, as the sworn enemy of an isolationist, overindividuated cultivation that insulates us from our deepest "crowd drives." In pointed contrast to his brother, Georg anoints himself—to borrow the title of Ernst Toller's well-known Weimar-era play—the novel's great "*Masse Mensch*" (crowd man). Here we catch him in the act of donning yet another, ill-fitting pseudophilosophical, hat. As the "Freudian" teller of the termite tale, he espouses a view quite incompatible with the very recently and earnestly espoused belief that the so-called crowd instinct is our deepest drive. With his claim that the sexual drive is both primordial and, in its naked quest for fulfillment, inherently opposed to social organization, he has clearly reversed himself. Whereas the "mass drive" (*Massentrieb*) made its appearance just a few pages prior as itself a kind of libido, somehow both mankind's first cause and destiny, here the sexual drive emerges as a decidedly less reliable friend of the "crowd." It functions as a force for social cohesion only as long as it is bound by sublimation. But Georg suggests that it is only a matter of time until it emerges unshackled and destructive. It will erupt even amidst a species as sexless as termites, and, by extension, within his "virtually sexless" (*beinah geschlechtslos*) elder brother; and in this push for erotic requital it operates (as Freud had argued) as a virulent solvent on social bonds. If this turnabout has eluded some critics, it is because Georg— no less than Pfaff—is a great manipulator of language. This individualistic drive for sexual gratification that dissolves the group into pleasure-seeking monads becomes within the space of a sentence a "mass hysteria" (*Massenwahn*), a term that may mask the otherwise blatant inconsistency with his previous position. Georg, it turns out, really is the protean player (*Schauspieler*) Kien accuses him of being; in championing a roughly Freudian view of culture, he is now simply following the latest fad.

All the pseudoscientific jargon notwithstanding, Georg was never really talking about instinctual theory per se, but about women. Freud simply presented Georg the opportunity to dress up the misogyny he hoped would please his older brother in the garb of a respectable scholarly illustration. Georg admits as much when, just before he deploys the termite tale, he sees as his primary mission the task of removing Therese: "Evidently [Kien] expected Georg to take her away."[112] By way of introduction to the termite parable, Georg remarks: "'I believe ... that you overestimate the importance of women. You take them too seriously, you think they are human beings like us. I see in women merely a passing necessary evil. Even some insects have it better than we do.'"[113] The subsequent story—or at least the first half, which holds out the prospect of firmly repressed sexuality—is meant to appease if not win over his brother; for the termites have in this segment already overcome this "necessary evil." Kien refuses to take the point, however, and instead launches a tirade against the creation of woman, which he concludes with the lamentation, "What misery for all time!"[114] This, in turn, provides Georg the opportunity to clarify the point of his parable: "Why for all time? We were just speaking a moment ago about the termites who have overcome sex. It is therefore neither an inevitable nor an invincible evil."[115]

In the second half of the story, which ostensibly represents a fundamental reversal, it remains clear that "sexuality" (*das Geschlecht*) is not to be read as libidinal drives in general, but more specifically as "woman." If the first half of the story functions as a carrot, the second half is meant as a stick. Even before he begins the story, Georg is evidently frustrated with his brother's unwillingness to submit to therapy. For Georg cannot perform his chimney-sweeping function unless Kien cooperates in revealing the source of his troubles with Therese. This is the passage, noted above, where Georg offers to play the eraser, "if only Kien would simply retrace the events... narratively back to their origin!"[116] The specter of the doomed termite orgy is Georg's threat of the return of the repressed, a warning he explicitly couches as the (otherwise unmotivated) burning of Kien's library. Submit to my therapy, Georg is saying, or suffer a similarly destructive fate. In denying the applicability of the termite allegory (and its implicit threat), Kien underscores the fact that he and Georg are talking about women and not sexual drives.[117] Spare me your idle threats, Kien is saying, for I have already killed off the woman at the root of my woes: "'Of my own free will, alone, leaning on no one—I had not even an accessory—I have liberated myself from a weight, a burden, a living death, a rind of accursed granite. Where would I be if I had waited for you?'"[118] Georg's termite parable is thus dismissed as superfluous. Kien has no need of grand psychosocial theories, for he has tended to the concrete problem in his own immediate vicinity.

Have the Kien brothers, in their predisposition to see women as the seat of sexuality and therefore as the real threat to culture, misread Freud? Not entirely. For while Freud intoned in *Civilization and Its Discontents* that "it is impossible to overlook the extent to which civilization is built upon a renunciation of instinct,"[119] he simultaneously succumbed to a tendency to identify instinct with women and the work of sublimation with men. "Women represent the sexual impulse," explains Frosh; "more prosaically, they are always trying to reclaim their menfolk from the clutches of the work of building culture (which forces men [according to Freud] to 'carry out instinctual sublimations of which women are little capable') into their isolated family units. Hence, civilisation opposes women by the same principle that it opposes love."[120] While the novel's parody certainly extends to this instance of slippage in Freud's own work—about which Freudian revisionists have had a good deal to say—it takes primary aim at the more popular Freudian reception. For it is within this larger orbit that popularizations, like Georg's termite narrative, would commingle Freudian "science" with deeply ingrained cultural prejudice. Here Canetti shows how the language of biology and positivistic inquiry could be used to camouflage if not justify real-world aggression toward women.

This is the cultural malaise with which Canetti confronts Freudian social psychology, and he does so through the improbable mouthpiece of Kien himself. By this point in the novel—we are just short of the comic resolution in which Georg buys the cooperation of Pfaff and Therese—it no longer matters that the protagonist himself is discredited. For the truth of this cultural diagnosis depends not on the benighted Kien, but on the data he musters, which we recognize as existing independently of the fictional novel. At the outset of this diatribe, we may be inclined to dismiss Kien's claim that "all really great thinkers are convinced of the worthlessness of women"[121] as the bluster of a madman. But just as Georg often inadvertently makes his case, Kien manages to give us pause, despite himself. When at first he cites Confucius and Buddha, we may still cling to the belief that we are in the hands of a merely idiosyncratic Orientalist. Yet Kien soon demonstrates that he has plenty of other illustrations at his disposal. "I will prove to you that all women deserve hate," he says to Georg. "You think I am expert only on the Orient. The proofs he needs, he's taken from his own area of specialty—or so you thought. I shall tear the blue down from the sky for you, and I will tell no lies. Truths, beautiful, hard, pointed truths, truths of every size and shape, truths of feeling and truths of understanding, even though in your case only your feelings function, you woman."[122]

Indeed, as Kien is able to pluck his "proofs" so readily from ancient Greek mythology and philosophy, and then quote whole passages from Homer in support of his case, not to mention his citation of the *Nibelungenlied,* Michelangelo's Sistine murals, Thomas Aquinas, Thomas More, a foray into ancient history, and so forth, it gradually becomes clear that this is no longer merely a case of private dementia. A symptom of the very cultural malady he illustrates, Kien powerfully demonstrates not "that all women deserve hate," but the extent to which misogyny has been a constituent element of the cultural canon. The picture we gain here is one of culture as a chauvinistic semiotic battlefield, not the product of successfully sublimated libido. The violence we witnessed in the single case of Anna is here multiplied in the imagination of artists and philosophers, and given high cultural standing in the process. Kien does not cite Freud in this misogynist pantheon; he is far too past-minded to take notice of this newcomer. But the novel does: not for promoting the kind of rabid hatred that Kien spews forth, but for propagating a grand theory that is at once amenable to this age-old prejudice and simultaneously diverts our attention from it. Though Freud knew of real-world violence—he famously sought to explain the barbarism of World War I—his psychological model would emphasize violence as intrasubjective and prior to the benefits of civilization. In one of the greatest, if bleakest, surveys of world literature and culture, *Auto-da-Fé* seems intent upon redirecting our attention to the fact that violence occurs within and in the name of civilization, as well as to the fact that the object of that violence is not in the first place some amorphously defined drives, but fellow human beings.

Rejection and Displacement: Freud as Foil

David Roberts asserted as recently as 1996 that "the rejection of psychoanalysis, fuelled by Canetti's encounter with and direct experience of the crowd, is already the driving impulse of his early novel, *Auto-da-Fé*."[123] While the foregoing has been concerned precisely to show in some detail how this "driving impulse" determines the particular shape of this complex novel, Roberts's thesis had to wait for verification until we could move beyond the assumption that Canetti's two principal works, *Auto-da-Fé* and *Crowds and Power*, respond to this psychoanalytic impulse in the same manner. Reading *Auto-da-Fé* as a kind of literary encryption of *Crowds and Power* has actually tended to emarginate Freud from the discussion of the novel; for Georg can hardly be seen as the simultaneous bearer of Canetti's truth *and* of Freud's error. This, too, was to prove a pitfall for Roberts, whose laudable impulse to align these two works vis-à-vis Freud results in the less than convincing proposition that Georg's crowd theory encapsulates a kind of alternate, group psychology that contrasts favorably with Freud's untenable individual psychology.[124] This simply entails too much reading backward and fails to respect the novel in its own right.

Looking back at the novel's literary engagement with Freud, we perceive thoroughgoing negation rather than the positive "counter image" of society Roberts would see in the novel. Now there can be no question of Freud receiving a fair hearing in *Auto-da-Fé*. Canetti's selection of recognizably Freudian notions, though hardly capricious, is undoubtedly polemic in that these ideas make their appearance only to be discarded as socially naive. In "The Good Father" we were reminded of psychoanalysis's predilection to psychologize real-world brutality; and in the person of Georg we noted an associated tendency to discredit socioeconomic determinants (e.g., the root causes of poor Jean Préval's misfortune) in favor of intrapsychic and mythological accounts. Similarly, the ultimate and unexpected applicability of Georg's termite parable to his elder brother's deeply sexist and isolationist practice of high culture illustrated the problematic limits of Freud's group psychology qua social theory. *Auto-da-Fé* thus echoes a standard critique of psychoanalysis's introverted gaze—though, given the novel's chronological priority, it would of course be more correct to say that these subsequent critics echo Canetti.[125] Hermann Broch perceptively observed that the novel leaves only destruction in its wake; it does not rebuild on the site of its ruin. Broch's comment is no less apropos of the novel's repudiation of Freud than any other system of ideas or set of cultural practices treated in this study. "There is something uncompromising about it that one has to respect," Broch observes. "But does that mean that you've given up hope? Does it mean that you yourself cannot find the way out, or does it mean that you are in doubt altogether about such a way out?"[126]

Broch did not live long enough to get the answer to his question, for the "way out" he sought but clearly missed in the novel would not emerge for another thirty years, that is, until the publication of *Crowds and Power* in 1960. It is tempting to say that, by viewing Freud as the unacknowledged *agon* motivating both works, the latter study presents the answer to the question posed by the novel. But this would simplify the way in which *Crowds and Power* makes its own complex and ambitious case against Freud with the quite different analytical tools available to a writer of nonfiction. Despite significant differences, it is nevertheless arresting to note how similar both works are in their general approach to Freud. Indeed, Adorno could be speaking of the novel when he says to Canetti: "Your critique seems to me to be extremely fruitful and correct in many points, for the very reason that Freud's basic tendency to replace the theory of society by individual psychology extended to the collectivity leads him time and again to the invariant fundamental quanta of the unconscious, neglecting essential historical modifications. As a result his social psychology remains somewhat abstract."[127] In the novel, Canetti was primarily concerned with clearing the way for further inquiry, that is, with negation, but not because he wished to promote a nihilistic worldview, as Peter Russell would famously accuse him. Freud's widespread acceptance, Canetti complained, simply led to complacency and to a dampening of intellectual curiosity. "The psychoanalytic epidemic had made advances," Canetti laments. "The most astounding things were occurring in the world, but it was always the same, arid background against which they placed these events. They spoke of these things and considered them explained, and the phenomena were no longer surprising. Where thinking should have *commenced,* there croaked instead an impudent choir of frogs."[128]

With *Crowds and Power* Canetti fulfills the very agenda he set forth in the novel. By then it was no longer enough to show the insufficiency of Freudian ideas, confronting them with stubborn facts of social reality. Now that he had killed off father Freud, he would replace him. Significantly, Canetti begins his study with the crowd (*"die Masse"*), viewing it as a fundamentally positive unit of social organization. The *sine qua non* of the crowd is an elemental human experience Canetti labels "discharge" (*Entladung*), which engenders a foundational sense of equality. "Before this the crowd doesn't really exist, it is the discharge which actually first constitutes it. This is the moment in which all who belong to the crowd rid themselves of their differences and feel as equals."[129] All subsequent egalitarian social theories, Canetti maintains, derive their power from the discharge phenomenon: "All demands for justice, all theories of equality draw their energy in the final analysis from this experience of equality, which everyone knows in his/her own way from the crowd."[130] Canetti very likely chose the term *Entladung* specifically to challenge—or dislodge—Freud's notion of psychic *"Abfuhr"* (discharge). For Canetti posits a fundamental, positive value to the individual's relationship to social organization in implicit contrast to Freud's notion of social groupings as the deeply conflicted by-product of libidinal sublimation. Society, in other words, is not a necessary evil (as in the Freudian schema), but a central good, albeit one eminently corruptible by the abuse of power.

Equally important was the need to dismantle and replace *the* central Freudian concept, namely the Oedipus complex. At Adorno's prodding, Canetti admitted that it was his ambition to retire the ill-defined Freudian concept, which he refered to as "identification," and replace it with his own notion of "transformation" (*Verwandlung*), a concept that allows for growth and development rather than the foreordained replay of the Oedipal conflict. Aware of the centrality of his own (and of the rival Freudian) concept, Canetti vowed to return to this issue in a second volume of *Crowds and Power* that never appeared in print during his lifetime. As his title (*Masse und Macht*) promises, Canetti lavishes a great deal of attention on the subject of power, espousing the proposition that violence and aggression are not primarily intrapsychic, but intersubjective, phenomena. Power circulates by way of "commands" (*Befehle*), which leave behind damaging "thorns" (*Stachel*).[131] This curiously mechanistic conception of power leaves no doubt in the reader's mind that violence breeds violence. Like Freud, Canetti acknowledges the profound influence of childhood experience in later adult life; but unlike Freud, Canetti is specifically worried that vulnerable children will become the repositories of thorns, which will in turn only lead to another cycle of violence in the next generation, when the victimized children become perpetrating adults—this time with them as perpetrators— later on in life. Guilt is redefined not as a function of Oedipal desires or as a response to the primordial crime of killing the father, but as the consequence of the misapplication of power. In case after case, Freud provides the antimodel, a kind of invisible grid that explains the content and structure of *Crowds and Power.*

This is not the place either to fully summarize or to critically assess the ideas put forth in *Crowds and Power.*[132] Yet enough may have been said to demonstrate that this work contains a positive fund of ideas meant to displace those of Freud and others. While there are clear and undeniable continuities between the novel and anthropological study at the level of fundamental attitude, there is much in the latter work that is not even hinted at in the former. The novel whets our appetite for the subsequent study by re-creating the curiosity Canetti claimed was destroyed by reverential and derivative Freudian disciples—followers not unlike Georg's fawning assistants at the asylum. But it is simply untenable to claim that those innovative ideas central to *Crowds and Power* ("discharge," "transformation," "command," "thorn," and so on) are present or even vaguely discernible in *Auto-da-Fé*. Having read about the brutal Pfaff and the abused Anna, we may appreciate better Canetti's later concern for children as particularly susceptible to becoming labile thorn repositories, but that is all. Canetti did not spend thirty years reformulating ideas that were essentially already complete in the novel. Moreover, the fictional Georg is not only *not* an illustration of the later work, he is a sometime exemplum of precisely that which *Crowds and Power* will reject. In stark contrast to this study's valorization of society, the novel depicts a world in which society seems dangerously to inhere in the minds of monomaniacal figures—a true "*Welt im Kopf*" (World in the

Head), to borrow the title from the novel's third book. In short, *Auto-da-Fé* speaks eloquently and hilariously about false approaches to the social, but is ignorant of the social concepts Canetti will propound in *Crowds and Power*.

All of which suggests that the most influential branch of scholarship on the novel has got it backward. It is not *Crowds and Power* that provides the theoretical key to the novel, but the novel that illuminates the concerns of the later study. The implications may prove mutually liberating: *Crowds and Power* can be released from its narrow literary-critical function and the novel can be further exposed to critical approaches at variance with Canetti's own views. This is hardly a radical proposition; for it was Goethe who long ago suggested that we approach a writer's work genetically, that is, by respecting the chronology and context of its genesis. Ironically, we owe this insight on the Canetti oeuvre to a man whose determinative influence Canetti never fully acknowledged — namely to Sigmund Freud.

Up to this point in this study, we have drawn upon an array of Weimar-era texts and contexts to illuminate the concerns of this ambitious novel. It may be helpful now to see how modernist and antimodernist critical paradigms of the post–World War II era can help us understand why *Auto-da-Fé* remains virtually in a class of its own, despite many obvious points of contact with literary high modernism. What is it about the novel — and the critics — that enforced this state of literary segregation? And in what sense might we think of this novel as an intentional boundary or endpoint to this movement?

6 Neither Adorno nor Lukács
Canetti's Analytic Modernism

A Productive Error

James McFarlane concludes his investigation into "The Mind of Modernism" with a panegyric to that veritable bible of the movement, T. S. Eliot's *The Waste Land,* which is said to embody a "peculiarly Modernist kind of vision." In this account, which focuses almost exclusively on intellectual history, literary modernism emerges as much more than an effect, or register, of the demise of traditional culture and the rise of the modern sciences. On the contrary, McFarlane's modernism is a central galvanizing agent of signal cultural importance—high modernism, in other words. Though he pays lip service to less lofty constructions,[1] McFarlane ultimately comes down squarely on the side of modernism as bearer of cultural coherence rather than mere barometer of fragmentation: "The defining thing in the Modernist mode is not so much that things fall *apart* but that they fall *together* . . . In Modernism, the centre is seen exerting not a centrifugal but a centripetal force; and the consequence is not disintegration but (as it were) superintegration."[2] This rather sanguine view, which ascribes an enormous synthesizing task to the modernist poet, was bound to find verification in *The Waste Land,* if only because this very reading of modernism is largely derived from Eliot himself. Less self-evident, however, is McFarlane's curious effort to fit *Auto-da-Fé*—which he supposes to be "an unexpected commentary" on Eliot—into this high modernist schema.[3] Though ultimately rather forced, this conjunction of Eliot with Canetti is fortunate in that it provides the opportunity to consider *Auto-da-Fé* within postwar discussions of American and European modernism, adding a context to Canetti's novel that not only has thus far been lacking in the critical literature, but one that illuminates the novel's distinctive traits particularly effectively. In resurrecting the so-called pretheoretical literary landscape of the novel's rediscovery in the early 1960s, we will come to see how *Auto-da-Fé* rather strenuously defies the affiliation

McFarlane so casually asserts. Sharing neither Adorno's marked sympathy for the epistemologically humbled modernist subject, nor meeting Lukács's demand for realistic depiction of an "objective totality," Canetti's novel fell between the chairs of the regnant literary paradigms and was thus destined to remain an outsider and a kind of curiosity until new views of modernism (and postmodernism) came into play.

Though this study has thus far profited precisely from these newer and more capacious orientations toward modernism, we now consciously step backward in time, a conceit that will help us appreciate *Auto-da-Fé* against the backdrop of the more familiar lights of high modernism. Since a discussion of the full range of modernist novels would be impossible — or amount to another book altogether — I will content myself instead with an ideal construct such as McFarlane himself provides. In leaping from the deeply conservative Eliot to the leftists Adorno and Lukács (with whom I am primarily concerned) we risk losing, one might object, high modernism's vast apolitical middle ground. Yet, given Adorno's propensity for cooptation by New Criticism, this need not be the case, as I argue below. Furthermore, by focusing on the modernist "epistemological shift" as the philosophical touchstone of modernism, as Randall Stevenson proposes,[4] we may indeed find ourselves in a position to capture a considerable number of high modernist works within a single conceptual framework. Additionally, though the texts customarily gathered under this rubric present a rich and apparently contradictory cluster of stances toward modernity,[5] they are unified, as Jameson argues, by their attempt to "manage" modernity, a strategy that includes constructing alternate aesthetic worlds, and one that certainly unites thinkers as different as Eliot and Adorno.[6] Lukács's self-imposed admonition, which he intones at the outset of his influential essay "The Ideology of Modernism," applies no less to this undertaking: "Of course, dogmas of this kind are only really viable in philosophical abstraction, and then only with a measure of sophistry."[7] In moving toward a new appreciation of the relationship of *Auto-da-Fé* to its modernist cousins, we will periodically cast a glance back on the foregoing study. In the end, we will see how *Auto-da-Fé* mounts a remarkable protest from within, announcing, as it were, an end to high modernism and the exigency of its own social and analytic agenda.

Before prematurely extricating *Auto-da-Fé* from McFarlane's clutches, let us first endeavor to understand his argument better. Canetti's protagonist seems so appealing because he appears to ratify modernism's investment in a fragmented and diffuse subjectivity that is actually enhanced by the superficial defect of blindness. Eliot (and then McFarlane) makes a virtue of these weaknesses in claiming that the blind Tiresias actually enjoys a very privileged kind of vision and, owing to his fluid boundaries and lack of distinct self-definition, a unique ability to unite all the disparate characters of this poem.[8] Taking his cue rather directly from Eliot, McFarlane views Tiresias's apparent liabilities as characteristically *modernist* assets: "His seeing blindness derives from a very Modernist logic, a logic which is then embodied in the structure of the poem as a whole."[9] It is crucial to note that the model proposed here contains a foregone conclusion: epistemological impairment — represented here above all as blindness — is from the outset to be seen as an ultimate bonus. And this, in turn, implies a perpetuation of the traditional model in which culture continues to assimilate the fragments of experience into a meaningful whole. We are to read *with* Tiresias, Eliot states in no uncertain terms: "What Tiresias *sees*, in fact, is the substance of the poem."[10]

It is not at all surprising that this emphasis on "seeing blindness" would call to mind Canetti's Peter Kien. "The hero of this novel, a professor of Oriental studies, also discovers for himself by chance the full visionary power of blindness (or at least of controlled 'defective' vision) as a cosmic principle."[11] McFarlane's scarcely contained enthusiasm for Kien is evident in his remark that "Canetti's hero recognizes . . . an active principle at work: in his kind of seeing-blindness he discovers a way of relating or linking things that would otherwise seem not in the least to relate to each other."[12] Like Tiresias, Kien exhibits the ability — precisely by means of an apparent perceptual deficiency — to unify dauntingly disparate phenomena. And, as with Tiresias, we are clearly meant to read *with* Canetti's professor. "Blindness becomes the means wherewith to come to terms with life," opines McFarlane, "permitting a wholly new philosophy of contingency. Canetti's hero decides that 'blindness is a weapon against time and space, and our existence a unique monstrous blindness.'"[13] A final ingredient to "this peculiarly Modernist kind of vision,"[14] and one that will be of crucial significance in our discussion of Adorno, below, is that of pain. The insights to be gleaned do not come without this price; Kien's "visionary blindness," we read, "like the blindness of eyes filled with tears or pain . . . yields much more reliable testimony about the real meaning of life than does the report of witnesses enjoying conventional good sight."[15] This in a nutshell comprises the high modernist recipe for ultimate recuperation of a disintegrating culture: a handicapped protagonist whose own fluid or fractured self and visionary blindness equips him, not without a measure of pain, to embrace (if not unite) a host of superficially discordant and incompatible phenomena. And it is this paradigm into which McFarlane rather forcibly inserts Kien.

Here one might object that this older view of modernism has already been superseded; that the newer views advocated, for example, by Bathrick and Huyssen in their *Modernity and the Text* already provide a more capacious framework that could easily accommodate the likes of *Auto-da-Fé*. This is admittedly true, and in fact informs the methodology of all the preceding investigations of this study. Yet while the fairly recent expansion of the term modernism, already fairly imprecise, by the way, in its more traditional usage, is undeniably more inclusive of a wider range of texts (and of a more diverse array of stances toward modernity), a degree of clarity may have been sacrificed in the process.

In an illuminating essay, "The Knower and the Artificer," intellectual historian David Hollinger acknowledges that modernism has of late been stretched in so many directions that it threatens to become an almost useless term,[16] but nevertheless concedes the appeal of maintaining it. "The advantages are manifest: one retains a claim to the most commanding, most talismanic word in the critical study of twentieth-century intellectual life."[17] Yet to do so does not mean that we reduce all constituent elements to some common denominator. Indeed, Hollinger is most concerned to retrieve that "cognitivist" aspect of modernism that both rivals and completes the more familiar figure of the "artificer"—a term he borrows from Joyce's iconic Stephen Dedalus—featured in the corpus of canonical literary modernism. As Hollinger rightly observes, "The Knower," while not entirely absent, "is less honored within the modernist literary canon." It will be my argument, below, that *Auto-da-Fé* presents the supreme exemplar of this minority tradition within the corpus of German modernist prose.

Hollinger's strategy of highlighting the cognitivist strain of modernist thought—which captures Canetti's undertaking extraordinarily well—is what most interests me in this context: he argues that we can best make sense of these divergent strands not by mingling the categories of the knower and the artificer, but by maintaining the traditional distinctions. Ultimately, Hollinger will underscore the interconnection of these two categories—he shows, for example, how both are present in certain key modernist novels.[18]

But his provisional strategy of segregation is quite fruitful and worthy of emulation here. Thus, in attending to McFarlane's and Eliot's confidence in the paradoxical prowess of the modernist protagonist (i.e., Hollinger's artificer), I do not seek to resurrect traditional conceptions for their own sake — or only because they happen to have been applied to Canetti — but also to reap a share of the conceptual clarity that will result from viewing *Auto-da-Fé* as an example of that minority cognitivist discourse that both constituted and rivaled canonical literary modernism.

Now, in his enthusiasm for what Lambert Zuidervaart would later dub the "deprivileged" modernist subject, McFarlane fails to inform us that Kien is not really blind, but is just pretending to be so. Furthermore, this blindness is not in any sense imposed by the modern world (whatever that would mean), but represents a scheme that issues from a quite integrated and devious consciousness. Moreover, Kien's pseudophilosophical method of expunging reality is, as we have seen above, problematic not only because it deprives ontological status to his fellow human beings (such as his nagging wife), which is in itself questionable, but because by losing sight of people in this manner he is actually overlooking a very real menace to his own well-being. Furthermore, if one were really seeking a true counterpart to Tiresias, particularly with regard to his capacity to host the most disparate of figures, one would more likely turn to Kien's equally problematic brother Georg — the psychic host par excellence, as we have had occasion to observe in the preceding chapter.

This affiliation of Kien with Tiresias, and thus of Canetti with Eliot, must be seen as part of a larger cultural dynamic that granted legitimacy to serious literature insofar as it participated in the developing modernist aesthetic. Indeed, the postwar era was an important period of canon formation for German modernism, as the additions of Franz Kafka (whose star rose dramatically in the 1950s) and Rainer Maria Rilke (whose only novel was first given its modernist imprimatur in the 1960s) clearly attest. Indeed, Canetti's novel reemerged into public consciousness just as *The Notebooks of Malte Laurids Brigge* (1910) was being ushered into the modernist pantheon. Why, to put it simply, was Canetti left out?

Clearly, *Auto-da-Fé* could only be shoehorned into the Elotian conception of high modernism with considerable effort. Both Kien and Georg contest the very fragmented subjectivity that high modernism enshrines; mythology serves in *Auto-da-Fé* not to counteract the chaos of history (as Eliot famously stated), but is itself the target of unrelenting parody; and, finally, the novel does not depict the loss of historical and social moorings as inevitable characteristics of the modern age that are somehow redressed by the ability of the precious individual to unite an increasingly disorienting world within himself. All of this—and this is quite substantial—is at odds with central strains of high modernism. But to demonstrate this, we need to move somewhat beyond Eliot and McFarlane to consider at least two of the major players in the construction of postwar modernism: Theodor W. Adorno and his principal aesthetic adversary, Georg Lukács.

Adorno and the Modernist Love Affair with the Fragmented Self

The influence of Adorno on definitions of modernity and modernist art in the postwar period can hardly be overestimated, particularly in light of his influential study (with Max Horkheimer) *Dialektik der Aufklärung* (Dialectic of Enlightenment, 1947) and the subsequent *Noten zur Literatur* (Notes to Literature, 1958–74). Indeed, in his *After the Great Divide* (1986), Andreas Huyssen baptizes Adorno the "high priest of modernism," "the theorist par excellence of the Great Divide, that presumably necessary and insurmountable barrier separating high art from popular culture."[19] Adorno's theory of modernism, which so powerfully maintained that divide, was motivated, Huyssen explains, by the "political impulse ... to save the dignity and autonomy of the art work from the totalitarian pressures of fascist mass spectacles, socialist realism, and an ever more degraded commercial mass culture in the West." This exclusionary gesture in turn "found its theoretically more limited expression in the New Criticism."[20] The link to New Criticism—dominant in America and England at this time—is significant because it demonstrates how Adorno's endorsement of modernism's "strategy of exclusion"—itself a politically motivated aesthetic—could be absorbed into a thoroughly apolitical approach to literature.[21] Frederic Jameson's assessment of Adorno's "proposal to see the classical stage of high modernism itself as the very prototype of the most 'genuinely' political art" as an ultimately "anti-political revival of the ideology of modernism" can help us to grasp the unholy alliance between Adorno and the New Critics regarding the high modernist canon.[22] Yet, even if Adorno may inadvertently have provided theoretical cover to traditionalist proponents of high modernism, we should not for our own part underestimate the distance separating Adorno's position, which ascribes a crucial contestatory power to modernist art, from Eliot's essentially compensatory view, which imagines a protagonist somehow capable of reconciling modernity's contradictions. To linger over this distinction, however, will not advance our understanding of *Auto-da-Fé*, above all, perhaps, because this very point of contrast became muddled in critical practice.[23] Let us therefore bridge the abyss between Adorno and Eliot, thereby recapitulating a New Critical practice, in order to see how that which is common to both the traditionalist and the Marxist, namely their sympathetic portrayal of the modernist protagonist, stands in stark and structural contrast to Canetti's treatment of Peter Kien.

Given his much-discussed indictment of instrumental reason in the *Dialectic*, the effective exclusion of *Auto-da-Fé* from membership among those lofty works that "enjoy what is today the only form of respectable fame" (Adorno's words in praise, here, of Beckett) is virtually foreordained.[24] For Canetti's novel is nothing if not analytic—mercilessly and unrelentingly "penetrating" as, for example, Erich Fried has observed.[25] In his widely read essay "Commitment" ("Engagement," 1965), Adorno argues—against Sartre and Brecht—that truly engaged literature has little to do with thematic political commitment and everything to do with modernist formal experimentation, that "*avant-garde* abstraction which provokes the indignation of philistines."[26] Adorno thus opposes modernist "autonomous" art to the well-meaning but often self-defeating category of "committed" art. His influential critique of traditional *litterature engagée* as moralizing, manipulative, and as the purveyor of unacknowledged consolation—perhaps above all in its capacity to aestheticize suffering—is widely known and has become part of our critical repertoire, as Lawrence Langer's work on Holocaust literature well attests.[27] Turning the traditional notion of engaged literature on its head, Adorno argues: "It is not the office of art to spotlight alternatives, but *to resist by its form alone* the course of the world, which permanently puts a pistol to men's heads."[28] The real virtue of those "very features defamed as formalism," we are told, is that they do not bespeak any political or social program—or much of anything, for that matter: "[Autonomous works of art] are knowledge as non-conceptual objects. This is the source of their nobility. It is not something of which they have to persuade men, because it has been given into their hands."[29] Lest this sound all too reminiscent of idealist aesthetics (one is reminded, for example, of Schiller's concept "naive poetry"), Adorno emphatically asserts that any formal contestation of empirical reality is dialectically related to that very empirical reality.[30]

Adorno's interest in art that presents "knowledge as non-conceptual objects" follows directly from his (and Horkheimer's) critique of instrumental reason in *Dialectic of Enlightenment,* their monumental effort to link the Enlightenment to that apogee of modernity (as they argue): the Holocaust. Art that holds out the promise of contesting commodification would have to do so, therefore, in a manner that eschews any heavy-handed teleological or manipulative component. This is why Adorno, in preparing for the discussion of his favorite modernists, Kafka and Beckett, hastens to remind us that "the *avant-garde* abstraction which provokes the indignation of philistines . . . *has nothing in common with conceptual or logical abstraction,*" that kind of instrumentalizing, nature-exploiting abstraction, in other words, which is the real culprit in the *Dialectic.*[31] Indeed, the nobility of Adorno's non-conceptual objects and their simple givenness reside in their (apparent) lack of tendentious purpose, lending them an aura of the naturalness — and thus the Schillerian reminiscence.

Adorno's argument usually achieves clearer contours when applied to actual literature. It may therefore be worthwhile to turn briefly to his discussion of Beckett for an illustration of what was dearest to him in modernist prose:

> Beckett's works . . . enjoy what today is the only form of respectable fame: everyone shudders at them, and yet no-one can persuade himself that these eccentric plays and novels are not about what everyone knows but no one will admit . . . They deal with a highly concrete historical reality: the abdication of the subject. Beckett's *Ecce Homo* is what human beings have become. As though with eyes drained of tears, they stare silently out of his sentences . . . However, the minimal promise of happiness [these works] contain, which refuses to be traded for comfort, cannot be had for a price less than total dislocation, to the point of worldlessness.[32]

Let us set aside the rather dubious claim regarding a critical consensus on the content of Beckett's works ("what everyone knows but no one will admit"), and focus instead on Adorno's discernment of the core concern of Beckett's oeuvre: the loss of the traditional will-dominated unified subject. For here Adorno — in good modernist company, by the way — is asserting a kind of mimesis; not the rich mimetic referentiality of nineteenth-century social realism, to be sure, but a rather definite homology between modernist protagonist and the real, extraliterary beings: "Beckett's *Ecce Homo* is what human beings have become." For Adorno, evidence of what we would today call a decentered subject is a truth ("a highly concrete historical reality") that manifests itself in modernist abstraction, a reality conveyed almost exclusively at the level of discourse rather than mere plot. Imbricated within this conception of modernism is Adorno's valorization of silence ("they stare silently out of his sentences") as well as his embrace of "dislocation" and "worldlessness" as the appropriate consequence of recognizing oneself in the text's "abdicated subject." Later in this same essay, Adorno returns to the topic of modernism's eloquent silence: "Yet paradoxically in the same [post–World War II] epoch it is to works of art that has fallen the burden of wordlessly asserting what is barred to politics."[33] "Wordless" here is, of course, Adorno's shorthand for a lack not of actual words but an absence of thematic social engagement. Resistance to empirical reality (whatever this would mean in practice) must issue forth from this "nonconceptual" silence. Adorno's modernist program resulted in his rather improbable championing of the reclusive aesthete Stephan George over the century's most accomplished committed artist, Bertolt Brecht.

Canetti, no less than Adorno, is concerned in *Auto-da-Fé* to resist the forces of cultural affirmation, as I have argued throughout this study. But whereas for Adorno this consists of "avoid[ing] popularization and adaptation to the market," that is, remaining at all costs on the proper side of that great divide, Canetti identifies and targets certain very specific trends within interwar culture—many of which haunt us still—and mercilessly parodies them. This literary strategy of "search and destroy" immediately suggests the fundamental distinction of Canetti's modernist prose: it is, in contrast to Adorno's veneration of the "nonconceptual object," decidedly conceptual, thematic, even argumentative. In fact, it would seem to enshrine all the hubristic evils of instrumental reason.

While this is surely somewhat of an exaggeration, it nevertheless serves to spotlight the epistemological grid that obtains within the novel and that operates between text and reader. Perhaps the clearest indicator of this novel's epistemic distinction among its modernists cousins is its peculiar wit, an often wicked humor that, as I reiterate throughout this study, operates over the heads of the benighted figures. This readerly sovereignty, however, is perceived to violate the modernist contract: the magisterial rationalist perspective is held to be an obsolete holdover from a discredited Enlightenment optimism; the comedic premise that social failings can be reliably isolated and corrected merely by identifying them, a kind of embarrassing naivete. And finally, the epic purview underwritten by a firmly interlocking epistemic narrative structure may appear to resurrect the quaint world of literary realism that was so widely repudiated by the modernists.

Canetti's analytic modernism cannot, however, be properly appraised by rhetoric that harbors its own foregone conclusion, such as the supposition that the presence of any analytical structure represents *eo ipso* a disreputable kind of ideological regression. For this assumption can blind us to the real innovation of *Auto-da-Fé*, which is to seduce readers into a state of epistemological security only later (with the arrival of Georg) to confront them with its radical insufficiency. In other words, analysis itself serves to critique traditional modes of analysis. The very readers who believe themselves superior to the erroneous constructions of characters given to relentlessly projecting themselves onto others are structurally drawn into precisely the same kind of error, and thus are fully implicated in the target of parody. In fact, as we have seen above in chapter 1, Canetti questions the fundamental premise of an epistemology based on identification: our need to affiliate ourselves with the beautiful (in the case of *Auto-da-Fé*, this is of course the handsome, erotically charged Georg) is hardly a reliable basis for making judgments about the world. In falling for Georg, as first-time readers of the novel typically do (and as a number of early critics of the novel did), we are knocked off our epistemological high horses.

Yet even the ability to make such confident distinctions between correct and misguided judgments implies an epistemological crow's nest that contrasts starkly with the tentative, radically contingent percipient subject of high modernism — a subject, after all, who cannot typically distinguish confidently between self and world, let alone make normative judgments about the latter. This is an important distinction, and one that will allow Canetti unique latitude, but it should not be exaggerated. Canetti's appropriation of realism's "panoptic" narrative structures is, ultimately, an analytic parody of realism — a burlesque, so to speak, that hardly recreates the confident, grand societal vistas of the great realists Fontane, Zola, or of his own favorite, Balzac.³⁴ The reader of *Auto-da-Fé* is sovereign, to be sure, but often over a Lichtenstein of literary reality. Like the protagonist Peter Kien, we know quite a lot about precious little.

Or do we? A closer analysis, undertaken in greater detail above in chapter 1, reveals that even this epistemological security is largely a chimera. Not only does the knowledgeable narrator turn out to be a sham, little more than an opportunity for the characters to masquerade their own bias as objective truth. More radically—and this has yet to be fully appreciated in the critical literature on the novel—the facts we possess often remain nothing more than uncontested (or uncontestable) claims of very biased players. How can we ever really know if Peter Kien is in fact a world-renowned sinologist, or if his brother Georg actually stands a chance of winning the Nobel prize for his innovations in the treatment of psychotic patients? The *ex post facto* discovery of ubiquitous self-interest and pervasive perspectivism parading as omniscience should leave *us* feeling epistemologically impaired. What provides the temporary illusion of epistemological security, on the other hand, is the fact that the narrative is constructed of extremely limited and mutually exclusive units. Each of the figural worlds remains utterly distinct, without the slightest overlap—a fact which thus far has been taken only as a symbol of the isolation of the individual in the modern world. Perhaps *Auto-da-Fé* can also be read to support this existential lament, but this highly artificial demarcation of rival belief worlds certainly serves another function as well. For it comprises the very precondition of our vaunted epistemological privilege. In this pared-down and schematized universe, unmasking a character's delusions and projections of self onto others is child's play. But is it our world?

Auto-da-Fé offers itself as a highly stylized model, not as a readily inhabitable simulacrum. In pointing to the world outside itself—to various cultural attitudes, beliefs, and practices of the interwar period—it simultaneously raises questions about the status and applicability of the very analysis it employs. The epistemological structure that underwrites the novel's humor becomes in the course of this monumental narrative also the object of the inquiry, a dialectical refinement that has not yet been fully appreciated. In the end, then, our epistemological sovereignty is somewhat of a pyrrhic victory. Like the infamous burrow in Kafka's short story of the same title, the narrative world of *Auto-da-Fé* begins to resemble an environment both terribly familiar and yet virtually impossible.

Certainly this analytic mode seemed foreign to classical high modernism, which viewed its more obviously skeptical model of epistemology as the product of numerous social upheavals—as, in other words, the child of modernity itself. Bradbury and McFarlane cite, for example, Strindberg's famous remark on the figures in his *Miss Julie* to demonstrate the point: "Since they are modern characters, living in an age of transition more urgently hysterical at any rate than the age that preceded it, I have drawn them as split and vacillating." They proceed to generalize this relationship to all of modernism: "This is much the sort of comment that might have been made by any Modernist writer between the 1880s and the 1930s; and, in its consonance between fragmentation, discontinuity, and the modern age of transition, it is itself modern."[35] Even Hermann Broch, who probably came closest to Canetti in diagnosing a cultural crisis—one thinks of the famous essay *"Zerfall der Werte"* (Disintegration of Values) that first appeared within the fictional context of *Die Schlafwandler*—took pains to portray his characters as psychograms of a disintegrating communal culture. Lukács noted this same, consonant relationship between what he called the erosion of the "outer world" or "reality" on the one hand and this new conception of "personality" on the other: "Attenuation of reality and dissolution of personality are thus interdependent: the stronger the one, the stronger the other."[36]

In contrast to Lukács, however, one finds among the modernists an implicit sympathy for the protagonists' fragmented consciousness as a consequence or expression of modernity itself. This is not to exclude the possibility of critique or protest encoded in such a figure, but one senses nonetheless, particularly in the postwar critical embrace of this fractured consciousness, a consensus on the necessity of this state of affairs—these men (it is typically a male protagonist) have no choice in the matter; they are products and victims of a fragmented age. Adorno's enthusiasm for Beckett, as we noted, certainly contains this same kind of empathetic identification: "everyone shudders ... [for this] is what human beings have become." This shudder of recognition reaches an apogee at that moment when Adorno reads himself into the actual position of the protagonist of Kafka's *"In der Strafkolonie"* (In the Penal Colony), who, it should be noted, actually loses consciousness in the process of his nightmarish torture: "Kafka and Beckett arouse the fear which existentialism merely talks about ... He over whom Kafka's wheels have passed"—for Adorno, a badge of honor—"has lost for ever both any peace with the world and any chance of consoling himself with the judgment that the way of the world is bad."[37] Apart from any particular attitude we may bear toward these protagonists, we are in most cases structurally constrained to read *with* them, which is to say that in order to make sense of the narrative we must assume their perspective. The consonance that we are told obtains between the fragmentation of modernity and the fragmented modernist protagonist replicates itself in this way at the level of text and reader.

But reading *with* these fellows is not always an easy task. For, whether it be Musil's *Törleß*, Rilke's *Malte*, or even Döblin's Franz Biberkopf, we are typically confronted with a protagonist who suffers from a certain diminished epistemological prowess; like Tiresias, they all are marked by compromised vision of some sort. One need only recall, for example, the establishing scene in *Berlin Alexanderplatz*, in which Biberkopf perceives the walls of a Berlin tenement courtyard to be falling in on him, though, of course, they are not. Perhaps these subjects have not fully abdicated, yet neither are they the realist heroes of yesteryear. This modern, fluid self, which Ernst Mach famously dubbed an *"ideelle denkökonomische, keine reelle Einheit"* (a thought construct, not a real unity) is simply less capable of knowing itself (or selves), the world, and of drawing a credible line of demarcation between the two. Indeed, this deprivileged modernist protagonist becomes the walking proof of the obsolete, or at least artificial, nature of these very subject-object distinctions. The typical protagonist of Expressionist drama presents, as Peter Szondi has shown, a parallel case in which the social world is refracted through an individual's consciousness and thereby subjected to notable distortion.[38] The debate—if there was one—as to whether this "seeing blindness" really represents a higher wisdom or rather a dangerous subjectivist misrepresentation becomes lost in the larger portrayal of this kind of handicapped perception as natural, even quintessentially modern. Biberkopf may be right about the menacing quality of the German metropolis. But in viewing himself as victim from the outset, is he not also perhaps laying the groundwork for exonerating himself of all responsibility for his own actions?[39] These questions, which are important to Canetti, tend to recede in the presence of these figures, because they are themselves merely the avatar of (and sometime antidote to) a larger-order social fragmentation. As Bradbury and McFarlane would have it, modernism "is the art consequent on the dis-establishing of communal reality and conventional norms of causality... The assumption that the age demands a certain kind of art, and that

Modernism is the art that it demands, has been fervently held by those who see in the modern human condition a crisis of reality, an apocalypse of cultural community."[40] In short, whether the modernist psyche reveals a rich inwardness or a tortured incoherence, whether we are to celebrate or condemn the world that drove the self both inward and apart, this fragmented mental state is not a free choice, but a given—Adorno's "highly concrete historical reality."

But what if this were not the whole truth? What if the celebrated crisis of subjectivity were, in part, hype, fad, or, worse yet, a kind of malleable persona through which one could exploit others—a feint, in other words, that served to conceal power? Furthermore, what if it were not a question of a homogenized generic self, but a gendered self, whose efforts at maintaining self-control, so to speak, revealed rich patterns of cultural misogyny? All of this, as I have argued above in chapter 2, is in fact strongly suggested by *Auto-da-Fé*. To modernism as it was constructed at the point of the novel's reemergence, and the time of Adorno's first American publications on aesthetics and politics, such would have been heresy. For this modernism was, as we have seen, largely predicated upon the sympathetic, or *consonant*, depiction of the fragmented self. *Auto-da-Fé* breaks modernism's empathetic spell over the reader and questions the political and social implications of a fragmented protagonist by, first of all, placing the notion of a universal, ungendered self into serious doubt.

To notice that *Auto-da-Fé* renders this hallmark of literary modernism in a markedly different manner is not to suggest that it necessarily *refutes* the consonant/sympathetic portrayal of consciousness in, say, Joyce's *Portrait of the Artist as a Young Man*. For this is not a matter of a simple binary, but rather of a cluster of possible positions. Yet coming at the end of a tradition that had tended to venerate the modernist protagonist, often rendering social reality only as refracted in this figure's own fragmented consciousness, Canetti was indeed intent on placing the phenomenon in a more critical light. Specifically, Canetti challenges the (often only implicit) consensus that the modernist protagonist is the inexorable end product of a world come unhinged, a victim of vanishing nineteenth-century certainties. *Auto-da-Fé* challenges Lukács's formula—if we may speak anachronistically—by suggesting that the loss of the communal may in part be attributable to the "inward turning" not only of modernist literature, but of a whole host of cultural currents in the Weimar era.

The strong epistemological structure of the narrative is of course hardly conducive to a sympathetic portrayal of the crisis of subjectivity: the reader is positioned outside and above, not with, the characters undergoing a crisis of subjectivity. The analytic cast of the novel thus asks us to think *about* this phenomenon, rather than read ourselves into it, a prospect that will yield insight if only we will allow the novel this liberty. In other words, we do not shudder in self-recognition (as Adorno did in the presence of Beckett and Kafka); we laugh at what we wish to see as distinct from ourselves. After all, overidentification, misidentification, and self-projection are the sins of the characters we recognize because we have as readers (at least until the introduction of Georg) been held at arm's length. The novel's analytic framework requires us to read Kien, not to read *with* Kien, as McFarlane would have us do in good high modernist fashion. *Auto-da-Fé,* does not, in other words, foster the modernist *"vision avec,"* but rather a stylized *"vision par derriere,"* to borrow a pair of terms used by Hans Binder in his analysis of Kafka.[41] If, in the end, we are deprived of the pleasures of identification, we are richly compensated with an aesthetic pleasure that is uncharacteristic of the high modernist mind-set: humor.[42]

Canetti's problematization of identification brings into focus the way in which high modernism had distanced itself from this commonplace manner of reading. In a pathbreaking essay on the television miniseries "Holocaust" (1978), Andreas Huyssen points to one of modernism's signal deficiencies: it fails to offer the opportunity for readers to identify. "What I am proposing," Huyssen explains, "is that certain products of the culture industry and their popular success point to shortcomings in avantgardist or experimental modes of representation."[43] While holding fast to modernism's "truth content," Huyssen faults these works for failing to meet "the socio-psychological need for identification with the Jews as victims."[44] What Huyssen identifies in his discussion of "Holocaust" can indeed be generalized (as his own book title suggests) to a much larger problematic: high art may have something to learn from lower—or more populist—forms of entertainment. Long disdaining identification as an obsolete if not vulgar relationship to the text, modernism made a virtue out of more cerebral modes of reception, though it was not, as we have noted, fully conscious of the implications of this practice. Owing fidelity variously to Brechtian "Verfremdung" (alienation) or to Adorno's belief in the powers of modernist form, traditional readerly identification with individual characters was rather forcefully shunned.[45] But this should not distract us from the way in which these works already fulfilled an identification function, if only for a certain clientele. Clearly Adorno saw himself (or his self) reflected in the fractured protagonists of Kafka and Beckett, even if many other readers never would experience this same degree of self-recognition. Because high modernism was touted as the only authentic response to modernity, and thus implicitly a natural or universal aesthetic, we may have overlooked the particular identification function operant in these avantgardist and experimental works. *Auto-da-Fé*, on the other hand, simply does not permit this kind of illicit identificatory pleasure, which elsewhere could of course take place without readers fully realizing that they are reading themselves into the respective modernist novel. In *Auto-da-Fé* the topic and practice are simply too prominently foregrounded for this to occur. Identification remains for Canetti a problem: both within the fictional world of the novel and at the level of reader and text, identification emerges as a vehicle for approaching *and* utterly distorting reality. There is no such thing here as sacred, Tiresian vision; identification as a hermeneutic principle is both necessary, and necessarily disfiguring. The novel in fact thrives on the insoluble tension between our ongoing need to identify on the one hand, and the inherent fallacy of this gesture, when raised to the level of epistemological criterion, on the other. *Auto-da-Fé* both appeases and thwarts this basic readerly urge, and in doing so flushes out into the open a foundational modernist aporia.

Canetti clearly did not draw the same conclusion for aesthetics as so many others did. On the contrary, he knew (as did Brecht) that analytic prose holds forth the possibility of a truly critical stance, including one that would take aim at the very framework that enables that analysis. Furthermore, Canetti believed that the subjectivist turn was something of a hoax, attributable in part to a culture of self-indulgence and solipsism that should be exposed, if not opposed.[46] Motivated, as we have seen, by a deep concern about the diminution of the public sphere as a consequence of inflated notions of subjectivity, *Auto-da-Fé* suggests the philosophical impossibility of conceiving of a fragmented self from the perspective of an equally fragmented consciousness. In "Self-Indulgent Philosophies of the Weimar Period" (chapter 3), I develop this thesis in some detail; but the conclusion may be restated here. Any time we imagine an inchoate self, we automatically do so from a position of a relatively more unified psyche: how else could we even recognize this phenomenon, let alone make meaningful comparisons with other notions of subjectivity? Rilke, in other words, is not Malte (or not *only* Malte) — even if on bad days he may have felt just like his psychically split protagonist — else he could not have written the novel. Similarly, if an age of economic and cultural dislocation had produced readers precisely and exclusively as fragmented as Malte, they could never recognize him as such.[47] Likewise, Adorno, despite his shudder of self-recognition in the face of true modernist art, is not exclusively to be equated with Kafka's exotically punished protagonist. When he is not under the wheels of Kafka's prose, he is (or was) an undeniably self-actuated theorist, quite capable of deploying a formidably analytic self.

Problematic as *Auto-da-Fé* demonstrates it to be, the analytic self cannot be checked at the door when one enters the realm of fiction. It is always there, Canetti seems to be suggesting, so perhaps it is best that we acknowledge it. What Canetti suggests by means of his unmistakably dissonant treatment of fragmented subjectivity, therefore, is not the inherent invalidity of the modernists' consonant or sympathetic rendering, but the essential bad faith in concealing the philosophically necessary discrepancy between the fragmented modernist protagonist and the necessarily less fragmented consciousness of author and reader. As a result of this kind of strong narrative, we are impelled to ask whether a charge that has often been laid at the feet of literary realism,[48] namely the concealment of ideology and the implication of its naturalness, may be just as apposite of high modernism.

Certainly Adorno himself can be faulted, as Frederic Jameson has suggested, for failing to recognize the irreducible role of the "transcendental subject" in his own Critical Theory.[49] Given Adorno's noted emphasis on our "unfreedom" in the face of the "administered universe," there seems to be in fact little role for the analytic self in political society. Freedom, agency, and the old Cartesian self that underlies both are simply comforting illusions, Adorno maintains. One could in fact argue that Adorno simply displaced reflective agency from individuals to modernist autonomous art. The Kantian autonomy of the individual becomes, with the requisite materialist alterations, the defining and redemptive characteristic of art.[50] Certainly Adorno is more sanguine about the prospects of modern art than he is about the individual's capacity to change society.[51] At the only point in the essay when he expresses explicit concern for social justice, Adorno links its attainment to modernist form rather than to traditional political activism.[52] "The Mind of Modernism," to use McFarlane's terminology, seems for Adorno to have mysteriously wandered into the modernist art object itself. Mindful that this critical subjectivity does not simply vanish into thin air, *Auto-da-Fé* poses the question about this mind's whereabouts, so to speak, once it has abdicated.[53]

One need not have been a leftist, politically astute Jewish intellectual in the final Weimar years—though the young Canetti was of course all of these things—to notice that these very same modern times had produced a whole array of other selves that had little in common with the modernist predilection for genuine fragmentation and dissolution. This is the context within which we must judge Georg's fascination with the gorilla man, a laughable figure meant to lampoon that ostensibly antibourgeois movement known as vitalism and loosely tied to Nietzsche. As I elaborate in chapter 3, Georg's enthusiastic conversion to this kind of primitivism harbors deeply reactionary and authoritarian tendencies. First, this apparently emancipatory persona is at root antisocial: his sense of reality consists of a highly protean bubble of consciousness that follows him around like an invalid's oxygen tent. Underlying this putatively liberating mode of consciousness is, as we have seen, the radical subordination of ontology not to epistemology per se, but to this single percipient individual's whim.

Georg's appropriation of this mind-set is, however, the most memorable critique in this context. He sits at the knees of the gorilla man in order to learn how to acquire not only his unique language—which is ultimately no language at all—but precisely his mode of consciousness, the radical malleability of which is thought by its very nature to contest the rigidities of bourgeois society. Georg's career, however, tells a different story. Underneath the facade of a vulnerable, permeable consciousness lurks a self every bit as hard-nosed and self-serving as his brother Peter. Georg presents the image of an intellectual's insidious retreat from an evermore daunting social reality under the cover of a pseudopolitical and specious antibourgeois ideology. Thirty years after Canetti wrote *Auto-da-Fé*, Lukács brought a similar, devastating charge against those enamored of the "dissolution of personality," which he attributed to a desire to dissociate oneself from political responsibility. Lukács termed this investment in fragmented subjectivity the "doctrine of the eternal incognito" because it provided an alibi to those men such as Martin Heidegger, Ernst Jünger, Carl Schmitt, and Gottfried Benn who participated in Nazism and later wished to believe that at a deeper level of selfhood they had in fact remained opponents. It was precisely the fragmented conception of the self to which they appealed in their self-defense.[54] Canetti could not of course have imagined the precise usefulness of Georg's infatuation to Nazi authorities, but the potential dangers are already clearly present in the novel.

This is a distinctive contribution. More than any other novel from within the movement, *Auto-da-Fé* contests the unlimited glorification of fragmented subjectivity, particularly when it becomes the arbiter of social reality. By means of a negative dialectic, the novel suggests that there is a limit, or endpoint, beyond which the veneration of individual consciousness—or, more accurately, an *individual's* consciousness—cannot proceed. It is not a simple matter of upholding some positive notion of the social that must, at all costs, be defended against the onslaughts of rampant subjectivity. Rather, *Auto-da-Fé* seems concerned to remind us that modernity has not eradicated the problem of power—and certainly not by means of retreat into a figure's rich psyche. More precisely, the novel suggests that power lurks in the very definition and deployment of fragmented consciousness. After reading *Auto-da-Fé*, one can never again take unreflective comfort in the inward turning of the novel; for we must always now ask ourselves whether the highly nuanced, layered consciousness we encounter may ultimately disguise authoritarian desires, or, by virtue of its manifest vulnerability, invite those of others. Otto Weininger sensed the widening gap between the traditional, will-dominated, "ethical" self and the modern, fragmented, "empirical" self. He wondered how such weakened empirical specimens (which he notoriously saw exemplified in women and Jews) could possibly survive with any dignity and meaning in the modern, materialistic world. Though infamous today for his misogyny and anti-Semitism, Weininger may deserve to be remembered also, as Steven Beller argues, for articulating the *civic* crisis posed by the rise of the empirical self. Certainly Canetti acknowledged the huge influence Weininger had on him and his entire generation. That impact is clearly felt in the novel, which asks, as we have seen, how this very modern self comports with notions of communal culture and civic responsibility. In the end, *Auto-da-Fé* forces us to bid farewell to the high modernist naturalization of the impaired self as the unexamined avatar of the modern age.

More the novel does not do. Both the use of radically reduced characters (with the partial exception of Georg) and the deployment of characters who construct artificially distinct and mutually exclusive worlds-units, instead of the radically more complex and overlapping portrayal of consciousness typical of Joyce or Woolf, suggest rather clearly that Canetti's critique is not meant directly to contest the rich and sophisticated minds we encounter in the fiction of the great masters of modernism, many of whom, as we know from his autobiography, he seems to have respected deeply. As we saw in chapter 5, Canetti explicitly renounced psychological realism over the protests of Broch; and one cannot help feeling that Canetti sensed the danger of undermining social critique by providing compellingly nuanced figures whose psychological appeal might serve to "explain" a set of practices we are meant to place in question.[55] *Auto-da-Fé* is, at any rate, simply incommensurate with such novels. Yet it may well serve as a necessary corrective, a function that is, as I hope is clear by now, directly ascribable to the author's choice of an epistemologically strong narrative structure.

Before concluding this topic altogether, it may be helpful to observe that our interest in the epistemological criterion of literary modernism has its own history. To be sure, the phenomenon of fragmented subjectivity is readily observable in the contemporary texts, both fictional and critical. Indeed, the Austrian critic Hermann Bahr used the term *"Nervenkunst"* (neuralgic art) to promote the trend that Anglo-American readers know, thanks to Henry James, as the "inward turning of the novel." Bahr advocated the application of the Naturalist technique, which in the work of Ibsen, Strindberg, and Hauptmann had so impressively captured social conditions, to the interior life of the mind. While this inward turn necessarily tended to valorize subjectivity, one does not notice among contemporary modernists the same degree of skepticism that later critics would bring to the discussion of modernism. Indeed, if one looks to the modernist practitioners themselves, one notes not a radical doubt, but a surprising confidence in their effort to portray the modern world. Different tools, foci, methods, conventions—all of these would, of course, be required. But the modernists were less despairing of their ability to produce a compelling literary perspective on modernity than committed to breaking with obsolete realist literary conventions. While any kind of summary statement runs the risk of oversimplification, it may be fair to say that the modernists themselves—as we saw in Eliot, above—viewed fragmented subjectivity as paradoxically enabling, not necessarily crippling. Certainly the New Critical love of paradox would sustain this potential to see loss as gain.

The investment in a radically decentered self became entrenched, it seems, with the ascent not only of Derrida and his disciples, but also of Lacan and Foucault on the critical horizon during the 1970s and 1980s. Their almost exclusive focus on literary modernism — and one could easily expand this list to include, for example, Kristeva's interest in modernist poetry as the privileged locus of the "semiotic" and Barthes's exaltation of the modernist "writerly" text — can in part be explained by the fact that such works offered prooftexts for a cluster of theories that similarly conceived of the self as essentially deprivileged,[56] that is, as an overdetermined *site* complexly constructed by impersonal forces rather than an autonomous, self-legislating subject. Modernism's vaunted "epistemological shift" (Stevenson) thus received a powerful boost by the canonization of these *critical* paradigms, such that the retrospective construction of modernism became significantly more skeptical about the modernist protagonist's epistemological prowess than the original authors themselves may have been. Approaching *Auto-da-Fé* through the prism of such theories of course made it even less likely that the novel would be admitted to the properly modernist (read: epistemologically skeptical) canon. In the case of *Auto-da-Fé*, this point may explain the curious fact that early reviewers of the thirties and forties clearly and repeatedly recognized the novel as modern, experimental, and anti-realist. Yet later critics of the seventies and eighties, influenced perhaps unwittingly by the centrality of subjectivity and epistemology in literary theory, were more ambivalent: Darby, whose study situates the novel within "disintegrative" anti-realist narrative strategies characteristic of modernism, is ultimately bewildered by the presence of a firm narrative structure. He delivers his verdict — which convicts the novel of harboring precisely the epistemologically strong narrative framework identified above — as if it had befallen him to unmask a beloved imposter. Likewise, Dieter Liewerscheidt, operating on the premise that only consonant modernism is valid modernism, acts as if he has discovered a cryptorealist novel masquerading as modernist, emblazoning his great discovery in the title of his article: "A Contradiction in the Conceptualization of the Novel."

Lukács and the Loss of the Social

In dramatizing fragmented consciousness not as the modern condition per se, but as something contingent and partial, Canetti approaches the substance of one of Georg Lukács's fundamental criticisms of modernism, namely that it universalizes and transcendentalizes subjective human experience. Writing of the modernist treatment of time, Lukács observes: "The uncritical approach of modernist writers—and of some modern philosophers—reveals itself in their conviction that this subjective experience constitutes reality as such. That is why this treatment of time can be used by the realistic writer to characterize certain figures in his novels, although in a modernist work it may be used to describe reality itself . . . We arrive, therefore, at an important distinction: the modernist writer identifies what is necessarily a subjective experience with reality as such, thus giving a distorted picture of reality as a whole (Virginia Woolf is an extreme example of this). The realist, with his critical detachment, places what is a significant, specifically modern experience in a wider context, giving it only the emphasis it deserves as a part of a greater, objective whole."[57]

If Georg's gorilla-fervor represents a particular instance of reactionary modernism—as I have proposed—rather than some quintessential expression of the modern age, then Canetti's critique does come very close to Lukács's protest against the uncritical exaltation of subjectivity over the intersubjective social whole. But as the passage above demonstrates, this similarity is itself only partial: for Lukács's touchstone of "critical realism" is, as he notes repeatedly, the literary representation of that "wider context," "a greater, objective whole." And precisely this is missing from *Auto-da-Fé*.

Though Canetti's novel lacks this *sine qua non* of Lukácsian critical realism, a common spirit of critique nevertheless inhabits the work of both. Lukács never tired of decrying, most memorably perhaps in his signature essay "The Ideology of Modernism," "the negation of outward reality," "the rejection of narrative objectivity," and the "attenuation of actuality," all lamentable characteristics he located in the work of the recognized modernists Joyce, Musil, Gide, and, of course, Kafka. Again and again, Lukács warned about mistaking a historical symptom (such as the individual's radical isolation) for a "natural" and therefore unalterable aspect of reality. In singling out Heidegger's concept of "thrownness-into-being" (*Geworfenheit ins Dasein*), Lukács furthermore opposes what he sees as the ruse of employing the "dignity" of philosophy in order to underwrite an essentially asocial worldview. "This implies," Lukács argues, "that man is *constitutionally unable* to establish relationships with things or persons outside himself."[58] McFarlane's rhapsodic endorsement of Kien's philosophy of blindness would seem to be a case in point.

Auto-da-Fé is thus solidly in line with this kind of critique, though of course it is not Heidegger, but philosophies popular during the Weimar period such as neoempiricism and neo-Kantianism, that form the principal target of the novel's parody of philosophy, as I have elaborated in chapter 3. Still, perhaps we need to ask how the novel can share the Lukácsian concern for the diminution, or outright abandonment, of the social without providing that putatively necessary corrective of "narrative objectivity." The answer derives from the dissonant narration described above. Rather than emanating from largely sympathetic consciousness—sympathetic in terms of epistemological stance rather than particular content—the text of *Auto-da-Fé* derives from figures from whom readers immediately feel distanced. In short, we witness and deplore the reduction of the social as a highly suspect function of their subjectivity; we watch as characters alternately illuminate and darken the social world according to a characteristic obsession, and—given the highly stylized epistemological privilege we enjoy—we recognize and condemn their mistakes. Thus, in contrast to Lukács's requisite wider context, the critical stance of *Auto-da-Fé* proceeds from the virtual absence—or at least the suspiciously ephemeral and malleable quality—of the social order.

At this point one might object that wringing critique from dearth of depiction is a very convenient interpretive gambit, and, furthermore, one that could just as easily apply to that body of consonant modernism that I have thus far sought to keep at some distance from *Auto-da-Fé*. The key difference, however, is that Canetti's novel foregrounds the figural process of reducing, refunctioning, and excluding the social. Just as Lukács arraigns Heidegger for lending a dubious respectability to modernism, the novel apprehends Kien in the very act of devising a curiously self-serving philosophy to authorize his exclusion of the larger world. I have already made brief reference to Georg's similarly suspect appropriation of the then-popular philosophical movement known as neoempiricism, which, despite superficial differences, he deploys to similarly solipsistic ends. But this is just one side of perception; in order to make the point, Canetti shows in some of the funniest passages of the novel how objects of perception—real places and cultural objects known to the reader independently of the text—are gradually denied, occluded, or remade in the image of the mad perceiver.

The largest of these cultural *données* is Vienna itself, which is both eerily present and absent in *Auto-da-Fé*. In fact, it is its occasional presence and unexpected reappearance that makes us feel the pervasive absence more acutely. Regarding the modernists' use of municipal settings, Lukács maintains that "Joyce uses Dublin, Kafka and Musil the Hapsburg Monarchy, as the locus of their masterpieces. But the locus they lovingly depict is little more than a backcloth: it is not basic to their artistic intention."[59] The Vienna of *Auto-da-Fé* is no mere backdrop in this sense. The evocation of the Austrian capital, particularly of two great institutions of the old dual monarchy, serves not to host but to contest the subjectivist proclivities of the figures. That architectural and cultural anchor of old Vienna, the Cathedral of St. Stephen, fails to ground or even orient the subjectivist fantasies of Peter Kien, who pauses at the landmark statue of Christ (the famous "Toothache Christ") only to see himself in this sculpture. Therese indulges similar subjectivist inclinations during her visit to the Cathedral: in the gilded painting of the Last Supper displayed over one of the side altars she is only able to see a "reflection" of her own small and venal world. This is clearly not the "seeing blindness" that McFarlane claimed for the novel; this is rank distortion. The glimpses we get of Vienna, though admittedly few and far between, provide us that which the figures utterly lack: a point of reference by which to gauge the partisan projections of the self-absorbed figures. The novel's much more extended focus on the "Theresianum," a thinly veiled reference to the real-world Viennese state-run auction house cum pawn shop known as the "Dorotheum," draws our attention not only to the particular economic crises of the Weimar years, but also to the way in which traditional culture was then subordinated in as yet unprecedented ways to the demands of naked commerce. The book-eating ogre whom Fischerle conjures in order to motivate Kien to ransom books is really just the humorous literalization of the Dorotheum's standard practice of commodifying and consuming art of all kinds. Though the novel's staging of this interwar crisis of values happens to overlap in part with Kien's own anxieties about disappearing cultural certainties, the evocation of the Theresianum fails to fully ratify the protagonist's nostalgia. In fact, both aspects of Vienna depicted in the novel—both the cathedral and the cathedral of commerce—serve to define rather than resolve widespread cultural anxieties characteristic of, but not limited to, the Austrian First Republic. Though this evocation of Vienna would seem too scant to fulfill Lukács's prescription for social critique,[60] we nevertheless garner precisely this critical vantage point from this modest municipal depiction.

Lukács memorably accused modernism not only of neglecting the wider social context, but also of the "rejection of history," citing Gottfried Benn's *Static Poems* as an exemplary realization of the subjectivist tendency that Henri Bergson is said to have sanctioned philosophically.[61] This concern for a lack of authentic historical consciousness resonates also within *Auto-da-Fé*, but with this caveat: whereas Lukács is concerned with the outright "denial of history," Canetti is more concerned with its perversion as a device for avoiding the anxieties of modernity.[62] As we noted earlier, this kind of spurious "historicism" makes its appearance in the novel not in the form of modern art (as Lukács held), but in the Weimar-era pulp fiction that has somehow found a place in Kien's august private library and is passed on to Therese as the fare appropriate to the barely literate. Canetti employs the then-wildly popular novel by Willibald Alexis, *The Trousers of Mr. Bredow*, which as we noted was published in school editions for courses on German history during the interwar period, to suggest the suspiciously historical appeal of this literature. Despite the historical veneer, this is sheer escapism, as we saw above in chapter 1, and is therefore rightly juxtaposed with Georg Kien's addiction to erotic French novels.[63] As in the matter of the requisite "wider social context," the critique here proceeds by way of negation—or, more precisely, by double negation: the novel rejects the characters' own dubious rejection of history.

The role of myth in *Auto-da-Fé* should be at least briefly mentioned in this context, for it is the integrating power of myth in high modernism that is typically opposed to the centrifugal force of history. Modernism's alleged denial of history, to which Lukács draws our attention, often went hand in hand with an embrace of myth. The classic expression of this doctrine is found in Eliot, who famously perceived in Joyce's *Ulysses* a certain "mythological method" credited as an effective means "of controlling, of ordering, of giving a shape and a significance to the immense panorama of futility and anarchy which is contemporary history."[64] This stabilizing or reconciling function, even if only as an aesthetic effect, has no counterpart in *Auto-da-Fé*. Though myth (differently conceived) would later assume great importance for Canetti in a positive sense, in the novel it serves primarily as grist for a stinging indictment of the "orientalist" construction of misogynistic high culture. Surely Kien's misogynist *tour de force* near the end of the novel, which draws so richly upon the mythological reserves of Western culture, reveals a cultural canon in crisis. The novel's unrelenting analytical modernism creates in the end a mass of deeply disturbing negations without promise of resolution. Canetti himself claims to have been left profoundly unnerved by the cultural wreckage *Auto-da-Fé* left in its wake.[65] Things finally do not fall together; they fall apart. The novel concludes in a state that is a far call from McFarlane's notion of "superintegration."

Underlying Lukács's entire critique of modernism is the assumption that we are insidiously positioned to side with the protagonist. Deprived of any independent perspective we would derive from a proper sociohistorical context, we are sucked into his subjective reality—subordinated, as it were, to his "unifying vision." Even if we don't particularly like the modernist hero, we run the risk, Lukács warns, of mistaking his particular fate as universal, ineluctable, and therefore unalterable. Lukács, in other words, concurs not only that high modernism is tantamount to what we have above termed consonant modernism, but argues that very point from additional angles.[66] Yet then, as now, *Auto-da-Fé*'s markedly dissonant posture complicates this dichotomy, for while it clearly does not qualify as an exemplar of Lukácsian critical realism, neither does it exhibit the ideological dangers against which Lukács so tirelessly inveighed. As we have had numerous occasions to observe thus far, the figures in the novel are schematically drawn, not psychologically nuanced approximations of real people, a point Canetti later underscored, though it is of course easily enough observed in the novel itself. These figures, hardly the subjectivist sirens of Lukács's antimodernist imagination, are instead quite consciously stylized vehicles for a whole array of social and cultural practices employed in doomed—and perhaps therefore humorous—ways to cope with the experience of modernity. When the novel's reclusive protagonist seeks to wall himself off from a threatening tide of humanity, ensconcing himself as the master researcher in a caricature of positivist inquiry, we see him as the expression of particular social and intellectual anxieties—not, as Lukács feared, as the timeless epitome of the human condition. Therefore it is precisely *without* directly depicting "the common life, the strife and togetherness of other human beings," that we come to see the "solitariness" of Kien and company as "a specific social fate, not a universal *condition humaine*."[67]

The fact that Canetti's novel shares so much of the spirit of Lukács's classic critique of modernism cannot, according to the prevailing ideas of the time, have encouraged postwar readers to consider *Auto-da-Fé* as authentically modernist. Given the fact that it ultimately confirms neither Adorno's positive nor Lukács's negative construction of literary modernism, the novel was virtually destined for emargination as long as these and similar views held sway. Yet as helpful as this context can be in situating *Auto-da-Fé* within what may be a more familiar literary-historical landscape, it may prove refreshing to note in conclusion the artificiality of this gambit. Not once in all of his writings does Canetti refer to modernism in the sense that we have been using it in this chapter. Canetti undoubtedly counted himself among those modern artists, who, as Ezra Pound put it, sought to "make it new," but he was just as likely to affiliate himself with modern music and sculpture as with literature. He relates feeling quite at home as a guest at Hermann Scherchen's symposium on modern music in Strassbourg in 1933, "because I had written 'Kant Catches Fire' [the manuscript title of *Auto-da-Fé*] and 'Wedding' and was conscious of the fact that with that I, like the composers in attendance, had done something *new*."[68] Indeed, Canetti contemplated writing the libretto for one of Scherchen's modernist compositions. In recounting Fritz Wotruba's approving reaction to the figures of *Auto-da-Fé*, Canetti furthermore invites a comparison between his own literary figures and the hard, uncompromising figures fashioned by this modernist sculptor.[69] Canetti felt an intense artistic "brotherhood" (his term) with Wotruba, about whom he later wrote a monograph, and saw his own literary accomplishment reflected in the musical innovations of his friend, Alban Berg. In other words, when Canetti conceived of modernism, his purview was hardly limited to literature alone.

This is not to suggest that Canetti was unfamiliar with the peculiarly literary avant garde of the 1930s. On the contrary, he reports: "During the last four or five years of independent Austria . . . one could hear a trinity of names, which was held high by the avant garde: Musil, Joyce and Broch, or Joyce, Musil and Broch."[70] All of whom, of course, were known to him well beyond mere hearsay. Joyce attended one of Canetti's salon readings (though he left at intermission because he was apparently put off by the Viennese dialect), while both Musil and Broch were Canetti's close friends. Nevertheless, Canetti dwelt less on what these (and other) modernists had in common with regard to technique, theme, or ideology, than with their shared goal of venturing something new and aesthetically challenging. In the end, this was Canetti's litmus test for respectable modern art: does it pander to conventional taste, and merely titillate, or does it risk "making it difficult," thereby resisting the allure of commercial success? The "odd trinity" (*die absonderliche Trinität*) of modernists mentioned above was bound together, at least for Canetti, not by some explicit aesthetic program or ideological doctrine, but merely by their desire to negate the literary status quo. "They belonged — this I never doubted — to a very small group of people who with literature made it difficult for themselves, who did not write for popularity or vulgar success. At that time this may have been more important for me than their work."[71] Authors like Stefan Zweig and Franz Werfel, on the other hand, were relegated to the category of the "mundane literature of those years" precisely for trimming their literary sails to market success. Canetti applied the same standard to modern music, as when he excoriated the Viennese public's "obduracy" in rejecting the experimental compositions of Alban Berg and Anton Webern.[72]

Canetti's broad, multimedia conception of modernism, which incidentally shares Adorno's own rigorous opposition to aesthetic commodification, provides a helpful reorientation, I think, as we conclude this discussion. Unbeholden to any of the high priests of modernism, Canetti continued to tread his own, sovereign path. At a time when modernism was in its heyday, Canetti penned an essay tellingly titled *"Realismus und Neue Wirklichkeit"* (Realism and New Reality), a piece that appears intent on scrambling the conventional wisdom. Indeed, in one of the very few places where he trains his attention explicitly on modern literature, Canetti pointedly eschews the language of literary modernism, advocating instead a brand of "new realism" that must rise to the challenge of our daunting "new reality." While it is undoubtedly instructive to contrast his novel, particularly its distinctive analytic structure, with better known high modernist schemas, we might finally permit *Auto-da-Fé* its own free berth. In these final pages, then, let us permit Canetti's own achievement — rather than the aesthetic criteria of others — to frame a concluding discussion of the author's subsequent oeuvre.

The End of Modernism and a New Beginning

The Nazi book burning and ban on "degenerate art" could not have come at a worse time for Canetti. Yet while these developments surely thwarted the reception of *Auto-da-Fé* in the German-speaking world, they do not fully explain the novel's marginal relationship to the high modernist canon in the postwar years. After all, *Auto-da-Fé* had been published in both Britain and the United States to critical acclaim and had even garnered a major literary award in France before the end of the 1940s. Though never as widely read as, say, Thomas Mann's *Der Zauberberg* (The Magic Mountain), it was certainly known to the cultural elite. We are forced therefore to face the conclusion that *Auto-da-Fé*'s status as a literary "Sonderling" (Auer) has less to do with world history, accident, or neglect than with the fact that it was effectively, though perhaps not consciously, excluded from the high modernist canon — and, of course, with the fact that it is indeed a very different kind of book.

As we have seen, these differences go well beyond the mere surface vagaries of mood, atmosphere, and style. It has been the frankly anachronistic task of this final chapter to transplant ourselves into the period when high modernism reigned supreme in order to work out consciously the ways in which *Auto-da-Fé* found itself at loggerheads with central, though not always explicit, tenets of this movement. Canetti was a modernist who loved Kafka and Musil, but also Balzac and Heinrich Mann (more than Thomas, by the way). If we chafe at McFarlane's belated and awkward attempt to bring Canetti into the modernist fold, we do so because of a profound sense of misalignment: Kien is simply no Tiresias. Indeed, whether we look to the standards of a traditionalist such as Eliot or to those of the Western Marxist Adorno, we see that *Auto-da-Fé* remains, at a fundamental level, delightfully different. The recent efforts to rewrite modernism as a broad set of cultural responses to the economic ruptures of modernity threaten to obscure the fact that the old elitist canon of great modernist masters was indeed held together by an identifiable and sometimes problematic core of qualities that happen to enshrine much of what *Auto-da-Fé* avidly contests. There were, in other words, good (or at least substantive) reasons for keeping Canetti's novel at arm's length. The inclusive, democratizing gesture of the new modernist paradigm should not, whatever other salubrious results it may have brought about, be used to conceal important conceptual differences.[73] As beneficiaries of this modernist perestroika, for example, we can now think of both Rilke and Canetti as suitably modernist, but we would only conflate these rather different novels at our own peril. Though today we might be inclined to read Rilke's *Malte* as a comment on the anomie of the modern metropolis, as critics have recently urged, what we most assuredly cannot do is read *Auto-da-Fé* as the celebration of the isolated, precious aesthete. In clashing with essential criteria of high modernism, Canetti earned his place on the sidelines. As a kind of rebel-participant, *Auto-da-Fé* self-consciously set a limit to the modernism of its day.

Yet this discussion, helpful as it may be in defining distinguishing features both of Canetti's prose and of high modernism's assumptions, threatens to become somewhat antiquarian. Surely it is an act of academic fancy to imagine *Auto-da-Fé* sitting in judgment on its modernist contemporaries — a kind of intellectual revenge fantasy, perhaps. This would be as misguided as it is fruitless. Though *Auto-da-Fé* can be said to articulate and foreshadow the very arguments that would later bring down the canon of the isolated great masters, this says nothing of the ongoing relevance of that characteristic feature of Canetti's prose that we have considered in some depth here, namely its markedly analytic quality.

Certainly this is a feature that characterizes all his later work. Canetti unabashedly employed fiction as well as nonfiction to investigate a world he felt to be both increasingly menacing and yet unfailingly awe-inspiring. His three allegedly absurdist plays (*Wedding, Comedy of Vanities,* and *The Numbered*) contain generous quantities of hyperbole and the grotesque, yet retain at bottom a recognizable social-critical agenda — and were for this very reason held by some critics to be insufficiently absurd.[74] The three-volume autobiography, the most successful of all Canetti's writings, was published to critical and popular acclaim. Yet, here too, critics lamented the fact that the narrator failed to engage in sufficient quantities of epistemological self-flagellation. He should have indulged in ritualistic expressions of his inability to narrate, they opine; or, at least, he might have foregrounded the incommensurability of the narrating and narrated selves. But here, as in the novel, Canetti thwarted readers' expectations.[75]

Canetti's captivating memoir of his visit to North Africa, *Die Stimmen von Marrakesch* (The Voices of Marrakesh, 1968) illustrates the paradox of this analytic prose particularly well. Canetti imparts a series of memorable aperçus into the lives of Arabs and Jews (his visit in the spring of 1954 preceded the Algerian Civil War of 1954–62) without renouncing his status as an outside observer. Ignorant of the native languages — but not of the colonial French — Canetti folds this linguistic handicap into the stories he tells; it becomes the self-conscious precondition of the experiences he relates and the pictures he paints. This frank acknowledgment of his own limited subject position stands not in the tradition of that high modernist, quasi-mystical

"Tiresian seeing-blindness," but instead demonstrates in an exemplary and timely manner the necessarily dual thrust of any multicultural undertaking: the irrepressible quest to know the other combined with the humility incumbent upon any foreign observer. These two factors, present also in *Auto-da-Fé*, produce remarkable glimpses into the lives of the native peoples. Their voices are recorded in the ears of the European intellectual, but are never fully translated. Canetti's very title, *The Voices of Marrakesh*, draws our attention to that which the author can never fully comprehend. Though realized in fascinatingly different ways, Canetti's analytic prose always contains the two elements we have observed throughout this study of *Auto-da-Fé*: a probing gesture toward discovery and an attendant reflection on the difficulty (and sometime futility) of that very undertaking.

With the conclusion of *Auto-da-Fé* Canetti himself was at a dead end. The social sphere he saw threatened by subjectivist fads and philosophies was something representable only indirectly in fiction and by means of negation because it existed for the author principally as unrealized potential. Canetti spent the next thirty-plus years pursuing a positive foundation that would justify his hope for the future of the human community in the face of the demonstrated barbarism of the two world wars. It was not something the young novelist factually knew, but something he fervently sought. Except for those few plays, the best of which, *Hochzeit* (Wedding, 1932), was contemporaneous with the novel and shared its fundamental critique of a radically diminished social sphere, *Auto-da-Fé* represents virtually the beginning and end of Canetti's fictional output.

Canetti's second "life's work," *Crowds and Power*, can appropriately be seen as an outgrowth of the novel in this larger sense. Not, of course, as a mere extension or repetition of the concerns we have thus far discussed, but as a response to the larger challenges posed in the novel. Indeed, the armchair anthropologist who narrates *Crowds and Power* represents a veritable "Anti-Kien" in that his insatiable hunger for the myths and legends of Asia, Africa, and the Americas exemplifies a constructive option to the eurocentric, misogynistic, and "orientalist" perversions of his fictional predecessor.[76] This new kind of mythological method that characterizes the pages of *Crowds and Power*—not Eliot's high modernist version—seeks to avoid the subjectivist dangers exhibited by both the Kien brothers by drawing upon the voices of the many, including emphatically those of the non-European peoples, past and present. If this can be seen as Canetti's effort to redeem reason and redefine "culture," it is a markedly literary and poetic undertaking as well. For this anthropological study—if we can after all call it that—not only eschews the accustomed scholarly apparatus in favor of masterful and riveting storytelling, but invokes the sovereignty of the poet in springing—sometimes capriciously and bemusingly—from insight to insight. As the novel is uncharacteristically analytical, this cross-cultural and interdisciplinary inquiry into the nature of masses and the sources of power is imbued with unexpected inflections of the poetic. And while *Crowds and Power* in a sense rebuffs the novel's protagonist, it also reprises him: this study's ambition, erudition, and, yes, bombast evoke nothing if not the ghost of Peter Kien.

Crowds and Power ventures this answer to the question posed in the novel—an incomplete answer, to be sure (Canetti had planned a second volume), but one that is based on a dauntingly expansive survey of world mythology, folklore, and anthropological reports: We are by nature social, and this is a fundamental characteristic, not an epiphenomenon of drive-sublimation, as Freud would have it. Furthermore, we possess the primal ability to evolve toward higher forms. In naming this most optimistic of qualities, Canetti borrowed a term from his beloved Kafka, "*Verwandlung*," thereby characteristically encoding a warning even at his most sanguine moment: the potential for human metamorphosis can go either way. Canetti's postulation of the transformative power recorded in myth comes only after hundreds of pages documenting patterns of atrocity and barbarism. It offers, finally, a whiff of optimism, a modicum of hope that contrasts starkly with—and responds to—the novel's dark and unpromising ending. In this way, then, Canetti's personal departure from literary modernism set the course for a creative new beginning.

NOTES

In the notes, *AF* refers to *Auto-da-Fé*, the Wedgwood English translation; *DB* refers to *Die Blendung*, the German original, as cited in the bibliography.

PREFACE

1. Denby, "Learning to Love Canetti," 107.
2. Up until 1993, the Harvard Department of Germanic Languages and Literatures listed *Auto-da-Fé* as a postwar novel on its reading list for graduate students.
3. Kimball, "Becoming Elias Canetti," 17.

INTRODUCTION

1. Kimball, "Becoming Elias Canetti," 23.
2. Canetti, *Das Augenspiel*, 39.
3. Ibid., 42.
4. See Darby's survey of the scholarly literature in *Structures of Disintegration*, 1–15, and Göpfert, *Canetti Lesen*.
5. Jay makes this point in both *The Dialectical Imagination* and *Adorno*.
6. Kimball, for example, remarks: "In tone, outlook, and texture, *Auto-da-Fé* may be described as a cross between Kafka . . . and the Borges of stories like 'The Library of Babel'" ("Becoming Elias Canetti," 23). Similarly, Denby observes: "The great European modernists—Yeats, Kafka, Mann, Musil—took on the burden of Europe's disintegration; Canetti, who had sorrowfully watched Austria fall apart between the wars, also sounds the authentic note of despair, the anguish of an impassioned humanism at bay" ("Learning to Love Canetti," 107).
7. Quoted in Rodney Livingstone, "Brecht's *Me-ti*," 68.
8. Canetti, *Das Augenspiel*, 142.
9. Ibid., 176.
10. Ibid., 176–77.
11. Göpfert, "Reception History," 304.
12. Ibid., 312.
13. Ibid., 302.

14. *Ein Dichter gegen Macht und Tod.*
15. Göpfert, "Reception History," 304.
16. For this story, as well as a source rich with early reception data, see "Weismanns Versuch."
17. Göpfert, "Reception History," 293.
18. Quoted in Peter Russell, "The Vision of Man," 30.
19. Reich-Ranicki, in *Ein Dichter gegen Macht und Tod*, remarks: "Es ist ein ganz großer Entwurf über die Tragödie des Intellektuellen in unserem Jahrhundert, eine Parabel von höchster Ambition."
20. Enzensberger, "Elias Canetti," 48.
21. Examples can be found in Barnouw, *Elias Canetti*, 29, and Lorenz, "Bezüge zwischen Roman und Massentheorie," 89.
22. Canetti, *Das Augenspiel*, 89.
23. See Murphy, *Canetti and Nietzsche*. For a more in-depth assessment of Murphy's monograph see Dagmar C. G. Lorenz's review in *German Quarterly* 71.2 (Spring 1998).
24. For a fuller account of German literary modernism than I can provide here, see Steven Dowden, *Sympathy for the Abyss*.
25. Dominick LaCapra and Walter Cohen, for example, take New Historicism to task for fostering "facile associationism" as well as "arbitrary connectedness"; in Cohn, "Optics and Power in the Novel," 96.
26. For example, Georg Eisler remarks, in *Ein Dichter gegen Macht und Tod*: "Canetti ist eminent weltanschaulich. Seine Arbeiten entstehen auf Grund einer sehr intensiven Betrachtung, eines sehr intensiven Anschauens, der Welt. Scheinbar steht er etwas abseits. Aber diese bohrende Art sich Fragen zu stellen, sich mit dem Wahrgenommenen auseinanderzustellen, geht natürlich auch ins Politische, ins in jeder Hinsicht Weltanschauliche."

CHAPTER 1

1. Canetti, "Das erste Buch," 250.
2. Ibid.
3. Ibid.
4. Liewerscheidt, "Ein Widerspruch," 356.
5. Darby, *Structures of Disintegration*, 101. For a contrastive study of narration in Canetti's two major works, see Werlen's *Narrative Strategies*.
6. Canetti, "Das erste Buch," 244. Here Canetti mentions also his translations of the American popular realist author Upton Sinclair for the leftist Malik Verlag of Berlin, 248–49.
7. Ibid., 249.
8. Canetti, *Auto-da-Fé*, 38. Henceforth all references to the Wedgwood transla-

tion will be abbreviated as *AF*. Those instances where I have modified Wedgwood are indicated by "trans. rev." The German text, cited in the notes according to the edition listed in the bibliography, is abbreviated as *DB*, as in the following: "Sollte es zu spät sein, dachte er, wie alt mag sie sein? Lernen kann man immer. Mit einfachen Romanen müßte sie beginnen" (*DB*, 37).

9. *AF*, 37; *DB*, 36.

10. *AF*, 42; "Für sie kam bloß ein Roman in Betracht. Nur wird von Romanen kein Geist fett. Den Genuß, den sie vielleicht bieten, überzahlt man sehr: sie zersetzen den besten Charakter. Man lernt sich in allerlei Menschen einfühlen. Am vielen Hin und Her gewinnt man Geschmack. Man löst sich in die Figuren auf, die einem gefallen. Jeder Standpunkt wird begreiflich. Willig überläßt man sich fremden Zielen und verliert für länger die eigenen aus dem Auge. Romane sind Keile, die ein schreibender Schauspieler in die geschlossene Person seiner Leser treibt. Je besser er Keil und Widerstand berechnet, um so gespaltener läßt er die Person zurück. Romane müßten von Staats wegen verboten sein" (*DB*, 41–42).

11. Terry Eagleton tells the story of the rise of English literature as an academic discipline in the British university—which occurred concurrently with the writing of *Auto-da-Fé* (1930-31)—in his "The Rise of English," in *Literary Theory*, 17–53.

12. *AF*, 43; "Sie schlug das Buch auf, las laut: 'Die Hosen . . .', unterbrach sich und wurde nicht rot. Ihr Gesicht bedeckte sich mit einem leichten Schweiß" (*DB*, 43).

13. "Roswitha las den Zettel durch und schnitt in der anderen Stube die letzte Zeile fort; sie genierte sich ihret- und ihrer Frau wegen, den Zettel in seiner ursprünglichen Gestalt abzugeben." In Fontane, *Effi Briest*, 198.

14. Effi instructs Roswitha: "du mußt mir nun auch Bücher besorgen; es wird nicht schwer halten, ich will alte, ganz alte" (ibid., 198). Fontane has included in this remark a barb against Alexis, with whom he felt a rivalry (see below): He has Effi suggest that it won't be difficult to find this Alexis novel in the library, because it is so dated. In this Fontane was simply wrong: Alexis's popularity continued unabated—even increased—during the Weimar period (see below).

15. Five times in Book 1 (*DB*, 42, 43, 45, 47, 121), and three times in Book 3 (*DB*, 379, 457, 458).

16. The nineteenth-century tendency to construct an idealized literary past—quite in contrast to historical reality—is well documented with regard to the "Ghettogeschichte" by Gabrielle von Glasenapp in her monograph *Aus der Judengasse*.

17. Thomas, "The Literary Reputation of Willibald Alexis," 195.

18. Adolf Stern writes that Alexis "ward nach einer üblen Gewohnheit . . . nur allzu oft als der deutsche Walter Scott bezeichnet" (in Thomas, ibid., 210 n. 3).

19. Ibid., 197.

20. Lynne Tatlock observes: "To this day he is remembered, if at all, as the German Walter Scott. Whereas in our own time his name means nothing to the gen-

eral public, educated Germans of an older generation tend to know the historical novel, *Die Hosen des Herrn von Bredow*" (*Willibald Alexis' Zeitroman "Das Haus Düsterweg"* and the *Vormärz*, 3).

21. This and the following publication information culled from Reinhard Oberschelp, ed., *Gesamtverzeichnis*, 418–19. Despite its title, this catalogue is not reliably comprehensive. Furthermore, printing quantities are only haphazardly given. Nevertheless, the global impression is that *Die Hosen* did a considerable business in the 1920s.

22. Though my account of the novel's publication history breaks off here, one might note that *Die Hosen des Herrn von Bredow* continued to be issued throughout the Nazi period.

23. Theodor Fontane, "Willibald Alexis," 422.

24. Alexis, *Die Hosen*, 49. Though no date of publication is printed in the book, 1926 is the year given in the *Gesamtverzeichnis* for the Insel printing of "22. bis 26. Tausend," which is printed on the final page of this edition.

25. Ibid., 29.

26. Ibid., 8, 74.

27. Ibid., 6.

28. *Der blaue Engel* opened in Berlin in 1930, though, of course, Heinrich Mann's novel, on which the film is loosely based, had already appeared almost twenty-five years earlier. Rath's enchantment at hearing the schoolgirls sing "Ännchen von Tharau" gives us an idea of the text through which he saw Lola-Lola.

29. With the metamorphosis of an obedient servant into a destroying shrew, Canetti combines gender representations often rigidly separated, namely the "real" subservient woman as against the "mythic" she-devil. On this see Maria Tatar, "'Wie süß ist es, sich zu opfern': Gender, Violence, and Agency in Döblin's *Berlin Alexanderplatz*," 514.

30. For an account and critical appraisal of this debate, see Saul Friedländer, *Probing the Limits of Representation*, especially 1–21.

31. Quoted in Thomas, "The Literary Reputation of Willibald Alexis," 195.

32. Ibid., 196.

33. Tatlock ("Willibald Alexis and 'Young Germany,'" 367) quotes Alexis himself on the collapse of the two time levels (the historical period treated and the period in which the novel is written) in this genre: "denn ist nicht jede Novelle =Roman [sic] eigentlich eine Zeitnovelle, wenn der Autor seine subjektive Auffassung in der Behandlung des Themas, möge es noch so weit in der Zeit zurückliegen, aus der Zeit, in der er lebt, mit hereinbringt?"

34. Thomas, "The Literary Reception of Willibald Alexis," 202.

35. Natter, *Literature at War*, 208.

36. *AF*, 114, my emphasis; "In der Liste der gefallenen Bücher figurierte als Nummer 39 ein dicker, alter Band über 'Bewaffnung und Taktik der Landsknechte.' Kaum war er mit schwerem Krach über die Leiter gekollert, als die blasenden Hausbesorger sich in Landsknechte verwandelten. Eine ungeheure Be-

geisterung packte Kien. Der Hausbesorger war ein Landsknecht, was denn sonst? ... Da jagte ihm die Faust keinen Schrecken mehr ein. Vor ihm saß eine wohlvertraute historische Figur. Er wußte, was sie tun und was sie lassen würde ... Armer, zu spät geratener Kerl, kam da als Landsknecht im zwanzigsten Jahrhundert auf die Welt ... ausgestoßen aus dem Säkulum, für das er geschaffen war, verschlagen in ein anderes, wo er immer fremd blieb! *In der harmlosen Ferne des beginnenden 16. Jahrhunderts schmolz der Hausbesorger zu nichts zusammen,* er mochte prahlen, soviel er wollte. *Um eines Menschen Herr zu werden, genügt es, ihn historisch einzureihen*" (DB, 119–20, my emphasis).

37. DB, 417.

38. Canetti visits the issues of "Vergangenheit," history, and historians repeatedly in the *Die Provinz des Menschen: Aufzeichnungen 1942–1972* and he is invariably negative. Canetti charges historians with preserving and propagating relationships of power, for failing to see what could have been (i.e., for encouraging the sense of historical inevitability), and for creating a false sense of security: "Die Geschichte gibt den Menschen ihr falsches Vertrauen zurück" (50). Other pertinent passages can be found at 13, 32–33 (where Canetti compares historians to blind termites who consume each other's waste), 36, 51.

39. See also Kien's paean to the past from the chapter "Die Erstarrung": "An allen Schmerzen ist die Gegenwart schuld. Er sehnt sich nach der Zukunft, weil dann mehr Vergangenheit auf der Welt sein wird. Die Vergangenheit ist gut, sie tut niemand was zuleid, zwanzig Jahre hat er sich frei in ihr bewegt, er war glücklich ... Er beugt sich vor dem Primat der Vergangenheit" (DB, 169).

40. AF, 398; "Lesen als Streicheln, eine andere Form der Liebe, für Damen und Damenärzte, zu deren Beruf feines Verständnis für die intime Lektüre der Dame gehörte" (DB, 436).

41. DB, 435; AF, 398.

42. AF, 398–99; "Die besten Romane waren die, in denen die Menschen am gewähltesten sprachen ... Eine solche Aufgabe bestand darin, die zackige, schmerzliche, beißende Vielgestalt des Lebens, das einen umgab, auf eine glatte Papierebene zu bringen, über die es sich rasch und angenehm hinweglas ... je öfter ein Geleise befahren war, um so differenzierter die Lust, die man ihm abgewann ... Georges Kien hatte als Frauenarzt begonnen. Seine Jugend und Schönheit fand ungeheuren Zulauf. In jener Periode, die nur wenige Jahre dauerte, ergab er sich den Romanen Frankreichs; an seinem Erfolg hatten sie wesentlichen Anteil ... Von zahllosen Frauen, zu seinem Dienst bereit, umgeben, verwöhnt, reich, wohlerzogen, lebte er wie Prinz Gautama, bevor er Buddah wurde. Kein besorgter Vater und Fürst schloß ihn vom Elend der Welt ab, er sah Alter, Tod und Bettler, so viele, daß er sie nicht mehr sah. Abgeschlossen war er doch, aber durch die Bücher, die er las, die Sätze, die er sprach, die Frauen, die sich als gierige, geschlossene Mauer um ihn stellten" (DB, 436).

43. Davis, *Resisting Novels,* 12.

44. Davis observes that "'Identification,' ... [a] major defense, in which we

convince ourselves that we are like certain 'ideal' figures, is so clearly a feature of novel reading that further discussion is not necessary . . . Suffice it to say that a novel can barely succeed unless we place ourselves in some special relation to the hero or heroine" (ibid., 21).

45. Ibid., 127.

46. Barnouw, *Elias Canetti*, 28.

47. *AF*, 395; *DB*, 432.

48. *AF*, 396; "Er war groß, stark, feurig und sicher; in seinen Zügen lag etwas von jener Weichheit, die Frauen benötigen, um sich bei einem Manne heimisch zu fühlen. Wer ihn sah, nannte ihn den Adam des Michelangelo" (*DB*, 433).

49. Davis notes that "ideologically speaking, then, character gives readers faith that personality is, first, understandable and, second, capable of rational change. As part of the general ideology of middle-class individualism, the idea that the subject might be formed from social forces and that change might have to come about through social change is by and large absent from novels. *Change is always seen as effected by the individual*" (*Resisting Novels*, my emphasis, 119).

50. Göpfert, "Reception History," 299.

51. Ibid., 303.

52. Georg's self-image as insightful "Menschenkenner" can be found at *AF*, 426, and *DB*, 466. The critics' love affair with Georg has continued down to Walter Sokel (1974) and Russell Berman (1986), both of whom will be discussed in the following chapter.

53. *AF*, 210; "'Sicher sind Sie ein guter Läufer!' Fischerle durchschaute die Falle und erwiderte: 'Was soll ich lügen? Wenn Sie einen Schritt machen, mach' ich einen halben. In der Schule war ich immer der schlechteste Läufer.' Er dachte sich den Namen einer Schule aus, für den Fall, daß ihn Kien danach fragte: in Wirklichkeit hatte er nie eine besucht. Aber Kien schlug sich eben mit wichtigeren Gedanken [namely the memory of his own physical shortcomings] herum. *Er stand vor dem größten Vertrauensbeweis seines Lebens. 'Ich glaube Ihnen!' sagte er schlicht. Fischerle frohlockte*" (*DB*, 229, my emphasis).

54. *AF*, 255; "weil ihm ihre Empörung gefiel" (279), trans. rev.

55. Canetti, *Das Augenspiel*, 132.

56. Davis, *Resisting Novels*, 102–61, especially 125.

57. Ibid., 137.

58. Ibid., 138.

59. Alexis, *Die Hosen*, 62.

60. Ibid., 185.

61. Ibid., 164.

62. Ibid., 49.

63. Davis, *Resisting Novels*, 142.

64. *AF*, 16–17, my emphasis, trans. rev. Readers of English may not immediately recognize Wedgwood's "Mut Strasse" as referring to a city street (*Straße* = street), and may also wish to know that there is some irony in the choice of this

name, which, though also a proper name (i.e., a real Viennese street name), literally means "courage street," indicating a quality totally lacking in the protagonist. "Da rief jemand laut jemand andern an: 'Können Sie mir sagen, wo hier die Mutstraße ist?' Der Gefragte entgegnete nichts. Kien wunderte sich; da gab es auf offener Straße *noch außer ihm* schweigsame Menschen. Ohne aufzublicken, horchte er hin. Wie würde sich der Fragende zu dieser Stummheit verhalten? . . . Wieder sagte er nichts. Kien belobte ihn . . . Noch immer sagte der zweite nichts . . . Der Vorgang spielte zu seiner Rechten. Dort tobte der erste: 'Sie haben kein Benehmen! . . .' Der zweite schwieg . . . Da bekam Kien einen bösen Stoß . . . Der zweite, der Schweiger und Charakter, der seinen Mund auch im Zorn beherrschte, war Kien selbst" (*DB*, 14–15, my emphasis).

65. Darby, *Structures of Disintegration*, 27.

66. Alexis, *Die Hosen*, 55, 56.

67. Ibid., 96–97.

68. Ibid., 68.

69. For the parallel story, see ibid., 87–89. Schneider Wiedeband, like Hedderich, is accused of selling fraudulent articles of clothing. Because of his talents as a tailor, and because "die sächsischen Herren" enjoyed playing him off against "die von Beelitz," Wiedeband was able to buy himself into nobility. But when he attempts revenge on his oppressors à la Michael Kohlhaas, both parties turn against him, and he is hanged.

70. The exchange in German runs as follows: "Plagt der Teufel den alten Krippenreiter, daß er einem Juden auflauert, der mit seinem Wagen nach Berlin fährt." "Einem Juden." "Oder so was" (ibid., 2:6).

71. Ibid., 2:12; see also 2:7–8.

72. An examination of Alexis's political affiliations can be found in Tatlock, "Willibald Alexis and 'Young Germany.'"

73. See Hal Draper, "Marx and the Economic-Jew Stereotype," in *Karl Marx's Theory of Revolution*, 1:591–608.

74. Alexis, *Die Hosen*, 2:12.

75. On this see Michael Brenner, *After the Holocaust*.

76. Alexis, *Die Hosen*, 1:23–24.

77. Thomas's statement on Alexis's "love of impartiality" certainly does not extend to this novel's anti-Semitism; nor does it seem appropriate in general to *Die Hosen*. See "The Literary Reception of Willibald Alexis," 207.

78. See also Alexis, *Die Hosen*, 2:157. Any critical position one might attempt to read into this representation seems further disallowed by Alexis's conception "of the hero as the representative of the reader, just as the chorus in ancient tragedy typifies public opinion" (Thomas, "The Literary Reception of Willibald Alexis," 210).

79. See, for example, Alexis, *Die Hosen*, 2:79, which marks the beginning of a passage that moves Lindenberg into a distinctly more positive light by portraying him as the enlightener of the youthful ruler.

80. Ibid., 62, 64.

81. Though also sprinkled throughout the book, such gnomic utterances can be found at 1:30 (fickle human nature), 1:92 (von Bredow as a dimwit), 1:60 (simple living is best).

82. Gilman, *Difference and Pathology*.

83. Some examples of Therese-focalization buried within an apparently objective narrative voice can be found at *DB*, 334 (the investigation), 80–81 (the furniture shopping excursion), and 107 (the discovery of Kien after his accident in the library). One example of unmarked Kien focalization is at *DB*, 181–82; others are strewn throughout the novel.

84. *AF*, 396; "in seinen Zügen lag etwas von jener Weichheit, die Frauen benötigen, um sich bei einem Manne heimisch zu fühlen" (*DB*, 433).

85. For a concise overview of these two Genettian terms ("zero focalization," "internal focalization") as well as Stanzel's parallel categories, see Dorrit Cohn, "Optics and Power in the Novel." A more extensive treatment of these key narratological terms can be found in Cohn's classic *Transparent Minds*.

86. See Canetti's 1965 essay "Realismus und neue Wirklichkeit."

87. Canetti, "Das erste Buch," 249.

CHAPTER 2

1. Sontag, "Mind as Passion," 88.

2. *AF*, 445; "Du bist immer höflich, du Weib, du bist wie die Eva . . . Ruh dich doch von der Weiblichkeit aus! Vielleicht wirst du wieder ein Mensch" (*DB*, 488). The title quotation is also spoken by Peter Kien to brother Georg. The German original has a somewhat different flavor: "Eigentlich bist du eine Frau. Du bestehst aus Sensationen" (*DB*, 479).

3. Lawson, *Understanding Elias Canetti*, 8.

4. Ibid., 41.

5. Ferrara, "Grotesque and Voiceless," 86, 93.

6. Foell, *Blind Reflections*, 186. Foell reaches a similar conclusion regarding a sexual encounter between Therese and Pfaff: "Canetti preserves the distance to Therese, leaving the reader disgusted at her . . . rather than sympathetic with her as victim of sexual assault. In effect, he perpetuates the myth that 'women want it'" (137). Though Foell claims to offer a more differentiated view (i.e., that Canetti both actively criticizes and passively reflects reigning gender theories of his day), the net effect of her study is to suggest that even in those cases where she perceives Canetti to have offered some revision of Weininger, that position is still decidedly misogynistic (see, for example, 57, 100, 148, 154, 188). More recently, Foell espouses the curious notion that *Auto-da-Fé* does not qualify as satire because it "cannot be a means of satire when the object of satire (here Weininger's 'W') is itself an absurd exaggeration"; see "Whores, Mothers, and Others," 248–

53. This stands in stark contrast to the more convincing position taken by Elfriede Pöder in "Spurensicherung."

7. Sontag, who once supposed that the novel "is animated by an exceptionally inventive hatred for women" ("Mind as Passion," 92), appears repeatedly as a kind of inspiration in subsequent feminist analyses of *Auto-da-Fé*. What her disciples have overlooked, however, is the more sophisticated "life and work" model implicit in Sontag's essay. Reflecting on language common to both the novel and the published notebooks (*Die Aufzeichnungen*), Sontag notes: "And this was not language suitable only for the mad bookman; Canetti later used it in his notebooks to describe himself, as when he called his life nothing but a desperate attempt to think about everything 'so that it comes together in a head and thus becomes one again,' affirming the very fantasy he had pilloried in *Auto-da-Fé*" (ibid., 93). This approach to "life and work," which is at once alert to inconsistencies and thematic parallels yet opposed to reductionist equations, seems to me the most promising for future Canetti scholarship, particularly as we anticipate the publication of the *Nachlaß* as well as a truly critical biography.

8. Felman, "Turning the Screw of Interpretation," 105.

9. Ferrara simply thinks that the novel's men are treated better by the narrator, who, for her, is interchangeable with Canetti himself ("Grotesque and Voiceless," 86–87, 92). Foell assumes a narrator so in charge of the story that silence itself tacitly endorses a *character's* misogynistic views. When Fischerle insults the school teacher by assuming she is a whore (recall that Fischerle thinks every woman is a whore), Foell rushes to her defense, lest the hapless reader be persuaded to adopt Fischerle's opinion: "The joke is at the teacher's expense...," we are told, "leaving the reader with Fischerle's viewpoint (which the narrator does not contradict) that this is not a 'real' woman because she is not a whore, not concerned with her attractiveness to men" (ibid., 141; see also 82).

10. On this see Foell (*Blind Reflections*, 125, 135, 139), who proposes that Kien is indeed an identification figure capable of inspiring misogyny in the reader.

11. Canetti, *Das Augenspiel*, 40.

12. Beller, "Otto Weininger as Liberal?"

13. *AF*, 184; *DB*, 200–201.

14. Bronfen, *Over Her Dead Body*, 415.

15. Ibid., 418.

16. *AF*, 177; *DB*, 192. The mother-son relationship is articulated later in the same chapter: "Sie hatte das Gefühl, daß sie am mißratenen Teil ihres Kindes mitschuldig sei" (*DB*, 199).

17. *AF*, 355; "Unters Bett wär' er zum Abschied gern gekrochen, weil er dort in der Wiege seiner Laufbahn lag. Da ... herrschte eine Ruhe wie in keinem Kaffeehaus" (*DB*, 388).

18. Tatar, *The Hard Facts of the Grimms' Fairy Tales*, 91.

19. Ibid., 182.

20. Ibid., 149.

21. *AF*, 368; "Bald nach dieser Veränderung starb die Frau, vor Überanstrengung . . . Am Tage nach der Beerdigung begann sein Wonnemond. Ungestörter als bisher verfuhr er mit der Tochter nach Belieben" (*DB*, 402).

22. Tatar, *The Hard Facts of the Grimms' Fairy Tales*, 150.

23. Ibid., 152–53.

24. *AF*, 370; "Das Futter gibt ihr . . ." "der gute Vater." / "Die Männer wollen sie . . ." "gar nicht haben." . . . / "Jetzt wird sie der Vater gleich . . ." "verhaften." / "Auf dem Vater seinem Schoß sitzt . . ." "die brave Tochter." / "Der Vater weiß, warum er sie . . ." "schlägt." / "Er tut der Tochter gar nicht . . ." "weh." / "Dafür lernt sie, was sich beim . . ." "Vater gehört" (*DB*, 404–5).

25. Concluding from Cox's study of 345 variants of "Cinderella," Tatar observes: "Cinderella and her folkloristic sisters are therefore almost as likely to flee the household because of their father's perverse erotic attachment to them or because of his insistence on a verbal declaration of love as they are to be banished to the hearth and degraded to domestic servitude by an ill-tempered stepmother" (*The Hard Facts of the Grimms' Fairy Tales*, 153). Tatar's analysis of the potential complementarity of the incestuous father/jealous mother plots reminds us that these may not, therefore, represent discrete alternative plots at the level of psychic motivation.

26. *AF*, 45, trans. rev.; *DB*, 45.

27. *AF*, 121; *DB*, 127.

28. *AF*, 43; "Umständlich suchte sie ein passendes [Stück Packpapier] aus und legte es dem Buche um, wie einem Kind ein Kleid . . . Er hatte sie unterschätzt. Sie behandelte die Bücher besser als er" (*DB*, 42).

29. Hauptmann employed this same female type elsewhere, as Karl S. Guthke has suggested, namely in the figure of Hanne Schäl (Frau Henschel), from *Fuhrmann Henschel* (1898).

30. Downing, "Repetition and Realism."

31. Hauptmann, *Bahnwärter Thiel*, 225, my emphasis. The German gives a slightly clearer sense of Lene's sexuality: "Drei Dinge jedoch hatte er, ohne es zu wissen, mit seiner Frau in Kauf genommen: eine harte, herrschsüchtige Gemütsart, Zanksucht und *brutale Leidenschaftlichkeit*. Nach Verlauf eines halben Jahres war es ortsbekannt, wer in dem Häuschen des Wärters das Regiment führte. Man bedauerte den Wärter."

32. For example, Werlen, *Narrative Strategies*, 12.

33. Hauptmann, *Bahnwärter Thiel*, 236.

34. Ibid., 238.

35. For more on this see Mieder, "'Spuren der schwarzen Spinne.'"

36. I explore this issue in greater depth in "The Kiss of the Spider Woman."

37. *AF*, 432, trans. rev.; "In der Spinne, dem grausamsten und häßlichsten aller Tiere, sehe ich die verkörperte Weiblichkeit. Ihr Netz schillert in der Sonne giftig und blau" (*DB*, 475).

38. Regarding pornography, Stewart wrote in the famous 1964 case of *Jacobellis*

v. Ohio: "I shall not today attempt further to define the kinds of material I understand to be embraced within that shorthand description; and perhaps I could never succeed in intelligibly doing so. But I know it when I see it."

39. Ryan, *Vanishing Subject*, 6–22; a somewhat fuller treatment of this topic can be found in her "Viennese Psychology and American Pragmatism."

40. Ryan, *Vanishing Subject*, 21.

41. For Weininger, the "Jew" no less than "Woman" represents the specter of the disunified empirical self. On the Jew as the quintessential Machian (or empirical) self, see Beller, *Vienna and the Jews*, 224. The opposition between the empirical and ethical selves is of central concern in Beller's "Otto Weininger as Liberal?"

42. In *Ein Dichter gegen Macht und Tod*, poet Erich Fried insightfully refers to Klaus Theweleit as Canetti's "rebellious student." Yet the affinity goes well beyond mere literary form (i.e., similar kinds of eclecticism and idiosyncratic essayistic form in both *Masse und Macht* and *Männerphantasien* [Male Fantasies]) to include a shared analysis of misogyny as rooted in a male identity crisis. Thus Theweleit's *Male Fantasies* is indebted as much to *Auto-da-Fé* as it is to *Masse und Macht*.

43. An instructive survey of Weininger's considerable influence can be found in Barbara Hyams and Nancy A. Harrowitz, "A Critical Introduction to the History of Weininger Reception."

44. Beller, "Otto Weininger as Liberal?," 97.

45. Ibid., 99.

46. Beller elaborates: "Man's mortal enemy is Woman, that is, the animal, the material, the earthly in each individual. What woman really represents is Weininger's fear that Man's higher self will be distracted from the pursuit of knowledge and meaning by the allures of hedonistic pleasure and the irrational realm of feelings" (ibid., 98).

47. *AF*, 239, trans. rev.; "Da der Philologe in ihm noch lebte, beschloß er, bis ruhigere Zeiten ins Land gekehrt wären, eine von Grund auf neue, textkritische Untersuchung der Evangelien vorzunehmen. . . . Er fühlte in sich Gelehrsamkeit genug, um das Christentum auf seinen wahren Ursprung zurückzuführen, und wenn er auch nicht der erste war, der die wirklichen Worte des Heilands in eine Menschheit warf . . . so hoffte er doch mit einigem inneren Grund, daß seine Deutung die letzte blieb" (*DB*, 261).

48. *AF*, 391; *DB*, 428.

49. *AF*, 385; "Die Wissenschaft hat uns von Aberglauben und Glauben befreit. Sie gebraucht immer die gleichen Namen, mit Vorliebe griechisch-lateinische, und meint damit die wirklichen Dinge. Mißverständnisse sind unmöglich" (*DB*, 421).

50. *AF*, 144; "Immer wieder zwang er sich, nach den japanischen Handschriften auf dem Tisch zu greifen. Kam er so weit, dann berührte er sie und zog die Hand, fast angewidert, gleich zurück. Was hatten die zu bedeuten? . . . Auf das begonnene Manuskript malte er, ganz gegen seine Gewohnheit, Zeichen, die keinen Sinn ergaben" (*DB*, 153).

51. *AF,* 130-31; "Es genügte ihm daß sie schwieg. Zwischen China und Japan sagte er sich einmal, das sei der Erfolg seiner klugen Politik . . . Viele Konjekturen gelangen ihm in diesen Tagen. Einen unglaublich verballhornten Satz stellte er in drei Stunden wieder her. Die richtigen Buchstaben regneten nur so aus seiner Feder . . . Ältere Litaneien meldeten sich in ihm zu Wort; darüber vergaß er die ihre" (*DB,* 138).

52. Kien is here referring to the discovery of Therese's finances, but the term—even in this context—remains apposite of his scholarly pursuits. *AF,* 144; *DB,* 153.

53. *AF,* 47-48; "Sie ist das beste Mittel, um meine Bibliothek in Ordnung zuhalten . . . Hätte ich eine Person nach meinen Plänen konstruiert, sie wäre nicht so zweckmäßig ausgefallen" (*DB,* 47).

54. *AF,* 148; "Damals sprach sie immer dasselbe; er lernte ihre Worte auswendig und war genaugenommen Herr über sie . . . aber da begann Therese wieder zu sprechen. Was sie sagte, war unverständlich und übte despotische Gewalt über ihn aus. Es ließ sich nicht auswendig lernen und wer sah voraus, was jetzt kam?" (*DB,* 158).

55. *AF,* 311; *DB,* 340, emphasis in original.

56. *AF,* 397, trans. rev.; "Er untersuchte sein Trugbild so lange, bis er sich davon überzeugte, was es war. Ganz anderen Gefahren, schadhaften Texten, fehlenden Zeilen, war er schon auf den Leib gerückt. Er entsann sich nicht, je versagt zu haben. Sämtliche Aufgaben, die er sich vorgenommen hatte, waren gelöst. Auch den Mord betrachtete er als eine erledigte Angelegenheit. An einer Halluzination zerbrach kein Kien . . ." (*DB,* 336). On this topic see also *DB,* 338, 349.

57. *AF,* 445; "Bücher sind stumm, sie sprechen *und* sind stumm, das ist das Großartige" (*DB,* 489, emphasis in original).

58. *AF,* 463; "Aus der ersten Zeile löst sich ein Stab und schlägt ihm eine um die Ohren. Blei. Das tut weh. Schlag! Schlag! Noch einer. Noch einer. Eine Fußnote tritt ihn mit Füßen. Immer mehr. Er taumelt. Zeilen und ganze Seiten, alles fällt über ihn her. Die schütteln und schlagen ihn, die beuteln ihn, die schleudern ihn einander zu. Blut . . . Zu Hilfe! Zu Hilfe! Georg!" (*DB,* 508).

59. Tatar, *Lustmord,* 10.

60. This incident is recounted in *DB,* 54-55.

61. Ibid., 18, 67, 183.

62. Ibid., 126.

63. *AF,* 322; "Solche Sachen stehen in den Büchern" (*DB,* 352).

64. *AF,* 438; "Georg sah sich hier als wichtigen Teil eines Mechanismus, den ein anderer zur Erhaltung seines bedrohten Selbstgefühls in Bewegung gesetzt hatte" (*DB,* 481).

65. In the most compelling chapter of *Lustmord,* "The Corpse Vanishes: Gender, Violence, and Agency in Alfred Döblin's *Berlin Alexanderplatz,*" Tatar concludes: "Franz and Reinhold may be indicted by the narrator and by the law for their murderous impulses and actions toward women, but the stories of the Whore of Babylon and Clytemnestra lift the burden of guilt from their shoulders" (151).

66. This misogynistic tour de force concludes, it should be noted, with yet another defense of the imagined Lustmord: "Seine Rede ging in die eines Verteidigers über, der vor Gericht erklärt, warum sein Klient die dämonische Frau ermorden mußte. Ihre Dämonie ersieht man aus dem unzüchtigen Leben, das sie gern geführt hätte, aus der aufreizenden Kleidung ... Welcher Mann hätte eine solche Frau nicht ermordet?" (*DB*, 493).

67. *AF*, 448; "Das Material war größer als sein Haß" (*DB*, 491; see also *DB*, 478).

68. *AF*, 111; "Am wohlsten fühlte er sich noch, wenn er sie dort unterbrachte, wo alles Platz fand, für das er trotz Bildung und Verstand keine Erklärung wußte. Von der Verrückten hatte er ein grobes und einfaches Bild. Er definierte sie als Menschen, die das Widersprechendste tun, doch für alles dieselben Worte haben. Nach dieser Definition war Therese — im Gegensatz zu ihm selbst — entschieden verrückt" (*DB*, 116; see also *DB*, 186).

69. Gilbert and Gubar, *The Madwoman in the Attic*.

70. *AF*, 395; "Er hielt es für seine eigentliche Lebensaufgabe, das riesige Material, über welches er verfügte, als Stütze für gangbare Bezeichnungen zu verwenden ... Er hing an der Fertigkeit des Systems und haßte Zweifler. Menschen, besonders Geisteskranke und Verbrecher, waren ihm gleichgültig ... Sie lieferten Erfahrungen, aus denen Autoritäten die Wissenschaft erbauten. Er selber war eine Autorität" (*DB*, 432–33).

71. *AF*, 396; "Verrückt, sagte er mit großem Nachdruck und blickte seine Frau durchdringend und durchschauend an, sie errötete, verrückt werden eben die Menschen, die immer nur an sich denken. Irrsinn ist eine Strafe für Egoismus ... Anderes hatte er seiner Frau nicht zu sagen. Sie war um dreißig Jahre jünger als er und verschönte seinen Lebensabend. Die erste Frau war ihm durchgebrannt, bevor er sie, wie später die zweite, in die eigene Anstalt steckte, als unheilbar egoistisch. Die dritte, gegen die er außer seiner Eifersucht nichts im Schilde führte, liebte Georges Kien" (*DB*, 433).

72. *AF*, 404; "Er tat ihnen [den Geisteskranken] den Gefallen und führte sie nach Ägypten zurück. Die Wege, die er dafür ersann, waren gewiß so wunderbar wie die des Herrn beim Auszug seines Volkes" (*DB*, 442).

73. *AF*, 405; "Seine Fachkollegen bestaunten und beneideten ihn ... Man beeilte sich, kleine Brocken von seinem Ruhm zu erschnappen, indem man sich zu ihm bekannte und seine Methoden in den verschiedenartigsten Fällen erprobte. Der Nobelpreis war ihm sicher" (*DB*, 443).

74. *AF*, 399; "Von zahllosen Frauen, zu seinem Dienst bereit, umgeben, verwöhnt, reich, wohlerzogen; [er] lebte wie Prinz Gautama, bevor er Buddha wurde" (*DB*, 436).

75. The Wedgwood translation captures the religious aura that attends Georg's repudiation of women: "He found the way to the wilderness in his twenty-eighth year" (*AF*, 399). The German text contains many humorous references to religious motifs in the surrounding text, but not in the sentence itself: "Den Weg in

seine Heimatlosigkeit fand er mit 28 Jahren" (*DB*, 436). Though Georg's conversion experience is thus riddled with irony, a number of critics take this transformation quite seriously. Hans Fabian, for example, refers to it as "Dieser Prozeß der Läuterung" and proceeds to identify it with "Canettis eigene Einstellung." See Fabian, "Die Sprache bei Elias Canetti," 504.

76. *AF*, 401, trans. rev.; "Wenn der Gorilla nur wieder sprach! Vor diesem einen Wunsch verschwanden alle Gedanken an Zeitknappheit, Verpflichtungen, Frauen, Erfolge, als hätte er von Geburt an den Menschen oder Gorilla gesucht, der seine eigene Sprache besaß" (*DB*, 439).

77. Clover, *Men, Women, and Chainsaws*, 97–113.

78. Beller, "Otto Weininger as Liberal?," 99.

79. *AF*, 401, 403; "Jeder Silbe, die er hervorstieß, entsprach eine bestimmte Bewegung. Für Gegenstände schienen die Bezeichnungen zu wechseln. Das Bild meinte er hundertmal und nannte es jedesmal verschieden; die Namen hingen von der Gebärde ab, mit der er hinwies ... Die Gegenstände hatten ... keine eigentlichen Namen. Je nach der Empfindung, in der sie trieben, hießen sie. Ihr Gesicht wechselte für den Gorilla, der ein wildes, gespanntes, gewitterreiches Leben führte. Sein Leben ging auf sie über, sie hatten aktiven Teil daran. Er bevölkerte zwei Zimmer mit einer ganzen Welt. Er schuf, was er brauchte, und fand sich nach seinen sechs Tagen am siebenten darin zurecht. Statt zu ruhen, schenkte er der Schöpfung eine Sprache" (*DB*, 439, 441).

80. For a somewhat different discussion of this concept with reference to *Auto-da-Fé*, see Pöder, "Spurensicherung," 59–60.

81. *AF*, 403; *DB*, 441.

82. No critic has, to my knowledge, fully appreciated the extent to which Georg actually creates this woman to appease the hallucinations of his patient Jean (see *DB*, 447, 448). The significance of this episode lies not primarily in Jean's fantasy of punishing the sexually "digressive" woman (a parallel to Kien's own hallucinatory fantasies of punishing Therese), nor in the fact that the assistants themselves make so much of this treatment as a test case of Georg's "therapy," but rather in the fact that it provides a frame for evaluating Georg's musings on the crowd (*DB*, 449–50). For a fuller treatment of this point, see below, chapter 5.

83. *DB*, 479, 488.

84. *AF*, 397; "Könige redete er untertänigst als Eure Majestät an ... Er wurde ihr einziger Vertrauter ... Er beriet sie ... als hätte er selbst ihre Wünsche, immer ihr Ziel und ihren Glauben im Auge, vorsichtig verschiebend ... Männern gegenüber nie autoritär ... schließlich sei er doch ihr Minister, Prophet und Apostel, oder zuweilen sogar der Kammerdiener" (*DB*, 434).

85. *AF*, 413; *DB*, 452.

86. *AF*, 421, trans. rev.; "Georg der Bruder eines Lustmörders. Schlagzeilen in allen Zeitungen ... Rücktritt von der Leitung einer Irrenanstalt. Fehltritt. Scheidung. Assistenten als Nachfolger. Die Kranken ... Sie lieben ihn, sie brauchen ihn, er darf sie nicht verlassen, ein Rücktritt ist unmöglich ... Peters Affäre muß

geregelt werden ... *Er* war für chinesische Schriften da, Georg für Menschen. Peter gehört in eine geschlossene Anstalt . . . Seine Unzurechnungsfähigkeit läßt sich beweisen. Auf keinen Fall tritt Georg von der Leitung seiner Anstalt zurück" (*DB*, 460–61).

87. *AF*, 456; "Sehnsucht nach dem Ort, wo er ein ebenso absoluter Herrscher war, wie Peter in seiner Bibliothek" (*DB*, 500).

88. Sokel, "The Ambiguity of Madness."

89. Barnouw, *Elias Canetti*, 25–26.

90. Berman, *The Rise of the Modern German Novel*, especially chapter 8, "The Charismatic Novel: Robert Musil, Hermann Hesse, and Elias Canetti," 179–204.

91. Notice in the following how Georg relates "die Masse" first to "the maternal" and then to madness, a term we have already established as, in the vocabulary of the novel, intrinsically "feminine": "'Die Menschheit' bestand schon lange, bevor sie begrifflich erfunden und verwässert wurde, als Mass. Sie brodelt, ein ungeheueres, wildes, saftstrotzendes und heißes Tier in uns allen, sehr tief, viel tiefer als die Mütter ... Zahllose Menschen werden verrückt, weil die Masse in ihnen besonders stark ist" (*DB*, 449–50). For a discussion of the feminization of the crowd in the novel, see Bernd Widdig, *Männerbünde und Massen*. Below, in chapter 5, I develop further the point that Georg offers us virtually no insight on crowd psychology, and that his views are only superficially similar to those enunciated by Canetti in *Crowds and Power*.

92. *AF*, 411, trans. rev.; "Zahllose Menschen werden verrückt, weil die Masse in ihnen besonders stark ist und keine Befriedigung findet. . . . Früher hatte er persönlichen Neigungen, seinem Ehrgeiz und den Frauen gelebt; jetzt lag ihm nur daran, sich unaufhörlich zu verlieren. In dieser Tätatigkeit kam er Wünschen und Sinnen der Masse näher, als die übrigen einzelnen, von denen er umgeben war" (*DB*, 450).

CHAPTER 3

1. Denby, "Learning to Love Canetti," 110.

2. My nonliteral translation aims to capture the spirit of Canetti's remark; compare *Das Augenspiel*, 131.

3. Ibid., 142.

4. Kien's interest in ancient Chinese texts indicates his total remove from contemporary concerns, and thus is not unrelated to the novel's critique in this regard. Yet a careful reading of the novel reveals that Kien's status as "sinologist" is more referred to than illustrated. The intellectual tradition associated principally with Kien and more consistently at stake throughout the novel is neo-Kantianism, as I argue below. Nevertheless, Kien's bastardization of Confucianism presents, as Ning Ying observes ("China und Elias Canetti," 155), a clear parallel to his capricious use of the Western philosophical tradition: "Kien verhält sich

tatsächlich nicht rigoros konfuzianisch, während er immer von den Ratschlägen der chinesischen Gelehrten redet."

5. The single episode which has thus far inspired a philosophical approach is Kien's pointedly pseudophilosophical diatribe against Therese's "blendende Möbel" (*DB*, 70–73); see Darby, "Perception and Perspective in Berkeley and Canetti."

6. In a rare moment of self-deprecation, Canetti remarks: "Ich hatte, wenn ich es heute zu bemessen versuche, noch wenig gelernt und jedenfalls nichts von dem, was sein besonderes Wissen ausmachte: die zeitgenössische Philosophie. Seine Bibliothek war hauptsächlich eine philosophische, er scheute im Gegensatz zu mir vor der Welt der Begriffe nicht zurück, er gab sich ihnen hin wie andere dem Besuch von Nachtlokalen" (*Das Augenspiel*, 27). Elsewhere in the autobiography Canetti remarks that he is simply not a "Begriffsmensch."

7. Regarding the professor of philosophy, Oskar Kraus, Canetti writes: "Daß er sich bei jeder Gelegenheit noch in seinem Alter auf seinen Meister, den Philosophen Brentano berief, hatte etwas Subalternes, wenigstens kam es mir so vor, da ich mich noch kaum mit Brentano befaßt und von der Vielfalt seiner Austrahlung eine unzureichende Vorstellung hatte" (ibid., 292; see also 291).

8. Unpublished letter of 1992 to the author. I rely in this chapter on Ryan (and later Copleston) to sketch in the philosophical information commensurate with Canetti's own understanding as well as with the novel's intention. It would be digressive and fundamentally mistaken, I think, to turn to philosophical tractates we know Canetti did not read, rather than attend to the level of discourse he clearly did imbibe at the university, Viennese coffee houses, and salons. My gratitude to my philosopher colleague, Steven Grossman, for reading this chapter for accuracy.

9. Ryan, *Vanishing Subject*, 6–22.

10. Ryan further delineates a third group of "empirical" psychologists (ibid., 2); but this distinction is not carried through in her own analysis and neither is it of relevance here.

11. Ibid., 9.

12. Ibid., 10. It is important to remember that "turn of the century" is a notoriously expandable term, often extended up to the Second World War. This is the sense in which Ryan uses it.

13. Ibid., 2.

14. See, for example, ibid., 12, where Ryan notes that "the two Austrian empiricists [were] on opposite sides of one of the greatest controversies of their time: the debate between holists and elementarists (the latter also being known as 'atomists')."

15. Ibid., 21.

16. Canetti, *Das Augenspiel*, 292.

17. This distinguishes Kafka, whose attitude toward neoempiricism Ryan deems to be parodic, from Canetti. Whereas Kafka also held up Brentano's notion of intentionality to parodic critique (Ryan, *Vanishing Subject*, 100–112), he does

not do so out of the same concern for the social world. An ironic treatment of empiricism does not therefore necessarily imply an unsympathetic treatment of the "fragmented self" of high modernism. See my discussion below in chapter 6.

18. *AF*, 273; "Vor seiner Firma blieb sie stehen. Die Buchstaben des Firmenschilds rückten nah an ihre Augen. Erst las sie Groß & Mutter, dann las sie Grob & Frau. Das hatte sie gern. Dafür gab sie ihre eilige Zeit auch her ... Da tanzten die Buchstaben vor Freude, und als der Tanz zu Ende war, las sie auf einmal Groß & Frau. Das paßte ihr gar nicht" (*DB*, 299).

19. Copleston, *History*, 7:431, my emphasis.

20. Locke does so as well; Hume offers a pragmatist solution (not unlike William James's) to the skepticism that arises from his version of empiricist philosophy; see ibid., 4:26.

21. Ibid., 6:206.

22. *AF*, 133–34; "Sie suchte sich die größte Kirche der Stadt, den Dom aus ... Da hing ein Bild mit dem Abendmahl, in teuren Ölfarben gemalt ... Den Beutel hätte man greifen können, dreißig schöne Silberstücke steckten drin ... Der Judas hielt ihn gepackt. Der hätt' ihn nicht hergegeben, der war ja so geizig. Der vergönnte niemandem was. Der war wie ihr Mann ... Ihr Mann ist mager, der Judas ist dick und hat einen roten Bart. In der Mitte von allen sitzt der interessante Mensch. So ein schönes Gesicht hat er, ganz blaß, und die Augen genauso wie es sich gehört. Der weiß alles ... Ihr Mann ist ein Schmutzfink. Der macht das für zwanzig Schilling ... Sie ist die weiße Taube. Die fliegt ihm grad über den Kopt. Die glänzt, weil sie so unschuldig ist. Der Maler hat es so wollen ... Sie ist die weiße Taube. Da soll es der Judas nur versuchen. Er kriegt sie doch nicht zu fassen. Sie fliegt ja wohin sie will. Sie fliegt zum interessanten Menschen, sie weiß, was schön ist. Der Judas hat nichts zu sagen. Der muß sich aufhängen ... Das Geld gehört ihr ... Gleich kommen die Soldaten ... Sie wird vortreten und sagen: 'Das ist nicht der Heiland. Das ist der Herr Grob, einfacher Angestellter bei der Firma Groß & Mutter. Dem dürfen Sie nichts tun. Ich bin die Frau...' Der Judas soll sich schon aufhängen. Sie ist die weiße Taube" (*DB*, 140, 141–42).

23. I develop this point further in "Elias Canetti's *Die Blendung* as a 'Viennese' Novel."

24. *AF*, 28; "Das Bewußtsein bewahre man für wirkliche Gedanken; sie nähren sich von ihm, sie brauchen es; ohne Bewußtsein sind sie nicht denkbar" (*DB*, 27).

25. Berkeley, *Principles of Human Knowledge*, 1:147.

26. Ibid., 5:233, my emphasis.

27. Ryan, *Vanishing Subject*, 12.

28. *AF*, 305, trans. rev.; "Er hatte Therese gepackt, nicht mehr zaghaft, mit aller Kraft hielt er sich an ihrem Rock fest, er stieß sie weg, er zerrte sie zu sich heran, er umspannte sie mit seinen langen, hageren Armen. Sie ließ es sich gefallen ... Bevor sie aufgehängt werden, bekommen Mörder eine letzte Mahlzeit ... Er drehte sie einmal um ihre eigene Achse und verzichtete auf die Umarmung ... Er glotzte sie aus zwei Zentimeter Entfernung an. Er strich mit zehn Fingern am Rock entlang.

Er streckte die Zunge heraus und schnupperte mit der Nase. Die Tränen traten ihm in die Augen, vor Anstrengung. 'Ich leide an dieser Halluzination!' bekannte er keuchend" (DB, 334).

29. AF, 305; "Ich lebe für die Wahrheit. Ich weiß, diese Wahrheit lügt" (DB, 333, emphasis in original).

30. AF, 305.

31. AF, 422; "Alle Morde, alle Ängste, alle Tücken der Welt waren zerstoben. Der Hausbesorger gefiel ihm. Sein Kopf erinnerte ihn an die aufgehende Sonne heute früh. Er war grob, aber erfrischend, ein unbändig starker Kerl, wie man sie in Kulturstädten und -häusern selten mehr sieht. Die Treppe dröhnte. Statt sie zu tragen, *schlug* Atlas die arme Erde" (DB, 462).

32. In the context of the interwar period it is perhaps not incidental to note that Georg's reinscription of Pfaff is predicated on an enthusiasm for nature and mythology (Pfaff becomes Atlas), both of which are opposed to "Kulturstädte." The nature interest and anti-urban sentiment remind us that Georg, as the great promoter of the "Naturmensch" (gorilla man) over against the decadent bourgeois citizen, can be situated among the contemporaneous "Lebensphilosophie" enthusiasts without compromising his neoempiricist aura.

33. AF, 376–77; "Sie ist nicht seine Tochter! . . . Irrtümlich erwähnte er einmal eine gewisse Poli. Seine Muskeln machten den Fehler sofort wieder gut. Der Name der Weibsperson, die er züchtigte, lautete auf Anna. Sie behauptete mit einer Tochter von ihm identisch zu sein. Er schenkte ihr keinen Glauben. Die Haare fielen ihr aus, und da sie sich wehrte, zerbrachen zwei Finger" (DB, 411-12).

34. Peter Russell argues, "If we are honest, we see *Auto-da-Fé* for what it is: a violently limited, eccentric and sadistic view of human existence," in "The Vision of Man," 32.

35. AF, 71; "*Esse percipi,* sein ist wahrgenommen werden. Was ich nicht wahrnehme, existiert nicht!" (DB, 73).

36. AF, 403; "Georges war Gelehrter genug, um eine Abhandlung über die Sprache dieses Irren zu veröffentlichen. Auf die Psychologie der Laute fiel neues Licht" (DB, 441).

37. AF, 405–6; "'Sie sehen, meine Herren,' sagte er ihnen etwa, wenn er allein mit ihnen war, 'was für armselige Einfaltspinsel, was für traurige und verstockte Bürger wir sind, gegen diesen genialen Paranoiker gehalten. Wir sitzen, er ist besessen; auf den Erfahrungen andrer wir, von eigenen er. Er treibt mutterseelenallein, wie die Erde, durch seinen Weltraum . . . Er glaubt an das, was ihm seine Sinne vortäuschen. Wir mißtrauen unseren gesunden Sinnen . . . Und er? Er ist Allah, Prophet und Moslim in einer Person. Bleibt ein Wunder darum kein Wunder mehr, weil wir ihm die Etikette Paranoia chronica aufkleben? Wir sitzen auf unserem dicken Verstand wie Habgeier auf ihrem Geld. Der Verstand, wie wir ihn verstehen, ist ein Mißverständnis. Wenn es ein Leben reiner Geistigkeit gibt, so führt es dieser Verrückte!'" (DB, 444).

38. AF, 410; "Wenn er müde war und von der Hochspannung, mit der ihn seine

irren Freunde luden, ausruhen wollte, versenkte er sich in die Seele irgendeines Assistenten. Alles was Georges tat, spielte in fremden Menschen" (*DB*, 449). Further, Georg thinks of himself in quintessentially empiricist terms, namely, as "a walking wax tablet," an image that expresses the interpenetrability so central to the empiricist model of consciousness. As a "tablet" it is an image of a considerably more passive self; yet as a "wax" tablet, it suggests a modicum of mutual interaction, of "entering" as well as receiving the stimulus. But as with so many other self-nominated images in the novel, we will see that this does not really fit what we know about Georg and his activities. It is a claim that, like so much of the narration in *Auto-da-Fé*, will have to be revised retrospectively.

39. Copleston, *History*, 7:440.

40. For Foucault, the tension between "the empirical and the transcendental" ("Man and His Doubles," 320) conceptions of the human being constitutes the dilemma par excellence of modern philosophy, as Gutting (in "Michel Foucault," chapter 9 of *French Philosophy in the 20th Century*) remarks: "The question of 'man' is particularly difficult because man is supposed to be simultaneously the source of representations (a subject) and an object of representation. Because of this, the question of how representation is possible becomes the question of how there can be a being that is both the ultimate subject of representation and a represented object. Developing a coherent conception of man in this sense has been the fundamental project of philosophy within the modern episteme (i.e., philosophy since Kant)." I cite this passage from the manuscript of Gutting's forthcoming study, generously provided to me by the author.

41. One needs to read the passage on Georg's "conversion" carefully, for it is focalized by him. He carries on an affair with the banker's wife, he admits, despite his intention to reform. To the very end, in fact, he attempts to solve problems erotically. Attempting to get Therese to agree to his conditions, Georg says, "Wenn ich nicht verheiratet wäre! . . . Sie haben doch, was eine Frau braucht. Nichts fehlt. Glauben Sie mir! . . . Und die Augen! Und die Jugend! Und der kleine Mund! Wie gesagt, wenn ich nicht verheiratet wäre—ich würde Sie zur Sünde verführen" (*DB*, 496–97).

42. Canetti, "Das erste Buch," 251–52.

43. For example, Dissinger argues (rather too creatively, I think) that the name "Kant" is a hidden contraction for "Canetti," and that both "Kant" and "Kien" are covert references (via the Latin *canis* and the French *chien*, respectively) to the word "dog." Dissinger undertakes these philological acrobatics in order to show that the brothers Kien represent the poet, about whom Canetti once said, "Der echte Dichter ist 'der Hund seiner Zeit,'" (*Vereinzelung und Massenwahn*, 129).

44. Canetti, *Das Augenspiel*, 44.

45. Copleston, *History*, 4:5.

46. *AF*, 18; "Wo immer eine Lehrkanzel für östliche Philologie frei wurde, trug man sie zu allererst ihm an. Er lehnte mit verächtlicher Höflichkeit ab" (*DB*, 16).

47. Copleston, *History*, 6:181–83.

48. All of this functions in the same manner as having Kien quote Berkeley irresponsibly, in ignorance of, or indifference to, the larger system of ideas (as Darby would have it). The reader, reasonably well informed on the Western philosophical and cultural tradition, perceives Kien's fraudulence without recasting the narrator in the image of Berkeley's God.

49. Canetti, *Das Augenspiel*, 44.

50. "Neukantianismus bezeichnet eine philosophische Schulrichtung . . . die um die Jahrhundertwende zur tonangebenden Philosophie in Deutschland avancierte und deren Ende gemeinhin mit dem Beginn des Zweiten Weltkriegs angesetzt wird" (Ollig, *Der Neukantianismus*, 1).

51. The leading figures in this disparate movement were Hermann Cohen, Wilhelm Windelband, Wilhelm Dilthey, and Ernst Cassirer, whose influential *Philosophie der symbolischen Formen* (1923–29) perhaps best epitomizes the neo-Kantian effort to reinvigorate the humanities as a philosophically cogent enterprise. Canetti's own contribution to this debate is only partially evident in *Auto-da-Fé*. A new, more positive sense of culture emerges first in *Crowds and Power*; see below, chapter 5.

52. *AF*, 123, my emphasis; "'Stimmt!' sagte er leise und nickte, wie immer wenn eine Wirklichkeit ihrem Urbild im Druck entsprach" (*DB*, 129).

53. *AF*, 246; "Er nahm die Rosen aus Fischerles Hand, entsann sich ihres Wohlgeruches, den er aus persischen Liebesgedichten kannte, und näherte sie seinen Augen, richtig, sie rochen. Das besänftigte ihn vollends" (*DB*, 269).

54. *AF*, 67, trans. rev.; "Die Oberfenster ließen Luft und Gedanken ein . . . Durchs Glas der Fenster spürte man den allgemeinen Zustand des Himmels, gedämpfter und stiller, als er in Wirklichkeit war. Ein mattes Blau sagte: die Sonne scheint, aber nicht bis zu mir. Ein ebenso mattes Grau, es wird regnen, aber nicht auf mich. Ein zartes Geräusch verriet fallende Tropfen. Ganz von ferne nahm man sie auf, sie berührten einen nicht. Man wußte nur: die Sonne strahlt, Wolken gehen, Regen fällt. Es war, als hätte sich jemand gegen die Erde verbarrikadiert; gegen alles bloß materielle Beziehungswesen, gegen alles nur Planetarische eine Kabine erbaut, eine ungeheure Kabine, so groß, daß sie für das Wenige ausreiche, welches an der Erde mehr als Erde und mehr als Staub ist, zu dem das Leben wieder zerfällt" (*DB*, 68–69). Kien's conception of the scholarly life as essentially insular—designed to keep the unknown at bay—is conveyed succinctly in the following line that continues the passage cited above: "Auf der Fahrt durch das Unbekannte war man wie auf keiner Fahrt" (*DB*, 69).

55. *AF*, 15–16; "Punkt acht begann die Arbeit, sein Dienst an der Wahrheit . . . Man näherte sich der Wahrheit, indem man sich von den Menschen abschloß. Der Alltag war ein oberflächliches Gewirr von Lügen . . . Wer unter den schlechten Schauspielern, aus denen die Masse bestand, hatte ein Gesicht, das ihn fesselte? Sie veränderten es nach dem Augenblick . . . *Er* legte seinen Ehrgeiz in eine Hartnäckigkeit des Wesens. Nicht bloß einen Monat, nicht ein Jahr, sein ganzes Leben blieb er sich gleich" (*DB*, 13–14).

56. *AF*, 16; "Der Charakter, wenn man einen hatte, bestimmte auch die Gestalt, schmal, streng und knochig" (*DB*, 14).

57. *AF*, 214; "'Sie wünschen!' / 'Ich—ich wollte in die Bücherabteilung.' / 'Die bin ich.' . . . / 'Was hatten Sie oben vor?' fragte Kien drohend. 'Ach, nur den Schiller'" (*DB*, 233).

58. *AF*, 215; "'Tun Sie das nie wieder, mein Freund! Kein Mensch ist soviel wert wie seine Bücher, glauben Sie mir!' . . . Warum gerade Schiller? Lesen Sie doch das Original! Lesen Sie *Immanuel Kant!*'" (*DB*, 234, emphasis in original).

59. *AF*, 444; "Es ärgert ihn, daß er nur an den kategorischen Imperativ und nicht an Gott glaubt. Sonst schöbe er diesem die Schuld zu" (*DB*, 487).

60. *AF*, 57, trans. rev.; "Jeder Mensch braucht eine Heimat, nicht eine, wie primitive Faustpatrioten sie verstehen, auch keine Religion, matten Vorgeschmack einer Heimat im Jenseits, nein, eine Heimat, die Boden, Arbeit, Freunde, Erholung und geistigen Fassungsraum zu einem natürlichen, wohlgeordneten Ganzen, zu einem eigenen Kosmos zusammenschließt. Die beste Definition der Heimat ist Bibliothek. Frauen hält man am klügsten von seiner Heimat fern. Entschließt man sich doch, eine aufzunehmen, so trachte man, sie der Heimat erst völlig zu assimilieren, so wie er es getan hat" (*DB*, 57; compare also 418).

61. See Ringer, *The Decline of the German Mandarins*, 253–449.

62. *AF*, 158–59; "An allen Schmerzen ist die Gegenwart schuld. Er sehnt sich nach der Zukunft, weil dann mehr Vergangenheit auf der Welt sein wird. Die Vergangenheit ist gut, sie tut niemand was zuleid, zwanzig Jahre hat er sich frei in ihr bewegt, er war glücklich. Wer fühlt sich in der Gegenwart glücklich? Ja, wenn wir keine Sinne hätten, da wäre auch eine Gegenwart erträglich . . . Er beugt sich vor dem Primat der Vergangenheit . . . Eine Zeit wird kommen, da die Menschen ihre Sinne zu Erinnerung und alle Zeit zu Vergangenheit umschmieden werden. Eine Zeit wird kommen, da eine einzige Vergangenheit alle Menschen umspannt, da nichts ist außer der Vergangenheit, da jeder glaubt: an die Vergangenheit" (*DB*, 169).

63. *AF*, 159; "Gott ist die Vergangenheit. Er *glaubt* an Gott" (*DB*, 169, emphasis in original).

64. Nicholas Boyle explicates the birth of German idealism within a culture of ex-theologians who transfer religious categories to philosophy and above all to "art" ("Kunst"), a quite questionable phenomenon, he argues, that continues down to our own day. See his "Learning from Germany."

65. Ollig remarks in this regard that neo-Kantianism "richtete sich gegen einen naturwissenschaftlich verbrämten Objektivismus, der die Subjektkomponente im Erkenntnisvorgang mehr oder weniger gänzlich unter den Tisch fallen lassen wollte" (*Der Neukantianismus*, 1–2).

66. Ibid., 2.

67. "Tölpel hantieren mit Elektrizität und komplizierten Atomen . . . Diese bedruckte Seite, so klar und gegliedert wie nur irgendeine, ist in Wirklichkeit ein höllischer Haufe rasender Elektronen. Wäre er sich dessen immer bewußt, so

müßten die Buchstaben vor seinen Augen tanzen . . . Am Tage brächte er eine schwache Zeile hinter sich, mehr nicht. Es ist sein Recht, die Blindheit, die ihn vor solchen Sinnesexzessen schützt, auf alle störenden Elemente in seinem Leben zu übertragen" (DB, 73).

CHAPTER 4

1. "Aus dem Prater ist natürlich auch die ungeheuerliche Figur—der Siegfried Fischerle in der Blendung—hervorgegangen, nicht? Also, der schrecklich zum Scheitern verurteilte Versuch einer Assimilation unter extremen Bedingungen": Gerald Stieg in Ein Dichter gegen Macht und Tod.

2. AF, 184–85; "Von den Sitten der Lokalität verstand er [Kien] wenig, aber eins schien ihm gewiß: hier strebte ein reiner Geist in elendem Körper seit zwanzig Jahren danach, sich über den Schmutz seiner Umgebung zu erheben . . . Therese [i.e., die Pensionistin] zog ihn ebenso beharrlich in den Schmutz zurück . . . Von der Welt des Geistes hat er nun einen winzigen Zipfel gefaßt und klammert sich daran mit der Kraft eines Ertrinkenden. Das Schachspiel ist seine Bibliothek . . . Kien stellt sich die Kämpfe vor, die dieser vom Leben geschlagene Mensch um seine Wohnung führt. Er bringt ein Buch mit nach Hause, um heimlich darin zu lesen, sie zerreißt es, daß die Fetzen fliegen. Sie zwingt ihn, ihr seine Wohnung für ihre entsetzlichen Zwecke zur Verfügung zu stellen. Vielleicht bezahlt sie eine Bedienerin, eine Spionin, um die Wohnung bücherrein zu halten, wenn sie nicht zu Hause ist. Bücher sind verboten, ihr Lebenswandel ist erlaubt . . . Sie reißt die Tür auf und stößt mit ihren plumpen Füßen das Schachbrett um. Herr Fischerle heult wie ein kleines Kind. Er befand sich gerade an der interessantesten Stelle seines Buches. Er sammelt die herumliegenden Buchstaben und wendet das Gesicht ab, damit sie sich über seine Tränen nicht freut. Er ist ein kleiner Held. Er hat Charakter" (DB, 201).

3. Two studies are of particular interest here: Ringer's The Decline of the German Mandarins and Marchand's Down from Olympus.

4. Marchand, Down from Olympus, 321.

5. Ibid., 312–14.

6. DB, 207, 210.

7. Marchand, Down from Olympus, 316.

8. Ibid., 322.

9. Ibid., 328. Marchand emphasizes the quietist character of this new humanism, a fact that strongly encourages the connection with Canetti's novel: "Thus the greatest failing of this devoutly antimodern pedagogy was its inability to confront nationalist and racialist classical studies with a credible, embracive cultural history . . . Jäger and his followers simply allowed themselves to become straw men— or uncomprehending internal émigrés like Thomas Mann's Serenus Zeitblom— under the reign of the antihumanist advocates of Aryan supremacy" (ibid., 330).

10. *AF*, 192, trans. rev.; "Überhaupt fürchtete er mit dem Bildungshunger des Kleinen in Konflikt zu geraten. Der würde ihm mit einem Anschein von Recht vorwerfen, daß da Bücher brachlägen. Wie sollte er sich verteidigen?" (*DB*, 209).

11. *AF*, 194; "Durch den täglichen Umgang mit solchen Mengen von Bildung würde der Hunger des Kleinen danach größer und größer; plötzlich würde man ihn dabei ertappen, wie er sich an ein Buch heranmachte und es zu lesen versuchte ... Man müßte ihn mündlich vorbereiten" (*DB*, 211).

12. *AF*, 194; "Wenn es einem gelang, diesen [gleichgesinnten Naturen] ein Stück Bildung, ein Stück Menschentum zu schenken, so hatte man etwas geleistet" (*DB*, 211). When Kien discovers that books are relegated to the top floor of the Theresianum, the least secure place in case of fire, he imagines his own behavior in the event of such a fire. Like a loving mother—he imagines—he stands before the dilemma of whether to abandon his "children" (i.e., books) to their certain death, or risk maiming them (or worse) by his rescue efforts. He opts for the latter: "Er bringt es [sie ins Feuer zu werfen] nicht übers Herz, *unter ihnen ist er zum Menschen geworden*" (*DB*, 225, my emphasis).

13. *AF*, 250; "Unter dem Druck der Bücher, die er nicht einmal las, veränderte sich der Zwerg zusehends. Kiens alte Theorie bestätigte sich glänzend" (*DB*, 273).

14. Beller, *Vienna and the Jews*, 211. Assimilation was also Kraus's answer to Herzl's call to Zionism; see Beller, 134.

15. Ibid., 211.

16. Beller notes that Cohen "could proclaim that Kant was the philosopher of the Jews, that Jews had become the carriers of the 'idealistic' mission because not of this world" (ibid., 140). This broader, self-conscious Jewish investment in the Enlightenment that acknowledged essential connections to Judaism Beller terms "the continuation of Judaism by other means beyond the Jewish identity" (ibid., 143). See also Nathan Rotenstreich, "Hermann Cohen."

17. Beller, *Vienna and the Jews*, 138.

18. Ibid., 125.

19. *AF*, 175, trans. rev.: "mächtige Nase" is better rendered as "immense nose" rather than Wedgwood's "majestic nose." "Da tauchte ein ungeheurer Buckel neben ihm [Kien] auf und fragte, ob es gestattet sei. Kien blickte angestrengt hinunter. Wo war der Mund, aus dem es sprach? Und schon hüpfte der Besitzer des Buckels, ein Zwerg, an einem Stuhl in die Höhe ... Die Spitze der stark gebogenen Nase lag in der Tiefe des Kinns. Der Mund war so klein wie der Mann, nur— er war nicht zu finden. Keine Stirn, keine Ohren, kein Hals, kein Rumpf—dieser Mensch bestand aus einem Buckel, einer mächtigen Nase und zwei schwarzen, ruhigen, traurigen Augen ... Plötzlich hörte [Kien] eine heisere Stimme unterm Tisch fragen: 'Wie gehn die Geschäfte?'" (*DB*, 189-90).

20. Paal, *Figurenkonstellation*, 31.

21. *AF*, 175; Kien "musterte die ausschließliche Nase des Kleinen, sie flößte ihm Verdacht ein" (*DB*, 190).

22. *AF*, 180; "Fischerle machte eine ganz kleine Pause, um die Wirkung des

Wortes 'jüdisch' auf sein Visavis zu beobachten. Kann man wissen? Die Welt wimmelt von Antisemiten. Ein Jude ist immer auf der Hut vor Todfeinden. Bucklige Zwerge und gar solche, die es trotzdem zum Zuhälter gebracht haben, sind scharfe Beobachter. Das Schlucken des anderen entging ihm nicht. Er deutete es als Verlegenheit und hielt von diesem Augenblick an Kien, der nichts weniger war, für einen Juden" (*DB*, 196).

23. *AF*, 234, trans. rev.; "Er vergaß, daß er in einer Kirche war. Vor Kirchen hatte er sonst Respekt und Scheu, weil seine Nase sehr auffällig war" (*DB*, 256).

24. *AF*, 245, trans. rev.; "Fischerle war überrumpelt, in einer Kirche fühlte er sich unsicher. Beinahe hätte er Kien wieder auf den Platz hinausgeschleift . . . Soll die Kirche einstürzen, der Polizei läuft er nicht in die Arme! Fischerle kannte schreckliche Geschichten von Juden, die unter den Trümmern krachender Kirchen begraben wurden, weil sie nicht hineingehörten. Seine Frau, die Pensionistin, hatte sie ihm erzählt, weil sie fromm war und ihn zu ihrem Glauben bekehren wollte" (*DB*, 268).

25. *DB*, 196, 200.

26. These bestial attributes of Fischerle can be found, respectively, at *DB*, 190, 315, 356, and 316.

27. *AF*, 250, trans. rev.; "Also undankbar sind Sie auch! Sie Saujud! . . . Von einem Saujuden hat man nichts anderes zu erwarten" (*DB*, 273).

28. *AF*, 352, trans. rev.: Wedgwood offers "Go boil your head!" for "Gehen Sie betteln mit Ihrer Nase!" which fails to capture the anti-Semitic imagery of the original: "Bei uns in Europa nennt man das Freßschach! Gehen Sie betteln mit Ihrer Nase!" (*DB*, 384). Since the word "Judennase" is so often on Fischerle's lips, one might even go so far as to read: "Go begging [or, get lost] with that Jew nose!"

29. Jutta Paal argues just this: "Vielmehr scheint es, daß Canetti die anti semitischen Tendenzen seiner Zeit kaum bemerkt hat, wenn er im *Augenspiel* erwähnt, daß er 'später, mit dem Fortgang der Ereignisse, über Fischerle oft Unbehagen empfand' und sich für diese Figur zu rechtfertigen suchte" (*Figurenkonstellation*, 31 n. 104). Paal's suggestion that the autobiography retracts this aspect of the novel is simply mistaken; the passage she cites supports no such assertion. It is at any rate astonishing to suggest that Canetti was oblivious to anti-Semitism, for he records in his autobiography horror at the assassination of Walter Rathenau; a sympathy for the situation of Austrian Galician Jews during the time of the First World War; and this reminiscence about Alma Mahler's anti-Jewish bigotry: "Did you ever see Gropius?"—Canetti recalls being asked—"A handsome, tall man. Exactly what one calls Aryan. The only man who suited me racially. Otherwise, it was always short Jews, like Mahler, who kept falling in love with me" (*Das Augenspiel*, 56). On the situation of the Galician Jews, see *Das Augenspiel*, 129; additional remarks about Alma Mahler's anti-Semitism and prejudice can be found there at 58, 155.

30. We know that Canetti reflected on Jewish self-hatred at the time he wrote this novel, because he reports in his autobiography that Otto Weininger's *Ge-*

schlecht und Character enjoyed a remarkable popularity among his peers at this juncture. More to the point, Canetti recorded in his diaries—some of which later became the *Aufzeichnungen*—just ten years after the first publication of the novel a reflection on "self-hatred" ("Selbsthaß"). Yet as the following *Aufzeichnungen* passage makes clear, this is not a case of confessing some shameful personal character flaw, nor is this observation necessarily limited in reference to Jews: "Es ist nur gut, sich manchmal zu hassen, nicht zu oft, sonst braucht man wieder sehr viel Haß gegen andere, um den Selbsthaß auszugleichen" (*Die Provinz des Menschen*, 89).

31. Nicola Riedner's *Canettis Fischerle* helpfully catalogues the full array of anti-Semitic stereotypes encoded in Fischerle in a more systematic manner than it is my purpose to do here. While Riedner correctly draws our attention to the key issue of assimilation, she ends up blaming the victim: Fischerle is presented as a negative example of over-assimilation, that is, as someone who has abandoned "die Quellen der eigenen Herkunft" (*Canettis Fischerle*, 143). This reading rests on a questionable view of Fischerle as someone who has a psyche capable of forgetting his identity, a disputable use of Canetti's autobiography, as well as an unsupported importation of key ideas from *Masse und Macht*.

32. Gilman, *The Jew's Body*, 43.

33. The depiction of Fischerle is indebted to a whole tradition of anti-Semitic caricature. Fischerle's most notorious cultural forebear with regard to physical resemblance is perhaps Wilhelm Busch's "Schmulchen Schiefelbeiner" (1882), in Peter Gay's words, the popular poet's "most obvious and most distasteful Jew." Gay notes further: "In several poems, Busch speaks of 'the' Jew, with his crooked nose and devious ways, physically ugly, morally corrupt, and financially unscrupulous. And he illustrates rhymes like these with savage drawings" (*Freud, Jews and Other Germans*, 207–8). We may therefore assume that Fischerle would easily have been recognized for his anti-Semitic pedigree by contemporary readers.

34. A striking example can be found in the caricature of the Jewish art critic for the *Neue Freie Presse*, which was intended to exhibit, Gilman notes, "the essential image of the Jew's body" (Gilman, *The Jew's Body*, 45). Further, Karl Arnold's caricature of the Berlin Jewish quarter, *Grenadierstraße, Berlin* depicts virtually every Jew as suffering from curvature of the spine (first printed in *Simplicissimus*, 1921; reprinted in Ruth Gay, *Jews of Germany*, 239).

35. Some readers will be reminded of Walter Benjamin's "bucklicht Männlein," which Hannah Arendt emphasizes in her introduction to the English edition of *Illuminations*, 5–7. In a general way, the association may be justified: the dwarf hunchback famous from *Des Knaben Wunderhorn* was an omen of bad luck and failure, and as such played into later anti-Semitic narrative and caricature. But Benjamin does not himself make this association. Nor is it possible that Canetti became aware of the little hunchback via Benjamin, because *Berliner Kindheit um Neunzehnhundert*, in which the reference appears, was not written until the late thirties and published only posthumously, in 1950.

36. *AF*, 186, my emphasis, trans. rev. Wedgwood softens the German and thereby obscures the reading I suggest below. By rendering "traurig" as "mistaken," she implies that Kien, who focalizes this passage, somehow regrets Fischerle's physical handicap, whereas the German suggests just the opposite, namely that Kien *justifies* Fischerle's physical misfortune in this manner: "ihr zerstörendes Treiben . . . galt dem Manne gegenüber, den die Natur durch eine traurige Etymologie ohnehin schon zum Krüppel geschlagen hatte" (*DB*, 202).

37. Fischerle's "etymology," which he repeats, is this: "Passen Sie gut auf: Stipendium ist ein feines Wort. Dieses Wort stammt aus dem Französischen und heißt dasselbe wie das jüdische Kapital!" (196).

38. *AF*, 180; "An ihrer Etymologie sollt ihr sie erkennen" (*DB*, 196).

39. *AF*, 343, trans. rev. Wedgwood has "dainty little nose" for the German "putzige Nase," a translation that excludes all valances of the word that connote "odd, funny, curious, queer, etc." — which, after all, are the principal meanings of the word. "Queer little nose" captures better the innkeeper's philosemitic condescension evident in the following hyperbole and use of diminutives: "Die Wirtin [schloß] Fischerles Buckel in ihre Arme. Sie überschüttete ihn mit Koseworten; sie hätte sich nach ihm gesehnt, nach seiner putzigen Nase, seinen krummen Beinchen und der lieben, lieben Schachkunst" (*DB*, 375).

40. Gilman, *The Jew's Body*, 38–59.

41. Pfaff and Therese are in the process of pawning Kien's library at the *Theresianum*. Pfaff tosses heavy books at Therese and seems to have second thoughts: "Er war auch damit unzufrieden, kam sich wie ein Schwächling vor und sagte manchmal, nächstens wird er noch ein Jud'" (*DB*, 312).

42. Gilman, *The Jew's Body*, 51–60.

43. In a reflection from 1942, Canetti indicated his opposition to the artificiality and pretense of characters that are to be taken for real people. Though he is here referring specifically to drama, we might recall that he elsewhere suggests that *all* his work is essentially dramatic: "Der Hauptwiderstand, den ich gegen die 'Entwicklung' von Charakteren empfand (so als wären sie wirkliche, lebende Menchen), erinnert daran, daß auch in der Musik die Instrumente gegeben sind" (*Die Provinz des Menschen*, 15–16).

44. Riedner veers toward attributing greater psychological dimension to Fischerle, claiming (improbably, I think) that he possesses more depth than Georg (*Canettis Fischerle*, 94). The assumption of psychological realism of some degree informs Riedner's conclusion, which presumes Fischerle to possess the capacity to choose one form of assimilation over another, as well as the ability to "transform" himself along the lines Canetti hinted at in *Masse und Macht* with his concept of "Verwandlung."

45. Gilman, *The Jew's Body*, 43, 52; Peter Gay, *Freud, Jews and Other Germans*, 210.

46. In his masterful study *Der Name als Stigma*, Bering elucidates the cultural and historical dimensions to the name "Siegfried": "Wie germanisch der

Name anmutete, so gut schien er später auch für Juden dienlich, die sich mit aller Macht 'germanisieren' wollten. Er wurde daher sehr bald antisemitisch markiert, Versatzstück in jüdischen Witzen und überhaupt Beweisstück, daß die Juden die deutschen Namen ganz verdorben hätten" (*Der Name als Stigma*, 425–26 n. 130; see also 18, 99, 244).

47. Ruth Gay, *The Jews of Germany*, 184. Regarding the *Nibelungenlied* as metaphor for Jewish assimilation to German culture, Peter Gay writes: "When [Hermann] Levi [the Jewish self-hating conductor of Wagner's *Parsifal*] lay ill, his father came to visit him, and . . . tried to read the *Nibelungenlied*, and asked his son questions. A substantial portion of German-Jewish history is summed up in this little domestic scene" (*Freud, Jews and Other Germans*, 218 n. 53).

48. See Panizza, *The Operated Jew*. From his tell-tale "Jewish" physical attributes, to his desire to unlearn his German-Jewish dialect, to his appetite for that seal of successful assimilation, the title of "Doctor," Panizza's Itzig mirrors the description (and fate) of Canetti's Fischerle.

49. Zipes, *Operated Jew*, 88.

50. World War I was the turning point in Jewish assimilation to German culture. On this point Peter Gay writes: "The decline of German liberalism and, even worse, the experience of war and its tempestuous aftermath went far toward closing the avenues of Jewish approaches to host cultures. The old fear returned, but under new conditions and hence under incomprehensible guises. The long ascent of Jewish integration into German culture was, if not exactly over, certainly imperiled" (*Freud, Jews and Other Germans*, 200).

51. Ibid., 197.

52. On the popularity of Wagner in the pre–World War II era, particularly among Jews, see Beller, *Vienna and the Jews*, 157–59.

53. Hanisch, "The Political Influence," 196.

54. Ibid., 197.

55. In Röhl, "Wilhelm II," 6.

56. Thomas Mann certainly took Wagner for granted as the cultural point of reference for a number of his works from the first part of the century. The best known of these, "Das Blut der Wälsungen" (first published 1921), features Jewish twins named for Siegfried's parents (Sigismund and Sieglinde), who, in the story's penultimate episode, attend Wagner's *Die Walküre*, the opera in *Der Ring des Nibelungen* that directly precedes *Siegfried*. The novella makes unmistakable use of anti-Semitic clichés, which has earned it the status of one of Mann's "Skandalgeschichten" (Vaget). Essentially this story depicts two Jewish siblings reading themselves longingly into a German cultural classic. Ironically, both the "Aryan"-looking parents of Siegfried (in the opera) and Mann's pointedly Jewish spectators see themselves as "outsiders," a narrative process that would seem to question the very German-Jewish dichotomy upon which the story depends. See Vaget, "Wälsungenblut," and Reed, "Der Fall Wagner."

57. The murderous passion is more readily evident in the original German:

"Seh' ich dir erst / mit den Augen zu, / zu übel erkenn' ich / was alles du thu'st: / seh' ich dich steh'n, / gangeln und geh'n, / knicken und nicken, / mit den Augen zwicken: / beim Genick' möcht' ich / den Nicker packen, / den Garaus geben / dem garst'gen Zwicker! / . . . / Alle Thiere sind / mir theurer als du: / Baum und Vogel, / die Fische im Bach, / lieber mag ich sie / leiden als dich" (Act 1, scene 1; 179). Wagner references are to the Norton critical edition, with English and German parallel text; accordingly, page numbers are identical for both languages.

58. "Da sah ich denn auch / mein eigen Bild; / ganz anders als du / dünkt' ich mir da: / so glich wohl der Kröte / ein glänzender Fisch; / doch kroch nie ein Fisch aus der Kröte!" (ibid., 181).

59. Again, the German is somewhat stronger in tone: "Ganz fremd bist du mir" (ibid., 182).

60. "So, hieß mich die Mutter, / möcht' ich dich heißen: / als 'Siegfried' würdest / du stark und schön" (ibid., 183).

61. Weiner, *Richard Wagner,* 170. Weiner maintains further: "Siegfried's voice, like Walther's in *Die Meistersinger,* is the voice of the *Volk,* whose deeper registers connote for Wagner the German essence. Mime's higher instrument, on the other hand, anticipates the voice of that most anti-Semitic and derisive of musical-dramatic constructions, Sixtus Beckmesser [also of *Die Meistersinger*]" (168).

62. See Borchmeyer, "The Question of Anti-Semitism." Borchmeyer is excellent on the issue of anti-Semitism in Wagner's own life. His analysis of the lyrical texts, however, is somewhat limited by *textimmanent* assumptions.

63. "Aus dem Wege dich zu räumen, / darf ich doch nicht rasten: / Wie käm' ich sonst anders zur Beute" (Act 2, scene 3; 238).

64. Trans. rev. "Schmeck' du mein Schwert, / ekliger Schwätzer!"; in translating the stage directions, I have followed the German Piper edition (232–33), according to which Siegfried "packt Mime's Leichnam auf, schleppt ihn nach der Höhle und wirft ihn dort hinein."

65. "In der Höhle hier / lieg' auf dem Hort! / Mit zäher List / erzieltest du ihn: / jetzt magst du des wonnigen walten!" (Act 2, scene 3; 238).

66. On the conflict between assimilated Western Jews and orthodox Eastern Jews, see Beller, *Vienna and the Jews,* 133; on tensions between Zionists and (other) Austrian Jews, consult Moser, "Die Katastrophe der Juden in Österreich," 77.

67. The call to rescind Jewish assimilation to German culture can be traced to 1918, when Müller von Hausen (who became infamous as the editor of the German version of the fraudulent *Protocols of the Elders of Zion*) published a demand for "eine deutsche Judenordnung" according to which, "Alle solche Personen gelten als Juden, deren Vorfahren am 11. März 1812 (Emanzipationsedikt für Preußen) Juden waren." Schubert, "Der Weg zur Katastrophe," 62. The culmination of this effort was of course the Nazi *Reichsbürgergesetz,* and the *Gesetz zum Schutze des deutschen Blutes und der deutschen Ehre,* both of 1935.

68. Kien protests that he is above taking filthy lucre for things of the mind, placing himself thus in the lofty idealist tradition of Plato ("Plato habe vergeblich

dagegen angekämpft"); to which Fischerle responds: "Plato ist gut!... Plato weiß ich. Plato ist ein reicher Mensch, du bist auch ein reicher Mensch" (*DB*, 289).

69. *AF*, 245; "Er glaubte an nichts, nur daran, daß 'Jud' zu den Verbrechern gehört, die sich von selbst bestrafen" (*DB*, 268).

70. Peter Gay remarks, "Impossible as it is to make dependable quantitative measurements of such matters, it seems most likely to me that Jewish cringing at Jewish conduct, the most common and most banal expression of Jewish self-hatred, grew markedly during the Weimar Republic, far beyond what it had been before World War I" (*Freud, Jews and Other Germans*, 200–201).

71. An English excerpt can be found in *The Weimar Republic Source Book*, 268–71.

72. *AF*, 197, trans. rev.; "Da soll einer sagen, die Juden sind feig. Die Reporter fragen ihn, wer er ist. Kein Mensch kennt ihn. Wie ein Amerikaner schaut er nicht aus. Juden gibt's überall. Aber von wo ist dieser Jud', der den Capablanca im Siegeszug hingemacht hat?" (*DB*, 215). The reference here is to the Cuban chess-master, José Raoul Capablanca (1888–1942).

73. *AF*, 364; "'Darling!' sagt die Millionärin und zupft ihn dran, sie liebt lange Nasen, kurze kann sie nicht schmecken" (*DB*, 397).

74. Fischerle's fantasy about marrying a rich gentile is an ironic reversal of yet another anti-Semitic stereotype: the impoverished protestant aristocrat marrying a wealthy Jewish heiress in order to save the family fortune. Intermarriage of this sort did, of course, occur; and this is part of the complex story of Jewish assimilation. But it also became the object of anti-Semitic satire, as Peter Gay notes: "A much-exploited theme for [the journal] *Simplicissimus* was the effete and impoverished Prussian aristocrat rescuing the family fortune with a suitable marriage to a Jewish heiress. The savagery of Bruno Paul's cover cartoon on this subject, published around 1900, is anything but exceptional. Entitled 'Aristocratic World View,' it depicts a hideous, stunted, obviously Jewish girl accompanied by her no less hideous, no less obvious father, marching to the altar with an impecunious nobleman" (*Freud, Jews and Other Germans*, 205). Therefore Fischerle's remark, "Sie heiratet meinen Namen, ich ihr Geld" (*DB*, 286), both evokes and parodies a well-known anti-assimilationist stereotype. The ironic reversal, however, is only partial: the Jew remains the physically disfigured person in both transactions.

75. These four references to World War I are found, respectively, in *DB*, 247, 253, 251, and 280. Further references can be found in *DB*, 218 (where standing in line reminds Fischerle of the war), 255 (where the prevaricating "blind" man claims to have learned to tell the truth in the war), and 318 (where the women in the crowd blame the lack of available men on the casualties of the Great War).

76. Moser, "Die Katastrophe der Juden in Österreich," 70.

77. *AF*, 326; "In einer Masse gab es eine Masse zu holen" (*DB*, 356).

78. *AF*, 328; "Fischerle hörte, was man ihm vorwarf... Für Zwerge gebe es 20 Jahre. Die Todesstrafe müßte wieder her. Krüppel gehören ausgerottet. Alle Verbrecher seien Krüppel. Nein alle Krüppel Verbrecher... Er solle lieber was

arbeiten. Er solle den Leuten nicht das Brot vom Mund wegnehmen. Was fange er mit den Perlen an, so ein Krüppel, und die Judennase gehöre abgehackt" (*DB*, 358).

79. For a recent critical assessment of this term in the context of German Studies, see Weninger, "Zur Dialektik des Dialektiks im deutschen Realismus."

80. *AF*, 331; "Die Menge fällt über sie her ... Die Fischerin stürzt zu Boden. Sie liegt auf dem Bauch und hält sich still. Sie wird furchtbar zugerichtet ... An der Echtheit des Buckels ist nicht zu zweifeln. Über ihn entlädt sich die Masse ... Dann verliert sie das Bewußtsein" (*DB*, 361).

81. Gilman, *The Jew's Body*, 236.

82. *AF*, 342; "Angst habe er doch. Er sei eben so gebaut. Wenn er wenigstens Dr. Fischer hieße, statt einfach Fischer, da hätte die Polizei gleich einen Respekt" (*DB*, 374).

83. *AF*, 359; "Der Anzug saß wie eine großartige Kombination. Was vom Buckel noch übrigblieb, verschwand unterm Mantel" (*DB*, 392; on the topic of camouflaging the "Jewish physique" with clothes, see also *DB*, 382, 385).

84. The cartoon "Jewish Metamorphosis" is reprinted in Ruth Gay, *Jews of Germany*, 233.

85. *AF*, 357; "Der Buckel [lag] in den letzten Zügen" (*DB*, 390).

86. This passage has all the markings of figural reworking, that is, it appears to me that Fischerle is protesting too much, and that, in the grand tradition of this novel, he is attempting to put a good face on a threatening incident. Such a judgment must, of course, remain somewhat speculative. However, I would point to those phrases where the language seems put to particular stress: "die Buben tobten und waren auf einmal erwachsen ... 'Meine Herren, was tut ihr!' Noch ein paar solche 'Herren' und sie blieben endgültig groß." Fischerle's desire to take these remarks as homage does not fully erase the suggestion of harassment and manhandling. In fact, he appears quite lucky to have escaped this gang.

87. *AF*, 357–58; "Einige Buben rotteten sich zusammen und warteten, bis der letzte Erwachsene verschwand. Plötzlich umringten sie Fischerle's Bank und brachen in einen englischen Chor aus. Sie heulten 'yes' und meinten 'Jud.' Vor seiner Reisefertigkeit fürchtete Fischerle Buben wie die Pest ... er war [jedoch] kein Jud' [mehr] und kein Krüppel, er war ein feiner Kerl und verstand sich auf Wigwams" (390–91). Fischerle's transformation into an American is here underscored by his alleged familiarity with American Indians. His reference to "wigwams" alludes to the immensely popular *Winnetou* novels by Karl May, who is credited with mediating images of the American "Wild West" to generations of Germans (up to the present), despite the fact that May himself only knew the United States from books. May's pseudohistorical realism is in many respects similar to Alexis's, discussed above in chapter 1.

88. *AF*, 360; "das Bild des wohlgeratenen Zwergs" (*DB*, 393). The larger context makes clear that the tailor takes pride in the fact that he has provided a suitable physique for Fischerle's beautiful spirit, the implication being that Fischerle's re-

cently acquired "cultivation" has fooled the tailor into believing that the dwarf truly is "well-bred." Thus we have a repetition (and modification) of the episode when Kien first meets Fischerle, in which "culture" means everything and nothing.

89. *AF*, 360; "Auf die Herzensbildung kommt es an" (*DB*, 393).

90. *AF*, 360; "ein frisch angezogener Mensch, verjüngt und hochgeboren" (*DB*, 393).

91. *AF*, 360; "Daraus entnahm Fischerle mit Recht und Stolz, daß er nicht mehr zu erkennen war" (*DB*, 394).

92. *AF*, 365; "Eine Faust schlägt ihm den Schädel ein. Der Blinde schleudert ihn zu Boden und holt vom Tisch in der Ecke des Kabinetts ein Brotmesser. Mit diesem zerfetzt er Anzug und Mantel und schneidet Fischerle den Buckel herunter. Bei der schweren Arbeit ächzt er, das Messer ist ihm zu stumpf, und Licht will er keines machen . . . Er wickelt den Buckel in die Fetzen des Mantels, spuckt ein paarmal drauf und läßt das Paket so liegen. Die Leiche schiebt er unters Bett" (*DB*, 398).

93. Fischerle's unawareness of his own use of Yiddish—because of the vulnerability it implies—appears much more tragic in historical hindsight and may well constitute one of those factors about this figure that gave Canetti pause in the post-Holocaust years; see below. In the context of the pre-Holocaust novel, however, there is legitimate, if undeniably dark, humor in Fischerle's total obliviousness to his language. His only hesitation in using the word "meschugge," it turns out, is that it might not make much of an impression on a psychiatrist, for whom, Fischerle reasons, insanity is an everyday complaint (see *DB*, 368).

94. *DB*, 453; *AF*, 414.

95. Canetti, *Das Augenspiel*, 201.

CHAPTER 5

1. Gay, *Freud*, 515.

2. Stieg concedes as much when he says: "Doch scheint mir der Roman selbst noch keine Antwort auf Freud zu enthalten, sondern eher die Drohungen der Epoche extrem zu artikulieren, bis hin zur Selbstvernichtung der Kultur" ("Canetti und die Psychoanalyse," 69).

3. In Adorno, "Canetti: Discussion with Adorno," 1–2.

4. Though Freud is on Adorno's mind throughout the conversation, the most substantial discussion of Canetti's dispute with Freud focuses on the disagreement over what constitutes a crowd (*Masse*). Canetti believes that Freud exaggerates the importance of the leader, and contends that Freud's whole concept of "identification" (by which he means, above all, the Oedipal bond) is "insufficiently reflected, too imprecise, not really clear" (ibid., 13). Clearly, Canetti wishes to substitute his cherished notion of "metamorphosis" (*Verwandlung*) for Freud's Oedipal complex. Adorno agrees that Canetti's social theories—particularly his insistence on seeing power as an external, social threat—represent an improve-

ment over Freud's overly abstract (and otherwise problematic) views on society. On this, see below.

5. Canetti, *Das Augenspiel*, 33.
6. Ibid., 42–43.
7. This, by the way, is the juncture where Broch advises Canetti to throw in the towel in this pursuit: "Es ist schade um die Zeit, die Sie daran wenden ... Sie können sich nicht einer Wissenschaft widmen, die keine ist und nie eine sein wird" (ibid., 43). So Canetti is clearly savoring a kind of retrospective victory when he recounts this episode.
8. Ibid., 40–41.
9. Ibid., 41.
10. Ibid., 44.
11. Gay, *Freud*, 405.
12. Canetti, *Das Augenspiel*, 237.
13. Ibid.
14. Ibid.
15. Ibid.
16. These events recounted in ibid., 167–73. Canetti often read his *Komödie der Eitelkeit* in tandem with "Der gute Vater," as on the evening of Max Pulver's remark quoted here (ibid., 169). Thus some of the reaction given in this paragraph might be construed to refer also to the *Komödie*. Nevertheless, as the following statement indicates, much of the negative reception was reserved explicitly for "Der gute Vater." It is important to know that Canetti read this chapter *after* the intermission, during the second half of the reading. "Man war noch eine ganze Weile beisammen, ich lernte so ziemlich alle kennen, die erschienen waren und jeder sagte mir's auf seine Weise, wie sehr ihn besonders der zweite Teil der Lesung geärgert habe" (ibid.).
17. Ibid., 169.
18. Ibid., 184.
19. The subjunctive mood in the following is apposite of the fact that the novel was of course still unpublished. Referring to the Zurich reading of 1935 (in the Stadelhoferstraße), Canetti relates: "Dafür hatte ich das Kapitel 'Der gute Vater' ausgesucht, aus dem Roman, der bald danach 'Die Blendung' betitelt werden sollte. Das hatte ich in Wien schon oft vorgelesen, privat und öffentlich und ich war seiner so sicher, als wäre es der unentbehrliche Teil eines allgemein bekannten und vielgelesenen Buches" (ibid., 169).
20. Ibid., 196.
21. *AF*, 88; "Jahre sehnte er sich schon danach, wieder einmal recht auf Weiberfleisch loszuschlagen" (*DB*, 91).
22. *AF*, 111; "'Die Weiber gehören totgeschlagen. Alle wie sie sind'" (*DB*, 116).
23. *AF*, 111–12, trans. rev.; "'Meine Frau, die ist aus den blauen Flecken nicht herausgekommen. Meine Tochter selig, die hab' ich gern gehabt, das war ein Weib,

wie man sagt, mit der hab' ich angefangen, wie sie noch ganz klein war'" (*DB*, 117).

24. *AF*, 286; "Wenn sie 40 Jahr' jünger wär.' Seine Tochter selig, ja, die war ein seelengutes Geschöpf. Die hat sich neben ihn legen müssen, wie er auf die Bettler gepaßt hat. Da hat er gezwickt und geschaut . . . Geweint hat sie. Es hat ihr nichts genützt. Gegen einen Vater gibt's nichts. Lieb war sie. Auf einmal war sie tot . . . Er hat sie halt gebraucht" (*DB*, 313–14). The last line, it should be noted, includes this alternate/supplemental meaning: "He simply used her."

25. *AF*, 289, trans. rev. While it is lexically possible to render "Parteien" as "tenants," that seems less appropriate in this context. Pfaff's anxieties are running high: he clearly fears the authorities, being arrested and prosecuted at this juncture. The "Parteien" he has in mind, therefore, are more likely the plaintiffs for the state in the trial he imagines will be conducted where he will be charged with the murder of his daughter. "Schänden" connotes a range of semantic possibilities — as I am sure Canetti intended — ranging from "rape" to "dishonor." But nowhere in this spectrum does one find "ferret out," as Wedgwood proposes. The tenants have no reason to be looking for the daughter. This correction is of some importance because this is a key passage where Pfaff convicts himself: the plaintiffs *continue* to violate his daughter, because this is a practice he has begun while she was under his care. Some ambiguity is inevitable, however, since Pfaff's manifest guilt punctures — but does not thoroughly clarify — the lies he has been at pains to put out. The German reads as follows: "Der Hausbesorger erstarrt. Er sieht, wie jemand jeden Ersten kommt und ihm die Pension wegnimmt, statt sie ihm zu bringen. Außerdem wird er eingesperrt . . . Alles kommt heraus, und die Parteien schänden seine Tochter noch im Grab. Er hat keine Angst . . . Er ist pensioniert. Er hat keine Angst. Der Doktor sagt selber, es sind die Lungen. Schicken Sie's fort! Ja wovon, lieber Herr? Die Pension braucht er zum Essen . . . Krankenkasse — ja was! Auf einmal kommt sie ihm mit einem Kind zurück. In das kleinwuzige Kabinett. Er hat keine Angst!" (*DB*, 316).

26. *AF*, 304, trans. rev. "Der Herr Professor redete von der Frau, aber er meinte die Tochter" (*DB*, 332; see also 321, 339).

27. *AF*, 370; "'Der Vater hat einen Anspruch . . .' 'auf die Liebe seines Kindes.' Laut und gleichmäßig wie in der Schule ratschte sie seinen Satz zu Ende . . . 'Zum Heiraten hat die Tochter . . .' — er streckte den Arm aus — 'keine Zeit.' 'Das Futter gibt ihr . . .' 'der gute Vater.' 'Die Männer wollen sie . . .' 'gar nicht haben'" (*DB*, 404).

28. *AF*, 374, trans. rev.; "Seit er sie zur Poli ernannt hatte, war er stolz auf sie. Die Weiber seien doch zu etwas gut, der Mann müsse es eben verstehen, lauter Polis aus ihnen zu machen" (*DB*, 409).

29. *AF*, 371; "Stundenlang liebkoste er sie" (*DB*, 405).

30. Two factors may, as I have said, inhibit our acknowledgment of the full extent of Pfaff's behavior: our own repulsion and the fact that Pfaff, though in-

consistent in his denials, is lying about the physical abuse. A prime example of his discordant assertions is to be found at the chapter's outset, where within the space of a paragraph he variously accounts for the death of his wife. In this passage, which serves as the exposition to Pfaff's affair with his own daughter, we witness him in the process of recasting the violent death as one attributable to "natural causes": "Bald nach dieser Veränderung starb die Frau, vor Überanstrengung. Sie kam der neuen Küche nicht nach . . . Oft wartete er volle fünf Minuten aufs Essen. Dann aber riß ihm die Geduld, und er prügelte sie, noch bevor er satt war. Sie starb unter seinen Händen. Doch wäre sie in den nächsten Tagen bestimmt und von selbst eingegangen. Ein Mörder war er nicht" (*DB*, 402). Though rendered in the ostensibly "objective" third person, this passage evinces a Pfaff no less in charge than in the coerced "dialogue" we witnessed above. The transparent efforts at self-justification ("eine volle fünf Minuten") and palpable pleading of his case ("Doch," "bestimmt") have left unmistakable traces of the building superintendent's pathetic "seelischer Haushalt."

31. *AF*, 369; *DB*, 404.

32. These nuptial terms can be found in *DB*, 402 and 405.

33. *AF*, 372, trans. rev. In translating the final clause as "she looks like a maiden fair," Wedgwood softens the passage unaccountably, overlooking, furthermore, the important conjunction "da," which links this clause to the preceding in the sense of "thus, so, as such." Canetti's German reads: "Sie nimmt das ganze Geld mit, übers Nachthemd wirft sie ihren eigenen Mantel, den sie nie tragen darf, nicht den alten des Vaters, da sieht sie wie eine Jungfrau aus" (*DB*, 406).

34. "Er findet ihren Mantel schön. Sie wird ihn tragen bis zu ihrem Tod, er ist noch neu" (*DB*, 407).

35. *AF*, 375; "während sie das Fleisch für sein Mittagessen weichschlug, klopfte er zum Vergnügen auf ihr herum. Sein Auge wußte nicht, was die Hand tat" (*DB*, 409).

36. *AF*, 369; "die Angst, die dieses Möbelstück ihr einflößte" (*DB*, 403).

37. *AF*, 378, trans. rev. "sie lebte noch mehrere Jahre als Dienstmädchen und Weib ihres Vaters" (*DB*, 413).

38. Hermann Broch was the first to see the influence of Edgar Allen Poe on *Die Blendung;* see Canetti, *Das Augenspiel*, 39.

39. At the comic conclusion of this subplot, where Georg pretends to be the Parisian police commissioner in order to appeal to the Hausbesorger's authoritarian mentality, Pfaff tenders the following unsolicited (and typically ignored) confession: "Benedikt Pfaff, der starke, rote Lümmel, zog seine Muskeln ein, kniete nieder, faltete die Hände und bat den Herrn Präsidenten um Vergebung. Die Tochter sei krank gewesen, *sie wäre von selbst auch gestorben*, bestens rekommandiere er sich, ihn nicht von seinem Posten zu vertreiben" (*DB*, 498, my emphasis).

40. This sealed-off room is itself a wonderful image of failed repression. Though Pfaff shuns the memory of the allegedly empty room ("Jede Erinnerung

an den leeren Raum daneben mied er"), the text of course speaks against him. When Kien, whose position at the peep-hole (*Guckloch*) now parallels precisely Anna's former reconnaissance assignment, refuses Pfaff's demand for food money, the latter considers as punishment incarcerating Kien in the very same room, "wo das Gemüt der seligen Tochter verlorengegangen ist" (ibid., 424). If not for the propitious arrival of Georg, Kien may indeed have suffered a similar fate. For Pfaff, it is only a matter of where to begin: "Was soll er jetzt zuerst? Ihm die Beine zerbrechen, den Schädel einschlagen, das Hirn verspritzen oder für den Anfang eine in den Bauch?" (ibid.).

41. Grünbaum, "Letters," 2.
42. Canetti, *Das Augenspiel*, 226.
43. This view was forcefully argued in the 1920s by Karen Horney and Ernest Jones; see Gay, *Freud*, 519-22.
44. Freud, "The Transformations of Puberty," 7:226.
45. Ibid., "The Dissolution of the Oedipus Complex," 19:178-79.
46. "In boys," Herman argues, "the suppression of incestuous wishes is rewarded by initiation into male privilege. The girl's renunciation of her incestuous wishes finds no comparable reward. It is rather through the consummation of incest that the girl seeks to gain those privileges which otherwise must forever be denied to her. Thus the girl has little inducement to overcome her infantile attachment to her father . . . The father's behavior toward his daughter thus assumes immense importance. If the father chooses to eroticize the relationship with his daughter, he will encounter little or no resistance. Even when the girl does give up her erotic attachment to her father, she is encouraged to persist in the fantasy that some other man, like her father, will some day take possession of her" (*Father-Daughter Incest*, 57).
47. In Herman, *Father-Daughter Incest*, 7.
48. See Gay, *Freud*, 73, and Herman, *Father-Daughter Incest*, 9. Gay commends Freud for being "severe with himself" (73), and goes on to suggest that this falsification was an effort to disguise the patient's identity (74). Thus Freud is seen to be in a dilemma: torn between the demands of science (full disclosure) and the demands of therapy (confidentiality). Herman suggests that Freud's motivations were less altruistic.
49. Gay argues that Freud's self-image as bourgeois critic impelled him toward advocating the female Oedipus complex. Commenting on the celebrated case of "Dora," in which Freud insists both that his female patient felt a sexual attraction for an older man who made an unwanted pass at her and that she was in love with her father, Gay observes: "Such a reading follows naturally from Freud's posture as a psychoanalytic detective and a critic of bourgeois morality. Intent on digging beneath polite social surfaces, and committed to the proposition that modern sexuality was screened by an almost impenetrable blend of unconscious denial and conscious mendacity, particularly among the respectable classes, Freud felt virtually obliged to interpret Dora's vehement rejection of Herr K. as a neurotic

defense" (*Freud*, 249). A defense, that is, against her own sexual desire. Dissatisfying in Gay's account is the fact that the exact opposite case might be made. Why, indeed, should Freud feel "obliged" to set aside Herr K.'s unseemly advance and postulate instead "a distinct feeling of sexual excitement" (249) on the part of his female analysand—which feelings, by the way, his patient firmly denied? More to the point for our purposes, perhaps, is the query, How does this move authorize Freud as "a critic of bourgeois morality"? Would he not in fact have qualified as a more radical critic of bourgeois hypocrisy had he confronted the illicit desire and violence of fathers? Herman suggests an antithetical reading, which attributes the utility of the Oedipus complex to its function in normalizing and internalizing an otherwise unsettling social phenomenon: "Freud concluded that his patients' reports of sexual abuse were fantasies, based on their own incestuous wishes. To incriminate daughters rather than fathers was an immense relief to him, even though it entailed a public admission that he had been mistaken" (*Father-Daughter Incest*, 10).

50. Canetti, "Macht und Überleben," 7.

51. In the conversation mentioned above, Canetti tells Adorno: "There is above all the question of the concept of identification. I consider this concept to be insufficiently reflected, too imprecise, not really clear. Freud says at many places in his work when talking of identification that it is a question of an exemplary model, of the child for example identifying with his father and wanting to be like his father. The father is the model. Now this is certainly right. But what really happens in this relation to the model has never been shown exactly . . . I have really made it my task to investigate all aspects of metamorphosis completely afresh, in order to be able to determine what a model actually is, and what really occurs between a model and the person who follows a model. Only then perhaps will we be able to have clearer ideas about identification. As long as this is not the case I am inclined to avoid the whole concept of identification" (Adorno, "Canetti: Discussion with Adorno," 13). In *Crowds and Power*, Canetti effectively replaces this notion with his own more positive concept of "Verwandlung," which also contains a fundamental aspect of identification. Canetti had planned to return to this topic in a second volume of *Crowds and Power*, but this, if written, was never published. For a more substantive explication and critique of the term "Verwandlung," see my "End of History."

52. Canetti, *Das Augenspiel*, 196.

53. Ibid., 183.

54. Wolff, *Child Abuse in Freud's Vienna*, 4.

55. Ibid. Wolff observes further: "Today there is heated controversy over the development of Freud's ideas about parents and children in the 1890s, but it has not been appreciated that Freud's Vienna was the scene of a great child abuse sensation, decades and decades before the formulation of the battered-child syndrome" (6).

56. Canetti, *Das Augenspiel*, 183.

57. Ibid., 201.

58. "Die Betroffene fühlt sich von einer überlegenen Macht gepackt, die sie nicht mehr losläßt. Es kann ein Mann sein, dem sie entkommen will, ein Mann, der sie geliebt hat und besitzt oder ein Mann wie Peleus, der sie erst besitzen wird. Es kann ein Priester sein, der die Kranke im Namen eines Gottes gefangen hält; es kann ein Geist oder Gott selber sein. In jedem Fall ist es wichtig, daß das Opfer die physische Nähe der überlegenen Macht fühlt, ihren unmittelbaren Griff auf sich" (Canetti, *Masse und Macht*, 383). Canetti's rather open challenge to Freud can be read in the section title, "Hysterie, Manie und Melancholie" (379–86).

59. Though Canetti is speaking of the novel as a whole when he remarks, "Es war ein erlösendes Gefühl . . . den Roman in den Händen zu halten, der von den dunkelsten Aspekten Wiens genährt war" (*DB*, 196), it seems clear from the context that "Der gute Vater" is uppermost in his mind; this is the juncture where Canetti refers to the "obligatory" reading of this chapter.

60. This, essentially, is the argument Gay makes (see above), though not with reference to Canetti. Throughout his magisterial study of Freud, Gay reminds us that Freud, though "revolutionary" in a very limited sense, was largely a social conservative. See, for example, Gay, *Freud*, 143, 149, 548.

61. *AF*, 372, trans. rev.; "'Zur Mutter,' sagte er, 'sie soll sich auch mal freuen'" (407).

62. *AF*, 372, trans. rev. Wedgwood's reading evades the oxymoron ("heimentführen," Canetti's neologism) in the German: "Ich entführe Sie heim" (*DB*, 406).

63. By, for example, citing the formula with which most fairy tales end: "Wenn ihre arme Mutter das erlebt hätte, sie wär' heut noch am Leben" (*DB*, 406).

64. See Gay, *Freud*, 519, and Herman, *Father-Daughter Incest*, 58.

65. *AF*, 372, trans. rev.; "Einen Mann will sie schon, damit sie von zu Hause wegkommt" (*DB*, 407).

66. This is reflected, for example, in the following: "Für sie hatte er gestohlen, aber er stellte sich ungeschickt an. Einem Ritter gelingt alles. Seit ihre Zigarette weg war, liebte sie ihn nicht mehr. Der Kopf des Vaters saß fester als je" (*DB*, 412).

67. *AF*, 377, trans. rev.; "Wohl nahm er seine Stieftochter vom Bett herunter und prügelte sie blutig" (*DB*, 411). It should be noted that Pfaff speaks here of a "stepdaughter" because since Anna rebelled against his authority and rejected the name "Poli," he denies that she really is his daughter, in much the same way that Kien denies Therese's existence.

68. "Sein lächerlicher Wunsch ist natürlich auf ein Jugenderlebnis zurückzuführen. Man müßte ihn einmal untersuchen . . . Die Vorstellung eines Geisteskranken ist von Jugend auf mit seiner Lust verbunden. Er fürchtet die Impotenz" (*DB*, 450).

69. "Er ist ein Mann, was hat jetzt zu geschehen? . . . Sobald es geschehen ist, wird sie ihn bewundern, weil er ein Mann ist. So sollen alle Frauen sein. Es geschieht also jetzt. Abgemacht. Er gibt sich sein Ehrenwort" (*DB*, 58).

70. *AF,* 57; "Aber die schweren Träume der letzten Zeit dürften mit seinem übertrieben strengen Leben zusammenhängen. Das wird jetzt anders" (*DB,* 57).

71. *AF,* 415, trans. rev.; "Was bedrängte ihn, ein beinahe geschlechtsloses Wesen?" (*DB,* 455).

72. *AF,* 421, trans. rev. Wedgwood skirts the issue of sexual abstinence entirely; "Peter gehört in eine geschlossene Anstalt. Er hat zu lange enthaltsam gelebt" (*DB,* 460-61).

73. Frosch, *Politics of Psychoanalysis,* 10.

74. Though Freud has of course been recruited for radical politics and wide-ranging cultural criticism, above all by the Frankfurt School, this inevitably involves redressing and modifying fundamental aspects of Freud's theory and practice. Above all, this has meant focusing on the social environment—as mediated by the father—in the socialization process. The Oedipus complex, in other words, has had to be opened up to include social, political, and cultural factors not emphasized by Freud. Stephen Frosh explicates and responds to the charge that psychoanalysis is essentially a "bourgeois discipline" (*Politics of Psychoanalysis,* 10). Indeed, his whole book should be seen as an attempt to rehabilitate Freud for social analysis. The amenability of traditional psychoanalysis to social conservatism is often cited in connection with the postwar popularity of psychoanalysis in the United States.

75. Stieg, "Canetti und die Psychoanalyse," 67 and 68, respectively.

76. *AF,* 431-32, trans. rev.; "Georg bemerkte sehr wohl, wann Peters Stimme überschnappte. Es genügte, daß seine Gedanken zur Frau oben zurückkehrten. Er sprach noch gar nicht von ihr und schon verriet sich in der Stimme ein schreiender, greller, unheilbarer Haß . . . Man mußte ihn zwingen, möglichst viel von seinem Haß preiszugeben. Wenn er doch einfach die Ereignisse, so wie sie sich ihm eingeprägt hatten, erzählend bis an ihren Ursprung zurückverfolgte! Georg verstand es, bei solchen Rückblicken den Radiergummi zu spielen, der alle Spuren auf dem empfindlichen Blatt der Erinnerung auslöschte" (*DB,* 473).

77. Gay, *Freud,* 65-66.

78. The allusion is to Breuer's phrase "wegerzählen," stemming from the early phase of psychoanalysis when Freud and Breuer were still collaborating. See ibid., 66 and 664 n. 65.

79. Freud, "Fragment of an Analysis of a Case of Hysteria," 7:116. Freud first came to recognize the phenomenon clearly in "Dora" (7-122); he would return to the topic specifically in the papers "The Dynamics of Transference" (12:99-108) and "Observations on Transference Love" (12:159-71).

80. Frosh, *Politics of Psychoanalysis,* 76. Frosh explicates the point further: "Thus, in the context of the relationship with the analyst, the patient reproduces her/his impulses, fantasies and desires which are directed towards other current and past objects... Distinctively when compared with some later theorists, Freud argues that although transference is experienced by the patient as real and as re-

ferring to the person of the analyst, it actually has nothing to do with current interactions" (77).

81. *AF,* 413; "Statt zu verarbeiten und zu entgegnen, nahm er mechanisch auf" (*DB,* 452).

82. Freud, "Recommendations to Physicians Practicing Psycho-Analysis," 12: 118.

83. Frosch, *Politics of Psychoanalysis,* 72.

84. *AF,* 397; "Da erwarb er, wenn er es noch nicht hatte, spielend das Vertrauen von Menschen, die sich jedem anderen gegenüber hinter ihre Wahngebilde versteckten. Könige redete er untertänigst als Eure Majestät an; vor Göttern fiel er auf die Knie und faltete die Hände. So ließen sich die erhabensten Herrschaften zu ihm herab und teilten ihm Näheres mit. Er wurde ihr einziger Vertrauter, den sie, vom Augenblick ihrer Anerkennung ab, über die Veränderung ihrer eigenen Bereiche auf dem laufenden hielten und um Rat angingen. Er beriet sie mit heller Klugheit, als hätte er selbst ihre Wünsche, immer ihr Ziel und ihren Glauben im Auge . . . schließlich sei er doch ihr Minister, Prophet und Apostel, oder zuweilen sogar der Kammerdiener" (*DB,* 434).

85. Frosh, *Politics of Psychoanalysis,* 77.

86. Ibid., 80.

87. *AF,* 397–98, trans. rev.: I have substituted "schizophrenia" for Wedgwood's "alternating personalities." Since the Greek root of "schizophrenia" actually means a splitting of the mind (Laplanche and Pontalis, *Language of Psychoanalysis,* 408), this term would seem to capture better "Bewußtseinsspaltungen." Of course, the ensuing text does not support the strict clinical definition of schizophrenia (which, however, is in its own right a disputed matter), but neither can this be expected of such a satirical passage. The German original reads: "Heftig umstritten war in der gelehrten Welt seine Behandlung von Bewußtseinsspaltungen der verschiedensten Art. Gebärdete sich zum Beispiel ein Kranker als zwei Menschen, die nichts miteinander gemein hatten oder sich bekämpften, so wandte Georges Kien eine Methode an, die ihm anfangs selbst sehr gefährlich erschien: er befreundete sich mit beiden Parteien . . . Dann ging er an die Heilung heran. In seinem eigenen Bewußtsein näherte er die getrennten Teile des Kranken, wie er sie verkörperte, und fügte sie langsam aneinander" (*DB,* 434–35).

88. Gay observes that this aspect of the "Dora" case left Freud open to considerable criticism: "This largely implicit claim to virtual omniscience invited criticism; it suggested Freud's certainty that all psychoanalytic interpretations are automatically correct, whether the analysand accepts them or disdains them. 'Yes' means 'Yes,' and so does 'No'" (*Freud,* 250). Freud later recanted—or, more accurately, qualified this position, but not until 1937, that is, well after the publication of *Auto-da-Fé* in 1935.

89. This from a remark about Broch where Canetti is discussing Broch's Freud enthusiasm: "Es war kein kaltes oder machtgieriges Schweigen, wie es von der

Analyse her bekannt ist, wo es darum geht, daß ein Mensch sich rettungslos einem anderen ausliefert, der sich kein Gefühl für oder gegen ihn erlauben *darf*" (*Das Augenspiel*, 34).

90. *AF*, 409; "'Aber Jean, sie liegt im Netz, siehst du sie nicht?' Immer hatte er recht. Der Freund öffnete den Mund, und schon war die Frau da" (*DB*, 447).

91. *AF*, 409, trans. rev. While Wedgwood's rendering fails to connote that Georg actually conjures Jeanne for his patient every day, I am perhaps guilty here of overcorrection. The German reads: "Alle Tage verhalf er Jean zu ihr" (*DB*, 448).

92. *AF*, 411, trans. rev.; "Von der viel tieferen und eigentlichsten Triebkraft der Geschichte, dem Drang der Menschen, in eine höhere Tiergattung, die Masse, aufzugehen und sich darin so vollkommen zu verlieren, als hätte es nie einen Menschen gegeben, ahnten sie nichts. Denn sie waren gebildet, und Bildung ist ein Festungsgürtel des Individuums gegen die Masse in ihm selbst" (*DB*, 449).

93. *AF*, 411, trans. rev. Because the English translation of *Masse und Macht* by Carol Stewart uses "crowd" for "Masse," I have done so here as well. Additionally, I have substituted "individuals" for Wedgwood's "single people" to avoid a misunderstanding (such as "unmarried"). I suspect one could go a step further here and add an adjective such as "monadic" or "isolated" to capture the contextual meaning of the "die übrigen einzelnen." The German reads: "Zahllose Menschen werden verrückt weil die Masse in ihnen besonders stark ist und keine Befriedigung findet. Nicht anders erklärte er sich selbst und seine Tätigkeit. Früher hatte er persönlichen Neigungen, seinem Ehrgeiz und den Frauen gelebt; jetzt lag ihm nur daran, sich unaufhörlich zu verlieren. In dieser Tätigkeit kam er Wünschen und Sinnen der Masse näher, als die übrigen einzelnen, von denen er umgeben war" (*DB*, 450).

94. *DB*, 450.

95. *AF*, 412; "Ein trauriger Tag, sagte er sich leise ... immer atmete er im Strom fremder Empfindungen. Heute spürte er nichts um sich, nur die schwere Luft" (*DB*, 451).

96. *AF*, 413; "Meine Frau langweilt mich" (*DB*, 452).

97. *AF*, 413, trans. rev.; "'Hau ihr nur eine herunter,' sagte Georges, diese zweiunddreißigjährige Treue hatte er satt. Jean schlug zu und schrie selbst für die Frau um Hilfe" (*DB*, 451).

98. *AF*, 413; "Außerdem war die Wachstafel im Schmelzen" (*DB*, 452).

99. *AF*, 414; "Warum geh' ich nicht endlich in die Wohnung? Weil die Frau dort auf mich wartet. Sie will Liebe ... Die Wachstafel drückte" (*DB*, 453).

100. *AF*, 406; "Seine Frau hielt es nach wenigen Wochen äußerster Armut nicht mehr bei ihm aus und brannte mit einem Unteroffizier durch" (*DB*, 444).

101. The very concept of transference short-circuits any effort to situate the analysand's projections onto the analyst within the context of economic, social, or adult intersubjective relationships. For, as Peter Brooks reminds us, "Transference is itself a kind of metaphor, a substitutive medium for the analysand's infantile experiences" (*Reading for the Plot*, 99). Laplanche and Pontalis elucidate further: "As

an expansion of the second Freudian theory of the psychical apparatus, the analytic treatment may be deemed to provide the ground on which intrasubjective conflicts—themselves the relics of the real or phantasied intersubjective relationships of childhood—can once more find expression in a relationship where communication is possible. As Freud noted, the analyst may for example find himself placed in the position of the super-ego; more generally, the whole interplay of identifications is given free rein to develop and to become 'unbound'" (*Language of Psychoanalysis*, 460).

102. "In seiner Wohnung richtete er Bett und Netz her, die Frau wäre endlich aufgetaucht. Jean träte leise herein und zöge das Netz zu" (*DB*, 448).

103. Canetti, *Das Augenspiel*, 135.

104. Gay, *Freud*, 552.

105. Stieg, "Canetti und die Psychoanalyse," 66.

106. Gay explains this as in part due to the state of biological science: "These conflicting appraisals [of the instincts] reach down to the fundamentals of psychology as a science. Freud was never completely happy with his theory of the drives, whether in its early or its late form. In 'On Narcissism' he lamented the 'complete lack of a theory of the drives'—Trieblehre—that might provide the psychological investigator with a dependable orientation. This absence of theoretical clarity was in large part due to the inability of biologists and psychologists to generate a consensus on the nature of drives or instincts" (*Freud*, 341).

107. Though he begins by suggesting that Freud's termite metaphor offers a fruitful point of comparison, and proceeds to argue, "daß Canetti hier auch ein ironisches Spiel mit der Psychoanalyse treibt" ("Canetti und die Psychoanalyse," 68–69), Stieg ends up postulating that Canetti actually employs Freud's concepts of repression and sublimation in order to mount a critique of high culture: "[Canetti] zeigt uns in der *Blendung* die Kultur in der Gestalt Peter Kiens als Ausdruck der extremsten Vereinzelung, der konsequentesten Distanz zu den anderen Menschen, allen voran den Frauen. Er zeigt sie uns als Hochkultur in einem durchaus Freudschen Licht als Exzesse der Verdrängung und Sublimation. Mit Freud zu sprechen, wäre Peter Kiens Ende eine radikale Wiederkehr des Verdrängten" (69).

108. *AF*, 432, trans. rev.; "Manche Insekten schon haben es besser als wir. Eine oder einige wenige Mütter bringen den ganzen Stock zur Welt. Die übrigen Tiere sind zurückgebildet. Kann man enger beisammenleben, als die Termiten es gewohnt sind? Welche furchtbare Summe geschlechtlicher Reizungen müßte ein solcher Stock vorstellen . . . besäßen die Tiere noch ihr Geschlecht! Sie besitzen es nicht, und die dazugehörigen Instinkte nur in geringem Maße. Selbst dieses Wenige fürchten sie. Im Schwarm, bei dem Tausende und Abertausende von Tieren scheinbar sinnlos zugrunde gehen, sehe ich eine Befreiung von der gespeicherten Geschlechtlichkeit des Stockes. Sie opfern einen kleinen Teil ihrer Masse, um den größeren von Liebeswirrungen freizuhalten. Der Stock würde an Liebe, wäre sie einmal erlaubt, zugrunde gehen" (*DB*, 474).

109. Laplanche and Pontalis, *Language of Psychoanalysis*, 214–17.

110. *AF,* 432–33, trans. rev.; "Ich weiß keine großartigere Vorstellung als die einer Orgie im Termitenstock. Die Tiere vergessen—eine ungeheuerliche Erinnerung hat sie gepackt—was sie sind, blinde Zellen eines fanatischen Ganzen. Jedes will für sich sein, bei hundert oder tausend von ihnen fängt es an, der Wahn greift um sich, *ihr* Wahn, ein Massenwahn, die Soldaten verlassen die Eingänge, der Stock brennt vor unglücklicher Liebe, sie können ja nicht paaren, sie haben kein Geschlecht, der Lärm, die Erregung, alles Gewohnte überbietend, lockt ein Ameisengewitter an, durch die unbewachten Tore dringen die Todfeinde ein, welcher Krieger denkt an Verteidigung, jeder will Liebe, der Stock, der vielleicht Ewigkeiten gelebt hätte, die Ewigkeiten, nach denen wir uns sehnen, stirbt, stirbt an Liebe, an dem Trieb, durch den wir, eine Menschheit, unser Weiterleben fristen! Eine plötzliche Verkehrung des Sinnreichsten ins Sinnloseste" (*DB,* 474).

111. Frosh, *Politics of Psychoanalysis,* 40.

112. *AF,* 432; "Offenbar erwartete er von Georg ihre Entfernung" (*DB,* 473).

113. *AF,* 432, trans. rev.; "Ich glaube, daß du die Bedeutung der Frauen stark überschätzt. Du nimmst sie zu ernst, du hältst sie für Menschen wie wir. Ich sehe in den Frauen ein nur vorläufig notwendiges Übel. Manche Insekten haben es besser als wir" (*DB,* 473–74).

114. *AF,* 444; "Welches Elend in alle Zukunft!" (*DB,* 487).

115. *AF,* 444, trans. rev.; "Warum in alle Zukunft? Wir sprachen doch vorhin von den Termiten, die das Geschlecht überwunden haben. Es ist also weder ein unbedingtes noch ein unausrottbares Übel" (*DB,* 487).

116. *AF,* 432, trans. rev.; "wenn (Kien) doch einfach die Ereignisse ... erzählend bis an ihren Ursprung zurückverfolgte!" (*DB,* 473; see also 478).

117. Which is not to say that Georg's threat falls on deaf ears. Indeed, it is clear that this image of the "Liebesaufruhr im Termitenstock" has burrowed itself deeply into Kien's consciousness, for he feels compelled to refute it throughout this chapter (see *DB,* 475, 487, 489, 490).

118. *AF,* 437, trans. rev.; "Aus eigenem Willen allein, von niemandem unterstützt, nicht einmal einen Mitwisser besaß ich, habe ich mich von einem Druck, einer Last, einem Tod, einer Rinde von verfluchtem Granit befreit. Wo wäre ich wenn ich auf dich gewartet hätte?" (*DB,* 479).

119. Freud, *Civilization and Its Discontents,* 21:97.

120. Frosh, *Politics of Psychoanalysis,* 45. Gay's exegesis of *Civilization and Its Discontents* corroborates Frosh's on this point: "Women, who have increasingly become love's guardians, are particularly hostile to civilization that corners the attention of their men and the service of their children" (*Freud,* 548).

121. *AF,* 433; "die wirklichen großen Denker sind vom Unwert der Frau überzeugt" (*DB,* 475).

122. *AF,* 437, trans. rev., though neither Wedgwood nor I has done justice to the idiomatic phrase "das Blaue vom Himmel herunterlügen," which means "to lie shamelessly" and is here cleverly reversed by Kien: "Ich werde dir beweisen, daß alle Frauen Haß verdienen; du meinst ich verstünde mich nur auf den Orient.

Die Beweise, die er braucht, holt er sich aus seinen Spezialgebieten — das denkst du dir. Ich werde dir das Blaue vom Himmel herunterholen, aber keine Lügen, Wahrheiten, schöne, harte, spitze Wahrheiten, Wahrheiten jeder Größe und Art, Wahrheiten fürs Gefühl und Wahrheiten für den Verstand, obwohl bei dir nur das Gefühl funktioniert, du Weib" (*DB*, 479).

123. Roberts, "Crowds and Power or the Natural History," 47.

124. Ibid., 49–50.

125. For example, Frosh notes that for Freud "there is no necessity to conceive of any inherent embeddedness of [the] individual in culture, a characteristic assumption of most progressive philosophies. Explanation of behaviour is provided by the vicissitudes of instinct; the environment is only relevant to the extent that it supports or opposes satisfaction" (*Politics of Psychoanalysis*, 27).

126. Canetti, *Das Augenspiel*, 42. Broch's remarks refer here to both *Die Blendung* and the contemporaneous play *Hochzeit*.

127. Adorno, "Canetti: Discussion with Adorno," 13; Adorno also takes approving notice of Canetti's emphasis on the violence within society that is often concealed from view (14).

128. Canetti, *Das Augenspiel*, 142–43.

129. Canetti, *Crowds and Power*, 12. In the orginal, Canetti underscores the sense of equality by italicizing the word "gleiche."

130. Canetti, *Masse und Macht*, 26.

131. Though Carol Stewart translates "Stachel" as "sting," I continue to prefer "thorn" because it more accurately represents Canetti's almost mechanistic concept and also provides a sense of the ongoing substantiality of this concept. "Sting" may suggest a pain that dissipates over time, possibly on its own. Canetti's curious notion of "thorns" is quite different.

132. For a brief overview, see my encyclopedia entry "Crowds and Power."

CHAPTER 6

1. Earlier McFarlane had rejected the characterization of modernism as either the "reconciliation of opposites" or as "ambivalence," claiming instead a much more complex model: "It is then as though the Modernist purpose ought to be defined as the resolution of Hegel with Kierkegaard; committing oneself neither wholly to the notion of 'both/and,' nor wholly to the notion of 'either/or,' but (as it were) to both — and to neither. Dauntingly, then, the Modernist formula becomes 'both/and and/or either/or'" ("Mind of Modernism," 88). In championing Eliot and Canetti, as we shall see, McFarlane appears to drop the Kierkegaardian side of his argument.

2. Ibid., 92.

3. Ibid., 91.

4. Stevenson's book is built around this notion, which he defines in this man-

ner: "philosophers such as Bergson, Nietzsche and William James all suggest a change in something as fundamental as the relation of mind and world—a kind of epistemological shift, from relative confidence towards a sense of increased unreliability and uncertainty in the means by which reality is apprehended in thought" (*Modernist Fiction*, 11). Stevenson qualifies this central idea by referring to Foucault's parallel concept of paradigm shifts, which is meant to remind us that philosophy should not naively be construed as the "cause" of changes in art: "Though it would obviously be misleading to rule out any possibility of philosophy influencing life or literature directly, relations between the various spheres need to be considered reciprocal rather than only hierarchical" (13).

5. On the rich variety of modernism, see, for example Bradbury and McFarlane: "In short, Modernism was in most countries an extraordinary compound of the futuristic and the nihilistic, the revolutionary and the conservative, the naturalistic and the symbolist, the romantic and the classical. It was a celebration of a technological age and a condemnation of it; an excited acceptance of the belief that the old regimes of culture were over, and a deep despairing in the face of that fear; a mixture of convictions that the new forms were escapes from historicism and the pressures of the time with convictions that they were precisely the living expressions of these things" ("Name and Nature of Modernism," 46).

6. Arguing against Lukács's claim that modernism wishes utterly to escape history and politics, Jameson argues that "the modernist project is more adequately understood as the intent . . . to 'manage' historical and social, deeply political impulses, that is to say, to defuse them, to prepare substitute gratifications for them" (in Stevenson, *Modernist Fiction*, 220).

7. Lukács, "Ideology of Modernism," 21.

8. Tiresias's visionary acumen, it must be stressed, derives not only from his paradoxical "visionary blindness," but from an almost mystical ontological status that permits him to "resolve within his own androgynous person" the full range of the poem's dramatis personae (McFarlane, "Mind of Modernism," 91).

9. Ibid.

10. Quoted in ibid., 90.

11. Ibid., 91.

12. Ibid., 92.

13. Ibid.

14. Ibid., 89.

15. Ibid., 92.

16. "The conventional use of the term *modernism* to denote the poets, novelists, and critics who reacted against the process of modernization—the advance of industrialization, bureaucracy, science, technology, and other institutions of modernity—has been rendered increasingly problematic by the more frequent use of the same term, within the same discourse, to refer to the theorists who inspired and defended this project of the mastery of nature, or who criticized it from a perspective more sympathetic than that displayed by T. S. Eliot and other

figures in the modernist canon" ("Knower and Artificer," 50). Hollinger goes on to note Marshall Berman's recent and ambitiously inclusive brief for modernism, which Hollinger attributes in part to Berman's struggle "against the hermeneutic imperialism of the postmodernists" (50).

17. Ibid., 29.

18. "The chief significance of the Knower and Artificer is not that so many intellectuals were willing to choose one absolutely over the other but that so many were willing to define the dilemmas and opportunities of modern culture so extensively in the terms of these two personae" (ibid., 36; see also 36–44).

19. Huyssen, *After the Great Divide*, ix.

20. This and the quotation directly preceding it can be found in ibid.

21. Ibid., vi.

22. Jameson, "Afterword," 209. The real proof of Adorno's error, Jameson argues, is the fact that capitalism has successfully commodified modernist art to an amazing extent. Commenting on Adorno's claim for the political efficacy of modernism, Jameson notes: "In retrospect, this now seems a most unexpected revival of a Lukács-type 'reflection theory' of aesthetics, under the spell of a political and historical despair that plagues both houses and finds praxis henceforth unimaginable. What is ultimately fatal to this new and finally itself once more anti-political revival of the ideology of modernism is less the equivocal rhetoric of Adorno's attack on Lukács or the partiality of his reading of Brecht, than very precisely the fate of modernism in consumer society itself" (209).

23. It is not the fact that high modernism is inherently ambivalent about the "disintegrating" modern world (as many commentators continue to believe) that collapses the opposition, but that in its very transcendent, conciliatory, unifying mode (à la Eliot) high modernism dissolves the distinction by encompassing both options—critique and resolution, or, better: resolution as critique—leaving the "ideology of modernism," so to speak, in the eye of the beholder.

24. Adorno, "Commitment," 190.

25. Fried in *Ein Dichter gegen Macht und Tod*.

26. Adorno, "Commitment," 190.

27. See, for example, Lawrence Langer's *Admitting the Holocuaust* and *The Holocaust and the Literary Imagination* as well as Alvin Rosenfeld, *A Double Dying* and *Thinking about the Holocaust*.

28. Adorno, "Commitment," 180, my emphasis.

29. Ibid., 193; the phrase quoted directly above ("the very features . . .") can be found in ibid., 188.

30. "The uncalculating autonomy of works which avoid popularization and adaptation to the market, involuntarily becomes an attack on them . . . Works of art that react against empirical reality obey the forces of that reality, which reject intellectual creations and throw them back on themselves. There is no material content, no formal category of artistic creation, however mysteriously transmitted and itself unaware of the process, which did not originate in the empirical

reality from which it breaks free" (ibid., 190). Yet how this actually works remains shrouded in mystery, and thus a vulnerable point in Adorno's aesthetic theory. That Schiller was in fact on his mind while writing this essay can be gleaned from this criticism of Sartre: "The content of his art becomes philosophy as with no other writer except Schiller" (ibid., 182).

31. Ibid., 190, my emphasis.
32. Ibid., 190–91.
33. Ibid., 194.
34. For a critical treatment of realism's "panoptic" epistemic privilege, see Dorrit Cohn, "Optics and Power in the Novel."
35. Bradbury and McFarlane, "Name and Nature of Modernism," 47.
36. Lukács, "Ideology of Modernism," 26.
37. Adorno, "Commitment," 191.
38. Szondi's observation, which derives from Lukács's pathbreaking assessment of Expressionism, is quoted in Schürer, "*Nebeneinander:* Aspekte der Kultur der Weimarer Republik," 402.
39. On other ways that the novel exonerates the protagonist, see Tatar, "Gender, Violence, and Agency in Döblin's *Berlin Alexanderplatz.*"
40. Bradbury and McFarlane, "Name and Nature of Modernism," 27.
41. Binder distinguishes "*vision par derriere* (Darstellung eines Erlebnisses vom Erzähl-Ich aus" from "*vision avec* (Darstellung eines Erlebnisses vom Erlebnis-Ich aus)," quoted in Jayne, *Erkenntnis und Transzendenz,* 18.
42. Significantly, it was not until the newer modernist paradigms displaced the traditional high modernist model that Kafka's humor was rediscovered. Though Kafka was known to laugh during his own readings, the high modernist construction of Kafka, which contains the most diverse and mutually exclusive of approaches, was dominated by a serious, even lugubrious, reading.
43. Huyssen, *After the Great Divide,* 97.
44. Ibid., 114.
45. In discussing Brecht (in "Commitment," 182), Adorno opposes modernist abstraction to identification.
46. See Canetti, *Das Augenspiel,* 131 and 142.
47. An early document of German literary modernism, Hofmannsthal's *Lord Chandos Brief,* provides a clear example of the contrast between the representation of individual psychic diffusion and general cultural anomie on the one hand, and the analysis of this situation, implicit in the very eloquent and sophisticated formulation, on the other. Lord Chandos's predicament cannot, in other words, be equated with Hofmannsthal's.
48. An example of this approach is Robert Holub's *Reflections of Realism.*
49. "Adorno's dismissal of Sartre's literary attempt to incite individual subjects to free and active choice was based on the premise that late capitalism had devised an all-inclusive 'administered universe,' a political order purged of contradiction and therefore of the objective possibility of choice . . . It should be added here

that the notion of a residual transcendental subject was structurally essential to Adorno's thought, furnishing the only point of leverage in a putatively totalitarian social order (and founding the possibility of a thought that could indict it as such). No assessment of his aesthetics can overlook this semi-miraculous persistence of the subject in a conceptual schema that posits its complete reification. Sartre's belief in the efficacy of individual engagement seems much less questionable than a theory in which the production of 'autonomous' works of art is little less than magical" (Jameson, "Presentation IV," 147).

50. On this see Zuidervaart's *Adorno's Aesthetic Theory*, especially chapter 6, "Political Migration" (122–49).

51. See, for example, this statement: "By dismantling appearance, [autonomous works of art] explode from within the art which committed proclamation subjugates from without, and hence only in appearance. The inescapability of their work compels the change of attitude which committed works merely demand" (Adorno, "Commitment," 191).

52. "The moment of true volition, however, is mediated through nothing other than the form of the work itself, whose crystallization becomes an analogy of that other condition which should be. As eminently constructed and produced objects, works of art, including literary ones, point to a practice from which they abstain: the creation of a just life" (ibid., 194).

53. Brecht's was surely one of the very few voices within modernism crying out in open support of this "analytic self"; indeed, his whole aesthetic program depends upon it. But Brecht's overtly Communist politics and his primary interest in drama, as well as Adorno's unsparing criticism of him, ensured that he would have little effect on the construction of Anglo-American high modernism. Though he praised Brecht's goals, Adorno derided his output as naively didactic, purveying "bad politics," and as amenable to readings from "official humanism" ("Commitment," 188). On Brecht's reception in the United States, see Mews, "An Un-American Brecht?"

54. Lukács, "Ideology of Modernism," 26–27.

55. This point—that rich psychological portrayal can serve to validate a state of affairs intended for critique—may in fact explain Broch's own doubts about the value of art. Still, as Roche points out, Broch's critique retains and indeed exemplifies "art's inherently proleptic function." See Roche, "National Socialism and the Disintegration of Values," 375.

56. Zuidervaart uses the term "deprivileged subject" as a designation for the epistemologically weakened, fragmented self: "Deep in this movement is the impulse to deprive the subject of its privileged position. In philosophy, this impulse opposes the constitutive knower first clearly articulated in Descartes's *cogito ergo sum*" (*Adorno's Aesthetic Theory*, 250); this, along with the phrase "deprivation of the subject," describes perhaps more helpfully what is commonly referred to as the modernist "fragmented self" or what Stevenson has called the "epistemological shift."

57. Lukács, "Franz Kafka or Thomas Mann?," 51.
58. Lukács, "Ideology of Modernism," 20–21.
59. Ibid., 21.
60. Lukács argues: "In any protest against particular social conditions, these conditions themselves must have the central place" (ibid., 29). Yet Canetti manages to keep wider social concerns on our mind without this sort of positive depiction. On the other hand, we come to see the subjectivist fantasies as themselves evidence of a highly problematic *social* practice.
61. Ibid., 35. Lukács rather directly blames philosophy, and Bergson in particular, for this subjectivist turn in literature: "Subjective Idealism had already separated time, abstractly conceived, from historical change and particularity of place. As if this separation were insufficient for the new age of imperialism, Bergson widened it further. Experienced time, subjective time, now became identical with real time; the rift between this time and that of the objective world was complete. Bergson and other philosophers who took up and varied this theme claimed that their concept of time alone afforded insight into authentic, i.e. subjective, reality. The same tendency soon made its appearance in literature" (ibid., 37).
62. It could be argued that Canetti is as close to Adorno as he is to Lukács in this rejection of historicism (understood as a form of "false consciousness"). But Canetti's method of engagement would undoubtedly have appalled Adorno, for he opts to distance himself from this form of populist diversion by means of parody rather than choosing an "unconsumable" modernist aesthetic; for this parody cannot function without resurrecting and reinscribing its realist target. Though allied in their rejection of the often disguised consolations of literature, Canetti and Adorno were, of course, to remain worlds apart regarding aesthetic policy: Adorno's almost masochistic aesthetic, developed in response to Nazism and the Holocaust (and preached, let us recall, to a specifically German audience), proscribes pleasure of almost any sort. The humor of *Auto-da-Fé*, resting as it does on the epistemological "superiority" of the reader, would undoubtedly have placed the novel beyond the pale of Adorno's conception of proper literary modernism. Laughing was simply verboten.
63. Georg evinces that second aspect of escapism affiliated in the novel with popular literature, namely "respectable" literature as a pleasurable, even erotic, form of dissipation. *Auto-da-Fé* wryly aligns the *Lebemann* Georg with this tendency, for he is from the very beginning introduced as someone seeking to cloak his lechery with more respectable cultural pursuits. The unproblematic and uncritical process of readerly identification—the slipping in and out of fictional characters—provides a kind of anesthetizing gratification that purveys in the end a sensual refuge from, rather than critical perspective on, the modern world.
64. This frequently quoted passage from Eliot has become a commonplace of high modernism; cited in Stevenson, *Modernist Fiction*, 212; McFarlane, "Mind of Modernism," 83; and elsewhere. It originally appeared in Eliot, "*Ulysses*, Order and Myth."

65. Canetti remarks: "'Kant fängt Feuer', so hieß der Roman, hatte mich verwüstet zurückgelassen. Die Verbrennung der Bücher war etwas, das ich nicht vergeben konnte... denn in der Bibliothek des Sinologen war alles enthalten, was für die Welt von Bedeutung war ... und zurück blieb eine Wüste, es gab nun nichts mehr als Wüste und ich selbst war an ihr schuld. Denn es ist kein bloßes Spiel, was in einem solchen Buch geschieht, es ist eine Wirklichkeit, für die man einzustehen hat" (*Das Augenspiel*, 9).

66. Lukács accuses the following intellectual trinity of aiding and abetting the modernist cause in this way: Heidegger, Freud, Bergson. Ironically, Lukács pays little attention in "Ideology of Modernism" to the wider social conditions that contributed to the rise of the deprivileged subject.

67. Lukács, "Ideology of Modernism," 20.

68. Canetti, *Das Augenspiel*, 61.

69. "Das scharf Umrissene der Figuren lag ihm" (ibid., 110).

70. Ibid., 162.

71. Ibid., 163; see also 122–23.

72. Ibid., 297; see also 83.

73. Indeed, the bulk of the foregoing study should in fact already have demonstrated the utility of newer approaches to modernism, which Huyssen and Bathrick describe rather succinctly as a "move away from the isolated masters of modernism toward history and politics" (*Modernity and the Text*, 2). An overview of this more capacious (and ever expanding) view of modernism can be found in Heller's review "New Life for Modernism," which discusses a number of relevant books on the topic.

74. Canetti, for example, held his play *Komödie der Eitelkeit* (published 1950, but written already in 1934) to be "eine legitime Entgegnung auf die Bücherverbrennung" of May 10, 1933 (*Das Augenspiel*, 115; see also 62), rather than an apolitical absurdist or existentialist drama.

75. This tendency is identified and refuted in Doppler's "Vor- und Gegenbilder."

76. I provide a more critical assessment of these matters, including a discussion of the elusive matter of "Verwandlung," in my "End of History."

BIBLIOGRAPHY

Adorno, Theodor. "Commitment" ("Adorno on Brecht"). In *Aesthetics and Politics: The Key Texts of the Classic Debate within German Marxism*, edited by Frederic Jameson and translated by Francis McDonagh, 177–95. London: New Left Books/Verso, 1977.
———. "Elias Canetti: Discussion with Theodor Adorno." *Thesis Eleven* 45 (1996): 1–15.
Alexis, Willibald. *Die Hosen des Herrn von Bredow. Vaterländischer Roman*. Leipzig: Insel, n.d. [1926].
Anderson, Mark. "Kafka and New York: Notes on a Traveling Narrative." In *Modernity and the Text: Revisions of German Modernism*, edited by Andreas Huyssen and David Bathrick, 142–61. New York: Columbia University Press, 1989.
Arnason, Johann P. "Canetti's Counter-Image of Society." *Thesis Eleven* 45 (1996): 86–115.
Auer, Annemarie. "Ein Genie und sein Sonderling—Elias Canetti und die Blendung." In *Zu Elias Canetti*, edited by Manfred Durzak, 31–53. Stuttgart: Klett, 1983.
Bahr, Hermann. "Das unrettbare Ich." In *Zur Überwindung des Naturalismus; theoretische Schriften, 1887–1904*, edited by Gotthart Wunberg, 183–92. Stuttgart: W. Kohlhammer, 1968.
Barnouw, Dagmar. *Elias Canetti*. Stuttgart: Metzler, 1979.
Bartsch, Kurt, and Gerhard Melzer, eds. *Experte der Macht: Elias Canetti*. Graz: Verlag Droschl, 1985.
Bathrick, David, and Andreas Huyssen. "Modernism and the Experience of Modernity." In *Modernity and the Text: Revisions of German Modernism*, edited by Andreas Huyssen and David Bathrick, 1–16. New York: Columbia University Press, 1989.
Beller, Steven. "Otto Weininger as Liberal?" In *Jews and Gender: Responses to Otto Weininger*, edited by Nancy A. Harrowitz and Barbara Hyams, 91–101. Philadelphia: Temple University Press, 1995.
———. *Vienna and the Jews 1867–1938: A Cultural History*. Cambridge: Cambridge University Press, 1989.
Benjamin, Walter. *Illuminations*. Edited and introduced by Hannah Arendt, translated by Harry Zohn. New York: Schocken, 1969.

Bering, Dietz. *Der Name als Stigma: Antisemitismus im deutschen Alltag 1812–1933.* Stuttgart: Klett-Cotta, 1988.
Berkeley, George. *Principles of Human Knowledge.* Vol. 1 of *The Works of George Berkeley, Bishop of Cloyne,* edited by A. A. Luce and T. E. Jessop. London, 1948.
Berman, Russell A. *The Rise of the Modern German Novel: Crisis and Charisma.* Cambridge: Harvard University Press, 1986.
Bettelheim, Bruno. *The Uses of Enchantment: The Meaning and Importance of Fairy Tales.* New York: Vintage Books, 1976.
Bischoff, Alfons-M. *Elias Canetti: Stationen zum Werk.* Frankfurt am Main: Peter Lang, 1973.
Borchmeyer, Dieter. "The Question of Anti-Semitism." In *Wagner Handbook,* edited by Ulrich Miller and Peter Wapnewski, translated by John Deathridge, 166–85. Cambridge: Harvard University Press, 1992.
Boyle, Nicholas. "'Art,' Literature, Theology: Learning from Germany." In *Higher Learning and Catholic Traditions,* edited by Robert E. Sullivan. Notre Dame: University of Notre Dame Press, 2001.
Bradbury, Malcolm, and James McFarlane, eds. *Modernism: A Guide to European Literature, 1890–1930.* 1976. London: Penguin, 1991.
Bradbury, Malcolm, and James McFarlane. "The Name and Nature of Modernism." In *Modernism: A Guide to European Literature, 1890–1930,* edited by Malcolm Bradbury and James McFarlane, 9–55. London: Penguin, 1991.
Brenner, Michael. *After the Holocaust: Rebuilding Jewish Lives in Postwar Germany.* Princeton: Princeton University Press, 1997.
Broch, Hermann. *Die Schlafwandler: eine Romantrilogie.* 1930–32. Vol. 1 of *Hermann Broch: Kommentierte Werkausgabe,* edited by Paul Michael Lützeler. Includes *Pasenow, oder Die Romantik, Esch, oder Die Anarchie,* and *Huguenau, oder Die Sachlichkeit.* Frankfurt am Main: Suhrkamp, 1986.
Bronfen, Elisabeth. *Over Her Dead Body: Death, Femininity and the Aesthetic.* New York: Routledge, 1992.
Brooks, Peter. *Reading for the Plot: Design and Intention in Narrative.* New York: Knopf, 1984.
Canetti, Elias. *Der andere Prozeß: Kafkas Briefe an Felice.* 1968. München: Carl Hanser, 1984.
———. *Das Augenspiel: Lebensgeschichte 1931–1937.* 1985. Frankfurt am Main: Fischer Taschenbuch, 1988.
———. *Die Blendung.* 1935. Frankfurt am Main: Fischer Taschenbuch, 1993. Translated as *Auto-da-Fé* by C. V. Wedgwood, 1946. New York: Farrar, Straus, Giroux, 1984.
———. *Dramen.* 1976. Frankfurt am Main: Fischer Taschenbuch, 1978.
———. "Elias Canetti: Discussion with Theodor W. Adorno." *Thesis Eleven* 45 (1996): 1–15.

———. "Das erste Buch: *Die Blendung*." In *Das Gewissen der Worte*, 241-54. Frankfurt am Main: Fischer Taschenbuch, 1981.

———. *Die Fackel im Ohr: Lebensgeschichte 1921-1931.* 1980. Frankfurt am Main: Fischer Taschenbuch, 1982.

———. *Die Fliegenpein: Aufzeichnungen.* Munich: Carl Hanser, 1992.

———. *Die gerettete Zunge: Geschichte einer Jugend.* 1977. Frankfurt am Main: Fischer Taschenbuch, 1979.

———. *Die gespaltene Zukunft.* Munich: Carl Hanser, 1972.

———. *Das Gewissen der Worte: Essays.* 1976. Frankfurt am Main: Fischer Taschenbuch, 1981.

———. "Macht und Überleben." In *Macht und Überleben: Drei Essays*, 7-24. Berlin: Literarisches Colloquium, 1961.

———. *Masse und Macht.* 1960. Frankfurt am Main: Fischer Taschenbuch, 1980.

———. *Der Ohrenzeuge: Fünfzig Charaktere.* 1974. Frankfurt am Main: Fischer Taschenbuch, 1983.

———. *Die Provinz des Menschen: Aufzeichnungen 1942-1972.* 1973. Frankfurt am Main: Fischer Taschenbuch, 1976.

———. "Realismus und neue Wirklichkeit." In *Das Gewissen der Worte*, 72-77. Frankfurt am Main: Fischer Taschenbuch, 1981.

———. *Die Stimmen von Marrakesch: Aufzeichnungen nach einer Reise.* 1967. Frankfurt am Main: Fischer Taschenbuch, 1980.

Clover, Carol. *Men, Women, and Chainsaws: Gender in the Modern Horror Film.* Princeton: Princeton University Press, 1992.

Cohn, Dorrit. "Optics and Power in the Novel." In *History and Literature: Essays in Honor of Karl S. Guthke,* edited by William Collins Donahue and Scott D. Denham, 91-106. Tübingen: Stauffenburg, 2000.

———. *Transparent Minds: Narrative Modes for Presenting Consciousness in Fiction.* Princeton: Princeton University Press, 1978.

Copleston, Frederick. *A History of Philosophy.* Vols. 5-7. 1963-64. New York: Image/Doubleday, 1985.

Curtius, Mechthild. *Kritik der Verdinglichung in Canettis Roman "Die Blendung": Eine Sozialpsychologische Literaturanalyse.* Bonn: Bouvier, 1973.

Darby, David. "'Esse Percipi, Sein ist Wahrgenommenwerden': Perception and Perspective in Berkeley and Canetti." *Neophilologus* 75 (1991): 425-32.

———. *Structures of Disintegration: Narrative Strategies in Elias Canetti's Die Blendung.* Riverside, Calif.: Ariadne, 1992.

Davis, Lennard J. *Resisting Novels: Ideology and Fiction.* New York: Methuen, 1987.

Denby, David. "Learning to Love Canetti: The Autobiography of a Difficult Man." *New Yorker* (31 May 1999): 106-13.

Der gelbe Stern in Österreich. Vol. 5 of *Studia Judaica Austriaca.* Edited by Kurt Schubert. Eisenstadt: Edition Roetzer, 1977.

Dissinger, Dieter. "Erster Versuch einer Rezeptionsgeschichte Canettis am Beispiel seiner Werke *Die Blendung* und *Masse und Macht.*" In *Canetti lesen*, edited by Herbert Göpfert, 90–105. Munich: Hanser, 1975.

———. *Vereinzelung und Massenwahn: Elias Canettis Roman "Die Blendung."* Bonn: Bouvier, 1971.

Döblin, Alfred. *Berlin Alexanderplatz: die Geschichte vom Franz Biberkopf.* Edited by Werner Stauffacher. Zurich and Dusseldorf: Walter Verlag, 1996.

———. "Die Ermordung einer Butterblume." In *Die Ermordung einer Butterblume: Ausgewählte Erzählungen 1910–1950*, edited by Walter Muschg, 42–54. Olten and Freiburg im Breisgau: Walter Verlag, 1962.

Donahue, William Collins. "Die Blendung, 1935." In *Encyclopedia of German Literature*, edited by Michael Konzett, 1:170–71. Chicago: Fitzroy Dearborn, 2000.

———. "Die Blendung: Elias Canetti's 'Viennese' Novel." *Sprachkunst: Beiträge zur Literaturwissenschaft* 30.2 (1999): 247–70.

———. "'Eigentlich bist du eine Frau. Du bestehst aus Sensationen': Misogyny as Cultural Critique in Elias Canetti's *Die Blendung.*" *Deutsche Vierteljahrsschrift für Literaturwissenschaft und Geistesgeschichte* 71.4 (December 1997): 668–700.

———. "The End of History: 'Eschatology' in Elias Canetti's *Masse und Macht.*" In *Fin de siècle—Fin du millénaire: Endzeitstimmungen in der deutschsprachigen Literatur*, edited by Helmut Koopmann and Hans-Jörg Knobloch. Tübingen: Stauffenburg, 2001.

———. "The Kiss of the Spider Woman: Gotthelf's 'Matricentric' Pedagogy and Its Postwar Reception." *German Quarterly* 67.3 (1994): 304–24.

———. "Masse und Macht, 1960." In *Encyclopedia of German Literature*, edited by Michael Konzett, 1:173–75. Chicago: Fitzroy Dearborn, 2000.

Doppler, Alfred. "Die Thematisierung der Konversation: Hugo von Hofmannsthals Lustspiel *Der Schwierige.*" In *Wirklichkeit im Spiegel der Sprache: Aufsätze zur Literatur des 20. Jahrhunderts in Österreich*, 65–78. Vienna: Europaverlag, 1975.

———. "Vor- und Gegenbilder (Gestalten und Figuren als Elemente der Zeit- und Lebensgeschichte in Canettis autobiographischen Büchern)." In *Elias Canetti: Londoner Symposium*, edited by Adrian Stevens and Fred Wagner, 33–44. Stuttgart: Verlag Hans-Dieter Heinz/Akademischer Verlag Stuttgart, 1991.

Dowden, Steven. *Sympathy for the Abyss: A Study in the Novel of German Modernism: Kafka, Broch, Musil and Thomas Mann.* Tübingen: Niemeyer, 1986.

Downing, Eric. "Repetition and Realism: The 'Ligeia' Impulse in Theodor Storm's *Viola tricolor.*" *Deutsche Vierteljahrsschrift für Literaturwissenschaft und Geistesgeschichte* 65.2 (1991): 265–303.

Draper, Hal. *Karl Marx's Theory of Revolution.* 2 vols. New York: Monthly Review Press, 1977.
Durzak, Manfred. *Zu Elias Canetti.* Stuttgart: Klett, 1983.
Eagleton, Terry. "The Rise of English." In *Literary Theory: An Introduction,* 17–53. 1983. Minneapolis: University of Minnesota Press, 1989.
Ein Dichter gegen Macht und Tod: Elias Canetti. Directed by Wolfgang Lesowsky and written by Krista Hauser and Wolfgang Lesowsky. Co-production of ORF, ZDF and SRG, 1985. Rebroadcast August 1994.
Elbaz, Robert, and Leah Hadomi. *Elias Canetti, or, the Failing of the Novel.* New York: Peter Lang, 1995.
———. "Text and Metatext in Canetti's Fictional World." *German Quarterly* 4 (1994): 521–33.
Elias Canetti's Counter Image of Society: Crowds and Power, Totalitarianism, Death, Transformation. Special Issue of *Thesis Eleven* 45 (1996).
Eliot, T. S. "Ulysses, Order and Myth." *Dial* 75 (1923): 480–83.
Enzensberger, Hans Magnus. "Elias Canetti: Die Blendung." *Der Spiegel* 32 (7 August 1963): 48–49.
Essays in Honor of Elias Canetti. Edited by Herbert G. Göpfert. New York: Farrar, Straus, Giroux, 1987. Translation, by Michael Hulse, of *Hüter der Verwandlung: Beiträge zum Werk von Elias Canetti.* Munich: Carl Hanser, 1985.
Fabian, Hans. "Die Sprache bei Elias Canetti: Exil als Asyl." In *Das Exilerlebnis: Verhandlungen des vierten Symposium über deutsche und österreichische Exilliteratur,* edited by Donald G. Daviau and Ludwig M. Fischer, 497–504. Columbia, S.C.: Camden House, 1982.
Falk, Thomas H. *Elias Canetti.* New York: Twayne, 1993.
Felman, Shoshana. "Turning the Screw of Interpretation." In *Literature and Psychoanalysis, The Question of Reading: Otherwise,* edited by Shoshana Felman, 94–207. Baltimore: Johns Hopkins University Press, 1982.
Ferrara, Jenna. "Grotesque and Voiceless: Women Characters in Elias Canetti's *Die Blendung.*" In *Proceedings and Commentary: German Graduate Students Association Conference at New York University,* edited by Patricia Doykos Duquette, Matthew Griffin and Inike Lode, 86–94. New York: n.p., 1994.
Fletcher, John, and Malcolm Bradbury. "The Introverted Novel." In *Modernism: A Guide to European Literature, 1890–1930,* edited by Malcolm Bradbury and James McFarlane, 394–415. London: Penguin, 1991.
Foell, Kristie A. *Blind Reflections: Gender in Elias Canetti's Die Blendung.* Riverside, Calif.: Ariadne, 1994.
———. "Whores, Mothers, and Others: Reception of Otto Weininger's *Sex and Character* in Elias Canetti's *Auto-da-Fé.*" In *Jews and Gender: Responses to Otto Weininger,* edited by Nancy A. Harrowitz and Barbara Hyams, 245–55. Philadelphia: Temple University Press, 1995.

Fontane, Theodor. "Willibald Alexis und sein Roman *Die Hosen des Herrn von Bredow.*" In *Gesammelte Werke in vier Bänden,* edited by Kurt Schreinert, 4:403–22. Gütersloh: Sigbert Mohn, 1961.
Foucault, Michel. "Man and His Doubles." In *The Order of Things: An Archeology of the Human Sciences,* translated by A. Sheridan. New York: Random House, 1970.
Freud, Sigmund. *The Standard Edition of the Complete Psychological Works of Sigmund Freud.* 24 vols. Translated from the German under the general editorship of James Strachey, in collaboration with Anna Freud, assisted by Alix Strachey and Alan Tyson. London: Hogarth Press, 1953–74.
Friedländer, Saul, ed. *Probing the Limits of Representation: Nazism and the "Final Solution."* Cambridge: Harvard University Press, 1992.
Frosh, Stephen. *The Politics of Psychoanalysis: An Introduction to Freudian and Post-Freudian Theory.* New Haven: Yale University Press, 1987.
Gardener, Sebastian. "Incurable Delusions: The Unresolved Conflict between Freudians and Their Foes." *Times Literary Supplement* 5039 (29 October 1999): 4–5.
Gast, Wolfgang. *Der deutsche Geschichtsroman im 19. Jahrhundert: Willibald Alexis. Untersuchungen zur Technik seiner "vaterländischen Romane."* Freiburg i. Br.: Universitätsverlag Becksmann, 1972.
Gay, Peter. *Freud: A Life for Our Times.* New York: W. W. Norton, 1988.
———. *Freud, Jews and Other Germans: Masters and Victims in Modernist Culture.* New York: Oxford University Press, 1978.
Gay, Ruth. *The Jews of Germany: A Historical Portrait.* Introduction by Peter Gay. New Haven: Yale University Press, 1992.
Gilbert, Sandra M., and Susan Gubar. *The Madwoman in the Attic: The Woman Writer and the Nineteenth-Century Literary Imagination.* New Haven: Yale University Press, 1979.
Gilman, Sander. *Difference and Pathology: Stereotypes of Sexuality, Race, and Madness.* Ithaca: Cornell University Press, 1985.
———. *Jewish Self-Hatred: Antisemitism and the Hidden Language of the Jews.* Baltimore: Johns Hopkins University Press, 1986.
———. *The Jew's Body.* New York: Routledge, 1991.
Glasenapp, Gabriele von. *Aus der Judengasse: Zur Entstehung und Ausprägung deutschsprachiger Ghettoliteratur im 19. Jahrhundert.* Tübingen: Niemeyer, 1996.
Göpfert, Herbert G., ed. *Canetti lesen: Erfahrungen mit seinen Büchern.* Reihe Hanser 188. Munich: Carl Hanser, 1975.
———. "The Reception History of Auto-da-Fé: A Documentation." In *Essays in Honor of Elias Canetti,* edited by Herbert G. Göpfert and translated by Michael Hulse, 289–319. New York: Farrar, Straus, Giroux, 1987.
Grünbaum, Adolf. "Letters to the Editor." *New York Times Book Review* (28 December 1998): 2.

Gutting, Gary. *French Philosophy in the 20th Century.* Cambridge: Cambridge University Press, forthcoming.
Hanisch, Ernst. "The Political Influence and Appropriation of Wagner." In *Wagner Handbook,* edited by Ulrich Müller and Peter Wapnewski, translated by John Deathridge, 186-201. Cambridge: Harvard University Press, 1992.
Hauptmann, Gerhart. *Bahnwärter Thiel.* In *Das Gesammelte Werk (Ausgabe letzter Hand),* 1:221-61. Berlin: Suhrkamp, 1943.
Heller, Scott. "New Life for Modernism." *Chronicle of Higher Education* 46.11 (5 November 99): A21-23.
Herman, Judith Lewis. *Father-Daughter Incest.* Cambridge: Harvard University Press, 1981.
Hinderberger-Burton, Tania. "The Quixotic in Canetti's *Die Blendung.*" *Modern Austrian Literature* 3/4 (1983): 165-76.
Hofmannsthal, Hugo von. *Der Schwierige.* In *Gesammelte Werke in Einzelausgaben: Lustspiele II,* edited by Herbert Steiner, 145-314. Frankfurt am Main: S. Fischer Verlag, 1954.
Hollinger, David A. "The Knower and the Artificer, with Postscript 1993." In *Modernist Impulses in the Human Sciences 1870-1930,* edited by Dorothy Ross, 26-53. Baltimore: Johns Hopkins University Press, 1994.
Holub, Robert C. *Reflections of Realism: Paradox, Norm, and Ideology in Nineteenth-Century German Prose.* Detroit: Wayne State University Press, 1991.
Huyssen, Andreas, and David Bathrick, eds. *Modernity and the Text: Revisions of German Modernism.* New York: Columbia University Press, 1989.
Huyssen, Andreas. *After the Great Divide: Modernism, Mass Culture, Postmodernism.* Bloomington: Indiana University Press, 1986.
———. "The Vamp and the Machine: Fritz Lang's *Metropolis.*" In *After the Great Divide,* 65-81. Bloomington: Indiana University Press, 1986.
Hyams, Barbara, and Nancy A. Harrowitz. "A Critical Introduction to the History of Weininger Reception." In *Jews and Gender: Responses to Otto Weininger,* edited by Nancy A. Harrowitz and Barbara Hyams, 3-20. Philadelphia: Temple University Press, 1995.
Jameson, Frederic. "Afterword." In *Aesthetics and Politics: The Key Texts of the Classic Debate within German Marxism,* edited by Frederic Jameson, translated by Francis McDonagh, 196-213. London: New Left Books/Verso, 1977.
———. "Presentation IV." In *Aesthetics and Politics: The Key Texts of the Classic Debate within German Marxism,* edited by Frederic Jameson, translated by Francis McDonagh, 142-50. London: New Left Books/Verso, 1977.
Jay, Martin. *Adorno.* Cambridge: Harvard University Press, 1984.
———. *The Dialectical Imagination: A History of the Frankfurt School and the Institute of Social Research, 1923-1950.* Boston: Little, Brown, 1973.
Jayne, Richard. *Erkenntnis und Transzendenz: Zur Hermeneutik literarischer*

Texte am Beispiel von Kafkas "Forschungen eines Hundes." Munich: Fink, 1983.
Johnston, William M. *The Austrian Mind: An Intellectual and Social History, 1848–1938.* Berkeley: University of California Press, 1972.
Kaes, Anton, Martin Jay, and Edward Dimendberg, eds. *The Weimar Republic Source Book.* Berkeley: University of California Press, 1994.
Kimball, Roger. "Becoming Elias Canetti." *New Criterion* 5.1 (1986): 17–28.
Koopmann, Helmut, ed. *Thomas-Mann-Handbuch.* Stuttgart: Kröner, 1990.
Kraus, Karl. "Er is doch e Jud." In *Untergang der Welt durch schwarze Magie,* 331–38. Vol. 8 of *Werke von Karl Kraus,* edited by Heinrich Fischer. Munich: Kosel, 1960.
Krumme, Detlev. *Lesemodelle: Elias Canetti, Günter Grass, Walter Höllerer.* Munich: Hanser, 1983.
Langer, Lawrence L. *Admitting the Holocaust: Collected Essays.* New York: Oxford University Press, 1995.
———. *The Holocaust and the Literary Imagination.* New Haven: Yale University Press, 1975.
Laplanche, J., and J.-B. Pontalis. *The Language of Psychoanalysis.* Translated by Donald Nicholson-Smith. New York: W. W. Norton, 1973.
Lawson, Richard H. *Understanding Elias Canetti.* Columbia: University of South Carolina Press, 1991.
Lessing, Theodor. *Der jüdische Selbsthaß.* Berlin: Jüdischer Verlag, 1930.
Liewerscheidt, Dieter. "Ein Widerspruch in der Erzählkonzeption von Elias Canettis *Die Blendung.*" *Wirkendes Wort* 28 (1978): 356–64.
Livingstone, Rodney. "Brecht's *Me-ti:* A Question of Attitude." In *Bertolt Brecht: Centenary Essays,* edited by Steve Giles and Rodney Livingstone, 62–73. No. 41 of *German Monitor.* Amsterdam: Rodopi, 1998.
Lorenz, Dagmar C. G. "Elias Canetti: *Masse und Macht* und *Die Blendung.* Bezüge zwischen Roman und Massentheorie." *Modern Austrian Literature* 3/4 (1983): 81–91.
Lukács, Georg. "Franz Kafka or Thomas Mann?" In *The Meaning of Contemporary Realism,* 47–92. London: Merlin, 1972.
———. "The Ideology of Modernism." In *The Meaning of Contemporary Realism,* 17–46. London: Merlin, 1972.
Luža, Radomír. *Austro-German Relations in the Anschluss Era.* Princeton: Princeton University Press, 1975.
McClelland, John. "The Place of Canetti's *Crowds and Power* in the History of Western Social and Political Thought." *Thesis Eleven* 45 (1996): 16–27.
McFarlane, James. "The Mind of Modernism." In *Modernism: A Guide to European Literature, 1890–1930,* edited by Malcolm Bradbury and James McFarlane, 71–93. London: Penguin, 1991.
Maia, Rousiley C. M. "Elias Canetti's *Auto-da-Fé:* From the Antithesis of the Crowd-Man to the Madness of Power." *Thesis Eleven* 45 (1996): 28–38.

Marchand, Suzanne L. *Down from Olympus: Archaeology and Philhellenism in Germany, 1750–1970*. Princeton: Princeton University Press, 1996.
Mews, Siegfried. "An Un-American Brecht?" *German Politics and Society* 13.3 (Fall 1995): 6–16.
Mieder, Wolfgang. "'Spuren der schwarzen Spinne': Elias Canetti und Jeremias Gotthelf." *Sprachspiegel* 50 (1994): 129–35.
Modern Austrian Literature. Special Elias Canetti Issue. 16.3-4 (1983).
Moi, Toril. *Sexual/Textual Politics: Feminist Literary Theory*. 1985. Reprint, London: Routledge, 1988.
Moser, Jonny. "Die Katastrophe der Juden in Österreich 1938–1945—ihre Voraussetzungen und ihre Überwindungen." In *Der gelbe Stern in Österreich*, edited by Kurt Schubert, 67–134. Eisenstadt: Edition Roetzer, 1977.
Müller, Ulrich, and Peter Wapnewski, eds. *Wagner Handbook*. Translated by John Deathridge. Cambridge: Harvard University Press, 1992.
Murphy, Harriet. *Canetti and Nietzsche: Theories of Humor in "Die Blendung."* Albany: State University of New York Press, 1997.
Musil, Robert. *Die Verwirrungen des Zöglings Törleß*. 1906. Reprint, Reinbek bei Hamburg: Rowohlt, 1988.
Natter, Wolfgang G. *Literature at War, 1914–1940: Representing the "Time of Greatness" in Germany*. New Haven: Yale University Press, 1999.
Oberschelp, Reinhard, ed. *Gesamtverzeichnis des deutschsprachigen Schrifttums (GV) 1911–1965*. Vol. 2. Verlag Dokumentation München, 1976.
Ollig, Hans-Ludwig. *Der Neukantianismus*. Stuttgart: Metzler, 1979.
Paal, Jutta. *Die Figurenkonstellation in Elias Canettis Roman "Die Blendung."* Würzburg: Königshausen & Neumann, 1991.
Panizza, Oskar. *The Operated Jew*. In *The Operated Jew: Two Tales of Anti-Semitism*, edited and translated by Jack Zipes, 47–74. New York: Routledge, 1991.
Pankau, Johannes G. "Körper und Geist: Das Geschlechterverhältnis in Elias Canettis Roman *Die Blendung*." *Colloquia Germanica* 23.2 (1990): 146–70.
Petersen, Carol. *Elias Canetti*. Berlin: Colloquium, 1990.
Piel, Edgar. *Elias Canetti*. Munich: C. H. Beck/edition text+kritik, 1984.
Pöder, Elfriede. "Spurensicherung: Otto Weininger in der *Blendung*." In *Blendung als Lebensform: Elias Canetti*, edited by Friedbert Aspetsberger and Gerald Stieg, 57–72. Königstein, Ts.: Athenäum, 1985.
Potgieter, Johan. "Elias Canetti: Individuum versus Masse. Eine sprachrealistische Veranschaulichung seiner Philosophie in *Die Blendung*." *Modern Austrian Literature* 27.3-4 (1994): 71–81.
Reed, Terence J. "Der Fall Wagner." In *Thomas-Mann-Handbuch*, edited by Helmut Koopman, 122–24. Stuttgart: Kröner, 1990.
Reinharz, Jehuda, and Walter Schatzberg, eds. *The Jewish Response to German Culture: From the Enlightenment to the Second World War*. Hanover, N.H.: University Press of New England, 1985.

Riedner, Nicola. *Canettis Fischerle: eine Figur zwischen Masse, Macht und Blendung.* Würzburg: Königshausen and Neumann, 1994.
Rilke, Rainer Maria. *Die Aufzeichnungen des Malte Laurids Brigge.* 1910. Vol. 6 of *Rainer Maria Rilke: Sämtliche Werke.* Edited by Ernst Zinn. Frankfurt am Main: Insel, 1966.
Ringer, Fritz K. *The Decline of the German Mandarins: The German Academic Community, 1890–1933.* 1969. Reprint, Hanover, N.H.: Wesleyan University Press, 1990.
Roberts, David. "Crowds and Power or the Natural History of Modernity: Horkheimer, Adorno, Canetti, Arendt." *Thesis Eleven* 45 (1996): 39–68.
Robertson, Ritchie. "Canetti as Anthropologist." In *Elias Canetti: Londoner Symposium,* edited by Adrian Stevens and Fred Wagner, 131–45. Stuttgart: Verlag Hans-Dieter Heinz/Akademischer Verlag Stuttgart, 1991.
———. "'Jewish Self-Hatred'? The Cases of Schnitzler and Canetti." In *Austrians and Jews in the Twentieth Century: From Franz Joseph to Waldheim,* edited by Robert S. Wistrich, 82–96. New York: St. Martin's Press, 1992.
Roche, Mark W. "National Socialism and the Disintegration of Values: Reflections on Nietzsche, Rosenberg, and Broch." *Journal of Value Inquiry* 26 (1992): 367–80.
Röhl, John C. G. "Wilhelm II.: 'Das Beste wäre Gas.'" *Die Zeit* 48 (2 December 1994): 6.
Rosenfeld, Alvin H. *A Double Dying: Reflections on Holocaust Literature.* Bloomington: Indiana University Press, 1980.
———. *Thinking about the Holocaust: After Half a Century.* Bloomington: Indiana University Press, 1997.
Rotenstreich, Nathan. "Hermann Cohen: Judaism in the Context of German Philosophy." In *The Jewish Response to German Culture: From the Enlightenment to the Second World War,* edited by Jehuda Reinharz and Walter Schatzberg, 51–63. Hanover, N.H.: University Press of New England, 1985.
Rothstein, Edward. "Dreams of Disappearance: The Secret Life of Elias Canetti." *New Republic* 2/3 (1990): 33–39.
Russell, Peter. "The Vision of Man in Elias Canetti's *Die Blendung.*" *German Life and Letters,* n.s., 1 (1974): 24–35.
Ryan, Judith. *The Vanishing Subject: Early Psychology and Literary Modernism.* Chicago: University of Chicago Press, 1991.
———. "Viennese Psychology and American Pragmatism." In *Fictions of Culture: Essays in Honor of Walter H. Sokel,* edited by Steven Taubeneck, 169–81. New York: Peter Lang, 1991.
Scherpe, Klaus R. "The City as Narrator: The Modern Text in Alfred Döblin's *Berlin Alexanderplatz.*" In *Modernity and the Text: Revisions of German Modernism,* edited by Andreas Huyssen and David Bathrick, 162–79. New York: Columbia University Press, 1989.

Schmidt, Hugo. "Narrative Attitudes in Canetti's *Die Blendung.*" *Modern Austrian Literature* 3/4 (1983): 93–109.
Schorske, Carl E. *Fin-de-Siècle Vienna: Politics and Culture.* New York: Vintage/Random House, 1981.
Schubert, Kurt. "Der Weg zur Katastrophe." In *Der gelbe Stern in Österreich,* edited by Kurt Schubert, 31–66. Eisenstadt: Edition Roetzer, 1977.
Schürer, Ernst. "Nebeneinander: Aspekte der Kultur der Weimarer Republik in Georg Kaisers 'Volksstück 1923.' " In *History and Literature: Essays in Honor of Karl S. Guthke,* edited by William C. Donahue and Scott D. Denham, 399–415. Tübingen: Stauffenburg, 2001.
Sebald, W. G. "Kurzer Versuch über System und Systemkritik bei Elias Canetti." *Études germaniques* 39 (1984): 268–75.
Sokel, Walter H. "The Ambiguity of Madness: Elias Canetti's Novel *Die Blendung.*" In *Views and Reviews of Modern German Literature: Festschrift for Adolf Klarmann,* edited by Karl S. Weimar, 181–88. Munich: Delp Verlag, 1974.
———. "Elias Canetti." In *European Writers: The Twentieth Century,* 12:2615–34. New York: Charles Scribner's Sons, 1990.
———. "Zum Verhältnis von Autobiographie und Roman bei Elias Canetti." In *Ist Wahrheit ein Meer von Grashalmen? Zum Werk Elias Canettis,* edited by Joseph P. Strelka and Zsuzsa Széll, 19–33. Bern: Peter Lang, 1993.
Sontag, Susan. "Mind as Passion." In *Essays in Honor of Elias Canetti,* edited by Herbert G. Göpfert, 88–107. New York: Farrar, Straus, Giroux, 1987.
Steinecke, Hartmut, ed. *Theorie und Technik des Romans im 20. Jahrhundert.* Tübingen: Niemeyer, 1972.
Stevens, Adrian, and Fred Wagner, eds. *Elias Canetti: Londoner Symposium.* Vol. 48 of *Publications of the Institute of Germanic Studies, University of London.* Stuttgart: Verlag Hans-Dieter Heinz/Akademischer Verlag Stuttgart, 1991.
Stevens, Adrian. "Creating Figures: Narrative, Discourse and Character in *Die Blendung.*" In *Elias Canetti: Londoner Symposium,* edited by Adrian Stevens and Fred Wagner, 105–18. Stuttgart: Verlag Hans-Dieter Heinz/Akademischer Verlag Stuttgart, 1991.
Stevenson, Randall. *Modernist Fiction: An Introduction.* Lexington: University Press of Kentucky, 1992.
Stieg, Gerald. "Canetti und Brecht oder: 'Es wird kein rechter Chor daraus . . .' " In *Zu Elias Canetti,* edited by Manfred Durzak, 138–50. Stuttgart: Klett, 1983.
———. "Canetti und die Psychoanalyse: *Das Unbehagen in der Kultur* und *Die Blendung.*" In *Elias Canetti: Londoner Symposium,* edited by Adrian Stevens and Fred Wagner, 59–73. Stuttgart: Verlag Hans-Dieter Heinz/Akademischer Verlag Stuttgart, 1991.
Swales, Martin. "The Problem of Nineteenth-Century German Realism." In

Realism in European Literature, edited by Nicholas Boyle and Martin Swales, 68–84. Cambridge: Cambridge University Press, 1986.
Széll, Zsuzsa. "Elias Canetti." In *Österreichische Literatur des 20. Jahrhunderts: Einzeldarstellungen,* edited by Hannelore Prosche, 461–79. Berlin: Volk und Wissen, 1988.
Tatar, Maria. *The Hard Facts of the Grimms' Fairy Tales.* Princeton: Princeton University Press, 1987.
———. *Lustmord: Sexual Murder in Weimar Germany.* Princeton: Princeton University Press, 1995.
———. "'Wie süß ist es, sich zu opfern': Gender, Violence, and Agency in Döblin's *Berlin Alexanderplatz.*" *Deutsche Vierteljahrsschrift für Literatur und Geistesgeschichte* 66.3 (1992): 491–518.
Tatlock, Lynne. "Willibald Alexis and 'Young Germany': A Closer Look." *German Life and Letters,* n.s., 34 (1980–81): 359–73.
———. *Willibald Alexis' Zeitroman "Das Haus Düsterweg" and the Vormärz.* Frankfurt am Main: Lang, 1984.
Theweleit, Klaus. *Male Fantasies.* 2 vols. Translated by Stephan Conway in collaboration with Erica Carter and Chris Turner. Minneapolis: University of Minnesota Press, 1987, 1989.
Thomas, L. H. C. "The Literary Reputation of Willibald Alexis as an Historical Novelist." *Modern Language Review* 45 (1950): 195–214.
Tietze, Hans. *Die Juden Wiens: Geschichte—Wirtschaft—Kultur.* 1933. Himberg bei Wien: Wiener Verlag, 1987.
Traverso, Enzo. *The Jews and Germany: From the "Judeo-German Symbiosis" to the Memory of Auschwitz.* Translated by Daniel Weissbort. Lincoln: University of Nebraska Press, 1995.
Vaget, Hans R. "Wälsungenblut." In *Thomas-Mann-Handbuch,* edited by Helmut Koopman, 576–80. Stuttgart: Kröner, 1990.
Volkov, Shulamit. "The Dynamics of Dissimilation: *Ostjuden* and German Jews." In *The Jewish Response to German Culture: From the Enlightenment to the Second World War,* edited by Jehuda Reinharz and Walter Schatzberg, 195–211. Hanover, N.H.: University Press of New England, 1985.
Wagner, Richard. *Der Ring des Nibelungen.* Edited by Julius Burghold. 1913. Reprint, Mainz and Munich: Schott and Piper, 1981.
———. *The Ring of The Nibelung.* Translated by Andrew Porter, illustrated by Eric Fraser. New York: Norton, 1976.
Weiner, Marc A. *Richard Wagner and the Anti-Semitic Imagination.* Lincoln: University of Nebraska Press, 1995.
Weininger, Otto. *Geschlecht und Charakter: Eine prinzipielle Untersuchung.* Vienna: W. Braumüller, 1903. Reprint, Munich: Matthes & Seitz, 1980.
"Weismanns Versuch, Canetti in Deutschland durchzusetzen." *Marbacher Magazin* 33 (1985): 27–45.

Weninger, Robert. "Zur Dialektik des Dialektiks im deutschen Realismus: Zugleich Überlegungen zu Michail Bachktins Konzept der Redevielfalt." *German Quarterly* 72 (1999): 115–32.
Werlen, Hans-Jakob. "Narrative Strategies in Elias Canetti's *Die Blendung* and *Masse und Macht.*" Ph.D. diss., Stanford University, 1988.
Widdig, Bernd. "Cultural Dimensions of Inflation in Weimar Germany." *German Politics and Society* 32 (1994): 10–27.
———. "Elias Canetti und die Inflation." *Merkur* 11 (1994): 985–97.
———. *Männerbünde und Massen: Zur Krise männlicher Identität in der Literatur der Moderne.* Opladen: Westdeutscher Verlag, 1992.
Wolff, Larry. *Child Abuse in Freud's Vienna: Postcards from the End of the World.* New York: New York Univeristy Press, 1995.
Ying, Ning. "China und Elias Canetti." In *Fernöstliche Brückenschläge: Zu deutsch-chinesischen Literaturbeziehungen im 20. Jahrhundert,* edited by Adrian Hsia and Sigfrid Hoefert, 151–61. Bern: Peter Lang, 1992.
Zipes, Jack, ed. and trans. *The Operated Jew: Two Tales of Anti-Semitism.* New York: Routledge, 1991.
Zuidervaart, Lambert. *Adorno's Aesthetic Theory: The Redemption of Illusion.* Cambridge: MIT Press, 1991.

INDEX

Abelard, 86
Abstraction: avant-garde, 180, 181; logical, 181
Abuse, child and spousal, 142–43, 147, 150, 152, 161, 242 (n. 55). *See also* Incest; Pfaff, Benedikt: abuses daughter; Rape
Adorno, Theodor W., xii, 5, 7, 15, 170, 171, 174, 176, 179–82, 185–86, 187, 188, 189, 190–91, 199–200, 201, 202, 242 (n. 51), 251 (n. 22), 252–53 (n. 49), 253 (n. 53), 254 (n. 62); *Notes to Literature,* 179; *Dialectic of Enlightenment,* 179, 180, 181
Aestheticism, 95
Alexis, Willibald (Wilhelm Häring), 3, 17, 22, 29, 41, 209 (n. 14), 210 (n. 33), 213 (nn. 77, 78), 236 (n. 87)
— *The Trousers of Mr. Bredow,* 19–20, 22–24, 26–27, 28, 32, 34–35, 37, 55, 198; and sex, 21; anti-Semitism in, 24, 37–40; plot of, 24–26
Alger, Horatio, 128
Allen, Walter, 11, 32
Anschluß, 11
Anti-Semitism, 1, 2, 13, 17, 39–40, 49–51, 59, 61, 105, 111, 114–15, 129, 192, 230 (n. 29); in Alexis, 24, 37–40; corporeal, 117, 118, 120, 123–25, 127, 129, 130, 131, 231 (nn. 34, 35); Canetti charged with, 134–36. *See also* Fischerle, Siegfried
Aquinas, Thomas, 168
Arendt, Hannah: *Illuminations,* 231 (n. 35)

Atwood, Margaret, 48
Austria, 11, 60, 61, 113, 117, 197, 200, 207 (n. 6)

Baboon, The, 115, 118, 128
Bahr, Hermann, 46, 193
Bakhtin, Mikhail, 130
Balzac, Honoré de, 19, 41, 184, 202; *Comédie humaine,* 90
Barnouw, Dagmar, 31, 32, 159
Barthes, Roland, 74, 194
Bathrick, David: *Modernity and the Text,* 177, 255 (n. 73)
Beckett, Samuel, 180, 185, 188, 189; *Ecce Homo,* 181–82
Beller, Steven, 46–47, 192, 217 (n. 46), 229 (n. 16); *Vienna and the Jews,* 61, 112
Benedikt, Friedl, xviii, 147
Benjamin, Walter, 119, 231 (n. 35)
Benn, Gottfried, 191; *Static Poems,* 198
Bennett, William: *Book of Virtues,* 8
Berg, Alban, 200, 201
Bergson, Henri, 198, 249–50 (n. 4), 254 (n. 61), 255 (n. 66)
Bering, Dietz, 232–33 (n. 46)
Berkeley, George, 77, 78, 81, 82, 86–87, 97, 100, 105, 226 (n. 48); *Principles,* 87
Berman, Marshall, 250–51 (n. 16)
Berman, Russell, xii, 212 (n. 52); *The Rise of the Modern German Novel,* 73–74
Bettelheim, Bruno, 54; *The Uses of Enchantment,* 151

Bildung, 2, 105, 106, 107, 109, 110, 111, 112, 118, 119, 127, 130, 134
Binder, Hans, 188
"Blinding," 1, 37, 85, 89, 149, 152
Blindness, 175–76, 186, 204
Blue Angel, The (film), 210 (n. 28)
Böll, Heinrich, xi
Boyle, Nicholas, 227 (n. 64)
Bradbury, Malcolm, 185, 186–87
Brecht, Bertolt, 8, 152, 180, 182, 188, 189, 251 (n. 22), 253 (n. 53)
Brentano, Franz, 60, 78–80, 81, 82, 87, 89, 92, 109, 222–23 (n. 17)
Broch, Hermann, 1, 3, 5, 14, 15, 45, 61, 77, 97, 98, 170, 185, 193, 200–201, 253 (n. 55); *Pasenow, oder Die Romantik 1888*, 7, 81; *The Sleepwalkers*, 15; and Freud, 139, 140–41
Bronfen, Elisabeth, 48
Brooks, Peter, 246–47 (n. 101)
Buddha, 67, 69, 168
Bürger, Peter, xii
Busch, Wilhelm, 231 (n. 33)

Canetti, Elias: *Crowds and Power*, xi, 3, 4, 5, 6, 8, 50, 73, 74, 85, 137, 138, 140, 142, 150, 159, 169, 170, 171–72, 204–5, 221 (n. 91), 246 (n. 93); autobiography of, xii, 4, 15, 33, 58, 138–39, 193, 203, 222 (n. 6), 230 (n. 29), 230–31 (n. 30); background of, 9; *The Play of Eyes*, 9–10; artistic goals of, 18, 19, 41–42, 200; Jewish identity of, 115–17; "Realism and New Reality," 201; *The Numbered*, 203; *Wedding*, 203, 204; *Comedy of Vanities*, 203, 255 (n. 74); *The Voices of Marrakesh*, 203–4; on historians, 211 (n. 38)
Cassirer, Ernst, 99, 226 (n. 51)
Chamberlain, Houston Stewart, 120
Christianity, 84, 130. *See also* New Testament
Christian Socialists, 112
Civilization, 165, 167, 169
Cixous, Hélène, 74
Clover, Carol, 70
Cohen, Hermann, 99, 112, 226 (n. 51), 229 (n. 16)
Cohen, Walter, 208 (n. 25)
Cohn, Dorritt, 214 (n. 85)
"Committed art," 180, 182
Confucius, 67, 168
Copleston, Frederick, 16, 82, 87, 93–94, 222 (n. 8)
Cox, Marian Roalfe, 216 (n. 25)
Crowd. *See* Canetti, Elias: *Crowds and Power*; Kien, Georg: and crowd
Culture, 17, 78, 103, 173, 198; French, 11, 109; U.S., 109; rise of, 162, 165, 167; fragmentation of, 175–77, 185, 186, 190; commercial mass, 179, 182, 188
—German, 2, 5–6, 8, 21, 24, 27, 47, 53, 56, 58, 65, 84, 101, 102, 103, 104, 106, 107, 111–12, 119, 187, 224 (n. 32); disintegration crisis of, 99, 105, 108, 112, 199; idealism in, 101, 112, 131; synthesis of, 110; assimilation of Jews into, 112, 113, 234 (n. 67); and physicality, 120, 124–25

Darby, David, 3–4, 19, 36, 77, 82, 90, 194, 226 (n. 48)
Darwin, Charles, 91
Davis, Lennard, 32, 34, 35, 40; *Resisting Novels*, 19, 30–31
Democritus, 85
Denby, David, xi, 76, 207 (n. 6)
Derrida, Jacques, 193
Dilthey, Wilhelm, 226 (n. 51)
Dissinger, Dieter, 225 (n. 43)
Döblin, Alfred: *Berlin Alexanderplatz*, 7, 19, 67, 90, 96, 186; "Murder of a Buttercup," 66
Dolezel, Lubomir, 36, 86

"Dorotheum," 197
Dowden, Steven: *Sympathy for the Abyss,* 208 (n. 24)
Downing, Eric, 56
Draper, Hal, 38

Eagleton, Terry, 209 (n. 11)
Egoism, 68, 73, 76, 81
Eisler, Georg: *Ein Dichter gegen Macht und Tod,* 208 (n. 26)
Elbaz, Robert, 3
Eliot, T. S., 174, 176, 178–79, 180, 193, 198, 202, 204, 249 (n. 1), 250–51 (n. 16), 251 (n. 23); *The Waste Land,* 173
Empiricism, 2, 60–61, 71, 76–96 passim, 99, 104, 109, 223 (n. 20), 225 (n. 40)
Enlightenment, 102, 106, 108, 112, 117, 181, 183, 229 (n. 16)
Enzensberger, Hans Magnus, xi, 4, 12, 40
Epistemology, 7–8, 33–34, 35, 36, 40, 45, 46, 63, 65, 77, 85, 103, 174, 176, 182–85, 186, 188, 189, 191, 193, 194, 196, 203, 249–50 (n. 4), 253 (n. 56), 254 (n. 62)
Escapism, 42, 95, 102. *See also* Literature, popular

Fabian, Hans, 220 (n. 75)
Felman, Shoshana, 44
Femininity. *See* Gender
Feminism: and literary criticism, 43–44, 45, 47, 142–43, 215 (n. 7)
Ferrara, Jenna, 43, 215 (n. 9)
Fichte, Johann Gottlieb, 94, 99
First Republic (Austria), 113, 197
Fischerin, 33, 48, 53, 54, 57, 59; and Fischerle, 49–51, 59; murder of, 50–51, 130, 133; and pathos, 51, 55; as prize, 59

Fischerle, Siegfried, 2, 9; and P. Kien, 32–33, 89, 100, 106, 111, 113, 114–15, 119, 128–29, 197; murder of, 40, 125–26, 129, 133, 135–36; and misogyny, 47, 60, 215 (n. 9); appearance of, 49, 50, 51, 59, 89, 113, 114, 115, 117–18, 120–23, 124, 127, 128, 129, 130–31, 133–34, 135, 231 (n. 33); and Fischerin, 49–51, 59; beating of, 50; as stereotype, 106, 113, 115, 117, 118, 125, 127, 128–30, 131, 231 (nn. 31, 33); and Pensionistin, 106–7, 115, 117; and assimilation, 112, 113, 118–19, 130–31, 133, 135, 231 (n. 31), 236–37 (n. 88); Jewish identity of, 113–15, 127–28, 133–34, 231 (n. 31), 237 (n. 93); anti-Semitism of, 115, 117, 127–28, 130; planned American escape of, 118–19, 127, 128, 131, 236 (nn. 86, 87); name of, 118–23, 127, 232–33 (n. 46); and G. Kien, 128, 133
Foell, Kristie, 43, 66, 73, 153, 215 (nn. 9, 10); *Blind Reflections,* 144, 214–15 (n. 6)
Fontane, Theodor, 22, 27, 90, 183; *Effi Briest,* 21, 209 (nn. 13, 14)
Foucault, Michel, 67, 74, 85, 94, 194, 225 (n. 40), 249–50 (n. 4)
Frankfurt School, 74, 244 (n. 74)
Freud, Sigmund, xii, 1, 6, 13, 34, 44, 55, 60, 61, 66, 74, 75, 138, 245 (n. 88), 255 (n. 66); and Oedipus complex, 54, 142, 147–49, 150, 152, 170, 171, 237–38 (n. 4), 241–42 (n. 49), 244 (n. 74); Canetti responds to, 136, 137–42, 149–52, 159, 169–72, 237–38 (n. 4); *Group Psychology and the Analysis of the Ego,* 138, 140–41; *Beyond the Pleasure Principle,* 141; *Civilization and Its Discontents,* 141, 162, 163, 167; and transference, 142, 155, 156–58,

244–45 (n. 80), 246–47 (n. 101); and sublimation, 142, 162–64, 165, 166, 167, 205, 247 (n. 107); and hysteria, 147, 148, 151; and incest, 147, 148, 170, 241 (n. 48), 242 (n. 55); *Introductory Lectures*, 148; *Studies on Hysteria*, 148; *Totem and Taboo*, 148, 162; and mythology, 161, 162, 170; and theory of drives, 163, 164, 247 (n. 106); and repression, 164, 165, 247 (n. 107); as misogynistic, 168–69

Freytag, Gustav, 22, 27

Fried, Erich, 180, 217 (n. 42)

Friedländer, Saul: *Probing the Limits of Representation*, 210 (n. 30)

Fries, Marilyn Silbey, 90

Frosh, Stephen, 155, 156, 157, 165, 167; *Politics of Psychoanalysis*, 244 (n. 74), 244–45 (n. 80), 249 (n. 125)

Frye, Northrup, 49

Gay, Peter, 16, 127, 137, 141; *Freud, Jews and Other Germans*, 231 (n. 33), 233 (n. 47), 235 (nn. 70, 74); *Freud*, 248 (n. 120)

Gay, Ruth, 119

Gender, 46, 47, 48, 71, 73, 187; and complementarity, 50; stereotypes of, 55, 56, 57–59, 61; and insanity, 68; and behavior, 69–70; and language, 74

George, Stefan, 95, 182

Germany, 113. *See also* Culture— German

Gide, André, 195

Gilbert, Sandra M., 68

Gilman, Sander, 40, 117, 130, 231 (n. 34)

Glasenapp, Gabrielle von: *Aus der Judengasse*, 209 (n. 16)

God, 69, 82, 87, 102, 104

Goethe, Johann Wolfgang von: *Faust*, 107, 108, 172

Gomperz, Theodor, 112

Gotthelf, Jeremias: *The Black Spider*, 58

Gottsched, Johann Christoph, 81, 82

Gorilla man, 60, 69, 70–71, 92, 93, 160, 163, 191

Grass, Günter Wilhelm, xi

Grimm, Brothers, 53

Grob, Herr (Mr. Brute), 58, 59, 81, 83, 84

Grolmann, Adolf von, 26

Grünbaum, Adolf, 147

Gubar, Susan, 68

Guthke, Karl, 216 (n. 29)

Gutting, Gary 225 (n. 40)

Gymnasien, 79, 105, 109

Hadomi, Leah, 3

Hanisch, Ernst, 120

Hanser Verlag, 11, 15

Häring, Wilhelm. *See* Alexis, Willibald

Hartung, Rudolf, 11

Hauptmann, Gerhart, 193; *Bahnwärter Thiel*, 56–59

Hausen, Müller von, 234 (n. 67)

Hegel, Georg Wilhelm Friedrich, 98, 99, 249 (n. 1)

Heidegger, Martin, 191, 195, 196, 255 (n. 66)

Heine, Heinrich, 11

Herman, Judith Lewis, 148

Hermeneutics, 33, 34, 36, 37, 78, 159, 189

"Historicism," 198, 254 (n. 62)

Hobbes, Thomas, 89

Hoepffner, Jean, 10

Hofmannsthal, Hugo von: *Der Schwierige*, 54; *Lord Chandos Brief*, 145, 252 (n. 47)

Hollinger, David, 14, 177–78
Holocaust, 6, 134, 135, 180, 181, 254 (n. 62)
"Holocaust" (television miniseries), 188
Homer, 67, 168
Horkheimer, Max: *Dialectic of Enlightenment*, 179
Humanism, 107–8
Humboldt, Wilhelm von, 108
Hume, David, 223 (n. 20)
Huyssen, Andreas, xii, 188; *Modernity and the Text*, 177, 255 (n. 73); *After the Great Divide*, 179

Ibsen, Henrik, 193
Idealism, 77, 88, 99–100, 102, 104, 110; German, 101, 112, 131, 227 (n. 64); aesthetics of, 181
Identification, 11, 30, 31, 32, 33–34, 73, 152, 171, 188–89, 199, 211–12 (n. 44)
Incest, 53–55, 143–47, 148, 149, 216 (n. 25), 241 (n. 46). *See also* Pfaff, Benedikt: abuses daughter
Insanity, 11, 12, 67–68, 70, 92–93, 95, 159; and women, 68, 72–73
Intellectualism, 13

Jäger, Werner, 2, 105, 110
James, Henry, 193
James, William, 60, 79, 89, 96, 109, 223 (n. 20), 249–50 (n. 4)
Jameson, Frederic, 174, 190, 250 (n. 6)
Jay, Martin, 5
Jesus, 83, 84
Jews: identity of, 9, 112, 113–14, 229 (n. 16); assimilation attempts of, 112, 113, 117, 118–20, 127, 133, 135, 233 (nn. 47, 50), 235 (n. 74); and self-loathing, 115–17, 127–28, 134, 230–31 (n. 30), 235 (n. 70); Viennese, 126;

and intra-Jewish debate, 127; as victims, 188. *See also* Judaism
Joyce, James, xii, 14, 140, 177, 193, 195, 197, 200–201; *Ulysses*, 7, 198; *Portrait of the Artist as a Young Man*, 187
Judaism, 5; "heritage" vs. religion of, 114, 117–18, 127. *See also* Jews
Judas, 83, 84
Jung, Carl, 61, 149
Jünger, Ernst, 191

Kafka, Franz, 15, 178, 181, 184, 185–86, 188, 189, 195, 197, 202, 205, 207 (n. 6), 222–23 (n. 17), 252 (n. 42); *In the Penal Colony*, 185, 190
Kant, Immanuel, 2, 80, 82, 88, 97, 98, 100, 102–3, 108, 110, 111, 112, 190, 229 (n. 16). *See also* Neo-Kantianism
Kant: as character name, 96–97, 225 (n. 43)
Kien, Georg, 2–3, 6, 7, 20, 67, 86, 191, 192; and sex, 29–30, 40, 57, 69, 70, 75, 198, 225 (n. 41), 254 (n. 63); and literature, 29–30, 40, 254 (n. 63); as narrator, 30, 40–41, 68–69, 159, 184, 204–5; appeal of, 31–32, 33, 41, 51, 73, 74, 159, 183, 188, 192, 212 (n. 52); and women, 41, 45, 46, 47, 62–63, 68, 94–95, 166–67, 219–20 (n. 75); and misogyny, 41, 47, 60, 166, 168; and femininity, 43, 46, 61–63, 69, 70, 71, 72, 73, 74, 221 (n. 91); and psychology, 67, 68–69, 71–73, 74, 75, 93, 95, 154; and gorilla man, 69, 70–71, 74, 93, 94–95, 191, 195, 224 (n. 32); treats P. Kien, 72, 153, 154–55, 162–67; and Therese, 72, 166, 168; and society, 74–75; and philosophy, 77, 80; as empiricist, 91–92, 94, 103, 104, 109, 152,

196, 224 (n. 32); and Fischerle, 128, 133; and termite parable, 142, 162–67, 170; as non-Freudian, 153, 154; as Freudian, 153–72 passim, 178, 220 (n. 82); and countertransference, 158, 159, 160–61, 162; and crowd, 158–61, 162, 165–66, 169, 221 (n. 91). *See also* Pfaff, Benedikt: and G. Kien

Kien, Peter, 5, 6, 7, 11, 71, 75, 78, 160, 180, 191; and Kant, 2, 96–98, 99, 102, 103; suicide of, 12–13, 40, 65, 73, 135–36; and Alexis, 19–20, 21, 26, 55, 198; and history, 28–29, 88, 103–4, 168; as narrator, 30, 35–36, 69, 184, 197, 204–5; and women, 43, 45, 46, 59, 166–67; and misogyny, 43, 47, 62, 67, 102, 154–55, 162, 166, 168, 198, 215 (n. 10); repulsiveness of, 57; as exile, 59–60; as academic, 59–60, 61–62, 72, 86, 93, 98, 110, 152, 159, 221–22 (n. 4), 226 (n. 54); and femininity, 61–62, 65, 69, 71, 73; interprets Therese as text, 63–65, 72, 73, 86; imagines murder of Therese, 65–67, 144; and philosophy, 77, 80, 85–86, 88, 91, 94, 112, 127, 196, 226 (n. 48), 234–35 (n. 68); identity of, 80–81, 93; self-mutilation by, 86; as idealist, 99–109 passim, 152; and books, 100–101, 102, 229 (n. 12); "mental library" of, 101, 111; misreads Fischerle and Pensionistin, 106–7, 108, 110–11, 135; anti-Semitism of, 117–18; and sex, 153–54; "blindness of," 176–77, 178, 195, 202. *See also* Fischerle, Siegfried: and P. Kien; Kien, Georg: treats P. Kien; Pfaff, Benedikt: and P. Kien; Therese: and P. Kien

Kierkegaard, Søren, 249 (n. 1)

Kimball, Roger, xii, 1

Kraus, Karl, 11, 112

Kraus, Oskar, 222 (n. 7)

Kristeva, Julia, 194

LaCapra, Dominick, 208 (n. 25)

Lang, Fritz: *Siegfried* (film), 126

Langer, Lawrence, 180

Language, 60, 70–71, 72, 74, 92, 93, 95, 109, 117, 130, 131, 133–34, 145, 166, 167–68, 191, 201, 203, 215 (n. 7), 221 (n. 91), 236 (n. 86), 237 (n. 93)

Lawson, Richard H., 43

Lessing, Theodor: *Jewish Self-Hatred*, 128

Liewerscheidt, Dieter, 18–19, 194

Literature, popular, 13, 18, 19, 20, 22, 38, 41, 44, 56, 152, 198; and sex, 21, 29–30, 31; and pleasure, 40; women in, 48, 65

Locke, John, 223 (n. 20)

Lorenz, Dagmar C. G., 208 (n. 23)

Lueger, Karl, 112

Lukács, Georg, xii, 77, 174, 179, 185, 187, 191–200 passim, 251 (n. 22), 254 (n. 62)

McFarlane, James, 173–74, 176, 178, 179, 185, 186–87, 188, 190, 195, 197, 199, 202, 249 (n. 1), 254 (n. 64)

Mach, Ernst, 9, 60, 61, 79, 87, 89, 91, 93, 186

Mahler, Alma, 230 (n. 29)

Malik Verlag, 41, 208 (n. 6)

Mann, Heinrich, 202; *The Blue Angel*, 210 (n. 28)

Mann, Thomas, 7, 14, 28, 202, 207 (n. 6), 228–29 (n. 9), 233 (n. 56); *The Magic Mountain*, 202

Marchand, Susan, 16, 108, 109, 110, 228–29 (n. 9)

Materialism, 99, 104–5, 192

May, Karl, 236 (n. 87)

Metamorphosis. *See* Transformation

Metaphysics, 79, 85, 87, 94, 99
Michelangelo, 168
Misogyny, 1–2, 13, 43–44, 45–46, 48, 51, 60, 61, 66, 115, 118, 135, 142–43, 149, 167–68, 192, 204, 215 (nn. 7, 10); cultural, 47, 67, 168–69, 187. *See also* Kien, Georg: misogyny of; Kien, Peter: misogyny of
Modernism, 173, 174, 176–77, 178–80, 183, 185, 188, 189, 190, 192, 198, 199, 201–3, 204, 251 (n. 23), 252 (n. 42)
Morality, 38, 82, 84, 86
More, Thomas, 168
Moser, Jonny, 129
Moses, 69
Mozart, Wolfgang Amadeus: *The Magic Flute*, 48–49, 50
Murphy, Harriet, 13
Musil, Robert, xii, 14, 195, 197, 200–201, 202, 207 (n. 6); *Die Verwirrungen des Zöglings Törleß*, 7, 81, 186
Mythology, 198–99

Narration, 30, 31, 34–38, 40–41, 44, 48, 55, 57–58, 59, 67, 68, 69, 90, 98, 113, 115, 127, 145, 146, 156, 183–84, 188, 190, 194, 196, 203, 215 (n. 9)
Nationalism: German, 27, 120; racist, 111, 120
Natter, Wolfgang, 27
Naturalism, 56, 57, 58, 193
Nature, 87
Nazis and Nazism, 5, 10, 12–13, 134, 191, 192, 201
Neoempiricism. *See* Empiricism
Neoidealism. *See* Idealism
Neo-Kantianism, 2, 78, 80, 96, 99, 102–3, 104, 110, 112, 196, 221–22 (n. 4), 227 (n. 65)
Nestroy, Johann, 11
New Criticism, 174, 179, 180, 193
"New reality," 41–42

New Testament, 5, 62, 109
Nietzsche, Friedrich, 11, 191, 249–50 (n. 4)
Novels. *See* Literature, popular
Nuremberg Laws, 9

Oberschelp, Reinhard: *Gesamtverzeichnis*, 210 (nn. 21, 24)
Objectivity, 104–5, 195, 196
Ollig, Hans-Ludwig, 104, 227 (n. 65)
Origen, 86

Paal, Jutta: *Die Figurenkonstellation in Elias Canettis Auto-da-Fé*, 113–14, 230 (n. 29)
Palace of Justice (Vienna), 4, 137
Panizza, Oskar: *Operated Jew*, 119
Pensionistin, 47, 49, 106–7; as Capitalist, 115, 117
Perception. *See* Subjectivity
Pfaff, Anna, 43, 48, 51, 146, 151–52. *See also* Pfaff, Benedikt: abuses daughter
Pfaff, Benedikt, 12, 118, 166; and P. Kien, 27–28, 50, 67, 88, 129, 145, 147, 240–41 (n. 40); misogyny of, 47, 55, 60, 143; abuses daughter, 53, 54–55, 57, 59, 89, 143–47, 149, 150, 152, 157, 168, 239 (n. 25), 239–40 (n. 30); and Therese, 58, 59, 143, 144, 214 (n. 6), 232 (n. 41); and G. Kien, 88–89, 147, 168, 224 (n. 32), 240 (n. 39); as stereotype, 134, 151; psychodrama of, 147
Philology, 62–63, 105, 108, 109, 110, 117, 118
Philosemitism, 115, 128
Philosophy: Eastern, 76–77, 221–22 (n. 4); Western, 77–78, 79, 80, 82, 86, 89, 91, 93–94, 99, 103, 104–5, 108, 109, 195–96, 221–22 (n. 4); 226 (n. 48)
Physics, 78

Plato, 234–35 (n. 68)
Pöder, Elfriede, 46, 215 (n. 6)
Poe, Egar Allan: "Tell-Tale Heart," 147
Pound, Ezra, 9, 200
Power, 85, 93, 140, 150, 171–72, 187, 211 (n. 38), 237–38 (n. 4); of psychoanalysts, 153, 156–58, 161, 192
Préval, Jean, 142, 158, 159, 160, 161, 162, 170, 220 (n. 82)
Protagonists, 186, 187, 190, 194, 199, 205, 252 (n. 47)
Prussia, 27
Psychoanalysis, 74, 137, 140, 141, 147, 151, 152, 153, 154, 155, 156, 157–58, 162, 164, 169, 170, 171, 244 (n. 74). *See also* Freud, Sigmund
Psychology, 67, 68–69, 71–73, 78, 79, 80, 81, 91, 92–93, 109, 139–41, 153, 154; social, 140–41, 170
Public sphere, 17, 189
"Public things," 142
Pulver, Max, 142

Raimund, Ferdinand, 11
Ranke, Leopold von, 26, 27
Rape, 43–44
Rath, Emanuel, 26, 210 (n. 28)
Rathenau, Walther, 120, 230 (n. 29)
Realism: psychological, 139, 140, 193; socialist, 179; literary, 183, 184, 190, 195. *See also* Literature, popular
Reichner, Herbert, 11
Reich-Ranicki, Marcel, 12, 40, 45
Reinvention, 9
Riedner, Nicole, 135; *Canettis Fischerle,* 231 (n. 31), 232 (n. 44)
Rilke, Rainer Marie, xii, 190, 202; *The Notebooks of Malte Laurids Brigge,* 7, 19, 81, 85, 178, 186, 202
Ringer, Fritz K., 103, 104

Roberts, David, 169
Russell, Peter, 89, 170, 224 (n. 34)
Ryan, Judith, 16, 46, 78, 79, 80, 82, 95, 222 (nn. 8, 10, 12, 14), 222–23 (n. 17); *The Vanishing Subject,* 60–61

St. Stephen, Cathedral of, 82, 197
Sartre, Jean-Paul, 180, 251–52 (n. 30), 252–53 (n. 49)
Saussure, Ferdinand de, 63, 70, 74
Scherchen, Hermann, 200
Schiller, Friedrich, 2, 101, 108, 135, 181, 251–52 (n. 30)
Schmitt, Carl, 191
Schnitzler, Arthur, 61; *Professor Bernhardi,* 111
Scholarship, 108, 109
Scott, Sir Walter, 22
Semiotics, 62, 65, 67, 68, 125, 145, 168
Sensation, 78, 79, 100. *See also* Subjectivity
Sex and sexuality, 21, 24, 26, 29–30, 31, 44, 46, 53–54, 57, 153–54, 167; and murder, 65–66, 72, 218–19 (n. 65), 219 (n. 66); sublimation of, 162–66
Sinclair, Upton, 41, 208 (n. 6)
Singer, Isaac Bashevis: *Shosha,* 78
Sinology, 62, 109, 168, 221–22 (n. 4)
Socialism, 96
Society, 90–91, 212 (n. 49); groupings in, 6; awareness of, 18, 21, 30, 76, 77, 84–85; fragmentation of, 31; behavior of, 50–51, 76; analysis of, 74; and liberation, 74; concerns of, 76, 77, 78; unrest in, 81, 99, 109, 185; environment of, 129; reality of, 139, 140, 151, 161–62, 172, 192, 193, 199; rise of, 162, 165, 167
Socioeconomics, 161, 170, 190, 197, 202

INDEX : 279

Sokel, Walter H., 73, 74, 212 (n. 52)
Sonne, Isaiah, 9–10, 33, 34, 76, 134, 135, 141, 150
Sontag, Susan, 14, 43, 215 (n. 7)
Spiders, imagery of, 58–59
Spiegel, Der, 4, 12
Stars of Heaven (pub), 50, 106, 113, 114
Stern, Adolf, 209 (n. 18)
Stevenson, Randall, 174, 194, 253 (n. 56); *Modernist Fiction*, 254 (n. 64)
Stewart, Potter, 60, 216–17 (n. 38)
Stieg, Gerald, 4, 11, 106, 137, 154, 163, 247 (n. 107)
Strindberg, Auguste, 193; *Miss Julie*, 185
Subjectivity, 46–47, 60–61, 71, 77–94 passim, 176, 178, 186–99 passim, 203–4, 254 (n. 61); male, 61, 66, 67
Szondi, Peter, 186

Tatar, Maria, 210 (n. 29); *The Hard Facts of the Grimms' Fairy Tales*, 53–54, 216 (n. 25); *Lustmord*, 65, 66, 218 (n. 65)
Tatlock, Lynne, 27, 209–10 (n. 20)
Theism, 87
Therese, 19–20, 26, 34, 37, 44, 45, 115; and P. Kien, 19–20, 21, 26, 27, 46, 50, 55–56, 59, 62, 63–66, 72, 82–84, 85, 86, 88, 89, 97, 101, 102, 105, 129, 153, 167; and sex, 21, 24, 26, 46, 47, 55, 57, 58, 81–82; and gender, 46, 48; as stereotype, 55, 56, 57, 58–59, 82, 83, 113, 134; and B. Pfaff, 58, 59, 143, 144, 214 (n. 6), 232 (n. 41); as text, 63–65, 72; madness of, 67–68; and G. Kien, 72, 166, 168; subjectivity of, 81–82, 83–84, 85, 89, 90, 94, 197

Theresianum, 3, 28, 101, 109, 129, 144, 197, 229 (n. 12), 232 (n. 41)
Theweleit, Klaus: *Male Fantasies*, 217 (n. 42)
"Third Humanism," 2, 110
Thomas, L. H. C., 22, 27
Tiresias, 176, 178, 186, 189, 202, 204, 250 (n. 8)
Toller, Ernst: *Masse Mensch*, 165
Toynbee, Philip, 11–12
Transformation (Verwandlung), 5, 6, 34, 150, 171, 172, 205, 237–38 (n. 4)
Tucholsky, Kurt, 119
Twain, Mark: *Tom Sawyer*, 24

Venus, 161
Verwandlung. See Transformation
Vienna, 3, 13, 76, 85, 90, 91, 126, 129, 139, 149, 150, 151, 196–97, 201, 242 (n. 55)
Vitalism, 108
Vulkan, 161

Wagner, Richard, 120; *Ring* cycle, 119, 123–27, 168, 233 (n. 47), 233–34 (nn. 56–57), 234 (nn. 58–61); *German Art and German Politics*, 120
Waldinger, Ernst, 32
Webern, Anton, 201
Wedgwood translation, xii, 11, 49, 81, 130, 142
Weimar Republic, 113
Weiner, Marc, 125
Weininger, Otto, 50, 56, 70, 71, 192, 214 (n. 6); *Sex and Character*, 46, 47, 61, 230–31 (n. 30)
Weismann Verlag, 11
Werfel, Franz, 9, 201
White, Hayden, 26
Wilhelm II, 120
Winckelmann, Johann Joachim, 108
Windelband, Wilhelm, 99, 226 (n. 51)

Wolf, Christa, xi
Wolff, Larry, 150
Women. *See* Gender; Insanity: and women; Literature: women in; Misogyny
Woolf, Virginia, 193, 195
World War I, 129, 169, 233 (n. 50), 235 (n. 75)
Wortruba, Fritz, 150, 200
Wundt, Wilhelm, 78, 80, 81

Yeats, W. B., 207 (n. 6)
Yitzchak, Abraham ben. *See* Sonne, Isaiah
Young Germany, 38

Zola, Émile, 41, 183
Zuckmayer, Carl, 9
Zuidervaart, Lambert, 178
Zweig, Stefan, 9, 11, 201

www.ingramcontent.com/pod-product-compliance
Lightning Source LLC
Chambersburg PA
CBHW021804220426
43662CB00006B/176